T0325642

Trust Management in Mobile Environments:

Autonomic and Usable Models

Zheng Yan

Xidian University, China & Aalto University, Finland

A volume in the Advances in Information Security, Privacy, and Ethics (AISPE) Book Series

Information Science REFERENCE

An Imprint of IGI Global

Managing Director:	Lindsay Johnston
Editorial Director:	Myla Merkel
Production Manager:	Jennifer Yoder
Publishing Systems Analyst:	Adrienne Freeland
Development Editor:	Christine Smith
Acquisitions Editor:	Kayla Wolfe
Typesetter:	Lisandro Gonzalez
Cover Design:	Jason Mull

Published in the United States of America by
Information Science Reference (an imprint of IGI Global)
701 E. Chocolate Avenue
Hershey PA 17033
Tel: 717-533-8845
Fax: 717-533-8661
E-mail: cust@igi-global.com
Web site: http://www.igi-global.com

Copyright © 2014 by IGI Global. All rights reserved. No part of this publication may be reproduced, stored or distributed in any form or by any means, electronic or mechanical, including photocopying, without written permission from the publisher. Product or company names used in this set are for identification purposes only. Inclusion of the names of the products or companies does not indicate a claim of ownership by IGI Global of the trademark or registered trademark.

Library of Congress Cataloging-in-Publication Data

Yan, Zheng, 1972-
 Trust management in mobile environments : autonomic and usable models / by Zheng Yan.
    pages cm
 Includes bibliographical references and index.
   ISBN 978-1-4666-4765-7 (hardcover) -- ISBN 978-1-4666-4766-4 (ebook) -- ISBN 978-1-4666-4767-1 (print & perpetual access) 1. Human-computer interaction. 2. Trust. 3. Mobile computing. 4. Computer users. I. Title.
  QA76.9.H85Y35 2014
  004.01'9--dc23
                              2013027741

This book is published in the IGI Global book series Advances in Information Security, Privacy, and Ethics (AISPE) (ISSN: 1948-9730; eISSN: 1948-9749)

British Cataloguing in Publication Data
A Cataloguing in Publication record for this book is available from the British Library.

All work contributed to this book is new, previously-unpublished material. The views expressed in this book are those of the authors, but not necessarily of the publisher.

For electronic access to this publication, please contact: eresources@igi-global.com.

Advances in Information Security, Privacy, and Ethics (AISPE) Book Series

ISSN: 1948-9730
EISSN: 1948-9749

MISSION

In the digital age, when everything from municipal power grids to individual mobile telephone locations is all available in electronic form, the implications and protection of this data has never been more important and controversial. As digital technologies become more pervasive in everyday life and the Internet is utilized in ever increasing ways by both private and public entities, the need for more research on securing, regulating, and understanding these areas is growing.

The **Advances in Information Security, Privacy, & Ethics (AISPE) Book Series** is the source for this research, as the series provides only the most cutting-edge research on how information is utilized in the digital age.

COVERAGE

- Access Control
- Device Fingerprinting
- Global Privacy Concerns
- Information Security Standards
- Network Security Services
- Privacy-Enhancing Technologies
- Risk Management
- Security Information Management
- Technoethics
- Tracking Cookies

IGI Global is currently accepting manuscripts for publication within this series. To submit a proposal for a volume in this series, please contact our Acquisition Editors at Acquisitions@igi-global.com or visit: http://www.igi-global.com/publish/.

The Advances in Information Security, Privacy, and Ethics (AISPE) Book Series (ISSN 1948-9730) is published by IGI Global, 701 E. Chocolate Avenue, Hershey, PA 17033-1240, USA, www.igi-global.com. This series is composed of titles available for purchase individually; each title is edited to be contextually exclusive from any other title within the series. For pricing and ordering information please visit http://www.igi-global.com/book-series/advances-information-security-privacy-ethics/37157. Postmaster: Send all address changes to above address. Copyright © 2014 IGI Global. All rights, including translation in other languages reserved by the publisher. No part of this series may be reproduced or used in any form or by any means – graphics, electronic, or mechanical, including photocopying, recording, taping, or information and retrieval systems – without written permission from the publisher, except for non commercial, educational use, including classroom teaching purposes. The views expressed in this series are those of the authors, but not necessarily of IGI Global.

Titles in this Series

For a list of additional titles in this series, please visit: www.igi-global.com

Research Developments in Biometrics and Video Processing Techniques
Rajeev Srivastava (Indian Institute of Technology (BHU), India) S.K. Singh (Indian Institute of Technology (BHU), India) and K.K. Shukla (Indian Institute of Technology (BHU), India)
Information Science Reference • copyright 2014 • 279pp • H/C (ISBN: 9781466648685) • US $195.00 (our price)

Trust Management in Mobile Environments Autonomic and Usable Models
Zheng Yan (Xidian University, China and Aalto University, Finland)
Information Science Reference • copyright 2014 • 352pp • H/C (ISBN: 9781466647657) • US $195.00 (our price)

Security, Privacy, Trust, and Resource Management in Mobile and Wireless Communications
Danda B. Rawat (Georgia Southern University, USA) Bhed B. Bista (Iwate Prefectural University, Japan) and Gongjun Yan (University of Southern Indiana, USA)
Information Science Reference • copyright 2014 • 413pp • H/C (ISBN: 9781466646919) • US $195.00 (our price)

Architectures and Protocols for Secure Information Technology Infrastructures
Antonio Ruiz-Martinez (University of Murcia, Spain) Rafael Marin-Lopez (University of Murcia, Spain) and Fernando Pereniguez-Garcia (University of Murcia, Spain)
Information Science Reference • copyright 2014 • 427pp • H/C (ISBN: 9781466645141) • US $195.00 (our price)

Theory and Practice of Cryptography Solutions for Secure Information Systems
Atilla Elçi (Aksaray University, Turkey) Josef Pieprzyk (Macquarie University, Australia) Alexander G. Chefranov (Eastern Mediterranean University, North Cyprus) Mehmet A. Orgun (Macquarie University, Australia) Huaxiong Wang (Nanyang Technological University, Singapore) and Rajan Shankaran (Macquarie University, Australia)
Information Science Reference • copyright 2013 • 351pp • H/C (ISBN: 9781466640306) • US $195.00 (our price)

IT Security Governance Innovations Theory and Research
Daniel Mellado (Spanish Tax Agency, Spain) Luis Enrique Sánchez (University of Castilla-La Mancha, Spain) Eduardo Fernández-Medina (University of Castilla – La Mancha, Spain) and Mario G. Piattini (University of Castilla - La Mancha, Spain)
Information Science Reference • copyright 2013 • 373pp • H/C (ISBN: 9781466620834) • US $195.00 (our price)

Threats, Countermeasures, and Advances in Applied Information Security
Manish Gupta (State University of New York at Buffalo, USA) John Walp (M&T Bank Corporation, USA) and Raj Sharman (State University of New York, USA)
Information Science Reference • copyright 2012 • 319pp • H/C (ISBN: 9781466609785) • US $195.00 (our price)

www.igi-global.com

701 E. Chocolate Ave., Hershey, PA 17033
Order online at www.igi-global.com or call 717-533-8845 x100
To place a standing order for titles released in this series, contact: cust@igi-global.com
Mon-Fri 8:00 am - 5:00 pm (est) or fax 24 hours a day 717-533-8661

Table of Contents

Section 2
Current Advances of Trust Management in Mobile Environments

Section 3
Autonomic and Usable Trust Management in Mobile Environments

Preface

Trust is firstly a social phenomenon. It is a multidimensional, multidisciplinary, and multifaceted concept. Various definitions exist in the literature. Common notions are confidence, belief, and expectation regarding the reliability, integrity, ability, or characters of an entity. In general, trust is subjective because acceptably sufficient trust levels differ for each entity. It is also dynamic, affected by many factors. It can further develop and evolve due to good experience. Bad experience, however, can cause decay due to sensitivity. From the digital system point of view, trust is an assessment on a trusting object based on the criteria of a trusting subject and a number of trust attributes (e.g., competence, security, dependability, and so on).

Trust plays a crucial role in our social life. With the rapid development of mobile communication and networking technologies, trust has become an important factor that influences the success of our digital life in mobile environments. Trust modeling and management are a useful means to control and manage trust in mobile computing systems. Transforming from a social concept of trust to a digital concept, trust modeling and management help in designing and implementing a trustworthy digital system, especially in emerging mobile computing systems and environments (e.g., self-organized mobile computing systems such as ad hoc networks and pervasive systems, etc.). Nowadays, trust management is emerging as a promising technology to facilitate collaboration among entities in a mobile environment where traditional security paradigms cannot be enforced due to lack of centralized control and incomplete knowledge of the environment.

The method to specify, evaluate, set up, and ensure trust relationships among entities is the trust model. The trust model aids the digital processing and/or controlling of trust. Trust management is concerned with: collecting the information required to make a trust relationship decision, evaluating the criteria related to the trust relationship as well as monitoring and reevaluating existing trust relationships, and automating the above process. However, an extension of this definition is needed to automatically ensure a dynamically changed trust relationship towards autonomic trust management. More importantly, due to the subjective characteristic of trust, trust management should also consider the role and influence of human beings. It is preferred that the design of trust management system is human-centric.

This book aims to provide a single record of current technologies and applications in Trust Management (TM), especially focusing on autonomic and usable TM in mobile environments. The overall objectives are to investigate various definitions or understandings of trust and extract its characteristics; study how to model trust in a digital approach and implement the model for establishing and managing trust in a mobile system; overview the literature of TM in mobile computing; summarize the achievement of TM in mobile cloud computing, mobile social networking, and future mobile Internet; and introduce autonomic and usable trust management solutions in the mobile domain. Regarding future research trends, the book indicates special issues needed to be solved for practical deployment of trust management systems in mobile computing environments.

Research on trust modeling and management is a prosperous area. It has become important in recent years because this technology can be applied to various areas to construct a trustworthy, secure, and dependable system, especially when collaboration of system entities is needed. Current research ultimately aims to empower individuals and organizations in building competencies for exploiting the opportunities of trustworthy mobile environments.

This book is designed for a professional audience who wishes to learn about the state of the art in trust modeling and management. More specifically, the book offers theoretical perspective and practical solutions to graduate and post-graduate students, researchers, and practitioners working in the areas of trust, security, and privacy in mobile computing systems (e.g., ad hoc networks, pervasive and ubiquitous computing, mobile computing platforms, social networking, grid computing, cloud computing, and software systems, etc.). This book is also suitable as a supplemental text or reference book for the graduate level or post-graduate level, as well as advanced undergraduate students in computer science, information science, computer engineering, Information Technology (IT), and electrical engineering.

This book integrates autonomic and usable trust management together and provides the latest research, development, and application results in this field to researchers, engineers, advanced undergraduates, and graduate students who are interested in the technologies and applications of TM. The proposed book will:

- Concern both subjective and dynamic characteristic of trust;
- Focus on autonomic and usable trust modeling and management technologies and solutions;
- Identify new requirements and challenges of TM in different scenarios of mobile environments;
- Present the latest research and development results in the focused topics;
- Investigate how some advanced technologies can be applied into mobile computing systems; and
- Be involved in more complete issues related to TM in mobile environments (e.g., privacy enhancement and key management, for practical system deployment).

Special attention will be paid to autonomic and usable trust modeling and management. More importantly, we aim to reveal how to achieve user trust and human-computer trust interaction and how to apply a human-centric trust modeling and management methodology into developing practical solutions.

The nine chapters of this book:

- Investigate various definitions or understandings of trust and its characteristics;
- Overview the literature of trust modeling and management in mobile networking, computing, and communications, analyzing current research issues and discussing future research trends;
- Study the recent advances of trust management in mobile environments and explore usable and autonomic trust management solutions for mobile cloud computing, unwanted traffic control, trustworthy pervasive social networking, and human-computer trust interaction; and
- Provide practical and comprehensive solutions for usable and autonomic trust management based on both trusted computing technology and trust evaluation by applying an inter-disciplinary methodology.

The prospective audience would be anyone who is interested in trust, security, and privacy; academics, technical managers, socialists, psychologists, and information security officers. The book can be used as a reference to achieve a general overview of trust modeling and management. It could serve as a textbook or reference materials for undergraduate and/or postgraduate teaching. IT industrial designers and architects may also refer to this book when designing and developing a practical trust management system in mobile environments.

ORGANIZATION OF THE BOOK

This book is organized into three sections, with a total of nine chapters. The first section introduces the technical background of trust modeling and management, which includes three chapters. This section also acts as tutorial material for a wide range of audiences, including advanced undergraduate students of IT.

Section 1: Background – Trust, Trust Modeling, and Trust Management

Chapter 1: Perspective and Characteristics of Trust – Understanding Trust in Different Disciplines

Chapter 1 introduces various perspectives of trust in different disciplines, investigates the factors that influence trust, and summarizes its basic characteristics. As the first chapter, it also introduces the contents and structure of the whole book, as well as the internal-relationships of the nine chapters.

Chapter 2: Trust Modeling and Computational Trust – Digitalizing Trust

Chapter 2 introduces the theories of trust modeling and computational trust. It classifies existing trust models based on different criteria, introduces a number of technologies applied in trust evaluation, and discusses the current problems and challenges in the literature.

Chapter 3: Trust Management and Its Challenges

Chapter 3 briefly introduces trust management technologies and gives a couple of concrete example solutions for the purpose of tutorial illustration. In addition, it discusses the current issues, problems, other interesting application scenarios, and future research trends in the area of trust management.

The second section introduces the current advances of trust management in mobile environments, focusing on mobile cloud computing, pervasive social networking, and the future Internet. It includes three chapters.

Section 2: Current Advances of Trust Management in Mobile Environments

Chapter 4: Trust Management in Mobile Cloud Computing

Chapter 4 introduces the advances of trust management technologies in cloud computing and mobile cloud computing. It analyzes the basic requirements of trust management in mobile cloud computing based on its architecture and distinct characteristics. This chapter further proposes a number of schemes in order to automatically control data access based on trust evaluation in a mobile cloud computing environment. Unsolved issues and future research challenges are also discussed.

Chapter 5: Trust Management for Unwanted Traffic Control

Chapter 5 discusses applying a trust management technology to conduct unwanted traffic control on the Internet, especially the mobile Internet. This chapter proposes a generic unwanted traffic control solution through trust management. It can control unwanted traffic from its source to destinations in a personalized manner according to trust evaluation at a Global Trust Operator and traffic and behavior analysis at hosts. Thus, it can support unwanted traffic control in both a distributed and centralized manner and in both a defensive and offensive way.

Chapter 6: Trust Management in Pervasive Social Networking

Chapter 6 reviews the literature with regard to how to build up trust in pervasive social networking. It explores whether pervasive social networking is demanded, considering many existing popular Internet social networking services. It proposes a trust management framework that holistically supports context-aware trust/reputation generation, trustworthy content recommendations, secure communications, unwanted traffic control, user privacy recommendation, and secure face-to-face pervasive social communications.

Although the chapters in Section 2 touch either autonomic or usable trust management solutions here and there in several concrete mobile domains, both autonomic and usable TM are not discussed in an oriented or specific manner. The third section further introduces a number of solutions for both autonomic and usable trust management in mobile environments. The contents of Section 3 further show the particular advance of trust management in mobile environments towards practical deployment, system intelligence, and social acceptance.

Section 3: Autonomic and Usable Trust Management in Mobile Environments

Chapter 7: User Trust and Human-Computer Trust Interaction

Chapter 7 explores the factors that influence trust in human-computer interaction (i.e., the construct of Human-Computer Trust Interaction [HCTI]) and proposes a number of instructions to improve user trust for human-computer interaction. This chapter discusses the ways for improving usability of trust management.

Chapter 8: Autonomic Trust Management in Mobile Environments

Chapter 8 introduces an autonomic trust management solution in mobile environments by applying both trusted computing and trust evaluation technologies. Its applicability is illustrated by applying it to a number of mobile application scenarios.

Chapter 9: Usable Trust Modeling and Management

Chapter 9 introduces a human-centric trust modeling and management method in order to design and develop a usable trust management solution that can be easily accepted by users towards practical deployment. Its effectiveness is illustrated by applying it to the design of a reputation system for mobile applications in order to achieve both usable and autonomic trust management.

Towards autonomic and usable trust modeling and management, the book covers the entire scope of studies for developing a trustworthy mobile system: from mobile Internet unwanted traffic control to mobile social networking, from mobile cloud computing to various mobile systems, from system framework and architecture to user interface and human-computer interaction. The book provides a comprehensive study on usable and autonomic trust management system development. Writing this book has been an enlightening and thought-provoking experience for me. I hope you enjoying reading this book. I will be happy if you find this book helpful and your interest in the field of trust modeling and management further aroused by reading the various perspectives presented herein.

Zheng Yan
Xidian University, China & Aalto University, Finland

Acknowledgment

I had a plan to write such a monograph several years ago when I was editing another book about trust modeling and management in digital environments in 2009. Most contents in this book are based on work conducted at the Nokia Research Center, Helsinki, Aalto University, Finland, and Xidian University, China. I would like to express my sincere gratitude to the Nokia Research Center for initiating my research on trust modeling and management. I would like to extend my gratitude to Prof. Raimo Kantola, Aalto University, for his support with writing the book. This work is also sponsored by the Fundamental Research Funds for the Central Universities under Grant K5051201032 and the initial grant of Chinese Educational Ministry for researchers returned from abroad.

This project began in May 2011 and ended in December 2012. Some contents of the book are based on my cooperation with a number of previous colleagues and students: Ms. Yu Chen, Ms. Yue Shen, Prof. Valtteri Niemi, Prof. Raimo Kantola, Dr. Silke Holtmanns, Prof. Christian Prehofer, Prof. Peng Zhang, Prof. Robert H. Deng, Prof. Yan Dong, Dr. Conghui Liu, and Dr. Piotr Cofta. My sincere thanks to all of them!

I would like to thank IGI Global for inviting me to develop this book and the editorial assistants whose efficient and cheerful assistance throughout the project made it an enjoyable experience.

I was fortunate in having great support and encouragement from my family. I feel deeply indebted to my husband, Peng, for his endless care in both my life and work, which has been a great source of inspiration in the completion of this book. Actually, it was he who motivated me to develop a book by myself in order to summarize my perspectives on usable and autonomic trust management. Last but not the least, my love and thanks to my son, Kuan, who is always the source of my happiness and my strength to overcome challenges in the life. The book is for my loves: Peng and Kuan.

Zheng Yan
Xidian University, China & Aalto University, Finland
December 3, 2012

Section 1
Background: Trust, Trust Modeling, and Trust Management

Chapter 1
Perspective and Characteristics of Trust:
Understanding Trust in Different Disciplines

ABSTRACT

Trust plays a crucial role in our social life to facilitate coordination and cooperation for mutual benefits. With the rapid growth of digital computing and networking technologies, especially in mobile domains, trust becomes an important aspect in the design, development, and maintenance of secure computing systems and mobile systems. Trust is a complicated concept. For understanding it in a comprehensive way, this chapter introduces various perspectives of trust in different disciplines, investigates the factors that influence trust and summarizes its basic characteristics. As the first chapter, it also provides a guideline for reading the whole book.

1. INTRODUCTION

Trust plays a crucial role in our social life. It is a key component to facilitate coordination and cooperation for mutual benefits. With the rapid growth of global digital computing and networking technologies, trust becomes an important aspect in the design, establishment and maintenance of a secure computing system and a mobile system. This raises the importance of trust between interacting digital entities. However, a traditional legal framework is not able to provide the needed trustworthiness for digital entities, e.g., in an electronic transaction and remote collaboration. Managing trust relationships has become critically important in the development of a digital system, especially in a mobile environment. In particular, for some emerging technologies, such as MANET (Mobile Ad Hoc Networks), ubiquitous computing, mobile social networking and cloud computing, trust management has been proposed as a useful solution to break through new challenges of security

DOI: 10.4018/978-1-4666-4765-7.ch001

Copyright © 2014, IGI Global. Copying or distributing in print or electronic forms without written permission of IGI Global is prohibited.

and privacy caused by the special characteristics of these systems, such as dynamic topology and mobility (Yan, Zhang, & Virtanen 2003; Yan 2006; Lin et al. 2004).

Trust is a very complicated phenomena attached to multiple disciplines and influenced by many measurable and non-measurable factors. It is defined in various ways for different purposes and based on disparate cultures, even though in the area of information technology. Thereby, it is difficult to give a common and comprehensive definition for this ordinary concept. Moreover, establishing a trust relationship in a mobile environment relates more aspects and issues than in the social world. This is because communications in a mobile computing network rely on not only relevant human beings and their relationships, but also digital components. On the other hand, the visual trust impression is missing and need somehow to be compensated. Additionally, it is more difficult to accumulate accurate information for trust assessment in mobile communications where information can be easily distorted or faked identities can be created. The mapping of our social understanding of trust into the digital world and the creation of trust models that are feasible in practice are challenging. Understanding the trust

relationship between two digital entities could help selecting and applying feasible measures to overcome potential security and privacy risks. Due to the complexity of trust, it is essential to understand various perspectives of trust in different disciplines and its basic characteristics.

This chapter reviews the perception of trust concept and analyzes its characteristics. We also summarize the factors that influence trust and comment which ones are particularly important in a number of specific scenarios.

2. PERCEPTION OF TRUST CONCEPT

What is trust? Referring to Figure 1, we can see that trust is the reliance of a kid on his/her parents. It is a risk to put your life into the hands of colleagues or friends; it is about secret sharing; it relates to loyal and truthful; it is collaboration for achieving a common target and gaining a mutual benefit; it is a kind of dependence facing a danger; it is also a belief on a person's skills, competence and capabilities with regard to professional knowledge and technologies, e.g., a doctor's medical treatment skills.

Figure 1. The concept of trust

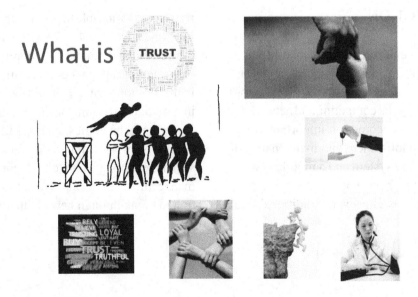

We can find various definitions of trust in the literature. For example, it can be loosely defined as a state involving confident positive expectations about another's motives with respect to oneself in situations entailing risk (Boon & Holmes, 1991). This definition highlights three main characteristics of trust. First, a trust relationship involves at least two entities: a trusting subject named trustor and a trusting object named trustee, reliant on each other for a mutual benefit. Second, trust involves uncertainty and risk. There is no perfect guarantee to ensure that the trustee will live up to the trustor's expectation. Third, the trustor has faith in the trustee's honesty and benevolence, and believes that the trustee will not betray his/her risk-assuming behavior.

Gambetta (1990) defined trust as trust (or, symmetrically, distrust) is a particular level of the subjective probability with which an agent will perform a particular action, both before [we] can monitor such action (or independently of his capacity of ever to be able to monitor it) and in a context in which it affects [our] own action. Mayer, Davis, and Schoorman (1995) provided the definition of trust as the willingness of a party to be vulnerable to the actions of another party based on the expectation that the other party will perform a particular action important to the trustor, irrespective of the ability to monitor or control that other party. These definitions point out another important main characteristic of trust: Trust is subjective. The level of trust considered sufficient is different for each individual in a certain situation. Trust may be affected by those actions that we cannot (digitally) monitor. The level of trust depends on how our own actions are in turn affected by the trustee's actions.

Trust is expressed in various ways in different context and technology areas. Herein, we list a number of examples.

- **On-Line Trust:** On-line trust is an attitude of confident expectation in an online situation of risk that one's vulnerabilities will not be exploited (Corritore, Kracher, & Wiedenbeck, 2003). This definition implies that trust is a kind of expectation or confidence in a specific context with regard to a risk.

- **Agent Trust:** In a multi-agent system, trust is a subjective expectation an agent has about another agent's future behavior (Mui, 2003). This definition indicates that trust is subjective and a kind of expectation related to a trustee's future behavior.

- **Software Trust:** In the area of software engineering, trust is accepted dependability in a software system (Avizienis, Laprie, Randell, & Landwehr, 2004). This definition points out trust is about a trustor's criteria on a trustee's quality (e.g., dependability).

- **MANET Trust:** For an ad hoc network, trust was defined as the reliability, timeliness, and integrity of message delivery to the intended next-hop of a node (Liu, Joy, & Thompson, 2004). In the concrete context of message delivery in MANET, trust is about the various quality attributes of a purpose.

- **Internet Application Trust:** Regarding Internet applications, trust is a qualified belief by a trustor with respect to the competence, honesty, security and dependability of a trustee within a special context (Grandison & Sloman, 2000). This definition implies that trust is the belief of a trustor on the trustee's various properties and this belief relates to a specific context.

In summary, trust is a multidisciplinary, multidimensional and multifaceted concept. The concept of trust has been studied in disciplines ranging from economics to psychology, from sociology to medicine, and to information and computer science (Yan, 2007). We can find various definitions of trust in the literature although researchers in different disciplines have agreed the importance of trust in the conduct of human affairs (Grabner-Kräuter & Kaluscha, 2003). Economists and sociologists have been interested in how institutions and incentives are created to reduce the anxiety and uncertainty associated with transactions (Granovetter, 1985; Zucker, 1986; Williamson, 1993). Personality psychologists traditionally have viewed trust as a belief, expectancy, or feeling that is deeply rooted in the personality and has its origins in the early psychological development of an individual (Rotter, 1967, 1971; Wrightsman, 1991). Social psychologists define trust as an expectation about the behavior of others in transactions, focusing on the contextual factors that serve either to enhance or inhibit the development and maintenance of trust (Lewicki & Bunker, 1995). In interpersonal communications, trust is a state involving confident positive expectations about another's motives with respect to oneself in situations entailing risk (Boon & Holmes, 1991). For making and breaking cooperative relations, Gambetta (2000) defined trust (or, symmetrically, distrust) as a particular level of the subjective probability. Mayer, Davis, and Schoorman (1995) viewed trust in organizational management as the willingness of a party to be vulnerable to the actions of another party.

In information science and computer science, expressions of trust are targeting at different contexts and technology areas that have their roots in different disciplines. Trust is a widely used term whose definition differs among researchers and application areas (Artz & Gil, 2007). Grandison and Sloman (2000) held an opinion that trust is a qualified belief by a trustor with respect to the competence, honesty, security and dependability of a trustee within a special context with regard to internet applications. On-line trust is an attitude of confident expectation in an online situation of risk that one's vulnerabilities will not be exploited (Corritore, Kracher, & Wiedenbeck, 2003). In a multi-agent system, trust is a subjective expectation an agent has about the future behavior of another agent (Mui, 2003). From a software engineering point of view, trust is accepted dependability (Avizienis et al., 2004). In an ad hoc network, trust has been interpreted as reputation, trusting opinion, probability, etc. (Sun et al., 2006). More concretely, trust could be defined as the reliability, timeliness, and integrity of message delivery to the intended next-hop of a node (Liu, Joy, & Thompson, 2004). Denning (1993) emphasized the importance of assessment for trust in a system, which is of particular importance in the digital environment where the entities often just have digital artifacts to base their trust judgment on. The current paradigm for trusted computing systems holds that trust is a property of a system. It can be formally modeled, specified, and verified. Trust is an assessment that an entity can be counted on to perform according to a given set of policies or standards with regard to some action. In particular, a system is trusted if and only if its users trust it. Trust itself is an assessment made by users based on how well the observed behavior of the system meets their own standards or expectation (Yan & Holtmanns, 2008).

McKnight and Chervany (2000, 2003) conducted analysis on the trust definitions and noted that trust is a concept hard to define because it is itself a vague term. Looking up the term "trust" in a dictionary may reveal many explanations since it is a cross-disciplinary concept. For example, from the sociologists' point of view, it is related to social structure. From the psychologists' point of view, it concerns personal traits. From the economists' point of view, it is a mechanism of economic choice and risk management (Yan & Holtmanns, 2008). Computer scientists pay more attention to the security and dependability of a digital system. The definitions of trust can be classified based on the consideration of structure, disposition, attitude, feeling, expectancy, belief, intention, and behavior.

Overall, trust has been defined by researchers in many different ways, which often reflect the paradigms of the particular academic disciplines of the researchers. There are literally dozens of definitions of trust, which many researchers find contradictory and confusing (Grabner-Kräuter & Kaluscha, 2003). Common to these definitions are the notions of confidence, belief, faith, hope, expectation, dependence, and reliance on the goodness, strength, reliability, integrity, ability, or characters of a person or thing (Yan, 2007). No matter what kind of trust is discussed, e.g., system trust, human trust, individual trust and institutional trust, a trust relationship generally involves at least two parties: a trustor and a trustee. The trustor is the trusting subject who holds confidence, belief, etc. on the reliability, integrity, ability, etc. of another person or thing, which is the object of trust - the trustee.

3. FACTORS THAT INFLUENCE TRUST

Trust is highly related to security. Many people think that trust is security. This is not true. In order to gain trust, especially in a digital system, ensuring system security and user safety is a necessity. However, trust is more than security. It relates not only security, but also many other factors, such as goodness, strength, reliability, availability, integrity, ability, or other characters of an entity. The concept of trust covers a bigger scope than security, thus it is more complicated to establish, ensure and maintain, in short manage trust than security.

Another important concept related to trust is privacy. The term *privacy* denotes the ability of an entity to determine whether, when, and to whom information about itself is to be released or disclosed (Yan & Holtmanns, 2008). Some researchers think that trust conflicts with privacy. In our social life, private information should be shared in order to gain trust. With trust, people are willing to share or reveal personal information. On the other hand, some people think trust helps ensuring privacy. A trustworthy digital system should firstly preserve its users' privacy. Trust

is beyond and will enhance system security and personal privacy. Trust, security and privacy are related crucial issues in the emerging technical areas in mobile environments.

As mentioned above, trust is a multifaceted concept, which is influenced by many factors. Since trust is also impacted by context. Its influencing factors could be different in different situations. The discussion of different trust concepts and constructs does not aim at reaching consensus on a single definition (Grabner-Kräuter & Kaluscha, 2003). Although the richness of the concept, we can still summarize the subjective and objective factors that are relevant to a decision of trust, as shown in Table 1. The factors influencing trust can be classified into five categories (Yan & Holtmanns, 2008):

- Trustee's objective properties, such as a trustee's security and dependability. Particularly, reputation is a public assessment of the trustee regarding its earlier behaviors.
- Trustee's subjective properties, such as trustee honesty.
- Trustor's subjective properties, such as trustor disposition to trust.

Table 1. Factors influencing trust

Trustee's objective properties	Competence; ability; security; dependability; integrity; predictability; reliability; timeliness; (observed) behavior; strength.
Trustee's subjective properties	Honesty; benevolence; goodness.
Trustor's objective properties	Assessment; a given set of standards; trustor's standards.
Trustor's subjective properties	Confidence; (subjective) expectations or expectancy; subjective probability; willingness; belief; disposition; attitude; feeling; intention; faith; hope; trustor's dependence and reliance.
Context	Situations entailing risk; structural; risk; domain of action; environment (time, place, involved persons), purpose of trust.

- Trustor's objective properties, such as the criteria or policies specified by the trustor for a trust decision.
- Context that the trust relationship resides in, such as the purpose of trust, the environment of trust (e.g., time, location, activity, devices being used, their operational mode, etc.), and the risk of trust. It specifies any information that can be used to characterize the background or situation of the involved entities (Dey, 2001). It is a very important factor influencing trust. It specifies the situation where trust exists. Dey defined the ability of a computing system to identify and adapt to its context as context-awareness (Dey, 2001).

If Te_o denotes the trustee Te's objective properties, Te_s denotes Te's subjective properties, Tr_o denotes the trustor Tr's objective properties, Tr_s denotes Tr's subjective properties, and C denotes the context of trust, the trust relationship R between Tr and Te can be simply expressed as the following formula:

$$R(Tr \rightarrow Te) = F(Te\_o, Te\_s, Tr\_o, Tr\_s, C) \quad (1)$$

In general, trust is subjective because acceptably sufficient trust levels differ for each entity. It is the subjective expectation of a trustor on a trustee related to the trustee's behaviors that could influence the trustor's belief in the truestee. It is also dynamic, affected by many factors. It can further develop and evolve due to good experience. Bad experience, however, can cause decay due to sensitivity. From the digital system point of view, trust is an assessment of the trustee based on the trustor's criteria and a number of trust attributes, e.g., competence, security, reliability, etc.

From the digital system point of view, we pay more attention to the objective properties of both the trustor and the trustee. For social human interaction, we consider the trustee's subjective and objective properties and the trustor's subjective properties. For economic transactions, we study the context for risk management. The context of trust is a very important factor that influences a trust relationship, e.g., the why and when to trust. Trust is influenced by many factors, but the impact of different factors could vary in dissimilar contexts.

Taking a concrete example, factors of software trust is illustrated in Figure 2. The software trust is related to software security that concerns avail-

Figure 2. Factors of software trust (Avizienis et al., 2004)

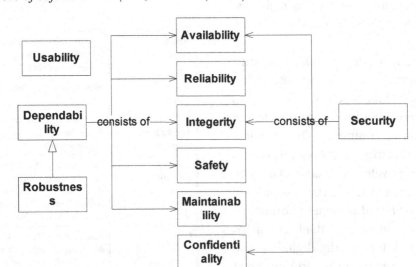

ability, integrity and confidentiality, and software dependability that relates to availability, reliability, integrity, safety and maintainability. Meanwhile, software trust is also highly influenced by software usability and the robustness of the system that runs the software. We can see that the software trust is mainly impacted by the objective properties of software. The subjective factors of a software user (i.e., trustor) could also influence user trust in software, considering software usability and the context of software usage (e.g., usage purpose).

4. CHARACTERISTICS OF TRUST

Despite the diversity among the existing definitions of trust, and despite that a precise definition is missing in the literature, there is a large commonality on the properties of trust. Rousseau, Sitkin, Burt, and Camerer (1998) also observed considerable overlap and synthesis in contemporary scholarship on trust. Particularly, the most common characteristics of trust, which play as the important guidelines for trust modeling are:

Trust is directed. This property says that trust is an oriented relationship between the trustor and the trustee. Entity A trusts Entity B doesn't mean B trusts A. For example, students trust their teacher to solve a question, while the teacher cannot trust his students to provide a right answer on the same question.

Trust is subjective. Trust is inherently a subjective or personal opinion. According to the survey conducted by Grandison and Sloman (2000), trust is considered a personal and subjective phenomenon that is based on various factors or evidence, and that some of those may carry more weight than others. Trust is different for each individual in a certain situation. This characteristic is also reflected in many existing definitions of trust. Taking an on-line payment toolkit as an example, a software engineer would like to trust and use it for on-line payment, while a retired English teacher dare not trust and use it at all. Different people hold different opinions on trust even in the same situation.

Trust is context-dependent. In general, trust is a subjective belief about an entity in a particular context. Taking a simple example to understand this, we trust our mathematics teacher to solve a mathematical problem, but we cannot trust him to drive a flight if he has no flight driving licence. Obviously, a trust relationship could be changed due to the change of context.

Trust is measurable. A trust value can be used to represent the different degrees of trust an entity may have in another. "Trust is measurable" also provides the foundation for trust modeling and computational evaluation. Current literature shows that trust can be measured in various ways based on a number of theories. In Chapter 2, we will illustrate in details how to evaluate trust in a digital way in order to get a quantified expression of trust: trust value.

Trust depends on history. This property implies that past experience may influence the present level of trust. The current trust value is normally inferred based on the knowledge and experiences accumulated in the past. Thus, it is a function related to the past value of trust.

Trust is dynamic. Trust is usually non-monotonically changed with time. The trust value is also a function of time. It may be refreshed or revoked periodically, and must be able to adapt to the changing conditions of the environment in which the trust decision is made. Trust is sensitive to be influenced due to some factors, events, or changes of context. In order to handle this dynamic property of trust, solutions should take into account the notion of learning and reasoning. The dynamical adaptation of the trust relationship between two entities requires a sophisticated trust management approach (Grandison and Sloman, 2000).

Trust is conditionally transferable. Information about trust can be transmitted/received along a chain (or network) of recommendations. The conditions are often bound to the context and the objective factors of the trustor. If Entity A trusts B and B trusts C, most possibly A could trust C under a certain condition.

Trust can be a composite property. "Trust is really a composition of many different attributes: reliability, dependability, honesty, truthfulness, security, competence, and timeliness, which may have to be considered depending on the environment in which trust is being specified" (Grandison and Sloman, 2000, pp. 3). Compositionality is an important feature for making trust calculations. Trust is not only established based on the personal experiences of a trustor, but also greatly impacted by the recommending opinions on a trustee provided by other entities that are trusted by the trustor. The final trust value is calculated by composing or aggregating of all above information.

Figure 3 shows a graphic expression of trust by considering its characteristics. It is a sign directed graph with feedback, consisting of nodes and weighted arcs. The nodes describe the entities that are connected by signed and weighted arcs representing their trust relationships and trust values. The value of Entity A's trust in B, denoted $Tv_{A,B}$ is a function of time t, trust relationship $R(A \rightarrow B)$ and past trust value $Tv'_{A,B}$, as described below:

$$Tv_{A,B} = TE\left\{t, R(A \rightarrow B), Tv'_{A,B}\right\} \qquad (2)$$

Since Entity A and C have no direct trust relationship but $R(A \rightarrow B)$ and $R(B \rightarrow C)$ exist (shown in solid arcs in Figure 3), $R(A \rightarrow C)$

(shown in a dash arc in Figure 3) can be inferred from $R(A \rightarrow B)$ and $R(B \rightarrow C)$ according to the property of "*Trust is conditionally transferable*".

5. A GUIDELINE OF BOOK READING

This book is organized into three sections, with a total of nine chapters. The first section introduces the technical background of trust, trust modeling and management in three chapters. Based on the understanding of trust concept and its characteristics, it is possible to conduct trust modeling especially in a mathematical way, while trust modeling is the basis for trust management. This section plays as a tutorial material for a wide range of audience including advanced undergraduate students of IT. It is designed for a professional audience who wishes to learn about the state of the art in trust modeling and management. The second section introduces the current advances of trust management in mobile environments, focusing on several hot topics like mobile cloud computing, pervasive social networking and the future Internet. This section offers theoretical perspective and practical solutions to graduate and post-graduate students, researchers and practitioners working in the areas of trust, security and privacy in mobile computing systems. The third section further introduces a number of solutions for both autonomic and usable trust management in mobile environments, starting from user trust and human-computer trust interaction, the book discusses autonomic trust management based on hybrid trust management technolo-

Figure 3. A graphic expression of trust

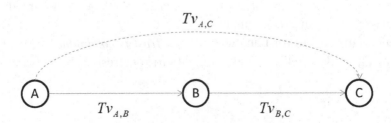

gies and investigates usable trust management by applying a user driven human-centric trust management methodology. The contents of this section further show the particular advance of trust management in mobile environments towards practical deployment, system intelligence and social acceptance. It is a good reading material for advanced professionals who are interested in human-centric trust management design and the deployment of intelligent trust management systems that can be easily accepted by mobile users. Chapter 7 requests readers to have a background of sociology, psychology and human-computer interaction (HCI). Figure 4 shows the structure of the book and specifies the target readers. The author suggests normal readers starting reading from the beginning and going ahead chapter by chapter. Advanced professionals in the area of trust management and trusted computing can directly jump to interesting chapters for reference. The exercises proposed at the end of each chapter aim to stimulate scientific thinking after reading. It can be applied in the post-graduate level teaching as classroom discussion topics or homework.

Some exercises request self-learning and serious thinking. Normal readers can ignore this part.

6. CONCLUSION

This chapter provides a brief review on perspective and characteristics of trust in order to understand trust from the view of different disciplines. We presented quite a number of existing trust definitions in the literature and analyzed them seriously in order to summarize the common understandings of trust and its general characteristics. We identified the relation and difference between trust and security, as well as privacy. Furthermore, the factors that influence trust were summarized in a comprehensive manner. As an example, we illustrated the factors of software trust in order to show the trust influencing factors are context-related. The comprehensive and sufficient understanding of trust could greatly help us modeling trust in an accurate measure by involving its influencing factors with context-awareness and considering its characteristics. A guideline of reading was provided at the end to instruct book audiences.

Figure 4. Structure of book

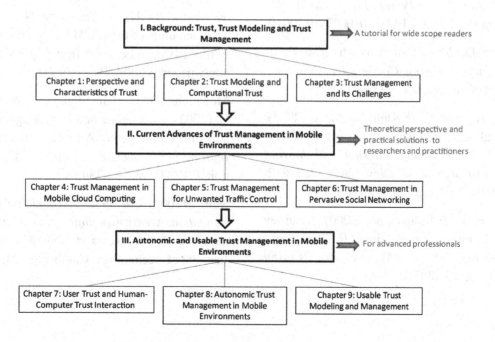

REFERENCES

Artz, D., & Gil, Y. (2007). A survey of trust in computer science and the semantic web. *Web Semantics: Science, Services, and Agents on the World Wide Web, 5*(2). doi:10.1016/j.websem.2007.03.002.

Avizienis, A., Laprie, J. C., Randell, B., & Landwehr, C. (2004). Basic concepts and taxonomy of dependable and secure computing. *IEEE Transactions on Dependable and Secure Computing, 1*(1), 11–33. doi:10.1109/TDSC.2004.2.

Boon, S., & Holmes, J. (1991). The dynamics of interpersonal trust: Resolving uncertainty in the face of risk. In R. Hinde, & J. Groebel (Eds.), *Cooperation and Prosocial Behavior.* Cambridge, UK: Cambridge University Press.

Corritore, C. L., Kracher, B., & Wiedenbeck, S. (2003). On-line trust: Concepts, evolving themes, a model. *International Journal of Human-Computer Studies. Trust and Technology, 58*(6), 737–758.

Denning, D. E. (1993). A new paradigm for trusted systems. In *Proceedings of the IEEE New Paradigms Workshop.* IEEE.

Dey, A. K. (2001). Understanding and using context. *Journal of Personal and Ubiquitous Computing, 5,* 4–7. doi:10.1007/s007790170019.

Gambetta, D. (2000). Can we trust trust? In *Trust: Making and Breaking Cooperative Relations.* Oxford, UK: University of Oxford.

Grabner-Kräuter, S., & Kaluscha, E. A. (2003). Empirical research in on-line trust: A review and critical assessment. *International Journal of Human-Computer Studies, 58*(6), 783–812. doi:10.1016/S1071-5819(03)00043-0.

Grandison, T., & Sloman, M. (2000). A survey of trust in internet applications. *IEEE Communications and Survey, 3*(4), 2–16. doi:10.1109/COMST.2000.5340804.

Granovetter, M. S. (1985). Economic action and socialstructure. *American Journal of Sociology, 91,* 481–510. doi:10.1086/228311.

Lewicki, R. J., & Bunker, B. (1995). Trust in relationships: A model of trust development and decline. In *Conflict, Cooperation and Justice.* San Francisco, CA: Jossey-Bass.

Lin, C., Varadharajan, V., Wang, Y., & Pruthi, V. (2004). Enhancing grid security with trust management. In *Proceedings of IEEE International Conf. on Services Computing,* (pp. 303-310). IEEE.

Liu, Z., Joy, A. W., & Thompson, R. A. (2004). A dynamic trust model for mobile ad hoc networks. In *Proceedings of the 10th IEEE International Workshop on Future Trends of Distributed Computing Systems* (FTDCS 2004), (pp. 80–85). IEEE.

Mayer, R. C., Davis, J. H., & Schoorman, F. D. (1995). An integrative model of organizational trust. *Academy of Management Review, 20*(3), 709–734.

McKnight, D. H., & Chervany, N. L. (2000). What is trust? A conceptual analysis and an interdisciplinary model. In *Proceedings of the 2000 Americas Conference on Information Systems* (AMCI2000). Long Beach, CA: AIS.

McKnight, D. H., & Chervany, N. L. (2003). The meanings of trust. *UMN University Report.* Retrieved December 2006, from http://misrc.umn.edu/wpaper/WorkingPapers/9604.pdf

McKnight, D. H., Choudhury, V., & Kacmar, C. (2002). Developing and validating trust measures for e-commerce: An integrative typology. *Information Systems Research, 13*(3), 334–359. doi:10.1287/isre.13.3.334.81.

Mui, L. (2003). *Computational models of trust and reputation: Agents, evolutionary games, and social networks.* (Doctoral dissertation). Massachusetts Institute of Technology, Cambridge, MA.

Rotter, J. B. (1967). A new scale for the measurement of interpersonal trust. *Journal of Personality*, *35*, 651–665. doi:10.1111/j.1467-6494.1967.tb01454.x PMID:4865583.

Rotter, J. B. (1971). Generalized expectancies for interpersonal trust. *The American Psychologist*, *26*, 443–452. doi:10.1037/h0031464.

Rousseau, D. M., Sitkin, S. B., Burt, R. S., & Camerer, C. (1998). Not so different after all: A cross-discipline view of trust. *Academy of Management Review*, *23*(3), 393–404. doi:10.5465/AMR.1998.926617.

Sun, Y., Yu, W., Han, Z., & Liu, K. J. R. (2006). Information theoretic framework of trust modeling and evaluation for ad hoc networks. *IEEE Journal on Selected Areas in Communications*, *24*(2), 305–317. doi:10.1109/JSAC.2005.861389.

Williamson, O. E. (1993). Calculativeness, trust and economic organization. *The Journal of Law & Economics*, *30*, 131–145.

Wrightsman, L. S. (1991). *Assumptions about human nature: Implications for researchers and practitioners*. Newbury Park, CA: Sage.

Yan, Z. (2007). *Trust management for mobile computing platforms*. (Doctoral dissertation). Helsinki Univ. of Technology, Helsinki, Finland.

Yan, Z., & Holtmanns, S. (2008). Trust modeling and management: From social trust to digital trust. In R. Subramanian (Ed.), *Computer Security, Privacy and Politics: Current Issues, Challenges and Solutions*. Hershey, PA: IGI Global. doi:10.4018/978-1-59904-804-8.ch013.

Yan, Z., Zhang, P., & Virtanen, T. (2003). Trust evaluation based security solution in ad hoc networks. In *Proceedings of the Seventh Nordic Workshop on Secure IT Systems* (NordSec03). NordSec.

Zucker, L. G. (1986). Production of trust: institutional sources of economic structure, 1840–1920. *Research in Organizational Behavior*, *8*, 53–111.

APPENDIX

Exercises and Questions

1. Please model trust in three different ways based on different definitions.
2. Please express the characteristics of trust in a mathematical way.
3. Please propose a model of trust based on its influencing factors.
4. Please propose a model of trust by considering its characteristics.
5. Please draw a picture with two persons to show trust characteristics.

Chapter 2
Trust Modeling and Computational Trust:
Digitalizing Trust

ABSTRACT

The trust model is the method to specify, evaluate, setup, and ensure trust relationships. It is the way to assist the process of trust in a digital system. This chapter introduces the technologies of trust modeling. The authors classify existing trust models based on different criteria and introduce a number of theories or technologies applied in trust evaluation. Furthermore, discussions on the current problems and challenges in the literature are presented.

1. INTRODUCTION

The method to specify, evaluate, set up, and ensure trust relationships among entities is the trust model (Yan & Holtmanns, 2008). It is the way to calculate trust (Yang, Sun, Kay & Yang, 2009). The trust model aids the digital processing and controlling of trust. Most existing trust models are based on the understanding of trust characteristics, accounting for factors influencing trust. Current work covers a wide area including ad hoc networks, ubiquitous computing, Peer-to-Peer (P2P) systems, multi-agent systems, web services, e-commerce, component software, and so on (Yan & Holtmanns, 2008).

Trust modeling has a history with about two decades. One of the earliest formalizations of trust in computing systems was done by Marsh (1994). In his approach, he integrated the various facets of trust from the disciplines of economics, psychology, philosophy and sociology. Since then, many trust models have been constructed for various computing paradigms such as ubiquitous computing, Peer-to-Peer (P2P) networks, and multi-agent systems. In almost all of these studies, trust is accepted as a subjective notion by all researchers, which brings us to a problem: how to measure trust? Translation of this subjective concept into a machine readable language is the main objective of trust modeling. Abdul-Rahman

DOI: 10.4018/978-1-4666-4765-7.ch002

Copyright © 2014, IGI Global. Copying or distributing in print or electronic forms without written permission of IGI Global is prohibited.

and Hailes (2000) proposed a trust model based on the work done by Marsh (1994). Their trust model focuses on online virtual communities where every agent maintained a large data structure representing a version of global knowledge about the entire network. Gil and Ratnakar (2002) described a feedback mechanism (i.e., a reputation mechanism) that assigns credibility and reliability values to sources based on the averages of feedback received from individual users.

There are various methodologies for trust modeling. They have been applied for different purposes. Some trust models are based on cryptographic technologies, e.g. Public Key Infrastructure (PKI) played as the foundation in a trust model (Perlman, 1999). A big number of trust models are developed targeting at some special trust properties, such as reputations, recommendations and risk studied by Xiong and Liu (2004) and Liang and Shi (2005). Seldom, they support multi-property of trust that is needed to take into account the factors of the trustee, the trustor and context. Many trust models have been constructed for various computing paradigms such as GRID computing, ad hoc networks, and P2P systems. These models use computational, linguistic or graphical methods. For example, Maurer (1996) described an entity's opinion about the trustworthiness of a certificate as a value in the scope of $[0, 1]$. Theodorakopoulos and Baras (2006) used a two-tuple in $[0, 1]^2$ to describe a trust opinion (refer to section 3.5). In Jøsang (1999), the metric is a triplet in $[0, 1]^3$, where the elements in the triplet represent belief, disbelief, and uncertainty, respectively. Abdul-Rahman and Hailes (2000) used discrete integer numbers to describe the degree of trust. Then, simple mathematical operations, such as minimum, maximum and weighted average, are used to calculate unknown trust values through concatenation and multi-path trust propagation. Jøsang and Ismail (2002) and Ganeriwal and Srivastava (2004) used a Bayesian model to take binary ratings as input and compute reputation scores by statistically updating beta probability density functions. Linguistic trust metrics were used for reasoning trust with provided rules by Manchala (2000). In the context of the "Web of Trust", many trust models (e.g., Reiter and Stubblebine (1998)) are built upon a graph where the resources or entities are nodes and trust relationships are edges.

One promising approach of trust modeling aims to conceptualize trust based on user studies through a psychological or sociological approach (e.g., a measurement scale). This kind of research aims to prove the complicated relationships among trust and other multiple factors in different facets. Two typical examples are the initial trust model proposed by McKnight, Choudhury, and Kacmar (2002) that explained and predicted user trust towards an e-vender in an e-commerce context, and the Technology Trust Formation Model (TTFM) studied by Li, Valacich, and Hess (2004) to explain and predict user trust towards a specific information system. Both models used the framework of the theory of reasoned action (TRA) created by Fishbein and Ajzen (1975) to explain how people form initial trust in an unfamiliar entity, and both integrated important trusting antecedents into this framework in order to effectively predict user trust. For other examples, Gefen (2000) proved that familiarity builds trust; Pennington, Wilcox, and Grover (2004) tested that one trust mechanism, vendor guarantees, has direct influence on system trust; Bhattacherjee (2002) studied three key dimensions of trust: trustee's ability, benevolence and integrity; Pavlou and Gefen (2004) explained that institutional mechanisms engender buyer trust in the community of online auction sellers. The trust models generated based on this approach are generally linguistic or graphic. They do not quantify trust for machine processing purposes. Therefore, the achieved results could only help people understanding trust precisely in order to work out a design guideline or an organizational policy towards a trustworthy digital system or a trustworthy user interface. Although little work has been conducted to integrate psychological, sociological and technological theories together, we believe, however, the psychological and sociological study results could further play as practical foundations of computational trust – modeling trust for a digital processing purpose,.

A typical approach can be found in recent researches regarding computational trust. In this approach, the characteristics of trust, principles or axioms are firstly presented; then they are modeled in a mathematical way; furthermore, the model is applied into trust evaluation or trust management for solving a specific issue. Examples of applying this method are Xiong and Liu (2004), Theodorakopoulos and Baras (2006), Song, Hwang, Zhou, and Kwok (2005), Liu, Joy, and Thompson (2004), and Sun, Yu, Han, and Liu (2006).

Modeling trust in a digital manner is crucial for autonomic trust management in order to sustain dynamically changed trust relationships in a digital system. Although a variety of trust models are available, it is still not well understood what fundamental criteria the trust models must follow. Without a good answer to this question, the design of trust models is still at an empirical stage and can never reach the expectation to simulate social trust to a satisfying degree. Current work focuses on concrete solutions in specific systems. Seldom, the usability of trust management is considered in order to achieve usable trust management for easy user acceptance. Basically, the trust model should reflect the characteristics of trust, consider the factors that influence trust, and thus support trust management in a feasible and usable way.

In the rest of this chapter, we firstly classify the trust models into different categories according to different criteria. Then, we introduce a number of prestigious trust evaluation technologies proposed in the literature. Finally, we analyze the problems of current research and specify challenges in trust modeling for future study.

2. TAXONOMY OF TRUST MODELS

The trust model aims to process and control trust using digital methods. Most of the modeling work is based on the understanding of trust characteristics and considers the factors influencing trust. The current work covers a wide area.

Trust models can be classified into various categories according to different rules or criteria. Table 1 shows the taxonomy of trust models and examples of each category. Based on the description methods, we can classify trust models into linguistic models, graphic models and mathematic models. Based on modeled contents, we can classify trust models into single-property models and multi-property models. For example, Xiong and Liu (2004) modeled the reputation as trust in P2P systems; while Yan and Prehofer (2011) considers a trustor's policy and a number of quality attributes of a trustee for autonomic trust management in a component based software systems. According to the expression of trust, we can classify trust models into models with binary ratings and models with numeral ratings, in which some work applied continuous ratings and some used discrete ratings. Based on the dimension of trust expression, we can classify trust models into the models with a single dimension, e.g., the trust models proposed by Maurer (1996) and Xiong and Liu (2004), and the models with multiple dimensions. Regarding the models with multiple dimensions, a trust value is generally expressed with several sub-values, indicating quantified dimensions of trust. For example, Jøsang (1999) described trust with three dimensions: belief, disbelief and unknown. Theodorakopoulos and Baras (2006) applied two dimensions to express trust in a comprehensive way: trust and the confidence on trust.

In addition, the trust models can also be classified based on the trusting objects into system trust model, human trust model, individual trust model and institutional trust model, and so on. For example, Yan and Prehofer (2011) proposed an adaptive trust model for component based

Table 1. Taxonomy of trust models

Criteria of Classification	Categories		Examples
Based on the description method	Models with linguistic description		Blaze, Feigenbaum, and Lacy (1996); Tan and Thoen (1998)
	Models with graphic description		Reiter and Stubblebine (1998)
	Models with mathematic description		Xiong and Liu (2004); Sun, Yu, Han, and Liu (2006)
Based on modeled contents	Single-property modeling		Xiong and Liu (2004); Sun, Yu, Han, and Liu (2006)
	Multi-property modeling		Zhou, Mei, and Zhang (2005); Wang and Varadharajan (2005); Yan and Prehofer (2011)
Based on the expression of trust	Models with binary ratings		
	Models with numeral ratings	Continuous ratings	Maurer (1996); Xiong and Liu (2004); weighted voting methods; Bayesian inference methods
		Discrete ratings	Liu, Joy, and Thompson (2004)
Based on the dimension of trust expression	Models with a single dimension		Maurer (1996); Xiong and Liu (2004)
	Models with multiple dimensions		Theodorakopoulos and Baras (2006); Jøsang (1999); Yan, Kantola and Shen (2011)
Based on the trusting objects	System trust model		Yan and Prehofer (2011)
	Human trust model		Muir (1994); Muir and Moray, (1996)
	Individual trust model		Yan et al. (2013); Li, Valacich, and Hess (2004); McKnight, Choudhury, and Kacmar (2002)
	Institutional trust model		McKnight, Cummings, and Chervany (1998); Bigley and Pearce (1998); Mayer, Davis, and Schoorman (1995)
Based on the development of trust	Initial trust model		McKnight, Choudhury, and Kacmar (2002); Li, Valacich, and Hess (2004)
	On-going trust model		Yan, Zhang, and Deng (2012); Yan et al. (2013)

software system. Muir (1994) and Muir and Moray (1996) studied human's trust in an automatic machine. The model proposed by McKnight, Choudhury, and Kacmar (2002) is about individual user trust in e-commerce. Mayer, Davis, and Schoorman (1995) explored an integrative model of organizational trust. Based on the development of trust, the trust models can be further divided into initial trust model and on-going trust model. For example, Yan et al (2013) studied the trust model of mobile application usage after initial trust is established, which belongs to the on-going trust model. The trust model about E-commerce explored by McKnight, Choudhury, and Kacmar (2002) and the Technology Trust Formation Model (TTFM) fall into the category of initial trust model.

Figure 1 illustrates a web trust model in the context of e-commerce explored by McKnight, Choudhury, and Kacmar (2002) through a user measurement scale. It is a linguistic model described by a graph. The model contains multiple properties, such as disposition to trust, institution-based trust, trusting beliefs and trusting intensions,

Figure 1. A web trust model (McKnight, Choudhury & Kacmar, 2002)

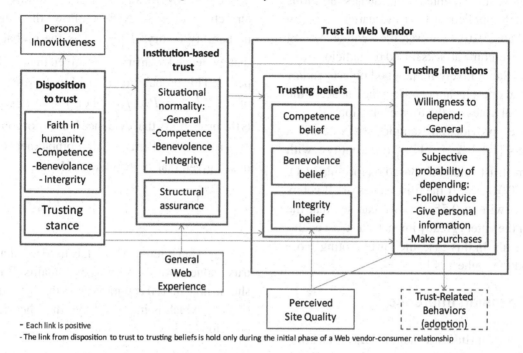

as well as other external impact factors (e.g., general web experience, perceived site quality and trust related-behaviors). It is about a user's trust model regarding e-commerce vendors, thus it is a human trust model in the stage of initial trust development and single dimensional.

3. TRUST EVALUATION TECHNOLOGIES

The main application of trust modeling is trust evaluation, especially evaluating trust in a digital manner. Trust evaluation is a technical approach of representing trust for digital processing, in which the factors influencing trust will be evaluated by a continuous or discrete real number, referred to as a trust value. Embedding a trust evaluation mechanism is necessary for providing trust intelligence in future computing and networking systems. Trust evaluation is the main aspect in the research for the purpose of digitalizing trust. In the literature, Bayesian inference, (weighted) average models,

Dempster-Shafer theory, subjective logic, fuzzy logic, entropy-based models, etc. are applied in trust modeling. In the rest of this section, we briefly introduce a number of promising theories or techniques for trust evaluation.

3.1. Weighted Voting

Trust in an object or event is evaluated based on the votes from many entities. As its names implies, Weighted Voting (WV) sums up all the votes v_k on the object with each vote weighted by the corresponding trust level of the voter T_k to output the combined trust level of the object/event T :

$$T = \frac{1}{K} \sum T_k v_k. \tag{1}$$

It should be noted here that decisions on composite objects/events are harder to be performed with this technique since it does not provide formalisms for handling unions and intersections of objects/events. Weighted voting and its variations are widely applied in trust evaluation in many areas (Yan, 2010). However, the weighted voting cannot overcome attacks raised by malicious voters to collaboratively frame good objects and/or boost bad ones. It cannot reflect the impact of the number of votes on the trust evaluation.

Table 2 provides an example list of votes from 10 voters $\{V1, V2, \ldots\ldots, V10\}$ on an entity e, with the same trust value 0.5. Based on formula (2.1), we get T_e=0.275. If the trust values of all voters are 1, T_e will be 0.55, thus we can see that the trust of the voters greatly impacts the trust evaluation result. In this case, the lowest voting score is 0 and the highest is 1.

3.2. Bayesian Inference

Among the data fusion techniques, Bayesian Inference (BI) is often used for trust evaluation (Pearl, 1988). In BI, the combined trust level corresponding to event α_i is the posterior probability of α_i given new evidence $e = \{e_1^j, e_2^j, e_3^j, \ldots\ldots, e_K^j\}$; it is expressed in terms of the prior probability $P[\alpha_i]$ using the Bayes' theorem:

$$P[\alpha_i/e] = \frac{P[\alpha_i]\prod_{k=1}^{K} P[e_k^j/\alpha_i]}{\sum_{h=1}^{I}\left(P[\alpha_h]\prod_{k=1}^{K} P[e_k^j/\alpha_h]\right)}, \qquad (2)$$

where we assume that evidence is independent for the sake of mathematical tractability. The computation of posterior probabilities for com-

posite events γ (recall that they are unions or intersections of basic events) follows the rules of probability theory. $P[e_k^i/\alpha_i]$ is the probability that evidence k confirms α_i, given that α_i happened. This probability is equal to the trust level of e_i^k: $T(e_k^i) = P[e_k^i/\alpha_i]$. For $j \neq i$, $P[e_k^j/\alpha_i]$ is the probability that evidence k does not confirm α_i (hence, it confirms $\overline{\alpha_i}$, the complement of α_i in Ω), given that α_i happened. Hence,

$$P[e_k^j/\alpha_i] = 1 - P[e_k^i/\alpha_i] = 1 - T(e_k^i).$$

Bayesian Inference is widely used to calculate trust value in various research domains. But we should note that BI cannot express the uncertainty of trust, which is improved by other theories as described below.

3.3. Dempster-Shafer Theory

The Dempster-Shafer Theory (DST), also known as the theory of belief functions, is a generalization of the Bayesian theory of subjective probability. It is a mathematical theory of evidence (Shafer, 1976), allowing one to combine evidence from different sources and arrive at a degree of belief (represented by a belief function) by taking into account all the available evidence. The theory was first developed by Dempster (1968) and Shafer (1976), but the kind of reasoning the theory uses can be found as far back as the seventeenth century. The theory came to the attention of Artificial Intelligence researchers in the early 1980s, when they were

Table 2. An example list of votes

Voter	V1	V2	V3	V4	V5	V6	V7	V8	V9	V10
v_k	0.1	0.2	0.3	0.4	0.5	0.6	0.7	0.8	0.9	1.0
T_k	0.5	0.5	0.5	0.5	0.5	0.5	0.5	0.5	0.5	0.5

trying to adapt probability theory to expert systems. Dempster-Shafer degrees of belief might combine the rigor of probability theory with the flexibility of rule-based systems. Subsequent work has made clear that the management of uncertainty inherently requires more structure than is available in simple rule-based systems, but the Dempster-Shafer theory remains attractive because of its relative flexibility. In particular, many researchers have proposed different rules for combining evidence, often with a view to handle conflicts in evidence better (Kari & Scott, 2002).

Whereas the Bayesian theory requires probabilities for each question of interest, belief functions allow us to base degrees of belief (or confidence, or trust) for one question on probabilities for a related question. These degrees of belief may or may not have the mathematical properties of probabilities; how much they differ from probabilities will depend on how closely the two questions are related. The Dempster-Shafer theory is based on two ideas: the idea of obtaining degrees of belief for one question from subjective probabilities for a related question, and Dempster's rule for combining such degrees of belief when they are based on independent items of evidence. The Dempster-Shafer theory can be applied into trust evaluation by expressing the trust by combining the degrees of belief generated from the probabilities of related factors.

In DST, the lack of knowledge about an event is not necessarily a refutal of the event. In addition, if there are two conflicting events, uncertainty about one of them can be considered as supporting evidence for the other. The major difference between BI and DST is that the latter is more suitable for cases with uncertain or no information. More precisely, in DST a node can be uncertain about an event, unlike in BI where a node either confirms or refutes the event. For example, if an entity A confirms the presence of

an event with probability p, in BI it refutes the existence of the event with probability $1-p$. In DST, probability is replaced by an uncertainty interval bounded by belief and plausibility. Belief is the lower bound of this interval and represents supporting evidence. Plausibility is the upper bound of the interval and represents non-refuting evidence. Hence, in this example, entity A has p degree of belief in the event and 0 degree of belief in its absence. In DST, the frame of discernment contains all mutually exclusive possibilities related to an observation. Hence, in our context, it is the set Ω defined previously. The belief value corresponding to an event α_i and provided by evidence k is computed as:

$$b_k\left(\alpha_i\right) = \sum_{q:\alpha_q \subset \alpha_i} m_k\left(\alpha_q\right), \qquad (3)$$

which means it is the sum of all basic belief assignments $m_k\left(\alpha_q\right)$, α_q being all basic events that compose the event α_i. In this case, only $\alpha_i \subset \alpha_i$ and hence $b_k\left(\alpha_i\right) = m_k\left(\alpha_i\right)$.

The plausibility value corresponding to event α_i represents the sum of all evidence that does not refute α_i and is computed as:

$$p_k\left(\alpha_i\right) = \sum_{r:\alpha_r \cap \alpha_i \neq 0} m_k\left(\alpha_r\right). \qquad (4)$$

Belief and plausibility are related by $p\left(\alpha_i\right) = 1 - b\left(\overline{\alpha_i}\right)$. The combined trust level corresponding to event α_i is the belief corresponding to α_i :

$$T_i = b\left(\alpha_i\right) = m\left(\alpha_i\right)$$
$$= \oplus m_k\left(\alpha_i\right), (k = 1, \ldots\ldots, K), \qquad (5)$$

where pieces of evidence can be combined using Dempster's rule for combination.

$$m_1\left(\alpha_i\right) \oplus m_2\left(\alpha_i\right)$$

$$= \frac{\displaystyle\sum_{q,r:\alpha_q \cap \alpha_r = \alpha_i} m_1\left(\alpha_q\right) m_2\left(\alpha_r\right)}{1 - \displaystyle\sum_{q,r:\alpha_q \cap \alpha_r = \varphi} m_1\left(\alpha_q\right) m_2\left(\alpha_r\right)}. \tag{6}$$

Herein, the basic belief assignment that confirms α_i is equal to the trust level of e_i^k: $T\left(e_k^i\right) = m_k\left(\alpha_i\right)$. For composite events γ, belief can be computed similarly using the above equations. For more information, see Shafer (1990) and the articles on the belief functions in Shafer and Pearl (1990).

Raya et al (2008) evaluated evidence with corresponding trust levels using weighted voting, Bayesian inference, and Dempster-Shafer Theory. Simulation results show that Bayesian inference and Dempster-Shafer Theory are the most promising approaches to evidence based trust evaluation, each one performing best in specific scenarios. More specifically, Bayesian inference performs best when prior knowledge about events is available whereas Dempster-Shafer Theory handles properly high uncertainty about events. In addition, the local processing approach based on either one of the above techniques converges to a stable correct value, which satisfies the stringent requirements of ephemeral networks, such as ad hoc networks.

3.4. Subjective Logic

Subjective Logic (SL) was introduced by Jøsang (2001). It can be used for trust representation, evaluation and update. It has a sound mathematical foundation in dealing with evidential beliefs rooted in Shafer's theory and the inherent ability to express uncertainty explicitly. Trust valuation can be calculated as an instance of Opinion in Subjective Logic. Subjective Logic expresses trust with multiple dimensions: belief, disbelief

and uncertainty. An entity can collect the opinions about other entities both explicitly via a recommendation protocol and implicitly via limited internal trust analysis using its own trust base. It is natural that the entity can perform an operation in which these individual opinions can be combined into a single opinion to allow a relatively objective judgment about another entity's trustworthiness. It is desirable that such a combination operation shall be robust enough to tolerate situations where some of the recommenders may be wrong or dishonest. Another situation with respect to trust valuation includes combining the opinions of different entities on the same entity together using a Bayesian Consensus operation; aggregation of an entity's opinions on two distinct entities with logical AND support or with logical OR support. A detailed description and demo can be found in http://folk.uio.no/josang/sl/.

Subjective Logic is a theory of opinion that can represent trust. It has been widely applied in many trust and reputation management systems (Yan, 2010). Its operators mainly support the operations between two opinions. It doesn't consider how to directly support context, such as time based decay, interaction times or frequency; trust standard/policy, like importance weights of different trust factors; popularity; etc. Concretely, how to generate opinions on recommendations based on credibility and/or similarity and how to overcome attacks on trust evaluation are beyond the theory of SL. These need to be further developed in real practice.

3.5. Semiring

Semiring was introduced by Theodorakopoulos and Baras (2006). The authors view the trust inference problem as a generalized shortest path problem on a weighted directed graph G(V, E) (trust graph). The vertices of the graph are the users/entities in the network. A weighted edge from vertex i to vertex j corresponds to the opinion that the trustor has about the trustee. The weight function is $l(i, j) : V \times V \rightarrow S$, where S is the opinion space. Each opinion consists of two numbers: the trust value, and the confidence value. The former corresponds to the trustor's estimate of the trustee's trustworthiness. The later corresponds to the accuracy of the trust value assignment. Since opinions with a high confidence value are more useful in making trust decisions, the confidence value is also referred to as the quality of the opinion. The space of opinions can be visualized as a rectangle (ZERO_TRUST, MAX_TRUST) × (ZERO_CONF, MAX_CONF) in the Cartesian plane ($S = [0, 1] \times [0, 1]$). Using the theory of Semirings, two nodes in an ad hoc network can establish an indirect trust relation without previous direct interaction. The semiring framework is also flexible to express other trust models.

Generally, two versions of the trust inference problem can be formalized in an ad hoc network scenario. The first is finding the trust-confidence value that a source node A should assign to a destination node B, based on the intermediate nodes' trust-confidence values. Viewed as a generalized shortest path problem, it amounts to finding the generalized distance between nodes A and B. The second version is finding the most trusted path between nodes A and B. That is, find a sequence of nodes that has the highest aggregate trust value among all trust paths starting at A and ending at B. In the trust case, multiple trust paths are usually utilized to compute the trust distance from the source to the destination, since that will increase the evidence on which the source bases its final estimate. The first problem is addressed with a "distance semiring", and the second with a "path semiring". Two operators are applied to combine opinions. One operator (denoted $\otimes$) combines opinions along a path, i.e., A's opinion for B is combined with B's opinion for C into one

indirect opinion that A should have for C, based on B's recommendation. The other operator (denoted $\oplus$) combines opinions across paths, i.e., A's indirect opinion for X through path p1 is combined with A's indirect opinion for X through path p2 into one aggregate opinion. Then, these operators can be used in a general framework for solving path problems in graphs, provided they satisfy certain mathematical properties, i.e., form an algebraic structure called a semiring.

3.6. Fuzzy Logic

Fuzzy logic (FL) is a form of many-valued logic; it deals with reasoning that is approximate rather than exact. In contrast with traditional logic theory, where binary sets have two-valued logic: true or false, fuzzy logic variables may have a truth value that ranges in degree between 0 and 1. Fuzzy logic has been extended to handle the concept of partial truth, where the truth value may range between completely true and completely false (Novák, Perfilieva & Močkoř, 1999). Furthermore, when linguistic variables are used, these degrees may be managed by specific functions. Fuzzy logic has been applied into many fields, from control theory to artificial intelligence, from expert systems to trust evaluation.

Fuzzy logic theory defines fuzzy operators on fuzzy sets. At present, Zadeh operators $\wedge$ and $\vee$ are commonly used to perform calculation and analysis. But they are so imprecise. Thus several general class fuzzy operators are proposed. To adapt to different sources of uncertainties in trust management, parameterized general intersection and union operators are needed. With different values of the parameters, these operators can flexibly express trust and capture uncertainty, e.g., Dubois-and-Prade operators (Dubois & Prade, 1980) can perform calculation and analysis, which are suitable for policy analysis and have clear semantic meaning. But for a concrete issue, the appropriate fuzzy operator may not be known. For this reason, fuzzy logic usually uses IF-THEN rules, or constructs that are equivalent, such as fuzzy associative matrices.

Fuzzy Logic has been applied by many researchers for developing an effective and efficient reputation system (Song, Hwang, Zhou & Kwok, 2005) and managing risk in E-commerce (Schmidt, Steele, Dillon & Chang, 2007; Tajeddine, Kayssi, Chehab & Artail, 2011). Herein, we briefly describe how to evaluate the trust relationship between entity A and B by applying Fuzzy Logic. It contains six steps.

1. Define fuzzy set F={f1,f2,...,f5} for different levels of evaluation, e.g., f1=Excellent; f2=Good; f3=Average; f4=Bad; f5=Risky;
2. Justify hierarchical trust factors that influence A's trust in B: the main factors and their sub-factors. For example, for e-commerce transactions, main factors influencing trust could be security technology, vender brand, and customer factor. For the main factor security technology, it contains such sub-factors as payment method, security techniques, and system availability;
3. Determine different weights for every hierarchical trust factors based on A's policy.

Suppose the weight's set of first hierarchical trust factors (i.e., main factors) is W={0.5,0.3,0.2} and the weights' sets of second hierarchical trust factors (i.e., subfactors) are W1={0.6,0.2,0.2}, W2={0.2,0.5,0.3},W3={0.3,0.3,0.4}.

4. Use statistical way of fuzzy to calculate the degree of second hierarchical trust factors to the set fi (i=1, 2, ..., 5);
5. Make trust evaluation with suitable fuzzy logic operators;
6. Generate unitary representation of evaluation on main factors and trust.

3.7. Fuzzy Cognitive Maps

A Fuzzy Cognitive Map is a combination of Fuzzy Logic and Neural Networks (Kosko, 1986). In a graphic illustration, FCM is a sign directed graph with feedback, consisting of nodes and weighted arcs. The nodes are used to describe the entities related to an investigated system. They are connected by signed and weighted arcs representing their causal relationships, see Figure 2.

All the values in the graph are fuzzy, so the nodes take values between [0, 1] and the weights of the arcs are in the interval [-1, 1]. Among nodes, three possible types of causal relationships express

Figure 2. An example of fuzzy cognitive map

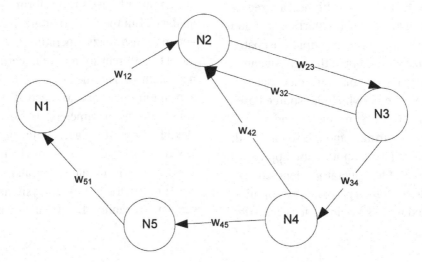

the type of influence from one node to another. A positive weight (e.g., $w_{12} > 0$) indicates that an increase in the value of one node (N1) leads to the increase of the value of another node (N2), and vice versa. Negative causality (e.g., $w_{51} < 0$) signifies that an increase in the value of one node (N5) leads to the decrease of the value of another node (N1), and vice versa. No causality (e.g., $w_{34} = 0$) occurs when an increase or decrease in the value of one node (N3) has no any influence on the value of another node (N4). FCM specifies the interconnections and influences between nodes. It also permits updating the construction of the graph, such as adding or deleting an interconnection or a node (Stylios, Georgopoulos & Groumpos, 1997).

A FCM can be used for evaluating trust. In this case, the concept nodes are trustworthiness and the factors that influence trust. The weighted arcs represent influencing relationships among these factors and the trustworthiness. FCM is convenient and practical for implementing and integrating trustworthiness and its influencing factors (Castelfranchi, Falcone & Pezzulo, 2003). It is a useful method in modeling and control of complex systems. It helps the system designer in decision analysis and strategic planning. Based on the FCM theory, a stable control performance could be anticipated based on a specific FCM configuration. Thus, we can utilize it to predict the performance of different trust control mechanisms in order to select the best ones (Yan & Prehofer, 2011). How to apply FCM to conduct autonomic trust management will be illustrated in Chapter 8.

3.8. Miscellaneous

3.8.1. Game Theory

Game theory is the formal study of conflict and cooperation (Myerson, 1991). It is a method of studying strategic decision making. Game theoretic concepts apply whenever the actions of several entities are interdependent. These entities may be individuals, groups, firms, or any combination of these. The concepts of game theory provide a language to formulate, structure, analyze, and understand strategic scenarios. Game theory is applied to study trust in E-commerce (Yao & Li, 2009). Chin (2009) proposed to use game theory to understand trust in networks. Game theory could be useful to study a strategy to establish trust for cooperation in order to gain maximum payoffs, e.g., in a mobile ad hoc network (MANET). It can be used to analyze the behavior strategies that are adaptively adopted by different entities in a system. But at present, it still lacks investigation to apply game theory for trust evaluation.

Trust models based on game theory in MANET can properly model the dilemma that a node has: to cooperate and gain trust, or not to cooperate and save battery. To face this dilemma, several pure and mixed strategies have been studied in game theory, especially different forms of tit for tat (Osborne, 2004). However, network conditions are dynamically changed in a MANET. Thus, game conditions can change over time, for which it is essential to make trust models evolve the strategies. Such kind of trust models is promising in MANET because they can dynamically adapt to the current network conditions. Mejia et al. (2011) proposed a trust model based on game theory that efficiently achieves both high adaptability to environment changes and quick convergence to almost optimal cooperation and energy saving values. Each node adapts its strategy to the dynamical characteristics of the network, trying to maximize its payoff in terms of packet delivery and resource saving.

3.8.2. Cloud Theory

Cloud model was firstly proposed by Li, Meng and Shi (1995). It is based on Gaussian function and uses *entropy* to express the ambiguity of the range of values. It also uses *hyper-entropy* to reflect the dispersion degree of cloud drops. Thus, the fuzziness and randomness can be integrated together in the cloud model. The qualitative and quantitative can also be transformed with each other. Cloud model is a promising theory to express uncertainty, thus suitable for modeling trust. Recently, it has been applied by a number of researchers to evaluate trust by defining trust cloud and using entropy and hyper-entropy to express the quality of trust. Cai, Li and Tian (2011) proposed using cloud theory to evaluate trust in E-commerce for choosing a transaction object. He, Niu, Yuan and Hu (2004) proposed to use a trust cloud model to do trust-based decision making in various security mechanisms in pervasive computing environments. Zhou, Xu and Wang (2011) applied cloud model to evaluate trust by proposing a Cloud-Based Weighted Trust Model (CBWT Model). This model includes the Weighted Trust Information Transfer Algorithm (WTIT Algorithm) and Weighted Trust Information Combination Algorithm (WTIC Algorithm), which preferably solves the problems of fuzziness and uncertainty in trust evaluation based on experimental results.

3.8.3. Information Theoretic Framework

Sun, Yu, Han, and Liu (2006) presented an information theoretic framework to quantitatively measure trust and model trust propagation in ad hoc networks. In the proposed framework, trust is a measure of uncertainty with its value represented by entropy. The authors develop four axioms that address the basic understanding of trust and the rules for trust propagation. Based on these axioms two trust models are introduced: entropy-based model and probability-based model, which satisfy all the axioms.

3.8.4. PeerTrust

Xiong and Liu (2004) presents five trust parameters used in PeerTrust, namely, feedback a peer receives from other peers, the total number of transactions a peer performs, the credibility of the

feedback sources, a transaction context factor, and a community context factor. By formalizing these parameters, a general trust metric is presented. It combines these parameters in a coherent scheme. This model can be applied into a decentralized P2P environment. It is effective against dynamic personality of peers and malicious behaviors of peers.

4. CURRENT PROBLEMS AND CHALLENGES

Trust is influenced by reputations (i.e., the public evidence of the trustee), recommendations (i.e., a group of entities' evidence on the trustee), the trustor's past experiences and context (e.g., situation, risk, and time). And each one of the above items except the context is impacted by the subjective and objective properties of the trustor and the trustee. Most of existing work focused on a singular trust value or level calculation by taking into account the previous behaviors of the trustee. The reputations, the recommendations and the trustor's own experiences are assessed based on the quality attributes of the trustee, the trust standards of the trustor and related context for making a trust or distrust conclusion. A number of trust models support the dynamics of trust. So far, some basic elements of context are considered, such as time and context similarity. The time element has been considered in many pieces of work, such as Wang and Varadharajan (2005) and Xiong and Liu (2004). For peer-to-peer systems, Sarkio and Holtmanns (2007) proposed a set of functions to produce a tailored trustworthiness estimation, which takes into account factors like age of reputation, value of transaction, frequency of transactions, reputation of the reputation giver, etc. However, no existing work gives a common consideration on all factors that influence trust in a generic way in digital environments, especially those subjective factors of the trustor and the trustee, as shown in Table 1 presented in Chapter

1. The existing trust evaluation technologies solve the uncertainty of trust, but they did not pay attention to the subjective of trust. It is still a challenge to digitally model the subjective factors related to the trustor and the trustee, especially when they are human-beings.

Despite the availability of various trust models, the fundamental criteria of trust models are still not well understood. Without sufficiently addressing this issue, the design of trust models is still at an empirical stage (Sun, Yu, Han & Liu, 2006). Yan and Prehofer (2011) proposed four criteria to evaluate the efficiency of a trust model: correctness, robustness, flexibility and adaptability. Most of existing work focuses on concrete solutions in specific systems. Additional examination is required before applying an existing solution into another domain. Most work focuses on trust evaluation (i.e., trust assessment), but does not consider how to ensure or sustain trust for the fulfillment of an intended purpose. It still lacks comprehensive discussions on how to automatically take an essential action according to a trust value. Although a number of trust models consider the influence of dynamic nature of trust and context, current literature does not adequately address context-aware adaptation of trust, especially in mobile domain (Hall, Heimbigner, Van Der Hoek & Wolf, 1997; Hermann, 2001, 2003; Malek et al, 2001; Mikic-Rakic, Malek & Medvidovic, 2008; Suryanarayana, Diallo, Erenkrantz & Taylor, 2006; Uddin, Zulkernine & Ahamed, 2008; Zhou, Jiao & Mei, 2005; Zhou, Mei & Zhang, 2005). In particular, we notify that literature lacks an inter-disciplinary approach or method to integrate the results of trust model study in different disciplines together.

5. CONCLUSION

This chapter introduced the concept of trust model. We briefly reviewed the methods applied for trust modeling and classify trust models into different categories based on different criteria. Taking a concrete example of web trust model, we specified its types under different classification rules. For digitalizing trust, trust evaluation plays an important role. Thus, we further introduced a number of promising trust evaluation technologies and indicated their limitations and advantages. The introduced evaluation technologies include Weighted Voting, Bayesian Inference, Dempster-Shafer Theory, Subjective Logic, Semiring, Fuzzy Logic, Fuzzy Cognitive Maps, Game Theory, Cloud Theory, Information Theoretic Framework, and PeerTrust. Based on the current state of arts, we commented the problems and challenges in the area of trust modeling, aiming to suggest future research directions.

REFERENCES

Abdul-Rahman, A., & Hailes, S. (2000). Supporting trust in virtual communities. In *Proceedings of the 33rd Hawaii International Conference on System Sciences*. IEEE.

Bhattacherjee, A. (2002). Individual trust in online firms: Scale development and initial test. *Journal of Management Information Systems*, *19*(1), 211–241.

Bigley, G. A., & Pearce, J. L. (1998). Straining for shared meaning in organization science: Problems of trust and distrust. *The Academy of Management Executive*, *23*, 405–421.

Blaze, M., Feigenbaum, J., & Lacy, J. (1996). Decentralized trust management. In *Proceedings of IEEE Symposium on Security and Privacy*, (pp. 164–173). IEEE.

Cai, H., Li, Z., & Tian, J. (2011). A new trust evaluation model based on cloud theory in e-commerce environment. In *Proceedings of the 2nd International Symposium on Intelligence Information Processing and Trusted Computing (IPTC)*, (pp. 139-142). IPTC.

Castelfranchi, C., Falcone, R., & Pezzulo, G. (2003). Integrating trustfulness and decision using fuzzy cognitive maps. In *Proceedings of the First International Conference of Trust Management (iTrust 2003) (LNCS)*, (vol. 2692, pp. 195-210). Berlin: Springer.

Chin, S. H. (2009). On application of game theory for understanding trust in networks. In *Proceedings of the International Symposium on Collaborative Technologies and Systems* (CTS '09), (pp. 106-110). CTS.

Dempster, A. P. (1968). A generalization of Bayesian inference. *Journal of the Royal Statistical Society. Series A (General)*, *30*, 205–247.

Dubois, D., & Prade, H. (1980). New results about properties and semantics of fuzzy set theoretic operators. In *Fuzzy Sets Theory and Applications to Policy Analysis and Information System*. New York: Plenum Press. doi:10.1007/978-1-4684-3848-2_6.

Fishbein, M., & Ajzen, I. (1975). *Beliefs, attitude, intention and behavior: An introduction to theory and research*. Reading, MA: Addison-Wesley.

Ganeriwal, S., & Srivastava, M. B. (2004). Reputation-based framework for high integrity sensor networks. In *Proceedings of the ACM Security for Ad-Hoc and Sensor Networks*, (pp. 66–67). ACM.

Gefen, D. (2000). E-commerce: The role of familiarity and trust. *Omega*, *28*(6), 725–737. doi:10.1016/S0305-0483(00)00021-9.

Gil, Y., & Ratnakar, V. (2002). Trusting information sources one citizen at a time. In *Proceedings of the 1st International Semantic Web Conference*. IEEE.

Hall, R. S., Heimbigner, D., Van Der Hoek, A., & Wolf, A. L. (1997). An architecture for post-development configuration management in a wide-area network. In *Proceedings of the 17th Int'l Conf. Distributed Computing Systems*, (pp. 269-278). IEEE.

He, R., Niu, J., Yuan, M., & Hu, J. (2004). A novel cloud-based trust model for pervasive computing. In *Proceedings of The Fourth International Conference on Computer and Information Technology*, (pp. 693-700). IEEE.

Herrmann, P. (2001). Trust-based procurement support for software components. In *Proceedings of the Fourth Int'l Conf. Electronic Commerce Research*, (pp. 505-514). IEEE.

Herrmann, P. (2003). Trust-based protection of software component users and designers. In *Proceedings of the First Int'l Conf. Trust Management*, (pp. 75-90). IEEE.

Jøsang, A. (1999). An algebra for assessing trust in certification chains. In *Proceedings of the Networking Distributed System Security Symposium*. IEEE.

Jøsang, A. (2001). A logic for uncertain probabilities. *International Journal of Uncertainty. Fuzziness and Knowledge-Based Systems*, *9*(3), 279–311.

Jøsang, A., & Ismail, R. (2002). The beta reputation system. In *Proceedings of the 15th Bled Electronic Commerce Conference*. Bled.

Kosko, B. (1986). Fuzzy cognitive maps. *International Journal of Man-Machine Studies*, *24*, 65–75. doi:10.1016/S0020-7373(86)80040-2.

Li, D., Meng, H., & Shi, X. (1995). Membership clouds and membership cloud generators. *Journal of Computer Research and Development*, *32*(6), 15–20.

Li, X., Valacich, J. S., & Hess, T. J. (2004). Predicting user trust in information systems: A comparison of competing trust models. In *Proceedings of the 37th Annual Hawaii International Conference on System Sciences*. IEEE.

Liang, Z., & Shi, W. (2005). PET: A personalized trust model with reputation and risk evaluation for P2P resource sharing. In *Proceedings of the 38th Annual Hawaii International Conference on System Sciences*. IEEE.

Liu, Z., Joy, A. W., & Thompson, R. A. (2004). A dynamic trust model for mobile ad hoc networks. In *Proceedings of the 10th IEEE International Workshop on Future Trends of Distributed Computing Systems* (FTDCS 2004), (pp. 80–85). IEEE. Kari, S., & Scott, F. (2002). *Combination of evidence in Dempster-Shafer theory*. Sandia National Laboratories SAND.

Malek, S., Esfahani, N., Menasce, D., Sousa, J., & Gomaa, H. (2009). Self-architecting software systems (SASSY) from QoS-annotated activity models. In *Proceedings of the Int'l Conf. Software Eng. (ICSE) Workshop Principles of Eng. Service-Oriented Systems*, (pp. 62-69). ICSE.

Manchala, D. W. (2000). E-commerce trust metrics and models. *IEEE Internet Computing*, *4*(2), 36–44. doi:10.1109/4236.832944.

Marsh, S. (1994). *Formalising trust as a computational concept*. (Doctoral Dissertation). University of Stirling, Stirling, UK.

Maurer, U. (1996). Modeling a public-key infrastructure. In *Proceedings of the European Symposium of Research on Computer Security* (LNCS), (vol. 1146, pp. 325–350). Berlin: Springer.

Mayer, R. C., Davis, J. H., & Schoorman, F. D. (1995). An integrative model of organizational trust. *Academy of Management Review*, *20*, 709–734.

McKnight, D. H., Choudhury, V., & Kacmar, C. (2002). Developing and validating trust measures for e-commerce: An integrative typology. *Information Systems Research*, *13*(3), 334–359. doi:10.1287/isre.13.3.334.81.

McKnight, D. H., Cummings, L. L., & Chervany, N. L. (1998). Initial trust formation in new organizational relationships. *Academy of Management Review*, *23*, 473–490.

Mejia, M., Peña, N., Muñoz, J. L., Esparza, O., & Alzate, M. A. (2011). A game theoretic trust model for on-line distributed evolution of cooperation in MANETs. *Journal of Network and Computer Applications*, *34*(1). doi:10.1016/j.jnca.2010.09.007.

Mikic-Rakic, M., Malek, S., & Medvidovic, N. (2008). Architecture-driven software mobility in support of QoS requirements. In *Proceedings of the First Int'l Workshop Software Architectures and Mobility*, (pp. 3-8). IEEE.

Muir, B. M. (1994). Trust in automation: Part I: Theoretical issues in the study of trust and human intervention in automated systems. *Ergonomics*, *37*, 1905–1922. doi:10.1080/00140139408964957.

Muir, B. M., & Moray, N. (1996). Trust in automation: Part II: Experimental studies of trust and human intervention in a process control simulation. *Ergonomics*, *39*, 429–460. doi:10.1080/00140139608964474 PMID:8849495.

Myerson, R. B. (1991). *Game theory: Analysis of conflict*. Boston: Harvard University Press.

Novák, V., Perfilieva, I., & Močkoř, J. (1999). *Mathematical principles of fuzzy logic*. Dordrecht, The Netherlands: Kluwer Academic. doi:10.1007/978-1-4615-5217-8.

Osborne, M. (2004). *An introduction to game theory*. Oxford, UK: Oxford University Press.

Pavlou, P., & Gefen, D. (2004). Building effective online marketplaces with institution-based trust. *Information Systems Research*, *15*(1), 37–59. doi:10.1287/isre.1040.0015.

Pearl, J. (1988). *Probabilistic reasoning in intelligent systems: Networks of plausible inference*. San Francisco, CA: Morgan Kaufmann.

Pennington, R., Wilcox, H. D., & Grover, V. (2004). The role of system trust in business-to-consumer transactions. *Journal of Management Information Systems*, *20*(3), 197–226.

Perlman, R. (1999). An overview of PKI trust models. *IEEE Network*, *13*(6), 38–43. doi:10.1109/65.806987.

Raya, M., Papadimitratos, P., Gligory, V. D., & Hubaux, J.-P. (2008). On data-centric trust establishment in ephemeral ad hoc networks. In *Proceedings of IEEE INFOCOM* (pp. 1912–1920). IEEE. doi:10.1109/INFOCOM.2008.180.

Reiter, M. K., & Stubblebine, S. G. (1998). Resilient authentication using path independence. *IEEE Transactions on Computers*, *47*(12), 1351–1362. doi:10.1109/12.737682.

Sarkio, K., & Holtmanns, S. (2007). Tailored trustworthiness estimations in peer to peer networks. *International Journal of Internet Technology and Secured Transactions*, *1*(1/2), 95–107. doi:10.1504/IJITST.2007.014836.

Schmidt, S., Steele, R., Dillon, T. S., & Chang, E. (2007). Fuzzy trust evaluation and credibility development in multi-agent systems. *Applied Soft Computing*, *7*(2), 492–505. doi:10.1016/j.asoc.2006.11.002.

Shafer, G. (1976). *A mathematical theory of evidence*. Princeton, NJ: Princeton University Press.

Shafer, G. (1990). Perspectives on the theory and practice of belief functions. *International Journal of Approximate Reasoning*, *3*, 1–40.

G. Shafer, & J. Pearl (Eds.). (1990). *Readings in uncertain reasoning*. San Francisco, CA: Morgan Kaufmann.

Song, S., Hwang, K., Zhou, R., & Kwok, Y. K. (2005). Trusted P2P transactions with fuzzy reputation aggregation. *IEEE Internet Computing*, *9*(6), 24–34. doi:10.1109/MIC.2005.136.

Stylios, C. D., Georgopoulos, V. C., & Groumpos, P. P. (1997). The use of fuzzy cognitive maps in modeling systems. In *Proceedings of the Fifth IEEE Mediterranean Conf. Control and Systems*. IEEE.

Subjective Logic. (n.d.). Retrieved from http://folk.uio.no/josang/sl/

Sun, Y., Yu, W., Han, Z., & Liu, K. J. R. (2006). Information theoretic framework of trust modeling and evaluation for ad hoc networks. *IEEE Journal on Selected Areas in Communications*, *24*(2), 305–317. doi:10.1109/JSAC.2005.861389.

Suryanarayana, G., Diallo, M. H., Erenkrantz, J. R., & Taylor, R. N. (2006). Architectural support for trust models in decentralized applications. In *Proceedings of the 28th Int'l Conf. Software Eng.*, (pp. 52-61). IEEE.

Tajeddine, A., Kayssi, A., Chehab, A., & Artail, H. (2011). Fuzzy reputation-based trust model. *Applied Soft Computing*, *11*(1), 345–355. doi:10.1016/j.asoc.2009.11.025.

Tan, Y., & Thoen, W. (1998). Toward a generic model of trust for electronic commerce. *International Journal of Electronic Commerce*, *5*(2), 61–74.

Theodorakopoulos, G., & Baras, J. S. (2006). On trust models and trust evaluation metrics for ad hoc networks. *IEEE Journal on Selected Areas in Communications*, *24*(2), 318–328. doi:10.1109/JSAC.2005.861390.

Uddin, M., Zulkernine, M., & Ahamed, S. I. (2008). CAT: A context-aware trust model for open and dynamic systems. In *Proceedings of the ACM Symposium on Applied Computing* (SAC '08), (pp. 2024-2029). ACM.

Wang, Y., & Varadharajan, V. (2005). Trust2: Developing trust in peer-to-peer environments. In *Proceedings of the IEEE International Conference on Services Computing*, (vol. 1, pp. 24–31). IEEE.

Xiong, L., & Liu, L. (2004). PeerTrust: Supporting reputation-based trust for peer-to-peer electronic communities. *IEEE Transactions on Knowledge and Data Engineering*, 16(7), 843–857. doi:10.1109/TKDE.2004.1318566.

Yan, Z. (2010). *Trust modeling and management in digital environments: From social concept to system development*. Hershey, PA: IGI Global. doi:10.4018/978-1-61520-682-7.

Yan, Z., Dong, Y., Niemi, V., & Yu, G. L. (2013). Exploring trust of mobile applications based on user behaviors: An empirical study. *Journal of Applied Social Psychology*. doi:10.1111/j.1559-1816.2013.01044.x.

Yan, Z., & Holtmanns, S. (2008). Trust modeling and management: From social trust to digital trust. In R. Subramanian (Ed.), *Computer Security, Privacy and Politics: Current Issues, Challenges and Solutions*. Hershey, PA: IGI Global. doi:10.4018/978-1-59904-804-8.ch013.

Yan, Z., Kantola, R., & Shen, Y. (2011). Unwanted traffic control via global trust management. [IEEE.]. *Proceedings of IEEE TrustCom*, *2011*, 647–654.

Yan, Z., & Prehofer, C. (2011). Autonomic trust management for a component based software system. *IEEE Transactions on Dependable and Secure Computing*, 8(6), 810–823. doi:10.1109/TDSC.2010.47.

Yan, Z., Zhang, P., & Deng, R. H. (2012). TruBeRepec: A trust-behavior-based reputation and recommender system for mobile applications. *Journal of Personal and Ubiquitous Computing*, 16(5), 485–506. doi:10.1007/s00779-011-0420-2.

Yang, Y., Sun, Y., Kay, S., & Yang, Q. (2009). Defending online reputation systems against collaborative unfair raters through signal modeling and trust. In *Proceedings of the ACM Symposium on Applied Computing* (SAC'09), (pp. 1308-1315). ACM.

Yao, L., & Li, Y. (2009). Research on trust in e-commerce of C2C based on game-theory. In *Proceedings of International Conference on Management and Service Science*, (MASS'09), (pp. 1-4). MASS.

Zhou, M., Jiao, W., & Mei, H. (2005). Customizable framework for managing trusted components deployed on middleware. In *Proceedings of 10th IEEE Int'l Conf. Eng. of Complex Computer Systems*, (pp. 283-291). IEEE.

Zhou, M., Mei, H., & Zhang, L. (2005). A multi-property trust model for reconfiguring component software. In *Proceedings of the Fifth International Conference on Quality Software*, (QAIC2005), (pp. 142–149). QAIC.

Zhou, Z., Xu, H., & Wang, S. (2011). A novel weighted trust model based on cloud. *Advances in Information Sciences and Service Sciences*, 3(3), 115–124. doi:10.4156/aiss.vol3.issue3.15.

APPENDIX

Exercises and Questions

1. Classify the introduced trust models based on different classification criteria.
2. Compare the introduced trust evaluation models by proposing a comparison model and indicate each model's advantages and disadvantages.
3. Please illustrate how to use the Bayesian inference to model multiple properties of trust.
4. Please illustrate how to apply the cloud model to model multiple dimensions of trust.

Chapter 3
Trust Management and Its Challenges

ABSTRACT

Trust management is the technology to collect information to make a trust decision, evaluate the criteria related to trust, monitor and reevaluate existing trust relationships, and ensure the dynamically changed trust relationships and automate the above processes. This chapter introduces trust management technologies. The authors classify them and discuss the advantages and disadvantages of each. Furthermore, they discuss the current issues, problems, and future research trends in the area of trust management.

1. INTRODUCTION

Trust management is concerned with: collecting the information required to make a trust relationship decision; evaluating the criteria related to the trust relationship; monitoring and reevaluating existing trust relationships; as well as ensuring the dynamically changed trust relationships and automating the process (Grandison & Sloman, 2000; Yan & Prehofer, 2011).

With the rapid development of computer and networking technology, trust has become an important factor that influences the success of our digital life. Trust management plays as a useful means

to control and maintain trust in digital systems. Transforming from a social concept of trust to a digital concept, trust modeling and management help in designing and implementing a trustworthy digital system, especially in mobile and distributed computing. Nowadays, trust management is emerging as a promising technology to facilitate collaboration among entities in an environment where traditional security paradigms cannot be enforced due to lack of centralized control and incomplete knowledge of the environment.

Various trust management systems are described in the literature. Two important systems are reputation based trust management systems

DOI: 10.4018/978-1-4666-4765-7.ch003

Copyright © 2014, IGI Global. Copying or distributing in print or electronic forms without written permission of IGI Global is prohibited.

and trusted computing enhanced trust management. Trust and reputation mechanisms have been proposed in various fields such as P2P systems (Kamvar, Scholsser & Garcia-Molina, 2003; Lee, Sherwood & Bhattacharjee, 2003; Liang & Shi, 2005; Singh & Liu, 2003; Song, Hwang, Zhou & Kwok, 2005; Walsh & Sirer, 2005; Xiong & Liu, 2004), e-commerce (Guha, Kumar, Raghavan & Tomkins, 2004), and web services (Resnick & Zeckhauser, 2002). Most of these focus on a specific system that is very different from each other. Recently, many solutions were developed for supporting trusted communications and collaborations among computing nodes in the domain of mobile and Internet computing and communications, e.g., a P2P system (Zhang, Wang & Wang, 2005), an ad hoc network (Sun, Yu, Han & Liu, 2006; Theodorakopoulos & Baras, 2006) and a GRID computing system (Lin, Varadharajan, Wang & Pruthi, 2004). Trusted computing based trust management applies sound security technologies in order to ensure the trustworthiness of a computer or communication system. It deals with root trust module, security policies, credentials, privacy and trust relationships. This kind of trust management has been applied not only in desk-top computers, but also mobile computing platforms (Yan, 2010).

In the rest of this chapter, we firstly classify the trust management technologies. Then we introduce a number of prestigious trust management systems or solutions proposed in the literature and discuss their advantages and disadvantages. Finally, we discuss the current issues, problems and future research trends in the area of trust management.

2. TAXONOMY OF TRUST MANAGEMENT SOLUTIONS

Current trust management solutions can be classified into three categories. The first category is security enhanced trust management solutions, e.g., trusted computing technology based solutions (TCG, 2003; Yan, 2010). This kind of solutions applies sound security technologies and cryptographic theories to ensure the trustworthiness of a computer, communication or networking system. It deals with root trust module, security policies, credentials, privacy and trust relationships. This kind of solutions provides security enhanced trust management. It mainly solves the security issue in a system, not comprehensively considers the multiple factors of trust, i.e., other properties of trust. Thereby, this solution generally did not ensure other properties of the system related to trust, such as usability and user's concern. It lacks intelligence to automatically control and maintain dynamically changed trust relationships.

The second category is trust evaluation based solutions, e.g., reputation systems (Yan, 2010). Trust evaluation is a technical approach of representing trustworthiness for digital processing, in which the factors influencing trust will be evaluated by a continuous or discrete real number, referred to as a trust value. Generally, a trust model is applied in order to specify, evaluate and set up trust relationships amongst entities for calculating, controlling and managing trust. The trust model could be linguistic, graphic and mathematic, corresponding to different researches conducted in different disciplines for different purposes. Embedding a trust evaluation mechanism is a necessity to provide trust intelligence in future computing devices, e.g., mobile smart devices. In particular, reputation is a measure that is derived from direct or indirect knowledge or experiences on entities and is used to assess the level of trust an entity puts into another entity. Thus, reputation based trust management (or simply reputation system) is a specific approach to evaluate and control trust. Trust and reputation mechanisms have been proposed in various fields of distributed systems, such as ad hoc networks, peer-to-peer systems, Grid computing, pervasive computing and e-commerce. This kind of solutions provides intelligence for trust decision, but lacks root trust support. Thus, it is hard to solve such an issue as the trustworthiness of trust management system.

The third category is a hybrid solution. It applies both the trusted computing and trust evaluation technologies in order to overcome the disadvantages of the above two kinds of solutions. The advantages of the third solutions are it can provide multiple properties of trust and meanwhile has the root trust support (Yan, 2010b). Thus, it can provide both system intelligence and trustworthiness. Notably, this kind of solutions is complicated. It has dependency on a root trust module, thus not so flexibly applied into various applications. However, current literature hasn't yet paid much attention to the hybrid solutions.

3. TRUST MANAGEMENT TECHNOLOGIES

In this section, we briefly introduce the main technologies of the above three trust management solutions.

3.1. Trusted Computing

The typical trusted computing technologies are specified in the specifications of TCG (Trusted Computing Group) (TCG, 2003), aiming to enhance the overall security, privacy and trustworthiness of a variety of computing devices. The current technologies for Trusted Computing Platform (TCP) are quite similar (Felten, 2003; England et al, 2003). The core of trusted computing technologies of TCG is Trusted Platform Module (TPM), a tamper-resistant module embedded in a platform. A TPM chip is designed to resist all software attacks and moderate hardware attacks. It encloses a non-volatile storage, a set of platform configuration registers (PCRs) and an engine for cryptographic operations. The TCG specifications define a suit of mechanisms including memory curtaining, secure I/O, secure storage, platform

measurement and remote attestation. All are based on the TPM chip and its supporting software called TCG Software Stack (TSS). As a fundamental secure computing module, it plays as the root trust module to establish security and trust in digital computing, communication and networking. Basically, it can provide secure booting and software installation, private data protection and digital rights management (DRM), as well as remote attestation based communications and collaboration. Herein, we introduce the basic security functions of TCP and its main applications.

3.1.1 Main Functions of TCP

3.1.1.1. Memory Curtaining

Memory curtaining is a hardware-enforced memory isolation scheme to guarantee the intactness of the process execution. One of the threats to the execution of security sensitive applications is the unauthorized memory access by malware residing in the same platform. The malware can spy on other processes' execution or even manipulate the data. Memory curtaining extends common memory protection techniques to provide full isolation of sensitive areas of memory—for example, locations containing cryptographic keys. Even the operating system does not have full access to curtained memory. When a process is running under memory curtaining protection, no adversarial process can read from or write to its memory space and CPU states. The exact implementation details are vendor specific. Some vendors (e.g., Intel) have already provided this feature.

3.1.1.2. Secure Storage and Sealed Storage

The sealed storage function defined by TCG can securely bind data encryption/decryption to a platform state or configuration. In the TCG specification, a hierarchy of storage encryption keys can be used to protect both the confidentiality and the integrity of data stored in hard disks. The root of the key hierarchy is the storage root key (SRK) which is stored inside the TPM chip when a user takes the ownership of the TPM. SRK is used to encrypt its children storage keys which can be further used to encrypt children keys in the next hierarchy level. To seal a data item, both the data itself and the relevant PCR values are encrypted together. The sealed data can only be decrypted by the TPM on which it was encrypted. To unseal the data item, the TPM decrypts it internally and compares the decrypted PRC values with the current ones. The data is released on the condition that both PCR values are the same. BitLocker Drive Encryption is a full disk encryption feature included with the Ultimate and Enterprise editions of Microsoft's Windows Vista, Windows 7, and the upcoming Windows 8 desktop operating systems, as well as the Windows Server 2008 and Windows Server 2008 R2 server platforms. It is designed to protect data by providing encryption for entire volumes. On-board Credential (ObC) (Ekberg, Asokan, Kostiainen & Rantala, 2008), a platform of credential management, extends the sealed storage function to the application level by supporting "credential program" to run in a secure execution environment.

3.1.1.3. Platform Measurement

Platform measurement is essential to compute the states or configurations of a platform. The TCG specifications introduce the root of trust for measurement (RTM) to reliably measure the platform states. To measure a process or application, RTM computes the hash value of the relevant software component and stores the hash in one of the TPM PCRs immediately before the program execution. Multiple rounds of measurements are stored in the same PCR by hashing the concatenation of a new measurement with the existing content of a PCR and then storing the output hash value in the register. A detailed record of all measured components is stored in the Stored Measurement Log (SML), which is maintained externally to the TPM chip. With platform measurement, a TCG-compliant platform can have either a secure booting or an authenticated booting. In both booting processes, the RTM measures every components the host is about to load, starting from BIOS, to the operating system loader and to the operating system. The secure booting is to detect malicious mutation of the platform. A component is allowed to be loaded only when its measurement is known to be trustworthy. In contrast, the RTM does not enforce such a matching policy during an authenticated booting. The platform only makes use of the measurements to convince others about the system it has booted into. In addition, platform measurement can also support conditional encryption and decryption.

3.1.1.4. Platform Attestation

Platform attestation is the process with which the platform measurement is signed and transported to a challenger for the purpose of checking the states of an attester platform. Figure 1 shows the involved parties and the process of remote attestation in TCG's specification. First, the challenger sends the remote attestation request with a random *nonce* to the attester platform. After receiving the challenge request, the attester platform retrieves the corresponding SML, and calls TPM to sign the relevant PCR values using the *nonce* and its Attestation Identity Key (AIK). Then the attester platform collects the credentials vouching for the TPM. The signature on the PCR values and related SML records, together with the credentials, are sent back to the challenger as the attestation response. The challenger verifies the signature and compares the received platform measurement with known-good ones, which can be retrieved from its local storage or a trusted third party.

Figure 1. Procedure of TCG remote attestation (Yan, 2010)

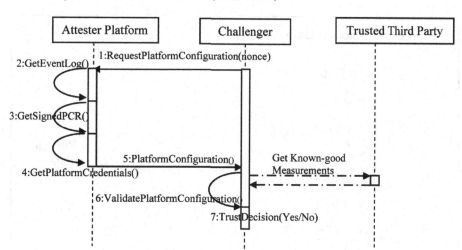

A requirement for the signatures in use is the anonymity of a TPM chip. The signatures are generated by using the AIK. A TPM chip may have multiple AIKs certified by a special certification authority called Privacy CA (P-CA). A certificate for an AIK does not reveal the TPM's identity. Instead, it only certifies that the key owner is compliant to the TCG specifications. Another approach to providing anonymity without the cost and risk of involving P-CA, is the Direct Anonymous Attestation (DAA) scheme (Brickell, Camenisch & Chen, 2004), which has been adopted by the TPMv1.2 standard as an option. A DAA issuer presents a zero-knowledge proof on its platform credential, without exposing its private information. Nonetheless, the computation cost of both signature generation and verification in DAA are higher than standard RSA signature operations.

3.1.2 Main Applications of TCP

The TPM chip and other TCP modules simply allow all hardware and software components to check whether they have woken up in trusted states. If not, they should refuse to work. It also provides secure storage for saving confidential information. Simply speaking, there are four basic applications supported by TCP.

3.1.2.1. Authenticated Booting and Software Installation

An authenticated boot service monitors what operating system software is booted and gives applications a sure way to identify which OS is running. Figure 2 illustrates the process of authenticated booting and trust challenge on remote platform or data.

A TPM chip takes charge when booting up. Its booting block checks the hardware specification against a known safe integrity metric (e.g., a certified hash code of hardware specification); and should that match, it then checks the OS loader. The OS loader, once proven safe, checks the OS kernel. The kernel knows how to check the list of legitimate software, which in turn can use OS resources to authenticate local and remote data, including software installation (TCG, 2003).

The TCP hardware keeps a tamper-evident log of the boot process, using a cryptographic hash function to detect any tampering with the log.

Figure 2. Authenticated booting and remote platform trust attestation

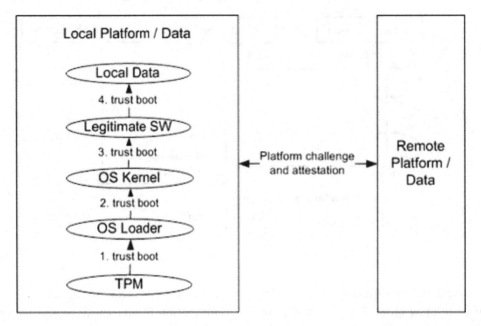

That is the loader calculates the hash code of the next software contributor and logs it in the TPM measurement storage. If the value derived from the log is same as the trusted value reported by the TPM, the check is passed.

What is more, the TCP hardware can make the configuration known to others, thus realize the trust attestation on remote platform/data. This is done through digitally certificating the configuration. Two levels of certifying are provided. The TPM certifies that a known OS version is running and then the OS can certify the precise configuration of a specific application.

3.1.2.2. Encryption and Decryption Services

Encryption service is the second major offer of TCP. It allows data to be encrypted in such a secure way that it can be decrypted only by a certain machine, and only if that machine is in a certain configuration.

This service is implemented by a combination of hardware and software facilities. The TPM hardware maintains a 'master secret key' for each machine, and it uses the master secret to generate a unique secret encryption key for every possible configuration of that machine. Thus, data encrypted for a particular configuration cannot be decrypted when the machine is in a different configuration.

This service can be extended from OS level to applications. This ensures that encrypted data can only be decrypted by desired version of desired applications when running on top of desired OS and on desired machine. So, we can transmit data to a remote machine in such a way that the data can be decrypted only if the remote machine is in a certain configuration. Figure 3 briefly shows the encryption service and corresponding decryption service provided by the TCP components. The encryption service provides a special control on digital data to make it accessible only when an expected platform environment is satisfied.

3.1.2.2. Privacy Support

The TCG specification provides a method described below for obtaining an anonymous user identity certificate from a Certificate Authority (CA) over a secure channel.

Figure 3. Encryption service and decryption service offered by TCP components

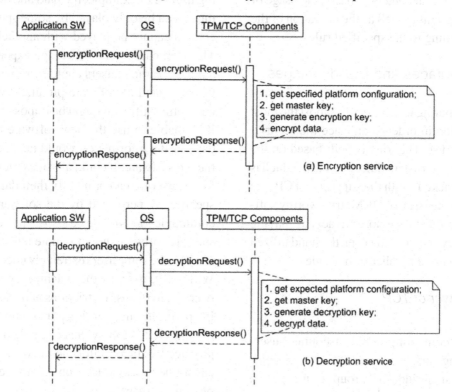

The TPM sends the public key (of the user that desires a certificate) and three credentials to the CA. The three credentials include:

- **A Public Key Certificate:** The endorsement certificate issued by the entity that endorses or certifies the TPM. It contains a null subject and the TPM endorsement identity's public key, among other things.
- **The First Attribute Certificate:** The platform credential containing a pointer to the endorsement certificate that uniquely identifies the platform's endorser and the model – hardware and software versions, TPM details, platform compliance with the TCG specifications, etc.
- **The Second Attribute Certificate:** The conformance credential, which asserts that the named TPM complies with the TCG specification.

The CA receives these three certificates, and verifies the information. Then the CA creates a TPM identity credential and sends it to its client via the secure channel. The TPM identity credential contains a null subject and the public key sent by the user in the certificate request. This procedure ensures that anonymous certificates are only issued to compliant devices.

3.1.2.3. DRM Support

The TCG specifications present several problems regarding to DRM. A TCG-enabled OS could prevent the user from running "unapproved" applications. Thus the applications with capability for copying, printing, and super-distributing digital contents are not allowed to play DRM-sensitive contents. Through extending the encryption service offered by the TCP, the TCG-enabled computing platform could control the access and execution of digital contents; master the usage of software programs as well as the operation of the system according to the specified rules.

3.1.3 Advantages and Disadvantages

Trusted computing technology is almost the most secure solution in order to enhance the security property of trust. The trust is built based on the belief of the root trust module, i.e., TPM, which is hard to be attacked. With the support of TCP, it is easy to solve the issue of DRM, trustworthy software installation and support privacy, by playing as a mandatory enabler. However, the standardized solution also has a number of bad sides.

3.1.3.1. Power of TCP

The trusted computing could discourage users from running software created by companies outside of a small industry group. Using trusted computing could shut out competition and engage in anti-competitive practices. Trusted Computing is seen as harmful or problematic to independent and open source software developers (Oppliger & Rytz, 2005). Anderson, R. (August 2003) pointed that "The fundamental issue is that whoever controls the Trusting Computing infrastructure will acquire a huge amount of power. Having this single point of control is like making everyone use the same bank, or the same accountant, or the same lawyer. There are many ways in which this power could be abused." This power will benefit limited computer manufacturers and software authors with increased control to impose restrictions on what users are able to do with their computers.

3.1.3.2. Usability Issue of TCP

The applications of TCP raise many usability issues. TCP is a security measure to control usage and access, protect and manage copy rights. However, the design is not motivated by concern-

ing users. For example, the paid and downloaded music can be only played by some specific players and cannot be played with another machine. This will cause very bad usage experience. For another example, users could be restricted to use the old brand of software product. Switching to competing software might be impossible because it is unable to use the new software to read old data, as the information would be "locked in" to the old software. It could also make it impossible for the user to read or modify their data except as specifically permitted by the software. Remote communications could be also restricted by using specific software due to remote attestation. This could make some users extremely uncomfortable. With TCP, user, as the machine owner, cannot override to bypass restrictions and use the secure I/O path, although this is a pure security solution. For a user, it is totally unacceptable if personally produced data or information or work results cannot be accessed later on due to the change of playing software.

3.1.3.3. Risk of Trust in Manufacturers and Vendors

How trustworthy is the root trust module? In order to trust the TPM, people have to trust the company that designed that check, the company that made that chip, those companies allowed to make software for the chip, and the ability and interest of those companies to not compromise the process. The standard is good, but incorrect implementation or flaw could be hidden from users and thus could undermine the integrity of the whole system without users being aware of the flaw.

3.1.3.4. Lack Dynamic Maintain of Trust

The focus on the security aspect of trust tends to, however, assume that other non-functional requirements, such as availability, reliability, and usability have already been addressed (Banerjee, Mattmann, Medvidovic & Golubchik, 2005). TCP is a solution to establish trust, but how to maintain trust in dynamically changed environments still lacks study. This 'hard' trust solution cannot support the subjective nature of trust. In addition, current trusted computing solution cannot handle the runtime trust management issues of software systems and autonomic trust management in pervasive computing.

3.2. Reputation Systems

An important category of trust management solutions is reputation based trust management system. Trust and reputation mechanisms have been proposed in various fields such as distributed computing, agent technology, grid computing, economics and evolutionary biology (Yan & Holtmanns, 2008). Reputation-based trust research stands at the crossroads of several distinct research communities, most notably computer science, information science, economics, and sociology.

3.2.1. A Brief Review

As defined by Aberer and Despotovic (2001), reputation is a measure that is derived from direct or indirect knowledge on earlier interactions of entities and is used to assess the level of trust an entity puts into another entity. Thus, reputation based trust management (or simply reputation system) is a specific approach to evaluate and control trust.

Reputation schemes can be classified into three different categories depending on what sort of reputation they utilize. Global reputation is the aggregation of all available assessments by other entities that have had interactions with the particular entity, and thus it has an n-to-1 relationship. On the other hand, the local reputation of an entity is each entity's own assessment based on past history of interaction with the particular entity, thus it is a 1-to-1 relationship. This reflects

the social situation that a person trusts another one. Personalized reputation is generated by aggregating all available assessments by tailoring them based on personal historical experiences.

Several representative P2P reputation systems currently exist, although the list we present is by no means exhaustive. The eBay and PeerTrust systems focus on trust management in securing commodity exchanges in e-commerce applications, as does the FuzzyTrust system by Song, Hwang, Zhou, and Kwok (2005). Other systems focus on generic P2P applications such as P2P file sharing and Web service-based sharing platforms.

The eBay (www.ebay.com) user feedback system described by Resnick and Zeckhauser (2002) is by far the simplest and most popular trust-management system, and is specifically tailored for e-auction applications. It applies a centralized database to store and manage the trust scores. Data is open to the general public, so a newcomer can easily obtain a peer score. It's a hybrid P2P system using both distributed client resources and centralized servers. This system tries to be user friendly by providing a limited amount of data to a user, but on the other hand the provided and processed information is not complete and does not provide a "full picture".

Singh and Liu (2003) presented Trustme, a secure and anonymous protocol for trust. The protocol provides mutual anonymity for both a trust host and a trust querying peer. Guha and Kumar (2004) developed an interesting idea about the propagation of distrust. In addition to maintaining positive trust values for peers, the system also allows the proactive dissemination of some malicious peers' bad reputations. Buchegger and Le Boudec (2004) designed a distributed reputation system using a Bayesian approach, in which the second-hand reputation rating is accepted only when it is compatible with the primary rating. This reputation scheme can detect mis-behavior nodes in ad hoc networks.

Several universities are working on the research projects involving trust management in P2P applications. For example, Xiong and Liu (2004) developed the PeerTrust model. Their model is based on a weighted sum of five peer feedback factors: peer records, scope, credibility, transaction context, and community context. PeerTrust is fully distributed, uses overlay for trust propagation, public-key infrastructure for securing remote scores, and prevents peers from some malicious abuses. Kamvar, Schlosser, and Garcia-Molina (2003) proposed the EigenTrust algorithm, which captures peer reputation in the number of satisfactory transactions and then normalizes it over all participating peers. The algorithm aggregates the scores by a weighted sum of all raw reputation scores. The fully distributed system assumes that pre-trusted peers exist when the system is initiated. It uses majority voting to check faulty reputation scores reported. Liang and Shi (2005) proposed the TrustWare system (retrieved from http://mist.cs.wayne.edu/trustware.html), a trusted middleware for P2P applications. Their approach consists of two models: the Multiple Currency Based Economic model (M-CUBE) and the Personalized Trust model (PET). The M-CUBE model provides a general and flexible substrate to support high-level P2P resource management services. PET derives peer trustworthiness from long-term reputation evaluation and short-term risk evaluation. Lee, Sherwood and Bhattacharjee (2003) proposed in the Nice project a scheme for trust inference in P2P networks. The trust inference consists of two parts for local trust inference and distributed search. After each transaction, the system generates cookies to record direct trust between peers. It also uses trust graphs to infer transitive trust along a peer chain. Credence is a robust and decentralized system for evaluating the reputation of files in a P2P file sharing system (Retrieved from http://www.cs.cornell.edu/people/egs/credence/index.html). Its goal is to enable peers to confidently gauge file authenticity, the degree to which the content of a file matches its advertised description. At the most basic level, Credence employs a simple, network-wide voting

scheme where users can contribute positive and negative evaluations of files. On top of this, a client uses statistical tests to weight the importance of votes from other peers. It allows the clients to share selected information with other peers. Privacy is ensured by not collecting or using any personally identifiable information in any way in the protocol. Each Credence-equipped client is supplied with a unique, randomly generated key pair that is not bound to any personal information for use in cryptographic operations.

Meanwhile, European Union (EU) project SECURE investigated the design of security mechanisms for pervasive computing based on the human notion of trust. It addresses how entities in unfamiliar pervasive computing environments can overcome initial suspicion to provide secure collaboration (Cahill et al., 2003). Another EU project Trust4All aims to build up trustworthy middleware architecture in order to support easy and late integration of software from multiple suppliers and still have dependable and secure operations in the resulting system (Retrieved from https://nlsvr2.ehv.compus.philips.com/).

3.2.2. An Example Reputation System: PeerTrust (Xiong & Liu, 2004)

PeerTrust is a dynamic reputation system for quantifying and assessing the trustworthiness of peers in P2P e-commerce communities. In PeerTrust, a peer's trustworthiness is defined by an evaluation of the peer with regard to providing service to other peers in the past. Such reputation reflects the degree of trust that other peers in the community have on the given peer based on their past experiences. Five factors are considered for such evaluation:

1. The feedback a peer obtains from other peers,
2. The feedback scope, such as the total number of transactions that a peer has with other peers,
3. The credibility factor for the feedback source,

4. The transaction context factor for discriminating mission-critical transactions from less or noncritical ones, and

5. The community context factor for addressing community-related characteristics and vulnerabilities.

The five parameters are formalized into a general trust metric that combines them in a coherent scheme. Given a recent time window, a peer and the community it belongs to, let $I(u, v)$ denote the total number of transactions performed by peer u with v, $I(u)$ denote the total number of transactions performed by peer u with all other peers, $p(u, i)$ denote the other participating peer in peer u's ith transaction, $S(u, i)$ denote the normalized amount of satisfaction peer u receives from $p(u, i)$ in its ith transaction, $Cr(v)$ denote the credibility of the feedback submitted by v, $TF(u, i)$ denote the adaptive transaction context factor for peer u's ith transaction (e.g., the size of a transaction between peer u and i), and $CF(u)$ denote the adaptive community context factor for peer u. The trust value of peer u denoted by $T(u)$ is defined in Formula 1.

$$T(u) =$$
$$\alpha * \sum_{i=1}^{I(u)} S(u, i) * Cr(p(u, i)) * TF(u, i) + \beta * CF(u),$$
$$\tag{1}$$

where α and β denote the normalized weight factors for the collective evaluation and the community context factor.

The metric consists of two parts. The first part is a weighted average of amount of satisfaction a peer receives for each transaction. The weight takes into account the credibility of feedback source to counter dishonest feedback, and transaction context to capture the transaction-dependent characteristics. This history-based evaluation can be seen as a prediction for peer u's likelihood of a successful transaction in the future. A confidence

value can be computed and associated with the trust metric that may reflect the number of transactions, the standard deviation of the ratings depending on different communities. The second part of the metric adjusts the first part by an increase or decrease of the trust value based on community-specific characteristics and situations. In PeerTrust, the incentive problem of reputation systems can be addressed by building incentives or rewards into the metric through community context factor for peers who provide feedback to others. For example, $CF(u)$ can be defined with a reward as a function of a ratio of total number of feedback peer u give others, denoted as $F(u)$, over the total number of transactions peer u has during the recent time window, that is $CF(u) = \frac{F(u)}{I(u)}$. The α and β parameters can be used to assign different weights to the feedback-based evaluation and community context according to different situations. The Formula 1 can be tailored into different expressions in order to reflect different scenarios. For more details, refer to Xiong and Liu (2004).

3.2.3 Advantages and Disadvantages

Reputation system is a 'soft trust' solution. TCP realizes trust management through hard security enforcement, while reputation systems realize trust through intelligent analysis according to all collected useful information or evidence. If we call TCP based solutions as 'hard trust' solutions, reputation systems can be named as 'soft trust' solutions. It overcomes the problem of the 'hard trust' solution by dynamically evaluate trust according to newly collected data. Thus, it can overcome the shortcoming of TCP.

However, current reputation systems still face a number of problems. First, they lack concern on system security. Reputation systems may face the problem of unfair ratings to artificially inflate or deflate reputations (Corritore, Kracher

& Wiedenbeck, 2003; Yang, Sun, Kay & Yang, 2009; Resnick & Zeckhauser, 2002; Resnick, Kuwabara, Zeckhauser & Friedman, 2000). They are vulnerable to a number of potential attacks, such as Sybil attack, on-off attack, independent bad mouthing attack, collaborative bad mouthing attack, and conflict behavior attack (Yang, Sun, Kay & Yang, 2009; Douceur, 2002; Sun, Han, Yu & Liu, 2006). The usage of pseudonyms introduces new challenges by making it hard to trace malicious behaviors. This also influences the accuracy of reputation. Sun et al. proposed a number of schemes to overcome some of the above attacks, but they did not consider the additional challenges caused by usability and privacy preservation (Sun, Han, Yu & Liu, 2006; Sun, Han & Liu, 2008). Most reputation systems didn't concern how to overcome the above attacks. Most solutions were proposed based on a number of security assumptions. Second, reputation systems cannot solve how to establish initial trust if no any information is available for trust/reputation evaluation. The users of such systems may face a potential risk at the beginning of usage. Third, incentives are required in order to encourage users to provide their feedback on interactions and their personal interests and profiles. However, due to privacy issue, many users are hesitate to provide their details [27, 28]. Particularly, the demand for human-computer interaction may raise a usability issue, especially for mobile users. Some people may feel uncomfortable or inconvenient to provide personal feedback, which could influence usage experience. Forth, the existing reputation systems based on user rating generally lack uniform criteria, which makes the rating a totally subjective behavior. Meanwhile, different users could treat and consider the reputation and recommendation information in different ways. These further complicate the users' decision and could negatively influence their usage behaviors. Feedback credibility is essential to generate a reliable reputation value in order to overcome the above potential attacks. But how to generate feedback credibility

in a usable way is an important issue that hasn't be seriously considered in the literature.

3.3 Hybrid Trust Management Solution

Few hybrid trust management solutions can be found in the literature. Balakrishnan and Varadharajan (2005) demonstrated the issues that might creep out in a security design, when a cryptographic technique alone is involved. They also suggested how to counter those issues through the combination of trust management with cryptographic mechanisms. Moreover, they proposed the need to introduce the notion of heterogeneity resource management in the security design to address the divergence among the nodes, which can be taken an advantage to diminish the packet drop attacks in ad hoc networks. To handle the dynamic nature of the medium, the authors proposed that the design of secure mobile ad hoc networks should envisage including trust management as another dimension apart from the cryptographic mechanisms. In addition, inclusion of trust management alone cannot guarantee secure communications due to some persisting issues such as packet dropping. Therefore, the resource should be also considered in order to provide a trustworthy system. Yan (2010b) presented an autonomic trust management solution for the mobile computing platforms that can support two levels of autonomic trust management: between devices as well as between services offered by the devices in the context of mobile communications, networking and computing. This solution is based on both a trusted computing technology and an adaptive trust control model. It supports autonomic trust control on the basis of the trustor device's specification, which is ensured by a Root Trust module at the trustee device's computing platform. This solution can effectively avoid or reduce risk by stopping or restricting any potential risky activities based on the trustor's specification. In order to ensure trustworthy services provided by the trustee device, the adaptive trust control model is applied to ensure that a suitable set of control modes are applied based on runtime trust evaluation in the trustee device in order to provide a trustworthy service expected by the trustor. Chapter 8 will introduce this solution in details.

Obviously, the hybrid solution can provide comprehensive trust management in terms of supporting multiple trust properties. It integrates the advance of both 'hard' and 'soft' trust solutions and overcomes the disadvantages of each. It can ensure initial trust and also provide intelligence on trust decision. Thus, it is a promising technology towards practical trust management. Notably, the current hybrid solutions are generally complicated. They didn't consider the concern of users and were not designed in a human-centric manner. Thereby, it cannot sufficiently support the usability property of trust.

4. CHALLENGES AND FUTURE RESEARCH TRENDS

4.1. Open Issues and Further Discussion

Trust management is an active research area in recent years. Trust is today's fashion in security (Gollmann, 2007). However, many interesting research issues are yet to be fully explored. We summarize some of them for interested readers.

First, it lacks a widely accepted trust definition across multiple related disciplines, as discussed in Chapter 1. Diverse definitions could easily make people confused. This fact could be the reason that a comprehensive trust model misses in the literature. Perhaps it is impossible to have such a generic trust management solution that can be commonly applied in various situations and systems.

Second, it lacks general criteria to assess the effectiveness of a trust management solution in the literature. Why is a trust model trustworthy?

Why and how is a trust management system effective? How can the trustworthiness of trust management be ensured? Most of the existing work overlooked these issues and missed discussions about them. New attacks or malicious behaviors could destroy a trust management system. Current prove is still based on empirical and experimental study. In order to explore the trustworthiness of trust management system, we should design and develop it by holistically considering multiple properties of trust, not only one or a couple of trust properties. The system should be seriously evaluated by testing its performance on all aspects of trust. However, no existing trust management system has achieved this goal.

Third, the literature lacks discussions on the competence of trust management. That is when and in which situation trust is possibly or impossibly managed, as well as how much it can be managed. Competence is an important factor that may influence the user's decision on trust. The competence of trust management directly influences the trustworthiness of the system. This is a very interesting and important issue worth our attention, especially for autonomic trust management.

Forth, it lacks study on trust behaviors, which is an objective reflector of subjective trust. Trust behavior is a user's actions to depend on an entity or believe it could perform as expectation. Numerous researchers have conceptualized trust as a behavior. Prior research has also confirmed a strong correlation between behavioral intentions and actual behaviors, especially for software and system usage (Venkatesh & Davis, 2000). At present, still very few studies examined trust from the view of trust behaviors (Grabner-Kräuter & Kaluscha, 2003). No much work explores trust behavior of software and system usage, especially for a mobile computing platform. However, the relationship between trust and interaction behavior is obvious since usage through human-device interaction implies trust. Lee and Moray found that trust in a system partially explained system use (Lee & Moray, 1992). Trust behaviors provide an important clue to indicate user feedback credibility and preference (Yan, Zhang & Deng, 2011). Designing and developing a trust management system based on trust behavior study could be a good way to overcome the current challenges of trust management.

Fifth, it lacks usable trust management study. As discussed already, trust management systems, no matter which category, are seldom designed driven by user concern. Thus, the proposed system is hard to be easily accepted by its users. How to design a usable trust management system that is practical and has sound usability is an interesting and significant research issue.

Sixth, it lacks autonomic trust management solutions and applications. Current work focuses mainly on how to evaluate trust, i.e., digitally expressing trust values. But the literature lacks discussion on how to make use of the trust values and how to apply this in concrete application scenarios towards autonomic trust management, which includes not only trust evaluation, but also trust control, maintenance, sustainment and assurance in order to successfully fulfill an intended purpose.

Finally, a number of important issues haven't been investigated for practical deployment of trust management system. These issues include trust/reputation value storage (Li & Singhal, 2007), usability of a trust management system (Yan & Niemi, 2009), trust policy management, trustworthy data collection and fusion for accurate trust evaluation, and how to extract user policy in a user-friendly interface. All above issues need further exploration. Obviously, the success of a practical trust management system requests sound usability with regard to user-device interaction. It should be accurate to evaluate trust/reputation, robust to overcome various potential attacks and efficient to dynamically manage trust relationships. A mechanism is expected to uniform the user's voting with trustworthy credibility. More importantly, the system should preserve user privacy to a certain level at the same time when it collects user data for trust and reputation generation.

4.2. Future Research Trends

This sub-section provides insights on future and emerging research trends with regard to trust management.

4.2.1. An Integrated 'Soft Trust' and 'Hard Trust' Solution

An integrated solution is expected to provide a trust management framework that applies both the 'hard trust' and 'soft trust' solutions. Theoretically, there are two basic approaches for building up a trust relationship. We name them as a 'soft trust' solution and a 'hard trust' solution. The 'soft trust' solution provides trust based on trust evaluation according to subjective trust standards, facts accumulated from previous experiences and history, and information derived from other people's experiences. The 'hard trust' solution builds up trust through structural and objective regulations, standards, as well as widely proved or accepted rules, mechanisms and sound security technologies. Both approaches are applied in practice. They can cooperate and support with each other in order to provide a trustworthy system. The 'hard trust' provides a guarantee for the 'soft trust' solution to ensure the integrity of its functionality. It solves secure communications and provides root trust. The 'soft trust' can determine which 'hard trust' mechanisms should be applied and at which moment. It provides intelligence for selecting a suitable 'hard trust' solution.

A number of basic functions should be supported by this integrated trust management framework: data collection and management for trust evaluation, trust standards extraction from the trustor, experience or evidence dissemination inside and outside the system, and a decision engine to provide guidelines for applying effective 'hard trust' mechanisms. In addition, how to collect, store, and propagate related information for trust evaluation and management is seldom considered in existing work. It is a relevant and practical issue for the deployment of trust management system. Human-device interaction is also crucial to transmit the trust standards and feedbacks of a user to the device and the device needs to provide its assessment on trust to its user. These factors influence the final success of a trust management system.

4.2.2. Usable and Autonomic Trust Management

The dynamic characteristic of trust requests trust management to be autonomic, especially in dynamically changed environments, e.g., mobile environments. The subjective characteristic of trust needs trust management to be humanistic and consider human's influence and demands in order to achieve usable trust management. However, few work in the literature studied both usable and autonomic trust management. Based on the above discussion and elaboration, usable and autonomic trust management is a future research direction and the key issue that needs to be solved in order to provide a practical trust management solution. This research is able to address the fundamental trust issues. It will open up a new research horizon on usable and autonomic trust management. The research results can be further applied into many domains such as distributed systems, software systems, cloud computing, pervasive/ubiquitous computing and social networking. This research contributes the literature by integrating both usable and autonomic trust management together.

There is a trend that all the processing for trust management is becoming autonomic. This is benefited from the digitalization of trust model. One of main reasons is for better system usability. Since trust relationship is dynamically changed, this requires the trust management should be context-aware and intelligent to handle the con-

text changes. Obviously, it does not suffice to require the trustor (e.g. most possibly a digital system user) to make a lot of trust related decisions because that would destroy any attempt at user friendliness. For example, the user may not be informed enough to make correct decisions. Thus, establishing trust is quite a complex task with many optional actions to take. Rather trust should be managed automatically following a high level policy established by the trustor. We call such trust management autonomic. Autonomic trust management automatically processes evidence collection, trust evaluation, and trust (re-)establishment and control. We need a proper mechanism to support autonomic trust management not only on trust establishment, but also on trust sustaining. In addition, the trust model itself should be adaptively adjusted in order to match and reflect real system situation. Context-aware trust management and adaptive trust model optimization for autonomic trust management are developing research topics (Campadello et al, 2005; Yan & Prehofer, 2007).

Trust management is a new research area. Except for a number of reputation systems in E-commerce (e.g., eBay reputation system) and trusted computing technologies, most research results haven't been deployed in practice. Towards further success, usable and autonomic trust management should be a fundamental issue to widely investigate.

4.2.3. Inter-Disciplinary Research and Future Internet Trust

Trust is a multidisciplinary, multidimensional and multifaceted concept. It has been studied in disciplines ranging from economics to psychology, from sociology to medicine, and to information and computer science (Yan, 2007). Future research will be inter-disciplinary in order to integrate the research results of multiple disciplines and take advantages of each.

One of the most promising inter-disciplinary research areas is future Internet trust. The Internet has revolutionized our life like nothing before. It has become the backbone of remote communications, networking, computing and services. It carries a vast range of information resources and services, such as the World Wide Web and email. It also gives birth to a wide range of novel applications, e.g., Voice over Internet Protocol (VoIP), Internet Protocol television (IPTV), Instant Messaging (IM), Blogging, cloud computing and social networking. It offers a wide range of electronic services, such as e-commerce, e-health, e-education, and e-government. At the same time when the Internet is evolving its infrastructure, driven by producers of contents (either professionally or consumer created) and extending itself to connect mobile devices and the "Internet of things", it still faces many issues and challenges related to trust. On the level of communication, e.g., spam, denial-of-service and distributed denial of services (DDoS) attacks, phishing, attacks that exploit software vulnerabilities (e.g., Internet worms), and malware that the user may download and invoke (e.g., spyware, viruses), spam — are some of the most visible symptoms. On the level of content delivery the chain of trust from producers to users is broken, thus the user cannot trust the content while the professional content producers feel that they are not adequately rewarded for their efforts. The Internet is not trustworthy enough due to equipment failures, software bugs, configuration mistakes and misplaced business incentives. The Internet's weak notions of identity, and particularly the ease of spoofing everything from IP addresses to domain names, from email addresses to routing information cause many security issues. The trustworthiness of contents input by amateur users into the Internet, the trust and privacy issues caused by today's Google, Wikipedia, YouTube and FaceBook phenomena introduce new challenges into future Internet trust research. With the rapid growth of Web 2.0, cloud computing and social networking, trust need to be seriously considered for the success of future Internet. This demand is clearly visible in many Future Internet

projects in the US, Europe, Japan and China that try to build trust, security and privacy into the architecture from the ground up rather than as an add-on like in the present architecture.

We can estimate that trust management will not only benefit security, but also other properties of the system, such as privacy, usability, dependability and Quality of Services. Combining trust management with other management tasks (e.g. resource management, power management, identity management, risk management and fault management) or applying it into other areas could produce cross-domain benefits and inter-disciplinary achievements. The research outcome will be a more intelligent system that helps users managing their increasing amount of digital trust relationships, while providing also good performance.

4.2.4. Trustworthy Data Fusion and Mining

As an indispensible part of future mobile Internet, the Internet of Things (IoT) is going to create a world where physical objects are seamlessly integrated into information networks in order to provide advanced and intelligent services for human-beings. The number of interconnected "things" such as sensors or mobile devices had overtaken the actual number of people population in the world since 2011, and it is expected to reach 24 billion by 2020. Various applications and services of IoT have been emerging into market, e.g. surveillance, health care, transport, food safety, location-based services, and distant object monitor and control. The future of IoT is promising.

As involved with a huge number of wireless sensor devices and based on wireless and mobile networks, as well as Internet cloud computing, IoT produces and processes large volumes of data. Data fusion and mining present an efficient way to manipulate, integrate, manage and preserve mass data collected from various "things". They have showed significance to extract and gain useful information based on the data collected from sensor networks, mobile devices or RFID streams, and have been playing a crucial role in IoT services and applications.

However, data in IoT are massive, multi-sourced, heterogeneous, redundant, dynamic and sparse. In order to guarantee a sensible thing-to-thing interaction, an effective aggregation of various data should be carried out to obtain holography of objects. Moreover, IoT is usually sensitive to information security, to assure the authenticity and reliability of the data resulting from aggregation and extraction is a challenge. On the other hand, the data collected often contain private information reflecting users' daily activities (e.g., mobility). Secure multi-party computations (SMC) is expected for preserving user privacy. But intelligently providing context-aware and personalized services based on data fusion and mining and at the same time preserving user privacy to an expected level causes a big challenge in current IoT research and practice.

Trustworthy data fusion and mining, in another term big data trust management, concern efficient, accurate, secure, privacy-preserved, reliable and holographic data process and analysis in a holistic manner. It has become crucial of importance for the future success of IoT. In recent years, trustworthy data mining and fusion in IoT have been paid an increasing attention and gained extensive studies towards being successfully applied into the practice of IoT applications and services. Data trust or big data trust management has also become a significant and promising research area towards future Internet.

4.2.5. Trust Management in Mobile Commerce

Due to always connection of the Internet with mobile devices, the past and current e-commerce will go to mobile. Mobile commerce is blooming in the recent decade. It becomes essential to ensure trust relationships involved in the mobile commerce.

Past trust management solutions for e-commerce can be updated to fit into the mobile domain. But a practical and successful solution should pay special attention to the particular characteristics of mobile commerce: limited computing capabilities of mobile devices and restricted user interface, which could greatly influence user experiences and final acceptance on a trust management solution for mobile commerce. Usable trust management and human-device trust interaction should be seriously studied herein.

4.2.6. Trust Behavior Research

Trust can be investigated from trust behaviors. Trust and trust behavior are different concepts: trust is the willingness to assume risk; trust behavior is the assuming of risk (Mayer, Davis & Schoorman, 1995). TRA theory posits that beliefs lead to attitudes, which lead to behavioral intentions, which lead to the behavior itself (Fishbein & Ajzen, 1975). Applying this theory, we propose that trusting beliefs (e.g., perceptions of specific computing system attributes) lead to trusting intentions (e.g., intention to engage in trust behaviors of using the computing system through human-computer interaction), which in turn result in trust behaviors (e.g., using the system in various context). Additionally, numerous researchers have conceptualized trust as a behavior, which has been validated in work collaboration and social communications (Anderson & Narus, 1990; Fox, 1974; Deutsch, 1973). Prior research has also confirmed a strong correlation between behavioral intentions and actual behaviors, especially for computing system usage (Sheppard, Hartwick & Warshaw, 1988; Venkatesh & Davis, 2000). Muir found a positive correlation between trust and use (Muir, 1994; Muir, 1996). The relationship between trust and interaction behavior is obvious since usage through human-device interaction implies trust. Lee and Moray found that trust in a system partially explained system use, but other factors (such as the user's own ability to provide manual control) also influenced the system use (Lee & Moray, 1992). All above studies indicate that a user's trust in a computing system can be evaluated based on the user's trust behaviors. However, still very few studies examined trust from the view of trust behaviors (Grabner-Kräuter & Kaluscha, 2003). Some work studies the trust behavior in e-banking behaviors (Grabner-Kräuter & Kaluscha, 2003). Existing trust behavior studies focus on human's trust in an automation and intelligent machine (Muir, 1994; Muir, 1996; Lee & Moray, 1992).

Trust behavior based trust management solutions, especially usable and autonomic trust management solutions could be an effective approach to overcome the challenges of current reputation systems. This is due to a number of reasons. First, trust behavior implies user trust and user preference. Conducting trust evaluation through trust behavior observation supports automatic useful information collection. Thus, trust management based on trust behaviors overcomes the challenge that trust evaluation lacks valid and useful data. Second, using trust behavior to play as the credibility of user feedbacks makes the trust evaluation have a uniform criterion. Thus, it is possible to overcome a number of potential security risks and support the trustworthiness of trust management. Third, using the correlations of trust behaviors to generate personalized reputation supports the subjective characteristic of trust. Finally, using trust behavior as a feedback to adaptively control trust can provide autonomic trust management, thus supporting the dynamic characteristic of trust. In summary, trust management based on trust behaviors is a promising method that is worth our study.

5. CONCLUSION

This chapter reviewed the technologies of trust management: their categories, advantages and disadvantages. Basically, the technologies of current trust management can be divided into three categories: security enhanced 'hard trust' solutions, trust evaluation based 'soft trust' solutions, a hybrid solution by integrating the 'hard trust' and the 'soft trust' ones. The chapter introduced the typical techniques of each type and discussed their pros and cons. Based on the review, the chapter further discussed the current issues, problems and limitations of current trust management research. We can see that there are still a number of open issues in the practice of trust management. At the end of the chapter, a number of future research trends in the area of trust management were proposed. The promising research topics include hybrid trust management, usable and autonomic trust management, inter-disciplinary future Internet trust research, trustworthy data fusion and mining, trust management in mobile commerce, and trust behavior research. Please note that all opinions presented in this chapter are the personal views of this book author. They are shared for promoting new research activities.

REFERENCES

Aberer, K., & Despotovic, Z. (2001). Managing trust in a peer-to-peer information system. In *Proceedings of the ACM Conference on Information and Knowledge Management* (CIKM), (pp. 310–317). ACM.

Anderson, J. C., & Narus, J. A. (1990). A model of distributor firm and manufacturer firm working partnerships. *Marketing*, 54(1), 42–58. doi:10.2307/1252172.

Balakrishnan, V., & Varadharajan, V. (2005). Designing secure wireless mobile ad hoc networks. In *Proceedings of the 19th International Conference on Advanced Information Networking and Applications* (AINA 2005), (vol. 2, pp. 5–8). AINA.

Banerjee, S., Mattmann, C. A., Medvidovic, N., & Golubchik, L. (2005). Leveraging architectural models to inject trust into software systems. In *Proceedings of the 2005 Workshop on Software Engineering for Secure Systems—Building Trust-worthy Applications*, (vol. 30, pp. 1-7). IEEE.

Brickell, E. F., Camenisch, J., & Chen, L. (2004). Direct anonymous attestation. In *Proceedings of the ACM Conference on Computer and Communications Security*, (pp. 132-145). ACM.

Buchegger, S., & Le Boudec, J. Y. (2004). A robust reputation system for P2P and mobile ad-hoc networks. In *Proceedings of the 2nd Workshop Economics of Peer-to-Peer Systems*. IEEE.

Cahill, V. et al. (2003). Using trust for secure collaboration in uncertain environments. *IEEE Pervasive Computing / IEEE Computer Society [and] IEEE Communications Society, 2*(3), 52–61. doi:10.1109/MPRV.2003.1228527.

Campadello, S., Coutand, O., Del Rosso, C., Holtmanns, S., Kanter, T., & Räck, C. … Steglich, S. (2005). Trust and privacy in context-aware support for communication in mobile groups. In Proceedings of Context Awareness for Proactive Systems (CAPS), (pp. 115-125). CAPS.

Corritore, C. L., Kracher, B., & Wiedenbeck, S. (2003). On-line trust: Concepts, evolving themes, a model. *International Journal of Human-Computer Studies. Trust and Technology, 58*(6), 737–758.

Deutsch, M. (1973). *The resolution of conflict: Constructive and destructive processes.* New Haven, CT: Yale University Press. doi:10.1177/000276427301700206.

Douceur, J. R. (2002). The sybil attack. In *Proceedings of the IPTPS'02* (LNCS), (vol. 2429, pp. 251-260). Berlin: Springer.

Ekberg, J.-E., Asokan, N., Kostiainen, K., & Rantala, A. (2008). Scheduling execution of credentials in constrained secure environments. In *Proceedings of the 3rd ACM Workshop on Scalable Trusted Computing*, (pp. 61-70). ACM.

England, P., Lampson, B., Manferdelli, J., Peinado, M., & Willman, B. (2003). A trusted open platform. *IEEE Computer, 36*(7), 55–62. doi:10.1109/MC.2003.1212691.

Felten, E. W. (2003). Understanding trusted computing – Will it benefits outweigh its drawbacks. *IEEE Security and Privacy, 1*(3), 60–62. doi:10.1109/MSECP.2003.1203224.

Fishbein, M., & Ajzen, I. (1975). *Beliefs, attitude, intention and behavior: An introduction to theory and research.* Reading, MA: Addison-Wesley.

Fox, A. (1974). *Beyond contract: Work, power, and trust relations.* London: Faber.

Gollmann, D. (2007). *Why trust is bad for security.* Retrieved May 2007, from http://www.sics.se/policy2005/Policy_Pres1/dg-policy-trust.ppt

Grabner-Kräuter, S., & Kaluscha, E. A. (2003). Empirical research in on-line trust: A review and critical assessment. *International Journal of Human-Computer Studies, 58*(6), 783–812. doi:10.1016/S1071-5819(03)00043-0.

Grandison, T., & Sloman, M. (2000). A survey of trust in internet applications. *IEEE Communications and Survey, 3*(4), 2–16. doi:10.1109/COMST.2000.5340804.

Guha, R., Kumar, R., Raghavan, P., & Tomkins, A. (2004). Propagation of trust and distrust. In *Proceedings of the 13th Int. Conf. on WWW*, (pp. 403-412). IEEE.

Kamvar, S., Scholsser, M., & Garcia-Molina, H. (2003). The EigenTrust algorithm for reputation management in P2P networks. In *Proceedings of 12th International Conf. of WWW*, (pp. 640-651). IEEE.

Lee, J., & Moray, N. (1992). Trust, control strategies and allocation of function in human-machine systems. *Ergonomics, 35*(10), 1243–1270. doi:10.1080/00140139208967392 PMID:1516577.

Lee, S., Sherwood, R., & Bhattacharjee, B. (2003). Cooperative peer groups in NICE. In *Proceedings of the IEEE Conf. on Computer Communications* (INFOCOM'03), (pp. 1272-1282). IEEE.

Li, H., & Singhal, M. (2007). Trust management in distributed systems. *Computer, 40*(2), 45–53. doi:10.1109/MC.2007.76.

Liang, Z., & Shi, W. (2005). PET: A personalized trust model with reputation and risk evaluation for P2P resource sharing. In *Proceedings of 38th Annual Hawaii Int. Conf. on System Sciences.* IEEE.

Lin, C., Varadharajan, V., Wang, Y., & Pruthi, V. (2004). Enhancing grid security with trust management. In *Proceedings of the IEEE International Conf. on Services Computing*, (pp. 303-310). IEEE.

Mayer, R. C., Davis, J. H., & Schoorman, F. D. (1995). An integrative model of organizational trust. *Academy of Management Review, 20*(3), 709–734.

Muir, B. M. (1994). Trust in automation part I: Theoretical issues in the study of trust and human intervention in automated systems. *Ergonomics, 37*(11), 1905–1922. doi:10.1080/00140139408964957.

Muir, B. M. (1996). Trust in automation part II: Experimental studies of trust and human intervention in a process control simulation. *Ergonomics, 39*(3), 429–469. doi:10.1080/00140139608964474 PMID:8849495.

Oppliger, R., & Rytz, R. (2005). Does trusted computing remedy computer security problems? *IEEE Security and Privacy, 3*(2), 16–19. doi:10.1109/MSP.2005.40.

Resnick, P., Kuwabara, K., Zeckhauser, R., & Friedman, E. (2000). Reputation systems. *Communications of the ACM, 43*(12), 45–48. doi:10.1145/355112.355122.

Resnick, P., & Zeckhauser, R. (2002). Trust among strangers in Internet transactions: Empirical analysis of eBay's reputation system. *Advances in Applied Microeconomics: The Economics of the Internet and E-Commerce, 11*, 127–157. doi:10.1016/S0278-0984(02)11030-3.

Sheppard, B. H., Hartwick, J., & Warshaw, P. R. (1988). The theory of reasoned action: A meta analysis of past research with recommendations for modifications in future research. *Consumer Res., 15*(3), 325–343. doi:10.1086/209170.

Singh, A., & Liu, L. (2003). TrustMe: Anonymous management of trust relationships in decentralized P2P systems. In *Proceedings of the IEEE Int. Conf. on Peer-to-Peer Comp.*, (pp. 142-149). IEEE.

Song, S., Hwang, K., Zhou, R., & Kwok, Y.-K. (2005). Trusted P2P transactions with fuzzy reputation aggregation. *IEEE Internet Computing, 9*(6), 24–34. doi:10.1109/MIC.2005.136.

Sun, Y., Han, Z., & Liu, K. J. R. (2008). Defense of trust management vulnerabilities in distributed networks. *IEEE Communications Magazine, 46*(2), 112–119. doi:10.1109/MCOM.2008.4473092.

Sun, Y., Han, Z., Yu, W., & Liu, K. J. R. (2006). A trust evaluation framework in distributed networks: Vulnerability analysis and defense against attacks. In *Proceedings of IEEE INFOCOM* (pp. 1–13). IEEE. doi:10.1109/INFOCOM.2006.154.

Sun, Y., Yu, W., Han, Z., & Liu, K. J. R. (2006). Information theoretic framework of trust modeling and evaluation for ad hoc networks. *IEEE Journal on Selected Areas in Communications, 24*(2), 305–317. doi:10.1109/JSAC.2005.861389.

TCG. (2003). *TCG TPM specification v1.2.* Retrieved from https://www.trustedcomputinggroup.org/specs/TPM/

Theodorakopoulos, G., & Baras, J. S. (2006). On trust models and trust evaluation metrics for ad hoc networks. *IEEE Journal on Selected Areas in Communications*, *24*(2), 318–328. doi:10.1109/JSAC.2005.861390.

Venkatesh, V., & Davis, F. D. (2000). A theoretical extension of the technology acceptance model: Four longitudinal field studies. *Management Science*, *46*(2), 186–204. doi:10.1287/mnsc.46.2.186.11926.

Walsh, K., & Sirer, E. G. (2005). Fighting peer-to-peer SPAM and decoys with object reputation. In *Proceedings of the Third Workshop on the Economics of Peer-to-Peer Systems*, (pp. 138-143). IEEE.

Xiong, L., & Liu, L. (2004). PeerTrust: Supporting reputation-based trust for peer-to-peer electronic communities. *IEEE Transactions on Knowledge and Data Engineering*, *16*(7), 843–857. doi:10.1109/TKDE.2004.1318566.

Z. Yan (Ed.). (2010). *Trust modeling and management in digital environments: From social concept to system development*. Hershey, PA: IGI Global. doi:10.4018/978-1-61520-682-7.

Yan, Z. (2010b). Security via trusted communications. In P. Stavroulakis, & M. Stamp (Eds.), *Handbook on Communications and Information Security*. Berlin: Springer. doi:10.1007/978-3-642-04117-4_33.

Yan, Z., & Holtmanns, S. (2008). Trust modeling and management: From social trust to digital trust. In R. Subramanian (Ed.), *Computer Security, Privacy and Politics: Current Issues, Challenges and Solutions*. Hershey, PA: IGI Global. doi:10.4018/978-1-59904-804-8.ch013.

Yan, Z., & Niemi, V. (2009). A methodology towards usable trust management. In *Proceedings of ATC09* (LNCS), (vol. 5586, pp. 179-193). Berlin: Springer.

Yan, Z., & Prehofer, C. (2011). Autonomic trust management for a component based software system. *IEEE Transactions on Dependable and Secure Computing*, *8*(6), 810–823. doi:10.1109/TDSC.2010.47.

Yan, Z., Zhang, P., & Deng, H.R. (2011). TruBeRepec: A trust-behavior-based reputation and recommender system for mobile applications. *Journal of Personal and Ubiquitous Computing*. doi: 10.1007/s00779-011-0420-2

Yang, Y., Sun, Y., Kay, S., & Yang, Q. (2009). Defending online reputation systems against collaborative unfair raters through signal modeling and trust. In *Proceedings of SAC'09*, (pp. 1308-1315). SAC.

Zhang, Z., Wang, X., & Wang, Y. (2005). A P2P global trust model based on recommendation. In *Proceedings of the 2005 Int. Conf. on Machine Learning and Cybernetics*, (vol. 7, pp. 3975-3980). IEEE.

APPENDIX

Questions and Exercises

1. What is the difference between trust modeling and trust management?
2. What is the difference between trust management and security management?
3. What are the characteristics of different trust management solutions? How about their advantages and disadvantages?
4. Please estimate the influence of future research trends of trust management on trust modeling research?

Section 2
Current Advances of Trust Management in Mobile Environments

Chapter 4
Trust Management in Mobile Cloud Computing

ABSTRACT

Cloud computing provides various computing resources delivered as a service over a network, particularly the Internet. With the rapid development of mobile networking and computing, as well as other enabling technologies, cloud computing is extended into the mobile domain. Mobile cloud computing concerns the usage of cloud computing in combination with mobile devices and mobile networks, in which trust management plays an important role to establish trust relationships in order to offer trustworthy services. This chapter briefly introduces trust management technologies in cloud computing. The authors analyze the basic requirements of trust management in mobile cloud computing by introducing its architecture and distinct characteristics. They further propose a number of schemes in order to realize autonomic data access control based on trust evaluation in a mobile cloud computing environment. Furthermore, the authors discuss unsolved issues and future research challenges in the field of trust management in mobile cloud computing.

1. INTRODUCTION

Cloud computing denotes computing resources delivered as a service over a network (e.g., the Internet). It offers a new way of Information Technology (IT) services by re-arranging various resources (e.g., storage, computing and services) and providing them to users based on their demand. Cloud computing provides a big resource pool by linking network resources together. It has desirable properties, such as scalability, elasticity, fault-tolerance, and pay-per-use. Thus, it becomes a promising service platform, rearranging the structure of IT.

With the rapid growth of mobile communications, networking, and computing, as well as wide usage of mobile devices, cloud computing is extended to mobile domain. People nowadays use

DOI: 10.4018/978-1-4666-4765-7.ch004

Copyright © 2014, IGI Global. Copying or distributing in print or electronic forms without written permission of IGI Global is prohibited.

their mobile devices to perform various activities. Cloud computing provides a most rational way for mobile devices to access services and resources at any time and in any place. Mobile cloud computing concerns the usage of cloud computing in combination with mobile devices and mobile networks, in which trust management plays an important role to establish trust relationships in order to offer trustworthy mobile services.

The same as the Internet based cloud computing, one important issue in mobile cloud computing is trust, which concerns security and privacy, as well as many other factors, such as dependability and usability. For example, personal data should be securely accessed at the data center or the cloud agent of the cloud service provider (CSP). Personal access of some data should not be tracked by unauthorized users. A data owner should have an effective way to audit its data integrity and the fulfillment of service level agreement (SLA) between the data owner and the CSP. In addition, privacy preservation in the utilization (e.g., search and query) of encrypted data outsourced on cloud servers in CSP is a challenge. However, distinct characteristics of mobile cloud computing (e.g., mobility and ubiquity) lead to a number of new challenges. Trustworthy service provision and usability of service consumption are important issues that impact the proliferation of mobile cloud computing. Furthermore, whether it is rational and dependable to provide cloud services in a pervasive manner in mobile domain? What is the concern and challenges with regard to trust management in mobile cloud computing, focusing on usability, security assurance, privacy preservation, autonomic trust establishment and management? All above issues are worth seriously investigating.

In the rest of this chapter, we introduce the basic concept of cloud computing and its foundational trust management technologies. We analyze the challenges of trust management in mobile cloud computing by introducing its architecture and distinct characteristics. We further propose a number of schemes in order to realize autonomic data access control based on trust evaluation in mobile cloud computing environments, which is a useful technique towards autonomic trust management. Furthermore, we discuss the current issues and future research trends in the field of mobile cloud computing trust management.

2. LITERATURE BACKGROUND

2.1. Cloud Computing

2.1.1. Concept and Characteristics

Cloud computing is a general term for anything that involves delivering hosted services over the Internet. What we traditionally mentioned web services (e.g., web emails) fall into the cloud computing. The name cloud computing was inspired by the cloud symbol that is often used to represent the Internet in flowcharts and diagrams. The cloud computing was initially invented by businessmen who would like to create a new business model to offer various digital services based on user demands and by applying a pay-per-use billing model. Like consuming electric power, we only pay cloud services when we consume them. Therefore, the distinct characteristics of cloud computing can be summarized as: 1) sold on demand based on a pay-for-what-you-use model; 2) elastic: a user can have as much or as little of a service as they want at any given time; 3) fully managed by providers: a user need nothing but a personal computer or device with Internet access.

2.1.2. Why Cloud Computing

The cloud computing draws an extensive attention from both academia and industry due to many reasons. First, it consists of significant innovations in virtualization and distributed computing. It provides an easy architecture and model for users to access various services, while no need to take care of or understand the technical details applied behind. For a user, the only need is a client device and network access. Thus, it makes professional and personal lives easier since it is one of the best and effective ways to make work be done efficiently and effectively. Second, it is a cost saving technique. It is an excellent way to help companies save money in any business policies and allow them focusing on their business objectives. For example, it can help a start-up company reduce up-front investment in IT infrastructure establishment and save cost of recruiting IT staffs. Third, the cloud computing provides scalable service access and sufficient data storage for its users. Cloud computing is one kind of model to use storage space online. Many data storage modes are available now but all of them don't allow their users to use more space. The users have to pay additional fee if they need more than pre-agreed space. But some cloud computing companies allow using enough storage space for anyone. There is no need to pay extra fee; the user only pays for used space. Thus, cloud computing eliminates the problem by offering an effective way to minimize the cost as well as to maximize the efficiency of a company. It reduces the cost in several ways and it is more economical than any fixed size storage modes. Whatever the reason, cloud computing is considered as a new and brilliant service architecture and an amazing service in IT sector. It is very possible to form a huge cloud computing market that is growing day by day.

2.1.3. Types of Cloud

Based on the deployment model of cloud computing, a cloud can be private or public or hybrid. A public cloud sells services to anyone on the Internet, for example, Amazon Web Services (http://aws.amazon.com) is the largest public cloud provider. A private cloud is a proprietary network or a data center that supplies hosted services to a limited number of people. When a service provider uses public cloud resources to create their private cloud, the result is called a virtual private cloud. Private or public, the goal of cloud computing is to provide easy and scalable access to computing resources and IT services. A hybrid cloud is a composition of at least one private cloud and at least one public cloud. A hybrid cloud is typically offered in one of two ways: a vendor has a private cloud and forms a partnership with a public cloud provider, or a public cloud provider forms a partnership with a vendor that provides private cloud platforms. Ideally, the hybrid approach allows a business to take the advantage of the scalability and cost-effectiveness that a public cloud computing environment offers without exposing mission-critical applications and data to third-party vulnerabilities. This type of hybrid cloud is also referred to as hybrid IT. Community cloud is a collaborative effort in which infrastructure is shared between several organizations from a specific community with common concerns in security, compliance, and jurisdiction. It can be managed internally or by a third-party and hosted internally or externally. This deployment model spreads costs over fewer users than a public cloud but more than a private cloud, thus some cost savings can be potentially realized based on a common demand.

2.1.4. Categories of Cloud Services

The cloud computing runs in a mode "X as a service (XaaS)", where X could be software, hardware, data storage, and etc (Armbrust et al, 2009). The cloud services are broadly divided into three categories: Infrastructure-as-a-Service (IaaS), Platform-as-a-Service (PaaS) and Software-as-a-Service (SaaS).

Infrastructure-as-a-Service provides virtual server instance API to start, stop, access and configure their virtual servers and storage. In the enterprise, cloud computing allows a company to pay for only as much capacity as is needed, and bring more online services as soon as required. Because this pay-for-what-you-use model resembles the way that electricity, fuel and water are consumed; it's sometimes referred to as utility computing. Examples of this type of cloud services are virtual machines and IT infrastructure services, such as Windows Azure Virtual Machines (http://www.windowsazure.com/en-us/), Google computer engine (https://cloud.google.com/products/compute-engine), and Amazon Web Service. In addition, storage as a service (STaaS), security as a service (SECaaS), and data as a service (DaaS) fall into this category.

Platform-as-a-service in the cloud is defined as a set of computing platform such as operating system, programming language execution environment, database, web server, software and product development tools hosted on the provider's infrastructure. Developers create applications on the provider's platform over the Internet. PaaS providers may use APIs, website portals or gateway software installed on the customer's computer. Google App Engine (https://developers.google.com/appengine/), Windows Azure Compute, and Force.com, (an outgrowth of Salesforce.com) are examples of PaaS. Developers need to know that currently, there are not standards for interoperability or data portability in the cloud. Some providers will not allow software created by their customers to be moved off the provider's

platform. In addition, test environment as a service (TEaaS) and API as a service (APIaaS) fall into this category.

In the software-as-a-service, the vendor supplies the hardware infrastructure and the software product, and interacts with the user through a front-end portal. SaaS is a very broad market. Services can be anything from Web-based email to inventory control and database processing. Because the service provider hosts both the application and the data, the end user is free to use the service from anywhere. The typical example of SaaS is Google Apps (http://www.google.com/enterprise/apps/business/), which features several Web applications with similar functionality to traditional office suites, including Gmail, Google Groups, Google Calendar, Talk, Docs and Sites. In addition, Desktop as a service (DESaaS) falls into this category.

2.1.5. Cloud Computing Architecture

The above three types of cloud computing services can be mapped into the architecture of cloud computing, as shown in Figure 1. It concerns the components and subcomponents required for cloud computing. Basically, it contains a front end

Figure 1. Cloud computing architecture

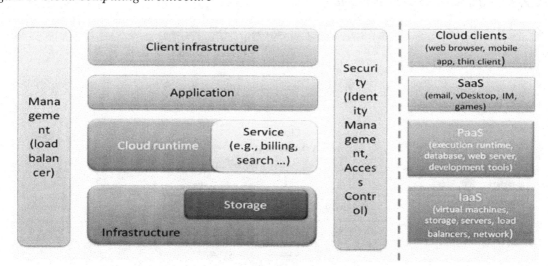

platform, named client infrastructure that consists of various cloud service access clients (e.g., fat client, thin client, and mobile device) and back end platforms (e.g., servers and storage), a cloud based delivery, and a network (e.g., Internet, Intranet, and Intercloud – the cloud of cloud). The back end platforms are structured into three layers:

- Infrastructure layer with storage utility offers IaaS, such as virtual machines, storage, servers, load balancers and network utilities.
- Cloud runtime and inside service layer contain runtime middleware that provides an effective method of distributing computations and allows developers to use the runtime's native language for all computations. This layer also provides a number of fundamental services for cloud computing, such as billing services and service search. This layer offers such cloud services as program language execution runtime, database, web server and development tools.
- Application layer contains various applications and software delivered as services. This layer can provide various kinds of SaaS, such as email, virtual desktop, instant messaging and games.

Both the front end platform and the back end platforms collaborate with the support of cloud computing management components and security components. The management component is applied to balance computing loads in order to achieve the best Quality of Services. The security component is responsible for ensuring the trust of cloud computing. Traditional security mechanisms include identity management for secure authentication and access control mechanisms for trustworthy authorization.

2.1.6. Pros and Cons

Obviously, cloud computing has a number of advantages such as agility of service encapsulation adaptive to the context changes of consumers, scalability and cost saving, shown in Figure 2. It could become the next generation service architecture. However, current cloud computing is still facing a number of challenges that could impede its further development. Security is the first issue. Allowing personal and private data to be stored at and managed by a CSP that cannot be fully trusted introduces a big risk for cloud service users. The data could be disclosed and the user privacy could be tracked by the CSP. It could be locked-in the CSP thus it is hard for the data

Figure 2. Pros and cons of cloud computing

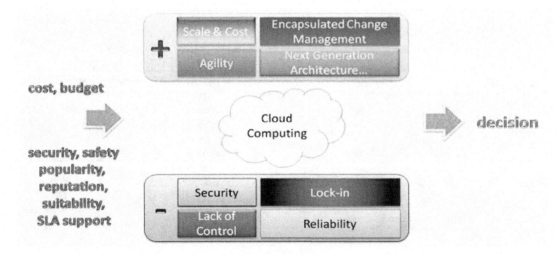

owner to control its own data and ensure that the SLA (service level agreement) has been reliably fulfilled. Reliability of CSP becomes crucial of importance since if the data is ruined at the CSP, the trust relationship between the user and CSP will be broken. Therefore, the decision of a user to adopt a cloud computing service should be made based on the current economic situation, business requirements and the concern of security, as well as the reputation of CSP. Without any doubt, trust plays a crucial role in cloud computing business.

2.2. Solutions of Trustworthy Cloud Computing

The technologies applied for ensuring a trustworthy cloud computing nowadays include data access control for secure data storage at CSP, identity management, privacy enhancement, and trust framework. Herein, we provide a brief review of these solutions since most of them can also be applied into some scenarios of mobile cloud computing when user data are stored at a third party, especially when making use of mobile Internet architecture.

2.2.1. Data Access Control

The traditional method to protect sensitive data outsourced to third parties is to store encrypted data on servers, while the decryption keys are only disclosed to eligible users. For example, traditional symmetric key cryptographic system is adopted to encrypt data to protect data security from a distrusted server. Before outsourcing, the data owner will first classify data with similar access control lists (ACLs) into a file-group, and then encrypt each file-group with a symmetric key. The symmetric key will be distributed to the users in the ACL, so that only the users in the ACL can access this group of files (Kallahalla et al., 2003). The main drawback of this approach is that the key size managed by the data owner grows linearly with the number of file-groups. Another approach is based on the combination of traditional symmetric key and public key cryptographic systems (Goh, Shacham, Modadugu & Boneh, 2003). The data owner first specifies an ACL for a data, and then encrypts the data with a symmetric key, which is encrypted with the public keys of users in the ACL. Therefore, only the users in the ACL can recover the data using their private keys. The main drawback of this approach is that the costs for encrypting data will grow linearly with the number of users in the ACL.

Obviously, there are several drawbacks about this kind of trivial solutions. First of all, such a solution requires an efficient key management mechanism to distribute decryption keys to authorized users, which has been proven to be very difficult. Next, this approach lacks scalability and flexibility; as the number of authorized users becomes large, the solution will not be efficient anymore. In case a previously legitimate user needs to be revoked, related data has to be re-encrypted and new keys must be distributed to existing legitimate users again. Last but not least, data owners need to be online all the time so as to encrypt or re-encrypt data and distribute keys to authorize users. Therefore, an ideal approach is to encrypt each data once, and distribute appropriate keys to users once, so that each user can only decrypt its authorized data.

Attribute-based encryption (ABE) turns out to be a good technique for realizing scalable, flexible, and fine-grained access control solutions (Sahai & Waters, 2005). In the ABE scheme, users are identified by a set of attributes rather than an exact identity. Each data is encrypted with an attribute-based access structure, such that only the users whose attributes satisfy the access structure can decrypt the data. For example, for data D, encrypted with the access structure a1 or a2, either users with attributes a1 or a2, can decrypt D. Attribute-based encryption has developed to two branches, key-policy ABE (KP-ABE) (Goyal, Pandey, Sahai & Waters, 2006) and ciphertext-policy ABE (CP-ABE) (Bethencourt, Sahai &

Waters, 2007; Muller, Katzenbeisser & Eckert, 2008), depending on how attributes and policy are associated with ciphertexts and users' decryption keys. In a KP-ABE scheme (Goyal, Pandey, Sahai & Waters, 2006), a ciphertext is associated with a set of attributes and a user's decryption key is associated with a monotonic tree access structure. Only if the attributes associated with the ciphertext satisfy the tree access structure, can the user decrypt the ciphertext. In a CP-ABE scheme (Bethencourt, Sahai & Waters, 2007), the roles of ciphertexts and decryption keys are switched; the ciphertext is encrypted with a tree access policy chosen by an encryptor, while the corresponding decryption key is created with respect to a set of attributes. As long as the set of attributes associated with a decryption key satisfies the tree access policy associated with a given ciphertext, the key can be used to decrypt the ciphertext. Since users' decryption keys are associated with a set of attributes, CP-ABE is conceptually closer to traditional access control models such as Role-Based Access Control (RBAC) (Bethencourt, Sahai & Waters, 2007). Thus, it is more natural to apply CP-ABE, instead of KP-ABE, to enforce access control of encrypted data.

The flexibility to control data access based on an attribute-based access structure makes ABE a promising cryptographic technique to secure data storage for cloud computing. Several schemes employed attribute-based encryption (ABE) for access control of outsourced data in cloud computing in order to achieve flexibility, scalability and fine-grained access control. Examples are a hierarchical attribute-set-based encryption (HASBE) for access control in cloud computing by extending ciphertext-policy attribute-set-based encryption (ASBE) with a hierarchical structure of users (Wan, Liu & Deng, 2012). The proposed scheme not only achieves scalability due to its hierarchical structure, but also inherits flexibility and fine-grained access control in supporting compound attributes of ASBE. In addition, HASBE employs multiple value assignments for access

expiration time to deal with user revocation more efficiently than existing schemes. Yu et al. (2010) proposed an access control mechanism based on KP-ABE for cloud computing, together with proxy re-encryption and lazy re-encryption for efficient user revocation. This scheme enables a data owner to delegate most of the computational overhead to cloud servers. It provides salient properties of user access privilege confidentiality and user secret key accountability. The use of KP-ABE provides fine-grained access control gracefully. Each file is encrypted with a symmetric data encryption key (DEK), which is in turn encrypted by a public key corresponding to a set of attributes in KP-ABE, which is generated according to an access structure. The encrypted data file is stored with the corresponding attributes and the encrypted DEK. If the associated attributes of a file stored in the cloud satisfy the access structure of a user's key, then the user is able to decrypt the encrypted, which is used in turn to decrypt the file. Wang, Liu and Wu (2010) proposed hierarchical attribute-based encryption (HABE) to achieve fine-grained access control in cloud storage services by combining hierarchical identity-based encryption (HIBE) and CP-ABE. This scheme also supports fine-grained access control and fully delegating computation to the cloud providers. Tang, Lee, Lui and Perlman (2012) presented FADE, a secure overlay cloud storage system that provides fine-grained access control and assured deletion for outsourced data on the cloud, while working seamlessly atop today's cloud storage services. In FADE, active data files that remain on the cloud are associated with a set of user-defined file access policies (e.g., time expiration, read/write permissions of authorized users), such that data files are accessible only to users who satisfy the file access policies. In addition, FADE generalizes time-based file assured deletion (i.e., data files are assuredly deleted upon time expiration) into a more fine-grained approach called policy-based file assured deletion, in which data files are assuredly deleted when the associated file access policies are revoked and become obsolete. However, existing access control solutions based on ABE applied complicated attribute structure into fine-grained access control, which makes computation load for key management very heavy. An efficient access control scheme based on ABE is expected in practice.

Several researchers have previously addressed access control issues for cloud computing from the architecture point of view. Nurmi et al. (2009) provided an authorization system to control the execution of virtual machines (VMs) to ensure that only administrators and owners could access them. Berger et al. (2009) promoted an authorization model based on both role-based access control (RBAC) and security labels to control access to shared data, VMs, and network resources. Calero et al. (2010) presented a centralized authorization system that provides a federated path-based access control mechanism. Almutairi et al. (2012) proposed distributed access control architecture by incorporating principles from security management and software engineering to address cloud computing security challenges. It is a comprehensive authorization design for access management by using an XML-based declaration of the access control policy towards practical implementation. All above researches concern how to fulfill access control policies in cloud computing.

A variety of researchers have looked into developing authorization models and systems related to cloud computing. Calero et al (2010) described a multi-tenancy authorization system suitable for middleware service in the PaaS layer. This authorization system provides access control to the information and services provided by different cloud services using cloud infrastructure. Each business can provide several cloud services that can collaborate with other services belonging either to the same organization or to a different organization. The system supports multi-tenancy, role-based access control (RBAC), hierarchical RBAC, path-based object hierarchies, and federation. But the system lacks support on

fine-grained control on the authorization information shared between organizations.

2.2.2. Identity Management (IdM)

The following organizations are working on standards related to identity management:

- The OpenID Foundation (OIDF; ht tp:// openid.net /foundation/) — OpenID 1.0/2, OpenID Connect
- OAuth (community site; http://oauth.net) — OAuth 1.0/OAuth Wrap
- Internet Engineering Task Force (IETF; www.ietf.org) — OAuth/WOES/Abfab/ HTTP
- World Wide Web Consortium (W3C; www.w3.org) — HTML/HTTP/SOAP
- Organization for the Advancement of Structured Information Standards (OASIS; www.oasis-open.org) — SAML/XML/ WS-*/XRI
- Shibboleth Project (www.shibboleth.net) — Shibboleth/OpenSaml 1.0/2.0
- US National Strategy for Trusted Identities in Cyberspace (NSTIC; www.nist.gov/ nstic)
- Open Identity Exchange (OIX; http:// openidentityexchange.org)
- Kantara Initiative (http://kantarainitiative. org) — proceeded by the Liberty Alliance
- InCommon Federation (www.incommon. org/about.html)
- US National Institute of Standards and Technology (NIST; www.nist.gov)
- Identity Commons (www.idcommons.net)
- Information Card Foundation (ICF; http:// informationcard.net/foundation)
- International Telecommunications Union (www.itu.int/ITU-T/studygroups/com17/ index.asp) — ITU-T Study Group 17
- International Organization for Standardization (ISO; www.iso.org)

Identity management becomes crucial of importance in cloud computing because a user might invoke services across multiple clouds. Identity management of cloud computing must support a mechanism to transfer a user's identifiers and credentials across layers and multiple clouds to access services and resources. This requirement includes a provision for a decentralized single-sign-on mechanism within the authorization model, which can enable persistent authorization for users in terms of their identity and entitlement across multiple clouds (Bhatti, Bertino & Ghafoor, 2006). Sanchez et al (2012) proposed a privacy enhanced and trust-aware identity management architecture compliance with SAMLv2/ID-FF standards. The aim is to provide an efficient identity management and access control, as well as dynamic, autonomic, and user-centric system for better scalability in cloud computing services. This architecture encourages cloud federation in a more active way by including reputation information and introducing Trust-Aware enhanced users. Likewise, the cloud providers make richer trust decisions when interacting with unknown entities. Furthermore, trust evolution by monitoring cloud providers and users' behavior allows rewarding or penalizing the current behavior, thus modeling the fact that trust changes over time. On the other hand, risk management enables to analyze the risk factors associated with each transaction. The architecture also empowers users to access cloud services and share digital contents without necessarily revealing their true identities to everyone by adopting multiple identities, for instance depending on the context. Olden (2011) suggested that identity management should be offered as an IaaS in order to architect a cloud scale identity fabric. However, identity management in the cloud is especially difficult because of the cross-cutting nature of identity and its impact across architectural and organizational domains (Olden, 2011).

A number of solutions were proposed in order to achieve federated identity management and provide identity privacy. Stihler et al (2012) proposed an architecture and a platform for federated identity management, mapping high level identities (i.e. from SaaS) to low level identities (i.e. for IaaS) to eliminate a multi-layer cloud computing integration gap. Fine grained accounting can be achieved by enabling the SaaS application developer to track resource usage on a user based fashion. It is also possible to apply security policies for individual users on the infrastructure level, obtain accurate auditing records, as the users are known on the whole cloud computing layers and deploy applications on multiple IaaS providers without losing identity unity. Angin et al (2010) presented an entity-centric approach for privacy and identity management in cloud computing. The advantage of an entity-centric identity management is that a disclosure of Personally Identifiable Information (PII) is no longer arbitrarily or at the will of CSP but is at the will of its owner. This approach is based on active bundles—each including PII, privacy policies and a virtual machine that enforces the policies and uses a set of protection mechanisms (such as integrity checks, apoptosis, evaporation, decoy) to protect themselves; and anonymous identification—to mediate interactions between an entity and cloud services using entity's privacy policies. Cloud computing can benefit from the entity-centric mechanism for protecting privacy of sensitive data throughout their entire lifecycle. Every entity's request for any service is bundled with the entity's identity and entitlement information. Thus, this approach allows the entity to create and manage its digital identities to authenticate in a way that does not reveal its actual identities or relationships between identities to vendors, service providers, etc; and to protect PII from unauthorized access.

2.2.3. Privacy Enhancement

Privacy in cloud computing is the ability of a user or a business to control what information they reveal about themselves over the cloud or to a cloud service provider, and the ability to control who can access that information (Angin et al, 2010). Data access control mechanism is one of important approaches for privacy enhancement, which has been reviewed in Section 2.2.1. Herein, we focus on other privacy enhancement schemes such as private auditing, data sharing accountability, private behavior preservation (e.g., privacy-preservation on searchable encryption), and so on.

Sundareswaran, Squicciarini and Lin (2012) proposed a Cloud Information Accountability (CIA) framework, based on the notion of information accountability. Unlike privacy protection technologies that are built on the hide-it-or-lose-it perspective, information accountability focuses on keeping the data usage transparent and traceable. By means of the CIA, data owners can track not only whether or not the SLAs are being honored, but also enforce access and usage control rules as needed. The applied approach leverages and extends the programmable capability of JAR (Java ARchives) files to automatically log the usage of the users' data by any entity in the cloud. Users will send their data along with any policies such as access control policies and logging policies that they want to enforce, enclosed in JAR files, to cloud service providers. Any access to the data will trigger an automated and authenticated logging mechanism local to the JARs. The integrity of the logging was solved by providing the JARs with a central point of contact that forms a link between them and the user. It records the error correction information sent by the JARs, which allows it to monitor the loss of any logs from any of the JARs. Moreover, if a JAR is not able to contact its central point, any access to its enclosed data will be denied.

Wang et al (2010) utilized and uniquely combined the public key based homomorphic authenticator with random masking to achieve the privacy-preserving public cloud data auditing system in order to ensure the integrity of outsourced data. The system can efficiently audit the cloud data storage without demanding the local copy of data, and introduce no additional on-line burden to the cloud user. In addition, the third party auditing process brings in no new vulnerabilities towards user data privacy.

In order to protect outsourced data privacy, sensitive data have to be encrypted before outsourced to the public cloud servers, which makes effective data utilization service a very challenging task. Although traditional searchable encryption schemes (e.g., Song, Wagner & Perrig, 2000; Goh, 2003; Boneh et al, 2004; Chang & Mitzenmacher, 2005; Curtmola et al, 2006) allow a user to securely search over encrypted data through keywords without first decrypting it, these techniques support only conventional Boolean keyword search and are not yet sufficient to meet the effective data utilization need that is inherently demanded by a large number of users and a huge amount of data files in cloud. Wang et al (2012) defined and solved the problem of secure ranked keyword search over encrypted cloud data. Ranked search greatly enhances system usability by enabling search result relevance ranking instead of sending undifferentiated results, and further ensures the file retrieval accuracy. Furthermore, Cao et al (2011) defined and solved the problem of privacy preserving multi-keyword ranked search over encrypted cloud data (MRSE) in order to extend previous work for supporting multi-keyword search and satisfy a set of strict privacy requirements for secure cloud data utilization. An efficient similarity measure of "coordinate matching", i.e., as many matches as possible, was adopted to capture the relevance of data documents to a search query. In addition, "inner product similarity" was applied to quantitatively evaluate such similarity measure. Privacy preservation on cloud data utilization is an important research topic in the current literature.

2.2.4. Trust Establishment

Cloud computing has opened up a paramount concern on trust. It introduces a different type of trust scenario, e.g., data owners are generally in different trust domains from data centers of CSP.

Thus, establishing trust among involved entities in cloud computing is essential. Khan and Malluhi (2010) looked at the trust in cloud computing from a user's perspective. They pointed out that control, ownership, prevention and security are key aspects that decide user trust in cloud services. Establishing trust in cloud computing can be achieved by a number of emerging technologies, such as remote access control, reflection, certification and private enclaves. Hwang and Li (2010) proposed using a trust-overlay network over multiple data centers to implement a reputation system for establishing trust between service providers and data owners. Data coloring and software watermarking techniques are applied to protect shared data objects and massively distributed software modules. These techniques not only safeguard multi-way authentications, but also enable single sign-on in the cloud and tighten access control for sensitive data in both public and private clouds.

Firdhous, Ghazali and Hassan (2011) conducted a survey on the trust management systems implemented on distributed systems with a special focus on cloud computing. They pointed that the existing trust models developed in distributed systems have not been used or tested in cloud computing environments. Hence the suitability of these models for use in cloud computing cannot be recommended without an extensive evaluation. In addition, the trust management systems proposed for cloud computing have been extensively studied with respect to capability, applicability in a heterogonous cloud environment and implementability. Based on this review, they commented that none of the proposed trust management systems were based on solid theoretical foundation and took any quality of service attributes to form trust scores. We notify that there exists a big opportunity in the research of trust management in the area of trust management.

Cloud computing has emerged as a promising service business. Quite a number of vendors, such as Google, Amazon, Microsoft, IBM, etc., have shipped cloud computing services into markets.

Many technologies have been proposed to enhance its trustworthiness. In this section, we only briefly introduced a limited number of advanced research results. However, the above solutions or techniques may not be sufficient enough to overcome challenges related to trust in mobile cloud computing, especially when cloud services are instantly offered by nearby computing resources carried by mobile devices.

3. MOBILE CLOUD COMPUTING

Mobile cloud computing is the usage of cloud computing in combination with mobile devices and mobile networking. Originally, cloud computing exists when tasks and data are kept on the Internet rather than on individual devices, providing on-demand access. With the emergence of high-end network access technologies like 2G, 3G, WiFi, WiMax and smart phones, a new derivative of cloud computing has emerged. This is referred as Mobile Cloud Computing (MCC). It can be defined as a composition of mobile technology and cloud computing infrastructure where data and their related processing will happen in the cloud with an exception that they can be accessed through a mobile device. Due to the advanced improvement in mobile browsers, nearly every mobile device can access cloud services. It's becoming a trend nowadays that many organizations are keen to provide accessibility to their employees to access an office network through a mobile device from anywhere.

Offloading computation from mobile devices to the cloud is in wide use today. Despite its success, however, it suffers from a number of shortcomings. These include the inflexibility in apportioning work between the mobile device and the remote cloud, the latency inherent in accessing remote cloud resources, and the inability to handle intermittent connectivity as a consequence of device mobility (Satyanarayanan et al, 2009). Normally, a mobile device often encounters many entities, including other mobile devices, capable of lending computational resources. Thus, a practical approach capable of handling connectivity disruptions is to leverage this additional computational power. Recent concept of mobile cloud computing extends the scenario of cloud computing in order to fully use computing resources available in vicinity and remotely.

3.1. Architecture and Distinct Characteristics

3.1.1. Architecture

We envision the spectrum of computational scenarios and classify the architecture of mobile cloud computing into three categories.

- **Mobile Access to Central Cloud:** At an extreme, a traditional MCC scenario is a mobile device intermittently connects to remote cloud resources maintained by a cloud service provider with which it has an established relationship, as shown in Figure 3 (a). This scenario has no difference from Internet cloud computing except that the cloud services are accessed by mobile devices through mobile connection points and mobile internetworking.

- **Mobile Access to Cloudlet:** Resource constraint is not just a temporary limitation, but is intrinsic to mobility. In this vision, mobile users generally like to seamlessly utilize nearby computers to obtain the resource benefits of cloud computing without incurring WAN delays and jitter. The second MCC scenario is the use of cloudlets on which service software is dynamically instantiated to enable the off-loading of computation from mobile devices, as shown in Figure 3 (b). Rather than relying on a distant "cloud", a mobile user instantiates a "cloudlet" on nearby infrastructure and uses it via a wireless LAN. Cloudlets are decentralized and widely dispersed Internet infrastructure. Their computing cycles and storage resources can be leveraged by nearby mobile computers. A cloudlet can be viewed as a "data center in a box" at a business premise. It is self-managed and requires little more than power, Internet connectivity, and access control for setup (Satyanarayanan et al., 2009). The cloudlet is generally decentralized and owned by local business. Unlike the traditional internet cloud, it can serve few users at a time. Most importantly, a cloudlet only contains soft state such as cache copies of

Figure 3. Three mobile cloud computing scenarios. a) mobile access to central cloud; b) mobile access to cloudlet; c) mobile access to pervasive cloud

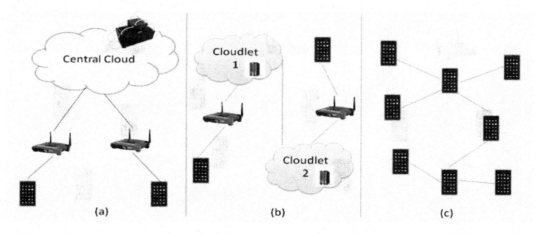

data or code that is available elsewhere. Loss or destruction of a cloudlet is hence not catastrophic.

- **Mobile Access to Pervasive Cloud:** At the other extreme, a mobile device only contacts with other mobile devices. This is a pervasive computational environment where both the computation initiator and the remote computational resources are mobile. The third MCC scenario is the use of computing resources instantly offered by mobile devices in vicinity to enable pervasive cloud services, as shown in Figure 3 (c). In this case, each mobile device could be a cloud service provider, called a pervasive cloud, which offers various services in a ubiquitous and instant manner. Although each mobile device's computing capability

is limited, it is still possible for a mobile device or a number of mobile devices cooperating together to provide expected services, especially in an urgent situation, e.g., disaster. Pervasive cloud services are provided based on self-organized mobile networks or through local connectivity.

For a long run, the environment of an initiator mobile device for remote computation will be, in the most general case, a hybrid of above scenarios. As such the mobile device needs to learn about the capabilities of its environment and adapt its remote computation decisions accordingly. Thus, the mobile cloud computing concerns new service architecture that is different from cloud computing, as shown in Figure 4. A mobile device can be served by three different levels of services:

Figure 4. Mobile cloud computing Architecture

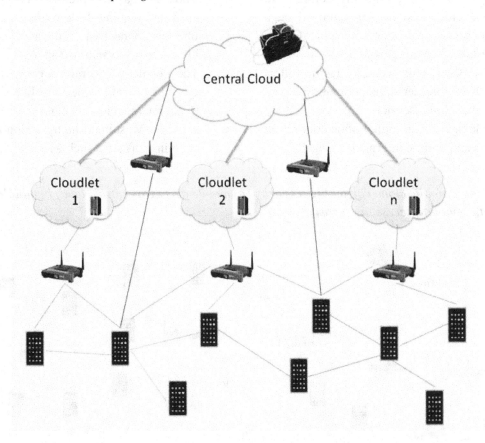

1) central cloud services located at the Internet provided by wireless or mobile networking; 2) cloudlet services offered by distributed business owners via wireless connection; 3) pervasive cloud services instantly provided by nearby mobile devices based on a self-organized network.

3.1.2. Distinct Characteristics

From the architecture of mobile cloud computing, we can summarize its distinct characteristics. First, mobile cloud computing only serves mobile clients. The service consuming clients are mobile computing devices. Second, the mobile cloud services can be offered by various devices or parties with different capabilities, such as Internet cloud service providers, cloudlet owners and other mobile devices. Wireless connection to an access point or other devices is essential to consume mobile cloud services. Third, the mobile cloud computing fully uses the computing resources of any third parties in order to achieve the best quality of services in different contexts. It aims to seamlessly convert services offered by one party to another without reducing quality. It attempts to provide always-available-services in any situations. Finally, the mobile device needs to learn about the capabilities of its environment and adapt its remote computation decisions accordingly. This causes special requirements and challenges on the design and development of the mobile cloud computing system (including its client).

3.2. Existing Trust Management Solutions for MCC

Few work related to trust management was found for mobile cloud computing in the literature. Existing work only focus on specific aspects for building up trust in mobile cloud computing. Zhang, Sun and Yan (2011) proposed a generic and flexible solution based on central cloud computing technology to realize trusted identity

management to achieve seamless roaming in a mobile heterogeneous environment, such as mobile cloud computing. Huang et al. (2010) proposed a new mobile cloud framework called MobiCloud to enhancing secure mobile computing based on MANET using cloud computing by addressing trust management, secure routing, and risk management issues in the network. MobiCloud is a secure mobile cloud computing framework, which transforms traditional MANETs into a new service-oriented communication architecture, in which each mobile device is treated as a Service Node (SN), and it is mirrored to one or more Extended Semi-Shadow Images (ESSIs) in the cloud in order to address the communication and computation deficiencies of a mobile device. However, this solution cannot support trust management in the scenario of "mobile access to pervasive cloud", where central cloud could be intermittently inaccessible. In MobiCloud, mobile users must trust the cloud service provider to protect the data received from mobile devices. However, it is a big concern for mobile users for storing their private sensitive information in a public cloud. Huang et al. (2011) addressed this privacy issue by presenting a new mobile cloud data processing framework through trust management and private data isolation. Jia et al. (2011) presented a secure data mechanism to solve the problem of data secrecy and privacy in mobile cloud computing. This mechanism outsources not only the data but also the security management to the mobile cloud in a trusted way. They explored identity based proxy re-encryption scheme to make mobile users easily implement fine-grained access control of data and also guarantee the data privacy in the cloud. To achieve this, they adopted an identity-based proxy re-encryption scheme which allows a mobile user to encrypt his data under his identity to protect his data from leaking and, at the same time, to delegate his data management capability to the mobile cloud. Furthermore the mobile user could delegate his access control capability to the cloud, which could grant the access of an authorized user by transforming the ciphertext encrypted with the data owner's identity to the one with the sharer's identity.

All the above researches made use of the security resources offered by central cloud to provide trust solutions (e.g., identity management and secure data access control) in mobile cloud computing environments. Existing work has not fully studied a comprehensive trust management solution to support all three scenarios of mobile cloud computing in a seamless way. Particularly, for mobile access to pervasive cloud, the literature lacks solutions on its trust management.

3.3. Research Requirements on Trust Management in MCC

In this subsection, we propose a number of special requirements towards comprehensive trust management in MCC.

1. **Usability Enhancement:** Since the mobile cloud services are normally consumed by mobile devices, the usability issue of MCC service provision and consumption should be paid special attention to. Furthermore, trust management for MCC should concern usability and user acceptance in order to support trustworthy user-service interaction. This requirement is more crucial in MCC, compared with cloud computing.
2. **Connection and Communication Security:** The secure wireless connection and communication among mobile devices, wireless access points and cloud service providers should be guaranteed.
3. **Individual Data Security and Privacy Assurance in All MCC Scenarios:** Any outsourced individual data of a data owner (mostly a mobile device user) to the central clouds, cloudlets or pervasive clouds should be securely controlled for access by authorized parties. In addition, the usage

(e.g., query or search), expected movement, operation and integrity of the data should be audited according to the data owner's expectation (e.g., data privacy should be preserved during the auditing) no matter where the data is stored (e.g., in either a central cloud data center, or a cloudlet, or a pervasive cloud). This requirement is different from and more stringent in MCC, compared with cloud computing.

4. **Intelligent and Seamless Service Conversion:** In order to achieve advanced quality of services, intelligent and seamless service conversion from one MCC scenario to another should be supported by the mobile device that accesses MCC services. Thus, the mobile device needs to learn about the capabilities of its environment and adapt its remote computation decisions accordingly. This requirement on mobile device is specific in MCC, but not needed in cloud computing.
5. **MCC Capability Management:** In order to achieve trustworthy mobile cloud computing, it is crucial to understand the computing capability of each mobile cloud service provider. The MCC system should load a service request based on the mobile cloud capability and dynamically adjust service provision and resource loading by adapting to the capability change.
6. **Trustworthy MCC Service Billing:** Because the MCC services could be offered and fulfilled by different types of parties (central clouds, cloudlet and pervasive clouds), pay-per-use should be shared among service providers in a trustworthy and acceptable way. The MCC service billing should be well processed and satisfied by each stakeholder. This requirement could cause additional challenges for the practical deployment of MCC.
7. **Trustworthy Identity Management:** For MCC service and billing, it is crucial of importance to manage mobile user/device

identity in a heterogeneous mobile computing environment with a trustworthy way.

4. AUTONOMIC DATA ACCESS CONTROL IN MCC BASED ON TRUST AND REPUTATION

In this section, we propose three schemes to control data access in MCC based on trust and reputation in a flexible and autonomic manner. The first scheme controls MCC data based on trust evaluation in mobile social networking. It can be applied into the situation that the personal data are stored in a central cloud data center, a cloudlet, or pervasive clouds and the data owner's mobile device is available or on-line. The second scheme relies on a reputation center to control data access. It is suitable to be applied to control data access at the central cloud data center, the cloudlet or pervasive clouds when the data owner's device is not available or on-line. The third scheme supports controlling data access by multi-dimensional trust and reputation levels that are assessed by multiple parties in a heterogeneous manner. It can be flexibly applied into various scenarios no matter the data owner's mobile device is available or not.

Using the level of trust and reputation to control MCC data access can greatly reduce the complexity of key management and computation load. The heterogeneous structure of access control attributes or policies can be considered and integrated into the process of trust evaluation or reputation generation, thus greatly reduce the size of keys and simplify key management.

4.1. Personal Data Access Control Based on Mobile Social Networking

4.1.1. Summary of Scheme

We propose using trust level assessed in mobile social networking to control personal data access at a mobile cloud data center (MCDC) (e.g., offered by a semi-trusted cloud computing service provider, a cloudlet or other mobile devices). Concretely, the trust level with regard to a concrete context (e.g., health treatment) can be assessed based on social networking activities, behaviors and experiences. According to the trust level and its linked context, the data owner encrypts his/her personal data by setting the trust threshold, specifying access context and indicating valid access period for the encrypted data access. The data owner issues the decryption keys to those eligible users to access its personal data. Thus, personal data access (with conditions like the trust level exceeds a threshold in a context and within a period of time) can be fully controlled by the data owner.

Due to the dynamically changed trust level, the data owner informs MCDC the blacklist of the users who is not eligible to access the data in the valid access period. Thus, those users who are not satisfied with the access control conditions cannot access the data any more through the control of the semi-trusted MCDC. We ensure the MCDC to perform the above access control following the data owner's request based on a reputation mechanism. Each MCDC's reputation is evaluated according to the user's feedback and published in order to encourage and ensure the good behavior of MCDC. Based on the reputation of MCDC, a mobile user can decide which MCDC should be adopted.

This scheme can be applied into such kind of scenarios that a mobile user saves its sensitive personal data at a MCDC. For ensuring the access of its data by a number of trustworthy users, he makes use of the trust clue accumulated from its individual social networking, especially mobile social networking records recorded by the mobile device to issue data decryption keys to eligible users and control the personal data access at MCDC.

4.1.2. Trust Assessment based on Mobile Social Networking

Trust can be assessed based on the clue showed in mobile social networking. We can accumulate the following information of social networking and communications through mobile devices.

- Mobile voice/video calls;
- Voice/video calls via mobile Internet (e.g., VoIP);
- Short messages;
- Instant messages;
- Pervasive interaction with a person based on local connectivity.

We classify them into three types: 1) calls; 2) messages; and 3) local instant interaction. The number of calls (called and received), messages (sent and received) and interactions can reflect the social closeness between two persons and their personal trustworthiness. This mobile social networking information can be automatically collected without intentional interaction with the mobile user. Thus, trust evaluation can be automatically conducted at backend with good usability. Herein, we propose a trust level assessment Formula 1 (presented in Box 1) to indicate the trust level of two persons based on mobile social networking. The notions used in the function are depicted in Table 1. Notably, we only show one example of trust evaluation function based on weighted voting herein. Other evaluation methods can be also applied in order to achieve good performance.

Notably, the above trust level can be optionally linked to a concrete context based on keyword extraction from messaging texts and voice/speech recognition. That is the $N\_c(i,j)$, $N\_m(i,j)$ and $N\_i(i,j)$ are recorded based on different context categories, thus $TL(i,j)$ is generated targeting at the trust level fell into different contexts. Based on the trust evaluation in different context, the data owner can set a data access control policy based on trust, context and time limitation.

4.1.3. Required Keys and System Setup

We apply the attribute-based encryption (ABE) to implement the scheme. During system setup, a public master key PK and a secret master key MK are generated; PK is available to every party in the MCC system, whereas MK is only known to the system user or a user agent. Every mobile user u maintains a public user key PK_u, which is used by a data owner to generate personalized secret attribute keys, and a secret key SK_u, which is used in the decryption operation related to PK_u.

Generation and distribution of PK_u and SK_u is the task of the user or the user agent. The user agent is required to verify the unique identifier of the user before these two keys are generated and issued during user registration into the system. Notably, the keys SK_u and PK_u are bound to the unique identifier of the user. This binding is crucial for the verification of the user's attributes.

Each user (e.g., a data owner) maintains a secret key SK_u, which is used to issue secret attribute keys to eligible users based on trust level (TL) evaluated in mobile social networking. It is also used to generate the public key of attributes - 'trust level' and 'time' of u. Parameter T denotes the public representation of the time attribute. For the attribute with representation of TL, or time T, there is a public key, respectively denoted PK_TL and PK_T, which is issued by u and is used to encrypt personal data of u in

Box 1.

$$TL(i,j) = f\left\{ TL'(i,j) + pl(i,j) * \begin{bmatrix} w1 * \theta(N\_c(i,j) + N\_c(j,i)) + w2 * \theta(N\_m(i,j) + N\_m(j,i)) \\ + w3 * \theta(N\_i(i,j) + N\_i(j,i)) \end{bmatrix} - pu(i,j) \right\}$$

$$(1)$$

Table 1. The notions used for trust assessment

Symbols	Description	Remark
N_c(i,j)	The number of calls made by i to j	
N_m(i,j)	The number of messages sent by i to j	
N_i(i,j)	The number of interactions initiated by i to j	
TL(i,j)	The trust level of j assessed by i; TL'(i,j) is the old value of TL(i,j)	
$\theta(I)$	The Rayleigh cumulative distribution function $\theta(I) = \left\{1 - \exp(\frac{-I^2}{2\sigma^2})\right\}$ to model the impact of integer number I, where $\sigma > 0$, is a parameter that inversely controls how fast the number I impacts the increase of $\theta(I)$. Parameter σ can be set from 0 to theoretically ∞, to capture the characteristics of different scenarios. We use $\theta(I)$ to model the influence of the number of calls, messages and interactions on social relationships.	
w1	The weight parameter to show the importance of voice call	w1+w2+w3=1
w2	The weight parameter to show the importance of messaging	
w3	The weight parameter to show the importance of instant interaction	
pl(i,j)	The priority level of j in i's social networks, e.g., a family member or close friend may have the highest priority level in various contexts	
pu(i,j)	The punishment factor of j in i's view, e.g., due to bad social interaction/communication experiences	
$f(x)$	The Sigmoid function $f(x) = \dfrac{1}{1 + e^{-x}}$, which is used to normalize a value into (0, 1) in order to unify an evaluated trust level into an expected scope	

order to control access based on the trust level and the time period. The corresponding secret attribute keys of PK_TL and PK_T, personalized for eligible users, are issued by u to the eligible users. To prevent collusion, every user gets a different secret attribute key that only he can use. A secret attribute key of an attribute TL, issued to an eligible user u' by u is denoted SK_(TL,u,u'). A secret attribute key of the attribute time T, issued to an eligible user u' by u is denoted SK_(T,u,u'). We call the set of secret keys that u' has (i.e., SK_u', SK_(TL,u,u') and SK_(T,u,u')) as its key ring. Table 2 summarizes the keys related to this scheme.

4.1.4. Secure Data Access Scheme

The proposed scheme consists of a number of fundamental algorithms: Setup, InitiateUser, CreateTrustLevelPK, IssueTrustLevelSK, CreateTimePK, IssueTimeSK, Encrypt and Decrypt. The description of the eight algorithms is as follows:

- **Setup:** The Setup algorithm takes as input the implicit security parameter 1^k. It outputs the public key PK and the master key MK. This process is securely conducted at the user's mobile device or a trustworthy user agent by a user request.

Table 2. Summary of applied keys

Key	Description	Usage
PK	The global key	An input for all operations
MK	The master key	For creation of user keys
PK_u	The public key of user u	The unique identifier of a user and the key for verification of the user's attributes, and personalized secret attribute key generation
SK_u	The secret key of user u	For decryption (to get a personalized secret attribute key)
PK_(TL,u)	The public key of attribute Trust Level generated by user u	For encryption (of personal data of user u)
SK_(TL,u,u')	The secret key of attribute Trust Level for user u' issued by u	For decryption (of personal data of user u)
PK_(TL,u)	The public key of attribute Time generated by user u	For encryption (of personal data of user u)
SK_(TL,u,u')	The secret key of attribute Time for user u' issued by u	For decryption (of personal data of user u)

- **InitiateUser(PK, MK, u):** The InitiateUser algorithm takes as input the public key PK, the master key MK, and a user identifier u (generally the unique user identity). It outputs a public user key PK_u, which will be used to issue secret attribute keys for u, and a secret user key SK_u, used for the decryption of ciphertexts. This process is also securely conducted at the user's mobile device or a trustworthy user agent by a user request.

- **CreateTrustLevelPK(PK, TL, SK_u):** The CreateTrustLevelPK algorithm is executed by the user u device whenever the user would like to control the access of its data based on trust assessment. The algorithm checks the TL related policies. If this is the case, the algorithm outputs a public attribute key for the TL of user u, denoted PK_(TL,u), otherwise NULL.

- **IssueTrustLevelSK(PK, TL, SK_u, u', PK_u'):** The IssuelTrustLevelSK algorithm is executed by the user u device by checking the eligibility of u'. The algorithm checks whether the user u' with public key PK_u' is eligible of the attri-

bute TL (i.e., the trust level of u' is equal or above an indicated level). If this is the case, IssueTrustLevelSK outputs a secret attribute key SK_(TL,u,u') for user u'. Otherwise, the algorithm outputs NULL. This process is executed by the user u based on the request from u'.

- **CreateTimePK(PK, T, SK_u):** The CreateTimePK algorithm is optionally executed by the user u device when the user would like to control the access of its data based on time. The algorithm checks the Time related policies. If this is the case, the algorithm outputs a public attribute key for the Time of user u, denoted PK_(T,u), otherwise NULL.

- **IssueTimeSK(PK, T, SK_u, u', PK_u'):** The IssueTimeSK algorithm is optionally executed by the user u device by checking the eligibility of u' with regard to time. The algorithm checks whether the user u' with public key PK_u' is eligible of the attribute T (i.e., the data can be accessed in an indicated time period by u'). If this is the case, IssueTimeSK outputs a secret attribute key SK_(T,u,u') for user u'. Otherwise, the algorithm outputs NULL. This process is executed by the user u based on the request from u'.

- **Encrypt(PK, M, A, PK_(TL,u), PK_(T,u)):** The Encrypt algorithm takes as input the public key PK, personal data M, an access policy A and the public keys PK_(TL,u), PK_(T,u) corresponding to the trust level, time occurring in the policy A. The algorithm encrypts M with the policy A and outputs the ciphertext CT. This process is conducted at a user device to protect its personal data. The encrypted data are uploaded to a data center for storage. Note that either PK_(TL,u), or PK_(T,u) or both can appear in the Encrypt, which depends on the access control policy defined in A. Concretely, if the user would like to control data access only based on the trust level, the Encrypt algorithm is simplified as Encrypt(PK, M, A, PK_(TL,u)). If the data access is controlled by both the trust level and the time, the Encrypt algorithm is kept as its original. Notably, M can be encrypted by a randomly generated symmetric key DEK, while DEK is protected by the Encrypt algorithm.

- **Decrypt(PK, CT, A, SK_u', SK_(TL,u,u'), SK_(T,u,u')):** The Decrypt algorithm takes as input a ciphertext produced by the Encrypt algorithm, an access policy A, under which CT was encrypted, and a key ring SK_u', SK_(TL,u,u') and SK_(T,u,u') for user u'. The algorithm Decrypt decrypts the ciphertext CT and outputs the corresponding plaintext M if the attributes were sufficient to satisfy A; otherwise it outputs NULL. This process is executed when an eligible user u' would like to access the data of another user u that are saved at a data center. The user u' firstly checks the encryption policy A, then conducts decryption with the key rings issued by user u.

Note that either SK_(TL,u,u'), or SK_(T,u,u') or both can appear in the Decrypt, which depends on the access control policy defined in A. Concretely, if the user controls data access only based on the trust level, the Decrypt algorithm is simplified as Decrypt(PK, CT, A, SK_u', SK_(TL,u,u')). If the user controls data access only based on the time, the Decrypt algorithm is simplified as Decrypt(PK, CT, A, SK_u', SK_(T,u,u')). If the data access is controlled by both the trust level and the time period, the Decrypt algorithm is kept as its original. If M is encrypted by a symmetric key DEK and DEK is protected by the Encrypt algorithm, the Decrypt algorithm is applied to get the plain DEK that is further used to get M.

4.1.5. Additional Access Control by MCDC

Due to the dynamic change of trust level, the previous eligible users could become distrusted. Thus the data owner won't allow them to access its data any more although it has already issued them the secret attribute keys and the valid access period has not been expired. In this case, the data owner informs MCDC the blacklist of the users who is not eligible to access the data in the valid access period. Thus, those users whose current trust level is below a threshold (i.e., unsatisfied with the access control conditions) cannot access the data any more through the control of the semi-trusted MCDC. MCDC can also block data access after the access time period is over and remind the data owner to upload newly encrypted data. Good behavior of MCDC is motivated by business profits that can be earned from providing expected MCC services. In addition, we apply reputation generation and publish the reputation of MCDC to the public to ensure good behaviors in MCC. Meanwhile, reputation information also assists mobile user decision on service selection.

4.1.6. Reputation Generation

We ensure the MCDC to perform the above additional access control following the data owner's instruction based on a reputation system. Each MCDC's reputation is evaluated according to the user's feedback and published in order to encourage and ensure the good behaviors of MCDC. For an untrustworthy MCDC, the user can select not using its services (i.e., not saving personal data at this MCDC). Thus this MCDC will lose its business customers. There are many existing reputation mechanisms can be applied to evaluate a MCDC's reputation based on user feedback. Herein, we provide a simple example method. Suppose that user k's voting on an MCDC at time t is V(k,t), and the user's own credibility of providing feedback at time t is C(k,t), we have the reputation value R of MCDC at time t_e as:

$$R(t_e) = \frac{\theta(K)}{O} \sum_{k=1}^{K} V(k,t) * C(k,t) * e^{-\frac{|t_e - t|^2}{\tau}},$$

where $O = \sum_{m} C(k,t) * e^{-\frac{|t_e - t|^2}{\tau}}$; K is the total number of votes on MCSP; t_e is the reputation evaluation time; t is the time of vote $V(k,t)$; parameter τ is used to control time decaying since we pay more attention to the current votes in order to overcome some potential attacks, such as collaborative bad mouthing attack. Function $\theta()$ has the same meaning as in Table 1. It is applied to model the impact of the number of votes on the reputation generation. C(k,t) can be generated based on the performance of user feedback by considering all the feedbacks provided by all users.

Note that the reputation generation service could be offered by a third party, e.g., another cloud computing service, or an authorized trusted party.

4.1.7. Procedure

Figure 5 illustrates the procedure of data access control based on trust evaluated in mobile social

Figure 5. A procedure of data access control based on trust evaluated in mobile social networking

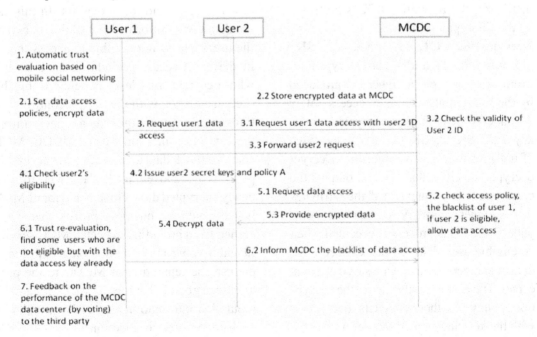

networking. We suppose that user 1 saved its sensitive personal data at an MCDC, while user 2 would like to access it with the authorization of user 1.

Step 1: User 1 conducts automatic trust evaluation based on mobile social networking activities, behaviors and experiences. This trust evaluation can be periodically executed or triggered by a social networking event.

Step 2: Based on the trust evaluation results, User 1 sets its sensitive data access policies (such as a trust level threshold and valid access time period). He further encrypts data based on the policies and stores the encrypted data at the MCDC.

Step 3: User 2 would like to access User 1's data. It requests the MCDC that checks the validity of its identifier in order to decide if forwarding its request to User 1 if it is not in the blacklist. User 2 can also request User 1 directly for data access.

Step 4: User 1 checks the eligibility of User 2 in order to generate personalized secret keys for User 2 to access the data stored at the MCDC data center. Data access controlled by multi-context based TL can be supported by the proposed scheme.

Step 5: User 2 accesses the encrypted data of User 1 with the issued secret keys. But before initiating the access, the MCDC firstly checks the access policy defined by User 1 and the blacklist of User 1 and verifies if User 2 is valid for data access. If the verification is positive, the MCDC allows the access. Then User 2 can decrypt the encrypted data.

Step 6: User 1 re-evaluates the trust based on mobile social networking. If there are the users who have been issued the secret keys are not eligible any more, User 1 will put them into its data access blacklist and inform the MCDC.

4.1.8. Further Discussion

The proposed scheme as described above has the following advantages:

- **Low Cost:** The scheme has low processing cost. This is reflected in two folds: a) low computational cost: the encryption is only conducted once using attribute-based encryption. Unlike many existing work, they apply both attribute based encryption and proxy-re-encryption (performed at MCDC or an agent) (Wang, Liu & Wu, 2010; Zhou et al., 2011). Herein, we ensure MCDC performs as the data owner expected by applying a reputation system to evaluate each MCDC's performance in order to help users select the best MCDC for personal data storage and process; b) the trust can be automatically evaluated based on mobile social networking records, thus greatly reduce the cost for collecting evidence for trust evaluation.

- **Simple Key Management:** In this scheme, revocation is handled by applying time as one attribute in the attribute-based encryption. The issued secret key is automatically expired when the time related condition is not satisfied. The valid data access time period can be flexibly defined in order to achieve as fine-grained as possible access control. Meanwhile, we make use of the blacklist issued by the data owner to conduct additional access control at MCDC even though some distrusted users still hold valid secret keys. This is achieved with the support of a reputation system. Therefore, we reduce the system complexity caused by key re-generation and management.

- **Low Transmission Load:** Transmission load can be also reduced by applying the scheme. As described already, there is no need to transmit new keys to new eligible users when some old eligible users are re-voked before data access time period is expired.

- **Security:** The security of this scheme is ensured by the attributed-based encryption theory. In addition, we apply reputation to encourage MCDC to perform as the user expects for extra data access control.

- **Privacy:** The scheme is based on such an assumption that the MCDC is semi-trusted. That is it is curious to know or could maliciously disclose user personal data, but in order to run business and earn profits, generally it performs according to the instruction of users. It provides such services as storing and maintaining user data, in order to deduce the computation and storing load of user mobile devices. The scheme supports data storage at MCDC in a secure way and enhances the user data privacy by hiding the plaintext from the MCDC. There is no way for the MCDC to know the plaintext of the user data. The valid access is only allowed to the users whom are trusted by the data owner.

- **Usability:** Since the trust evaluation is performed based on automatically collected mobile social networking data, the usability regarding trust evaluation can be greatly improved.

In summary, the proposed scheme as described above employs usable and autonomic trust evaluation and can control mobile cloud data access based on the evaluated trust level in mobile social networking, which is an efficient way to support autonomic trust management in MCC.

4.2. Control MCC Data Access Based on Reputation

4.2.1. Summary of Scheme

We propose introducing a reputation center (RC) to support data owners to control the access of

their personal data during mobile cloud service fulfillment. The RC can help the data owner to control the access to their personal data stored at MCDC when the owner has no concrete idea how to perform access control and/or when the owner is off-line. This is a very normal situation in practice.

We suppose that each data owner's data are encrypted and stored at the MCDC. When data access is needed, the data requester requests the RC to issue a reputation certificate by agreeing with RC an insurance agreement, which indicates the punishment of illegal data disclosure. For acting data access, the RC firstly checks the access policy of the data owner and evaluates the recent reputation of the data requester. If all are positive, RC informs the MCDC to re-encrypt the data (or the secret key used for encrypting the data) in order to make it only decrypted by the eligible data requester.

The punishment specified in the insurance agreement is decided based on the reputation of the requester. The reputation evaluation is based on the feedback of the requester's users, performance observation on the services provided by the requester, and performance records reported from the consumers of the services provided by the requester, as well as the certificates issued by the third authorized parties.

This proposed scheme can be applied into such a scenario that a mobile user saves its sensitive personal data (e.g., social security and health data) at a MCDC. In order to avoid its data to be disclosed by the MCDC, the user encrypts the data to limit access. It only would like to assign the entity with good reputation to access the data. Critically, it is hard for the user to see the trust and reputation of those entities that could be mobile cloud service providers (MCSP) collaborating with its private MCSP for offering a complete service, but are hidden from the user since they are not the MCSP directly handling the request of the user. Thus, it is hard for the user itself to control the data access. The RC handles trustworthy data access on behalf of the mobile user in such a situation.

4.2.2. System Structure

The scheme can be applied into such a system structure as shown in Figure 6. The mobile cloud services are offered by a number of MCSPs, such as central cloud service providers that are either private or public, cloudlet owners and pervasive cloud providers. Those MCSPs are either private for a specific user or public for all users. Each MCSP has its own data center (either huge or trivial) for data storage, a resource center that can offer various services and a management center that is responsible for service request and provision management. When the private cloud cannot satisfy a user's demand, it could collaborate with other MCSPs to provide demanded services for the user. A reputation center plays as an independent party to evaluate the reputation of each MCSP or each system entity.

4.2.3. Reputation Generation

We use $R(t_e)$ to denote the reputation of an entity at time t_e. It contains two parts: the reputation

contributed by the user feedback, denoted Rf and the reputation contributed by performance monitoring and reporting, denoted Rp. There are many existing reputation mechanisms can be applied to evaluate an entity's reputation based on user feedback. We apply Formula 2 again herein. Suppose the user k's voting on the entity at time t is V(k,t), and the user's own credibility of providing feedback at time t is C(k,t), we have the reputation value Rf of the entity contributed by the user feedback as:

$$Rf(t_e) = \frac{\theta(K)}{O} \sum_{k=1}^{K} V(k,t) * C(k,t) * e^{-\frac{|t_e-t|^2}{\tau}}, \quad (2)$$

where C(k,t) can be generated based on the performance of user feedback by considering the feedback provided by all users of the entity's service and the performance monitoring and reporting.

C(k,t) is generated at RC. If the feedback V(k,t) provided by k doesn't match the final evaluation result, that is $\delta = \frac{1}{2} - |V(k,t) - R(t)| \leq 0$,

Figure 6. One example application system structure

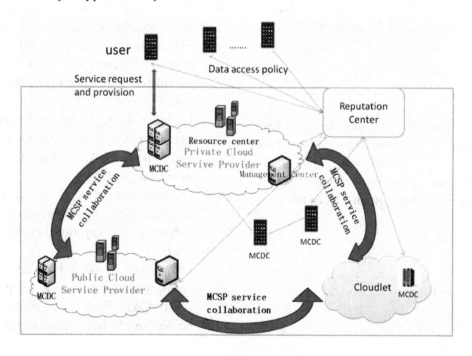

$\gamma++;$ If $V(k,t)$ matches the fact, that is $\frac{1}{2} - |V(k,t) - R(t)| > 0$, or no $V(k,t)$ is provided, γ is not changed. The C(k,t) of k at time t is:

$$C(k,t) =$$
$$\begin{cases} C(k,t) + \omega\delta & (\gamma < thr) \\ C(k,t) + \omega\delta - \mu\gamma & (\gamma \geq thr) \end{cases} = \begin{cases} 1 & (C(k,t) > 1) \\ 0 & (C(k,t) < 0) \end{cases},$$
(3)

where γ is a parameter to record the number of mismatching, μ is a parameter to control the deduction of C(k,t) caused by bad voting performance, δ is a deviation factor to indicate the deviation between a user's vote and the real reputation, and ω is a parameter to control the adjustment scale of C(k,t).

For generating the reputation based on the performance observation and performance records on the services provided by the entity, suppose the monitored performance or recorded performance is p_m, while the threshold performance is p_t, if p_m is better than p_t, the positive number of performance P is increased by 1, otherwise, the negative number of performance N is increased by 1. We have the reputation value Rp of the entity contributed by performance monitoring and recording at time t_e based on the Bayes' theorem as:

$$Rp(t_e) = \frac{P}{P + N + o}(o = 1),$$
(4)

where o is a parameter controlling the rate of loss of uncertainty for different scenarios (we often take $o = 1$).

Thus the final reputation of an entity can be aggregated by combining Rp and Rf as below:

$$R(t_e) = \frac{\theta(K_{Rp})}{\theta(K_{Rp}) + \theta(K_{Rf})} Rp(t_e) +$$
$$\frac{\theta(K_{Rf})}{\theta(K_{Rp}) + \theta(K_{Rf})} Rf(t_e),$$
(5)

where K_{Rp} is the total number of performance monitoring reports from the entity and performance records provided by the entity's users. K_{Rf} is the total number of feedback records. We use function $\theta()$ to model the influence of the number of evidence resources on the reputation generation. The weight of two different kinds of evidence sources is decided by the radio measured by $\theta()$.

4.2.5. Required Keys and System Scheme

We employ the proxy re-encryption (PRE) theory developed by Blaze, Bleumer and Strauss (1998). It allows a proxy to transform a ciphertext computed under Alice's public key into one that can be decrypted using Bob's privacy key. During ciphertext transformation, referred to as re-encryption, the proxy learns nothing about the underlying plaintext. The PRE enables us to apply RC to issue a proper key to an authorized entity.

A proxy re-encryption scheme is represented as a tuple of (possibly probabilistic) polynomial time algorithms (KG; RG; E; R; D) (Ateniese et al., 2005; Green & Ateniese, 2007):

- (KG; E; D) are the standard key generation, encryption, and decryption algorithms for an underlying public key encryption scheme. On input the security parameter 1^k, KG outputs a public and private key pair (pk_A; sk_A) for entity A. On input pk_A and data m, E outputs a ciphertext CA = E(pk_A; m). On input sk_A and ciphertext CA, D outputs the plain data m = D(sk_A; CA).
- On input (pk_A; sk_A; pk_B), the re-encryption key generation algorithm, RG, outputs a re-encryption key rk_A→B for the proxy.
- On input rk_A→B and ciphertext CA, the re-encryption function, R, outputs R(rk_A→B; CA) = E(pk_B; m) = CB which can be decrypted using private key sk_B.

The RC as well as every entity in the system each has a public and private key pair under the public key encryption scheme (KG; E; D). Let (pk_RC; sk_RC) denote the public and private key pair of the RC and (pk_u; sk_u) denote the public and private key pair of entity u. The RC works as follows for managing keys and controlling the data access. The RC, on input (pk_RC; sk_RC; pk_u) to the algorithm RG, generates the re-encryption key rk_RC→u for u if it satisfies the access policy of the data owner based on the latest reputation evaluation on u at RC and an insurance agreement agreed by both RC and u. The RC then forwards rk_RC→u and access control policies to the MCSP. A data owner p encrypts its secret key k_p using the public key of the RC to obtain E(pk_RC, k_p) and publishes it along with its data encrypted by k_p (data_p) to the MCSP. If an entity u is allowed to access the data, the MCSP computes (based on the approval of RC) R(rk_RC→u; E(pk_RC; k_p)) = E(pk_u; k_p) and gives it to the entity u. The entity u decrypts E(pk_u; k_p) using its private key sk_u to obtain k_p and then uses it to get the plain data. In this scheme, the MCSP functions as the proxy in the proxy re-encryption scheme, it indirectly distributes secret keys of data decryp-tion to other authorized entities while without learning anything about these secrets (e.g., k_p and data_p). Note that, the access polices could be defined by the data owner and sent to the MCSP to ensure them. Thus, personalized private data protection can be ensured. Algorithm 1 is applied to grant an access right to an eligible entity. Note that RC and MCSP do not collude, i.e., RC itself is not allowed by the MCSP to access the user's personal data.

The algorithm for revoking entity u from the access of data_p is below.

4.2.6. Punishment Generation

In the insurance agreement between an entity and RC, punishment pu(u, data_p) on data_p disclosure is set based on the reputation level of the entity. The higher the reputation, the lower the punishment rate is set in the agreement. With this way, the system entity is encouraged to perform well. The intrinsic reason of the RC to run its business is caused by the profit of insurance business. The RC sells insurance to cloud service users in order to compensate their lost if there is any illegal private data disclosure. Optionally, MCSP

Algorithm 1. Grant an access right to entity u - grant (u)

Policy(u) = { <u; data_p, time granted> | p ∈ P}, where P is the set of data owners whose data records are allowed to be accessed by entity u, time is the time period of allowed access or allowed times of access, for example.
1. Entity u generates (pk_u; sk_u):

(pk_u; sk_u) = KG(1^k)
Note: Step 1 is skipped if it has been executed once and the values of (pk_u, sk_u) and (pk_RC, sk_RC) remain unchanged.
4. Entity u requests transformed ciphertext of the secret key k_p of the data owner p.
5. MCSP's MCDC forwards the request to RC
6. RC checks Policy(u) and issue MCSP rk_RC->u = RG(pk_RC; sk_RC; pk_u) to transform E(pk_RC; k_p) into E(pk_u; k_p) if Policy(u) authorizes u to access p's data: R(rk_RC->u; E(pk_RC; k_p)) = E(pk_u; k_p). RC also provides Policy(u) to MCSP.
Note: rk_RC->u calculation can be skipped if it has been executed already and the value of (pk_u, sk_u) and (pk_RC, sk_RC) remain unchanged.
7. Entity u obtains k_p if passing the eligibility check of MCSP by decrypting E(pk_u; k_p) using its private key sk_u: k_p = D(sk_u; E(pk_u; k_p)), and then it can access data_p at MCSP.

Algorithm 2. Revoke one entity from accessing data_p - revoke (u, data_p)

If an entity u is not eligible to access data_p, RC informs MCSP to block its access to data_p.

pays annual fee to RC for making RC to issue it rk_RC->u for transforming E(pk_RC; k_p) into E(pk_u; k_p). This is essential for MCSP to run its cloud services. Note that the cloud service user could be another MCSP. At the initial stage of deployment, the user insurance fee charged by RC could be free in order to encourage the usage of RC to guarantee user data privacy. Introducing this insurance mechanism will encourage users to store sensitive data at MCDC.

4.2.7. Procedure

Figure 7 illustrates the procedure of data access control based on the invention. We suppose that User 1 saves its sensitive personal data at MCSP 1 data center, while User 2 (which can be another MCSP 2) would like to access it with the authorization of RC.

Step 1: User 1 encrypts data_1 with a secret key k_1 and sends the data access policy to RC. User 1 uploads the encrypted data and E(pk_RC, k_1) to MCSP 1;

Step 2: User 2 requests MCSP 1 to access data_1, and MCSP 1 forwards the request to RC;

Step 3: RC evaluates user 2's reputation and checks if it satisfies with data_1's access policy. Based on the reputation level, RC sets punishment rate pu(u2, data_1) and generates rk_RC->u2 if access is allowed;

Step 4: RC and user 2 set an insurance agreement based on pu(u2, data_1);

Step 5: RC issues rk_RC->u2 and access policy to MCSP 1 that re-encrypts the k_1 to get E(pk_u2, k_1);

Step 6: MCSP 1 sends E(pk_u2, k_1) to User 2 who decrypts it to get k_1 with its private key sk_u2 to access data_1 stored at MCSP 1;

If later on, User 2 wants to access data_1 again and/or other data in MCSP 1, but RC indicates that it doesn't satisfy with the access policy, RC will inform MCSP 1 to block User 2's access.

4.2.8. Further Discussion

The above scheme has the following advantages:

- **Low Cost:** The scheme encrypts each data once, and distributes appropriate keys to authorized entity once. The number of

Figure 7. A procedure of data access control based on reputation

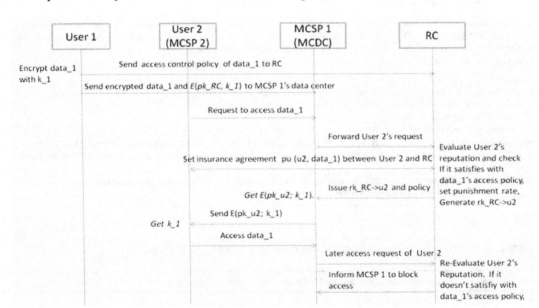

keys managed for data encryption/decryption won't change due to the change of the number of data requesters.

- **Release Computational Load of Data Owner and MCSP:** The main problem of ABE and PRE based approaches is that the data owner should be online in order to send the PRE keys to the CSP or MCSP in a timely fashion, to prevent the revoked user from accessing the data (Wang, Liu & Wu, 2010). The delay of issuing PRE keys may cause potential security risks. This scheme overcomes this problem by introducing a reputation center to delegate the data owner to handle the re-encryption. Meanwhile, due to the large scale of data management and processing limitation of some MCSPs, MCSP's computational load should not be heavy in order to improve its efficiency. This scheme also releases the re-encryption load of MCSP. There is no need for MCSP to re-encrypt the data itself on behalf of the data owner. It only re-encrypts the symmetric key used for encryption and decryption.

- **Simple Key Management:** In this scheme, revocation is handled by RC and MCSP by applying reputation evaluation at RC and policy based access control at MCSP. The system only need generate the public key pairs for each system entity. The secret key k_p used for data encryption is maintained by the data owner. The public key of RC (pk_RC) is public for each data owner. Key generation and management are simple.

- **Security:** The security of this invention is ensured by the proxy re-encryption, symmetric key encryption and public key encryption theories. In addition, we apply insurance agreement to ensure the data security after access. Additionally, digital watermarking technologies can be applied to watermark plain data before encryption

and then it is possible to track illegal usage or disclosure of data after a user gains the plain data.

- **Privacy:** The scheme is designed based on such an assumption that the MCSP is semi-trusted. That is it is curious to know or could maliciously disclose user personal data. But in order to run business and earn profits, generally it can perform well as users and RC instruct. It provides such services as storing and maintaining user data, in order to reduce the corresponding load of user device. The scheme supports data storage at MCDC in a secure manner and enhances the user data privacy by hiding the plaintext from the MCSP. There is no way for the MCSP to know the plaintext of the user data although they are stored at its data center. The valid access is only allowed to the users who are reputable based on public evidence although the data owner may not have any direct experience or interaction with them. In addition, although the data owner encrypts k_p with RC's public key and provides the encrypted key to MCSP, RC has no way to know the plain key k_p since MCSP won't share it. Even though MCSP and RC could collude, RC, as an insurance company, is responsible for guaranteeing the privacy of data if user pays for the insurance service.

- **Compatibility:** This scheme is compatible with the previous scheme. It handles the case that the data owner has no idea of the trust of a data requester, thus has no way to authorize an access right. When the data owner can decide the data access and would like to be involved into the access control, this scheme can cooperate with the previous scheme to conduct data access control by applying both individual trust evaluated by the data owner and the public reputation generated by a reputation center.

4.3. Heterogeneous Data Access Control in MCC

We recall the previous scenario: a mobile user's personal health data are stored at the data center of MCSP. In order to avoid his data to be disclosed by the MCSP, the user encrypts the data for limited access. He would like to assign the people he trusts with regard to his health treatment to access these data. He also would like to assign the entity (e.g., a MCSP) with good reputation in his health treatment to access the data. How to ensure secure personal data access by a trustworthy entity (e.g., a person, a service provider, or a service) is an important issue. Some people or MCSPs are user preferred and trusted based on past experiences. But in many cases, it is hard for the data owner to justify the trust and reputation of all entities involved in the fulfillment of a requested service (e.g., some of them could be MCSPs that are involved due to MCSP collaboration, but they could be hidden from the user since they are not the MCSP responding the request of the user). In this case, it is hard for the data owner to control the data access. How to ensure trustworthy data access in heterogeneous situations is a practical problem in MCC.

4.3.1. Summary of Scheme

We further propose 2-dimensional or multidimensional control on cloud data access based on individual trust evaluated by the data owner and/or public reputation evaluated by one or more reputation centers (RCs) during cloud service fulfillment. Concretely, the data owner encrypts its data with a symmetric secret key K and separates K into two parts: K1 and K2. It respectively encrypts K1 with RC's public key pk_RC and K2 with a public attribute key pk_IT with regard to individual trust attribute. It uploads the encrypted data and the above two parts of encrypted key to an MCSP. For accessing the data, a user requests MCSP. If the user is not in a blacklist, MCSP forwards its request to RC and/or the data owner. RC checks the user's reputation and generates a re-encryption key for the user to decrypt K1 if it is eligible. MCSP also forwards request of the user to the data owner based the owner's access policy. The owner issues the personalized secret key to the user to assist him to get K2 if its trust level satisfies the access condition. By achieving both K1 and K2, the user can access the encrypted data.

In case that the user is not eligible to access the data (e.g., the reputation/trust of the user is below a threshold), RC and/or the data owner will inform MCSP to put it into access blacklist of the data. In later access, MCSP will block this user's access. If the user becomes eligible to access the data, RC and/or the data owner will inform MCSP to put it into access whitelist of the data.

K1 and K2 can be flexibly set based on different application scenarios. If the data owner would like to control data access only by itself, K1 is null and K2=K. If the data owner would like to control data access only by RC, K1=K and K2 is null. If the data owner would like to control its data access by both individual trust and public reputation (i.e., by both the owner and RC), neither K1 nor K2 is null, and aggregating K1 and K2 can get K. If the data owner would like to control its data access by either the individual trust or public reputation (i.e., by either the owner or RC), K1=K2=K. If the data owner doesn't want to control its data access, K1=K2=K=null.

Notably, the data encryption key K can be divided into multiple parts in order to support various control strategies. For example, the data owner would like to control its data access based on reputation evaluation by multiple RCs in order to highly ensure data security and privacy, especially when it is off-line. In this case K can be separated into multiple parts K1, K2, ..., Kn (n>=2). The data owner encrypts different parts of K with different RC's public keys. Later on, the data access can be jointly controlled by each

RC (e.g., with regard to different reputation properties) by issuing re-encryption keys to decrypt different parts of K.

4.3.2. System Structure

The scheme can be applied into such a system structure as shown in Figure 8. The cloud services are offered by a number of MCSPs, which are either a private MCSP of a user or a public MCSP for all users. Each MCSP has its own data center for data storage, a resource center that can offer various services and a management center that is responsible for service request and provision management. When a private MCSP cannot satisfy a user's demand, it could collaborate with other public MCSPs to provide demanded services for the user. One or more RC plays as an independent party to evaluate each MCSP's (or each system entity's) reputation. The user (i.e., data owner) controls personal data access based on individual trust evaluation on different system entities. The evaluation is based on direct interaction or experiences with those entities. Publishing reputation of each MCSP by RCs encourages and ensures good behaviors of MCSP.

4.3.3. Required Keys and Scheme

Every user u maintains a public user key pk_u, which is used by a data owner to generate personalized secret attribute keys, and a secret key sk_u, which is used in the decryption operation related to pk_u. The user can be a data owner or a data requester. Each user can verify the individual trust of a system entity (e.g., a user and a MCSP). A data requester can be a MCSP or a user. Each RC maintains a public key pk_RC and a secret key sk_RC. The data owner generates a symmetric key K to protect its personal data. The symmetric key can be divided into a number of parts K1, K2, ..., Kn depending on the data owner's data access control policy. Normally, K is separated into two parts: K1 and K2. In what follows, we illustrate how the data access is controlled by the data owner and/or one RC based on individual trust and/or public reputation.

We apply attribute-based encryption to realize data access control based on data owner evaluated individual trust level. The advance is the data owner can issue K2 to a number of eligible users at the same time with one encryption computation, and different users cannot collude with each other.

Figure 8. An example system structure

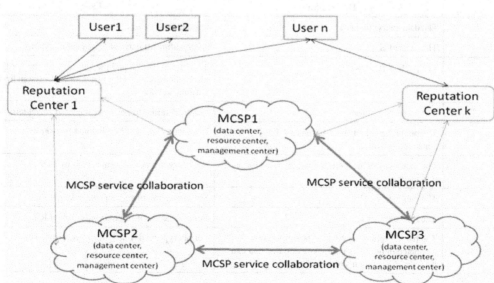

Each user maintains a secret key sk_u that is used to issue secret attribute keys to eligible users based on individual trust (IT). It is also used to generate the public key of attributes IT and other attributes (e.g., 'time') for protecting the data of user u. We denote the public representation of individual trust attribute as IT. For the attribute IT, there is a public key, respectively denoted pk_IT, which is generated by the user u and is used to encrypt K2 in order to control data access based on the individual trust level. The corresponding secret attribute keys of pk_IT, personalized for eligible users, are issued by the user u. To prevent collusion, each user gets a different secret attribute key only used by himself. A secret attribute key of an attribute IT, issued for an eligible user u' by user u is denoted SK_(IT,u,u'). We call the set of secret keys that a user u' has (i.e., SK_u' and SK_(IT,u,u')) as its key ring.

In addition, we employ proxy re-encryption theory that enables to apply RC to issue K1 to an authorized entity. Proxy re-encryption allows a proxy (e.g., MCSP) to transform a ciphertext computed under RC's public key into the one that can be decrypted using a user's privacy key.

During ciphertext transformation, referred to as re-encryption, the proxy learns nothing about the underlying plaintext. Table 3 summaries the keys used in this scheme.

The scheme consists of a number of fundamental algorithms: CreateEncryptionKey, DivideKey, CombineKey, CreateIndividualTrustPK, IssueIndividualTrustSK, Encrypt2, Decrypt2, ReencryptionKeyGeneration, Encrypt1, ReEncryption, Decrypt1, Encrypt, and Decrypt. The description of the algorithms is as follows:

- **CreateEncryptionKey():** The CreateEncryptionKey algorithm generates a symmetric key K to encrypt data.
- **DivideKey(K, n):** The DivideKey algorithm divides input K into n parts.
- **CombineKey(K1, K2, ..., Kn, n):** The CombineKey algorithm aggregates partial keys (K1, K2, ..., Kn) together to get a complete key K.
- **CreateIndividualTrustPK(IT, sk_u):** The CreateIndividualTrustPK algorithm is executed by the user device whenever the user would like to control the access of its

Table 3. Summary of applied keys

Key	Description	Usage
K	The data encryption key	For data encryption
K1, K2, ...	The parts of K	Aggregating all parts of K can get a complete K
pk_u	The public key of user u	The unique ID of u and the key used for the verification of u's attributes, and the generation of personalized secret attribute key for u
sk_u	The secret key of user u	For decryption (to get a personalized secret attribute key)
pk_(IT,u)	The public key of attribute Individual Trust generated by user u	For encryption of K2 (generated by user u)
sk_(IT,u,u')	The secret key of attribute Individual Trust for user u' issued by u	For decryption of K2 (encrypted by user u)
pk_RC	The public key of RC	For generation of re-encryption key at RC
sk_RC	The secret key of RC	For generation of re-encryption key at RC
rk_RC→u	The re-encryption key to decrypt a ciphertext computed under RC's public key into one that can be decrypted using u's privacy key.	For decryption of one part of symmetric key K: K1

data based on the individual trust evaluation. The algorithm checks the IT related policies. If this is the case, the algorithm outputs a public attribute key for the IT of user u, denoted pk_(IT, u), otherwise outputs NULL.

- **IssueIndividualTrustSK(IT, sk_u, u', pk_u'):** The IssueIndividualTrustSK algorithm is executed by the user device by checking the eligibility of u'. The algorithm checks whether the user u' with public key pk_u' is eligible of the attribute IT (i.e., the trust level of u' is equal or above an indicated threshold level). If this is the case, IssueIndividualTrustSK outputs a secret attribute key sk_(IT, u, u') for user u'. Otherwise, the algorithm outputs NULL.

- **Encrypt2(K2, pk_(IT, u)):** The Encrypt2 algorithm takes as input the partial key: K2 and the public keys pk_(IT, u), corresponding to the individual trust occurring in the data access policy A of user u. The algorithm encrypts K2 with the policy A and outputs the cipher-key CK2. This process is conducted at a data owner device to protect its personal data. The owner publishes it along with its data to the MCSP.

- **Decrypt2(CK2, sk_u', sk_(IT, u, u')):** The Decrypt2 algorithm takes as input a cipher-key produced by the Encrypt2 algorithm and a key ring sk_u', sk_(IT, u, u') for user u'. The algorithm Decrypt2 decrypts the cipher-key CK2 and outputs the corresponding plain key K2 if the attribute is sufficient to satisfy the policy A used for encryption; otherwise it outputs NULL.

- **ReencryptionKeyGeneration(pk_RC, sk_RC, pk_u):** The ReencryptionKeyGeneration algorithm, on input (pk_RC; sk_RC; pk_u) to the algorithm, generates the re-encryption key rk_RC→u for entity u if it satisfies the access

policy of the data owner based on the latest reputation evaluation on entity u at RC. The RC then forwards rk_RC→u to the MCSP.

- **Encrypt1(pk_RC, K1):** A data owner encrypts its partial secret key K1 using the public key of the RC to obtain E(pk_RC, K1) and publishes it along with its data to the MCSP.

- **ReEncryption(rk_RC→u; E(pk_RC; K1)):** If an entity u is allowed to access the data, the MCSP computes ReEncryption(rk_RC→u; E(pk_RC; K1)) = E(pk_u; K1) = CK1 and gives it to the entity u. The entity u decrypts E(pk_u; K1) using its private key sk_u to obtain K1 and uses it to gain a complete key. In this scheme, the MCSP functions as the proxy in the proxy re-encryption scheme, it indirectly distributes partial secret key of data decryption to authorized entities while without learning anything about these secrets (i.e., K1 and data). Note that RC and MCSP don't collude with each other. RC itself is not allowed by the MCSP to access the user's personal data.

- **Decrypt1(sk_u, E(pk_u; K1)):** The Decrypt1 algorithm takes as input a cipher-key produced by the ReEncryption algorithm and sk_u. The algorithm Decrypt1 decrypts the cipher-key E(pk_u; K1) = CK1 and outputs the corresponding plain key K1.

- **Encrypt(K(K1, K2), M):** The Encrypt algorithm takes as input K and data M to get encrypted data CT. The data owner publishes CT to the MCSP.

- **Decrypt(CT, CombineKey(K1, K2, 2)):** The Decrypt algorithm takes as input a cipher-text CT produced by the Encrypt algorithm and all parts of K to output the plaintext M.

Concretely, the data owner u1 encrypts its data with a symmetric secret key K. It separates K into two parts: K1 and K2. It respectively encrypts K1 with RC's public key pk_RC and K2 with a public attribute key pk_IT with regard to the individual trust attribute. It uploads the encrypted data, data access policy and the above encrypted partial keys to MCSP. For accessing the data, a user u2 requests MCSP. If the user is not in a blacklist, MCSP forwards its request to RC and the data owner. RC checks the user's reputation and generates a re-encryption key ReEncryption(rk_RC→u2; E(pk_RC; K1)) = E(pk_u2; K1) = CK1 for the user to decrypt K1 if it is eligible. MCSP also forwards the request to the data owner based the owner's access policy, who issues the personalized secret key sk_(IT, u1, u2) to u2 to get K2 if u2's trust level satisfies the access condition. By achieving both K1 and K2, u2 can access the encrypted data.

In case that the user is not eligible to access data (e.g., the reputation/trust of the user is below a threshold), RC and/or the data owner will inform MCSP to put it into the blacklist of the data. In later access, MCSP will block this user's access.

If the user becomes eligible to access the data, RC and/or the data owner will inform the MCSP to put it into the whitelist of the data.

4.3.4. Procedure

Figure 9 illustrates the procedure of data access control based on the above scheme. We suppose that User 1 (u1) saved its sensitive personal data at a MCSP's data center, while User 2 (u2) would like to access it with the authorization of u1 and an RC.

Step 1: User 1 generates an encryption key K and separates it into two parts K1 and K2. It encrypts data M with the secret key K to get CT. It generates the data access policy A with regard to individual trust level threshold and public reputation threshold for M. User 1 uploads the encrypted data CT, policy A and encrypted K1=E(pk_RC, K1) and encrypted K2=E(pk_IT, K2) to MCSP; User 1 sends A to RC.

Step 2: User 2 would like to access User 1's data. It requests MCSP that checks the validity

Figure 9. Procedure of heterogeneous data access control

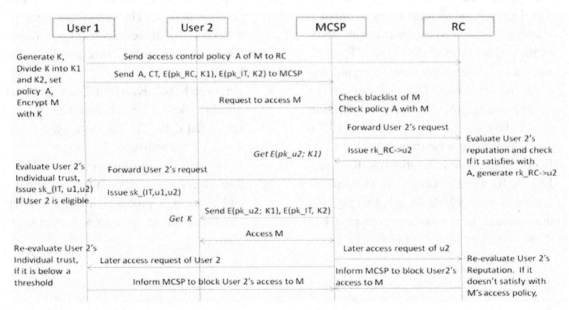

86

of its ID in order to decide if forwarding its request to User 1 and RC if it is not in the blacklist.

Step 3: RC evaluates User 2's reputation and checks if it satisfies with M's access policy A. Based on the reputation level, RC generates rk_RC->u2 if access is allowed; meanwhile, User 1 checks the eligibility of User 2 in order to generate personalized secret keys sk_(IT,u1,u2) for User 2 to decrypt K2 in order to access the data stored at the MCSP's data center.

Step 4: RC issues rk_RC->u2 to MCSP that re-encrypts the K1 to get E(pk_u2, K1) if the re-encryption was never conducted; User 1 issues sk_(IT,u1,u2) to User 2.

Step 5: MCSP allows the access by providing the encrypted data CT and encrypted keys E(pk_u2; K1), E(pk_IT, K2) to User 2.

Step 6: User 2 decrypts the encrypted K1 and K2 with the issued secret keys from User 1 and its private key sk_u2. By combining K1 and K2, User 2 can get a complete K to decrypt CT and get M;

Step 7: User 1 re-evaluates the trust of other users based on past and newly accumulated experiences. If there are the users who have been issued the secret keys are not eligible any more, User 1 will put them into its data access blacklist and inform MCSP. RC can also re-generate reputation of users. If RC indicates that User 2 doesn't satisfy with access policy A, RC will inform MCSP to block User 2's access.

4.3.5. Heterogeneous Access Control Support

K1 and K2 can be flexibly set based on different application scenarios. If the data owner would like to control data access only by itself, K1 is null and K2=K. If the data owner would like to control data access only by RC, K1=K and K2=null. If the data owner would like to control

its data access by both individual trust and public reputation (i.e., by both the owner and RC), neither K1 nor K2 is null, and aggregating K1 and K2 can get K. If the data owner would like to control its data access by either individual trust or public reputation evaluation (i.e., by either the owner or RC), K1=K2=K. If the data owner doesn't want to control its data access, K1=K2=K=null. Thus, this scheme is an integration of the two schemes described in Section 4.1 and 4.2.

Notably, the data encryption key K can be divided into multiple parts in order to support various control strategies. For example, the data owner would like to control its data access based on reputation evaluation by multiple RCs in order to highly ensure data security and privacy, especially when it is off-line. In this case K can be separated into multiple parts K1, K2, ..., Kn (n>=2). The data owner encrypts different parts of K with different RC's public keys. Later on, the data access should be controlled by each RC according to local reputation evaluation (e.g., with regard to different reputation properties or dimensions) by issuing re-encryption keys to decrypt different parts of K. The procedure to control data access by multiple RCs and/or the data owner is similar to Figure 9. The main approach is we apply the proxy re-encryption at RC_i to generate rk_RC_i->u2 if the reputation evaluated by RC_i satisfies A. The scheme makes MCSP re-encrypt Ki to get E(pk_u2, Ki), which can be further decrypted by User 2.

4.3.6. Further Discussion

The advantages of this scheme are discussed as below.

Personalization. The access polices can be flexibly defined by the data owner regarding who and how to securely control data access. For who, the data owner can indicate which authorized party can control its data access except for itself. For how, multi-dimensional trust/reputation levels are applied for access control. The trust/reputation can be evaluated based on many factors and evidence, analyzed and processed by the data owner and/or different reputation centers authorized by the data owner. Thus, personalized private data protection can be supported by this scheme.

Low cost. The scheme encrypts each data once, and distributes appropriate keys to authorized entity once. The number of keys managed for data encryption/decryption won't change due to the change of the number of data requesters.

Flexibility. The scheme supports various control strategies, which are handled by the data owner and/or RC. Free control of data access can also be supported without changing the system design. It won't request the data owner to be always online. In this case, one or multiple reputation centers can delegate the data owner to control data access. Meanwhile, due to large scale data management and the limitation of some MCSPs, MCSP's computational load should not be heavy in order to achieve sound efficiency. This scheme can also release the re-encryption load of MCSP. If the re-encryption is conducted, no need for MCSP to do it again. We apply blacklist and whitelist to control data access at MCSP when a user is revoked or re-authorized.

Multi-dimensional access control. In this scheme, data access is control by trust individually evaluated by the data owner, and/or public reputation evaluated by one or more reputation centers. Thus, the access control is more trustworthy than other existing solutions. Note that other control attributes or reputation properties can be applied by this scheme. Possible implementation approaches are: a) we apply attribute-based encryption by adding new control attributes at the data owner; b) we apply multiple RCs to control different attributes or reputation properties at RC.

Security. The security of this scheme is ensured by the proxy re-encryption, and attribute-based encryption theory, as well as symmetric and public-key encryption theories.

Comprehensive. This scheme is a complement of previous two schemes. It handles heterogeneous cases of cloud data access. This comprehensive solution supports various cloud data access policies that are applied in different application scenarios.

5. UNSOLVED RESEARCH PROBLEMS AND CHALLENGES

Based on the review of current literature, we can see that there are a number of unsolved issues towards trustworthy mobile cloud computing. Existing research and industrial products provide some valuable solutions to achieve connection and communication security, secure data access control and privacy assurance, mainly for cloud computing, but not targeting MCC. Due to the distinct characteristics of MCC, additional research problems should be solved and many challenges need to be overcome. Herein, we list some important issues.

First, usability is an important issue in MCC due to the use of mobile devices to access cloud services. MCC client solution should concern usage experience during mobile cloud service consumption. This issue hasn't been deeply studied in the past.

Second, it lacks a comprehensive solution to ensure data security and privacy in all MCC scenarios. So far, there is no serious study on how to ensure data security and privacy if the data need to be transferred among the central cloud, cloudlets and pervasive clouds. It is a challenge to ensure data security and privacy if it needs to be moved among multiple different types of distrusted or semi-trusted parties during the fulfillment of a service.

Third, deep investigation hasn't yet been done for the purpose of providing MCC client intelligence. MCC aims to fully use all kinds of computing resources in order to achieve the best quality of services. But this requires more on a mobile device to be capable of detecting its environment and adapt cloud computing decision accordingly. How to integrate MCC with other technologies, such as internet of things, could be an interesting research topic.

Fourth, trustworthy and usable identity management in a heterogeneous mobile cloud computing environment is still an open issue although a few solutions have been proposed. Techniques for managing authentication and authorization are critical to the mobile cloud computing. Cloud-based services and rapidly expanding mobile platforms will depend on identity management to provide a seamless user experience. Although a number of standards have been advanced, an Internet scale identity solution with widely accepted usability remains elusive (Lynch, 2011). Identity management should be usable and easily accepted by mobile device users. More efforts should be made in this area.

Fifth, capability management of MCC has not been paid much attention to in current literature and industry. How to adaptively manage computing loads in MCC according to the changes of a heterogeneous mobile computing environment is a challenge.

Finally, a trustworthy billing solution for MCC services hasn't been seriously studied and developed. In MCC, a service could be offered by a central cloud, cloudlets and pervasive clouds in parallel. How to pay for the CSPs, cloudlet owners and pervasive cloud providers in a secure manner is a problem worth our efforts to investigate. This is also a practical issue demanded to be solved for MCC deployment.

6. CONCLUSION

Mobile cloud computing extends the vision of cloud computing to provide mobile users a wide range of computing resources delivered as a service over mobile networks, mainly based on wireless communication technologies and mobile Internet. In this chapter, we introduced the basic of cloud computing and its characteristics. We reviewed the current advance of building trust of cloud computing in the aspects of data access control, identity management, privacy enhancement and trust establishment. Furthermore, we explore the concept and distinct characteristics of mobile cloud computing by introducing three typical MCC scenarios and MCC architecture. Literature review showed that few studies have been conducted to provide a comprehensive trust management in MCC, thus we proposed a number of requirements for establishing trust in MCC. In addition, we proposed three schemes in order to realize autonomic data access control based on trust/reputation in MCC in a comprehensive and flexible manner. These schemes support autonomic and usable trust management in mobile cloud computing. However, trust management research in MCC is still in its infancy. There are quite many unsolved issues and challenges that request our further efforts towards trustworthy mobile cloud computing that can be easily accepted by mobile users.

REFERENCES

Almutairi, A., Sarfraz, M., Basalamah, S., Aref, W., & Ghafoor, A. (2012). A distributed access control architecture for cloud computing. *IEEE Software*, 29(2), 36–44. doi:10.1109/MS.2011.153.

Amazon Web Services (AWS). (n.d.). Retrieved from http://aws.amazon.com

Angin, P., et al. (2010). An entity-centric approach for privacy and identity management in cloud computing. In *Proceedings of 29th IEEE Symposium on Reliable Distributed Systems*, (pp. 177-183). IEEE.

Armbrust, M., et al. (2009). *Above the clouds: A Berkeley view of cloud computing* (Tech. Rep. USB-EECS-2009-28). Berkeley, CA: University of California.

Ateniese, G., Fu, K., Green, M., & Hohenberger, S. (2005). Improved proxy re-encryption schemes with applications to secure distributed storage. In *Proceedings of the 12th Annual Network and Distributed System Security Symposium*, (pp. 29–43). IEEE.

Berger, S. et al. (2009). Security for the cloud infrastructure: Trusted virtual data center implementation. *IBM Journal of Research and Development*, *53*(4), 560–571. doi:10.1147/JRD.2009.5429060.

Bethencourt, J., Sahai, A., & Waters, B. (2007). Ciphertext-policy attribute based encryption. In *Proceedings of the 2007 IEEE Symposium on Security and Privacy*, (pp. 321–334). IEEE.

Bhatti, R., Bertino, E., & Ghafoor, A. (2006). X-federate: A policy engineering framework for federated access management. *IEEE Transactions on Software Engineering*, *32*(5), 330–346. doi:10.1109/TSE.2006.49.

Blaze, M., Bleumer, G., & Strauss, M. (1998). Divertible protocols and atomic proxy cryptography. In *Proceedings of International Conference on the Theory and Application of Cryptographic Techniques* (EUROCRYPT), (pp. 127–144). EUROCRYPT.

Boneh, D., Crescenzo, G. D., Ostrovsky, R., & Persiano, G. (2004). Public key encryption with keyword search. In *Proceedings of Int'l Conf. Advances in Cryptology* (EUROCRYPT '04). EUROCRYPT.

Calero, J. M. A., Edwards, N., Kirschnick, J., Wilcock, L., & Wray, M. (2010). Toward a multi-tenancy authorization system for cloud services. *IEEE Security and Privacy*, *8*(6), 48–55. doi:10.1109/MSP.2010.194.

Cao, N., Wang, C., Ren, K., & Lou, W. (2012). Privacy-preserving multi-keyword ranked search over encrypted cloud data. [IEEE.]. *Proceedings of INFOCOM*, *2011*, 829–837.

Chang, Y. C., & Mitzenmacher, M. (2005). Privacy preserving keyword searches on remote encrypted data. In *Proceedings of Int'l Conf. Applied Cryptography and Network Security (ACNS '05)*, (pp. 442-455). ACNS.

Curtmola, R., Garay, J. A., Kamara, S., & Ostrovsky, R. (2006). Searchable symmetric encryption: Improved definitions and efficient constructions. In *Proceedings of ACM Conf. Computer and Comm. Security* (CCS'06), (pp. 79-88). ACM.

Firdhous, M., Ghazali, O., & Hassan, S. (2011). Trust management in cloud computing: A critical review. *International Journal on Advances in ICT for Emerging Regions*, *4*(2), 24–36.

Goh, E., Shacham, H., Modadugu, N., & Boneh, D. (2003). Sirius: Securing remote untrusted storage. In *Proceedings of Network and Distributed Systems Security Symposium* (NDSS), (pp. 131–145). NDSS.

Goh, E. J. (2003). *Secure indexes*. Retrieved from http://eprint.iacr.org/

Google. (n.d.). *Computer engine*. Retrieved from https://cloud.google.com/products/compute-engine

Google Apps. (n.d.b). *Engine*. Retrieved from http://code.google.com/appengine/

Google Apps. (n.d.a). Retrieved from http://www.google.com/enterprise/apps/business/

Goyal, V., Pandey, O., Sahai, A., & Waters, B. (2006). Attribute-based encryption for fine-grained access control of encrypted data. In *Proceedings of the 13th ACM Conference on Computer and Communications Security*, (pp. 89–98). ACM.

Green, M., & Ateniese, G. (2007). Identity-based proxy re-encryption. In *Proceedings of the International Conference on Applied Cryptography and Network Security* (ACNS), (pp. 288–306). ACNS.

Huang, D., Zhang, X., Kang, M., & Luo, J. (2010). MobiCloud: Building secure cloud framework for mobile computing and communication. In *Proceedings of the Fifth IEEE International Symposium on Service Oriented System Engineering* (SOSE), (pp. 27-34). IEEE.

Huang, D., Zhou, Z., Xu, L., Xing, T., & Zhong, Y. (2011). Secure data processing framework for mobile cloud computing. In *Proceedings of 2011 IEEE Conference on Computer Communications Workshops* (INFOCOM WKSHPS), (pp. 614–618). IEEE.

Hwang, K., & Li, D. (2010). Trusted cloud computing with secure resources and data coloring. *IEEE Internet Computing*, *14*(5), 14–22. doi:10.1109/MIC.2010.86.

Jia, W., Zhu, H., Cao, Z., Wei, L., & Lin, X. (2011). SDSM: A secure data service mechanism in mobile cloud computing. In *Proceedings of 2011 IEEE Conference on Computer Communications Workshops* (INFOCOM WKSHPS), (pp. 1060–1065). IEEE.

Kallahalla, M., Riedel, E., Swaminathan, R., Wang, Q., & Fu, K. (2003). Plutus: Scalable secure file sharing on untrusted storage. In *Proceedings of the USENIX Conference on File and Storage Technologies* (FAST), (pp. 29–42). USENIX.

Kaufman, L. M. (2009). Data security in the world of cloud computing. *IEEE Security and Privacy*, *7*(4), 61–64. doi:10.1109/MSP.2009.87.

Khan, K. M., & Malluhi, Q. (2010). Establishing trust in cloud computing. *IT Professional*, *12*(5), 20–27. doi:10.1109/MITP.2010.128.

Lynch, L. (2011). Inside the identity management game. *IEEE Internet Computing*, *15*(5), 78–82. doi:10.1109/MIC.2011.119.

Microsoft Azure. (n.d.). Retrieved from http://www.microsoft.com/azure/

Muller, S., Katzenbeisser, S., & Eckert, C. (2008). Distributed attribute-based encryption. In *Proceedings of the 11th Annual International Conference on Information Security and Cryptology*, (pp. 20–36). IEEE.

Nurmi, D., et al. (2009). The eucalyptus open-source cloud-computing system. In *Proceedings of 9th IEEE/ACM Int'l Symp. Cluster Computing and the Grid* (CCGRID 09), (pp. 124–131). IEEE/ACM.

Olden, E. (2011). Architecting a cloud-scale identity fabric. *Computer*, *44*(3), 52–59. doi:10.1109/MC.2011.60.

Pirretti, M., Traynor, P., McDaniel, P., & Waters, B. (2010). Secure attribute based systems. *Journal of Computer Security*, *18*(5), 799–837.

Sahai, A., & Waters, B. (2005). Fuzzy identity-based encryption. In *Proceedings of 24th International Conference on the Theory and Application of Cryptographic Techniques*, (pp. 457–473). IEEE.

Sanchez, R., Almenares, F., Arias, P., Diaz-Sanchez, D., & Marin, A. (2012). Enhancing privacy and dynamic federation in IdM for consumer cloud computing. *IEEE Transactions on Consumer Electronics*, *58*(1), 95–103. doi:10.1109/TCE.2012.6170060.

Satyanarayanan, M., Bahl, P., Caceres, R., & Davies, N. (2009). The case for VM-based cloudlets in mobile computing. *IEEE Pervasive Computing / IEEE Computer Society [and] IEEE Communications Society*, *8*(4), 14–23. doi:10.1109/MPRV.2009.82.

Song, D., Wagner, D., & Perrig, A. (2000). Practical techniques for searches on encrypted data. In *Proceedings of the IEEE Symp. Security and Privacy*, (pp. 44-55). IEEE.

Spring, J. (2011). Monitoring cloud computing by layer, part 1. *IEEE Security and Privacy*, 9(2), 66–68. doi:10.1109/MSP.2011.33.

Stihler, M., Santin, A. O., Marcon, A. L., & da Silva Fraga, J. (2012). Integral federated identity management for cloud computing. In *Proceedings of the 5th International Conference on New Technologies, Mobility and Security* (NTMS), (pp. 1-5). NTMS.

Sundareswaran, S., Squicciarini, A., & Lin, D. (2012). Ensuring distributed accountability for data sharing in the cloud. *IEEE Transactions on Dependable and Secure Computing*, 9(4), 556–568. doi:10.1109/TDSC.2012.26.

Tang, Y., Lee, P. P. C., Lui, J. C. S., & Perlman, R. (2012). Secure overlay cloud storage with access control and assured deletion. *IEEE Transactions on Dependable and Secure Computing*, 9(6), 903–916. doi:10.1109/TDSC.2012.49.

Wan, Z., Liu, J., & Deng, R. H. (2012). HASBE: A hierarchical attribute-based solution for flexible and scalable access control in cloud computing. *IEEE Transactions on Information Forensics and Security*, 7(2), 743–754. doi:10.1109/TIFS.2011.2172209.

Wang, C., Cao, N., Ren, K., & Lou, W. (2012). Enabling secure and efficient ranked keyword search over outsourced cloud data. *IEEE Transactions on Parallel and Distributed Systems*, 23(8), 1467–1479. doi:10.1109/TPDS.2011.282.

Wang, C., Wang, Q., Ren, K., & Lou, W. (2010). Privacy-preserving public auditing for data storage security in cloud computing. [IEEE.]. *Proceedings - IEEE INFOCOM, 2010*, 1–9. doi:10.1109/INFCOM.2010.5462173.

Wang, G., Liu, Q., & Wu, J. (2010). Hierachical attibute-based encryption for fine-grained access control in cloud storage services. In *Proceedings of the ACM Conf. Computer and Communications Security* (ACM CCS). Chicago, IL: ACM.

Windows Azure Virtual Machines. (n.d.). Retrieved from http://www.windowsazure.com/en-us/

Yu, S., Wang, C., Ren, K., & Lou, W. (2010). Achieving secure, scalable, and fine-grained data access control in cloud computing. [IEEE.]. *Proceedings - IEEE INFOCOM, 2010*, 534–542.

Zhang, P., Sun, H., & Yan, Z. (2011). Building up trusted identity management in mobile heterogeneous environment. In *Proceedings of IEEE 10th International Conference on Trust, Security and Privacy in Computing and Communications (TrustCom)*, (pp. 873-877). IEEE.

Zhou, M., Mu, Y., Susilo, W., & Yan, J. (2011). Piracy-preserved access control for cloud computing. In *Proceedings of TrustCom11* (pp. 83–90). TrustCom.

APPENDIX

Questions and Exercises

1. What is the difference between cloud computing and mobile cloud computing?
2. What are the distinct characteristics of mobile cloud computing?
3. What are the challenges of mobile cloud computing with regard to trust management?
4. Can you propose a comprehensive trust management framework for mobile cloud computing?

Chapter 5
Trust Management for Unwanted Traffic Control

ABSTRACT

The Internet has become the backbone of remote communications, networking, and computing. It offers an incentive platform for many services and applications. People's lives have been dramatically changed by the fast growth of the Internet. However, it also provides an easy channel for distributing contents that are unwanted by users. Unwanted traffic includes malware, viruses, spam, intrusions, unsolicited commercial advertisements, or unexpected contents. This chapter discusses applying trust management technology to automatically conduct unwanted traffic control in the Internet, especially the mobile Internet. The authors propose a generic unwanted traffic control solution through trust management. It can control unwanted traffic from its source to destinations in a personalized manner according to trust evaluation at a Global Trust Operator and traffic and behavior analysis at hosts. Thus, it can support unwanted traffic control in both a distributed and centralized manner and in both a defensive and offensive way. Simulation-based evaluation shows that the solution is effective with regard to accuracy and efficiency for Botnet intrusion and DDoS intrusion via reflectors. It is also robust against a number of malicious system attacks, such as hide evidence attack, bad mouthing attack, on-off attack, malicious attack of ISP, and combinations, which are playing in conjunction with various traffic intrusions. Meanwhile, the solution can provide personalized unwanted traffic control based on unwanted traffic detection behaviors. A prototype system is implemented to illustrate its applicability for SMS spam control.

1. INTRODUCTION

The Internet has become the backbone of remote communications, networking, and computing. It carries a vast range of information resources and services, such as the World Wide Web and email.

It also gives birth to a wide range of applications, e.g., Voice over Internet Protocol (VoIP), Internet Protocol Television (IPTV), Instant Messaging (IM), E-Commerce, Blogging, and social networking. Nowadays, these applications can be also widely accessed by mobile devices.

DOI: 10.4018/978-1-4666-4765-7.ch005

Copyright © 2014, IGI Global. Copying or distributing in print or electronic forms without written permission of IGI Global is prohibited.

At the same time as the Internet provides a great social value, it is bogged down by unwanted traffic, which is malicious, harmful or unexpected for its receiver. While some of the traffic is clearly malicious from the point of view of any benevolent user, some might be viewed as unwanted by one user while another is interested in it. The main tool for distributing unwanted traffic is Botnets. According to the statistics of the Organization for Economic Co-operation and Development (OECD), on average 1.5% of the Internet connected hosts were infected by bots in OECD countries [1]. In some countries the level of infection is more than 5%. Botnets are used to spread malware, send spam, attack hosts and networks, collect sensitive information from users and earn money from fraud. The builders and users of Botnets form an ecosystem of shady and criminal activities.

The fact that the Internet does its best to deliver what a sender is sending while it does not ask for the consent of a receiver, causes additional costs to its users. The receivers have to pay for the unwanted traffic in the form of wasting time, investing into and operating spam filtering, firewalls, virus scanning, malware and intrusion detection and cleaning up after infections. What is missing is a systematic way to reform the existing ecosystem of the shady and criminal activity.

However, controlling unwanted traffic is actually difficult due to many technical and social reasons. First, the subjective notion of unwanted traffic and various types of Internet traffic make it difficult to develop a generic solution. Second, any unwanted traffic control system could be the target of hackers. This fact requests that the designed system should be robust against various attacks. Third, we note that security issues are difficult for ordinary users to comprehend leading to low security awareness. This implies that it is preferred to have a usable, automatic and intelligent solution with minimum involvement of the users.

This chapter studies applying trust management technology to conduct unwanted traffic control in the Internet, especially the mobile Internet.

We propose a generic unwanted traffic control solution through trust management. It can control unwanted traffic from its source to destinations in a personalized manner according to trust evaluation. We propose to build a trust management system that includes all Internet Service Providers (ISPs), their subscribers (i.e., hosts), and a newly introduced global trust operator (GTO) to evaluate the trust of each system entity in order to decide how to control the unwanted traffic from a specific source. The trust of an entity contains two parts: the global trust that indicates the probability and nature of unwanted traffic sourced from the entity and the detection trust that specifies the detection performance of each entity. We assume that system effectiveness and feasibility follows from three characteristics: accuracy, efficiency and robustness. Accuracy means that the trust value of an entity must reflect the share of unwanted traffic that is sent by hosts subscribed or belonging to the entity. Efficiency means that malicious senders are spotted quickly. Robustness means that the system will continue performing its task accurately and efficiently under any feasible attack strategy of malicious hosts.

Concretely, we evaluate the global trust of each involved system entity in order to figure out if the traffic from it should be controlled for a receiver. The system entity can be a host, a corporate network or an ISP. The evaluation is based on both unwanted traffic detection reports sent from the hosts and traffic monitoring and checking at ISP. The system controls unwanted traffic in both a distributed and centralized manner. The host itself is capable of blocking traffic targeting on it based on local traffic and behavior analysis. We define that a counter approach to unwanted traffic is defensive if it is focused on protecting hosts and networks from the unwanted traffic through traffic and content analysis and blocking it based on local knowledge. The approach is offensive if it seeks to control unwanted traffic as well as punish malicious or indifferent behaviors and encourage good behaviors of hosts and ISPs. Therefore, the proposed system can filter unwanted traffic at each host in a defensive way and automatically control traffic from a distrusted source in an offensive manner based on GTO. Unlike previous work (Tang, Krasser, He, Yang & Alperovitch, 2008), the proposed solution reduces the overhead of ISP traffic monitoring by triggering the monitoring according to the analysis of the detection reports from hosts. In order to overcome potential attacks, we apply both global trust and detection trust to certify the reports from the hosts and ISPs, and make use of reporting correlation to provide personalized unwanted traffic control. Our design aims to provide a generic solution for various types of unwanted traffic over the Internet, which is efficient in controlling unwanted traffic based on personal preferences and robust against various system attacks.

Although a number of trust and reputation mechanisms have been proposed for controlling spam (Zheleva, Kolcz & Getoor, 2008; Zhang, Han & Liang, 2009; Liu, Aggarwal & Duan, 2009; McGibney & Botvich, 2007; Zhang, Duan, Liu & Wu, 2009; Tang, Krasser, He, Yang & Alperovitch, 2008; Janecek, Gansterer & Kumar, 2008; Zhang, Xu, Peng & Xu, 2010), spim (i.e., Instant Messaging spam) (Bi, Wu & Zhang, 2008), SPIT (Spam over Internet Telephony) (Kolan & Dantu, 2007) and web pages (Wu, Goel & Davison, 2006; Page, Brin, Motwani & Winograd, 1998; Liu, Gao, Liu, Zhang, Ma, He & Li, 2008; Gyongyi, Garcia-Molina & Pedersen, 2004), to our knowledge, such a generic and personalized solution as what we propose in this chapter is still lacking in the literature.

The rest of the chapter is organized as follows. Section 2 gives a brief overview of literature background. Section 3 introduces the structure of the proposed trust management system followed by a procedure to control unwanted traffic. The algorithms used in the system are described in Section 4. We further evaluate the effectiveness of the designed algorithms through simulations and analysis in Section 5. Thereafter, we discuss the practical significance and additional issues of the proposed solution in Section 6. Finally, conclusions and future work are presented in the last section.

2. LITERATURE BACKGROUND

2.1. Unwanted Traffic Detection Technology

An effective and intelligent mechanism is still expected to control unwanted traffic although a number of anti-spam techniques and applications have been proposed in the literature. Examples of existing solutions are whitelists/blacklists, header/content checks and rule-based filtering (e.g., SpamAssassin (Schwartz, 2004)), Bayesian analysis (e.g., SpamBayes (Meyer & Whateley, 2004), sender authentication (e.g., Sender Policy Framework (Wong & Schlitt, 2006), Yahoo DomainKeys (Allman, Callas, Delany, Libbey, Fenton & Thomas, 2007), etc.), challenge/response (e.g., TMDA), Blackhole listing (e.g., SORBS, Kelkea MAPS), and distributed checksums (e.g., DCC, Vipuls Razor) (Haskins & Nielsen, 2004). A problem of whitelists and blacklists is that they leave a sizable set of senders in the middle of the spectrum that are not classified. This is because there was not enough credible information or feedback to make a binary decision about these senders. We further argue that spam filters, intrusion detection systems, and firewalls are defensive tools, i.e., they concentrate on defending against malware and intrusion attacks. They are good at collecting the evidence of suspect behaviors. An offensive tool would set the goal of winning the war against the shady and criminal ecosystem by making that ecosystem or at least as many of its businesses as possible unprofitable. Firewalls may reside in routers, separate boxes and on hosts. A network based firewall for battery powered mobile devices can be efficient while on the device a firewall is not practical: attacks or unwanted traffic could deplete the battery. Thus, a network based offensive solution is preferred for the mobile Internet.

On the other hand, a personalized solution for unwanted traffic control is needed in practice. Obviously, whether the traffic is treated as unwanted is often a subjective opinion. Some traffic treated unwanted by a host could be expected by others. A network based solution, controlled by a policy dynamically tailored for different hosts, looks like an attractive option. The reports of various detection tools installed at a host can play as valuable inputs to the personalized control of unwanted traffic. The solution proposed in this chapter partially depends on the evidence collected from each system entity involved in the global Internet system. The evidence can be contributed by various existing tools and extracted from the behaviors or activities of users.

2.2. Unwanted Traffic Control Through Trust Management

Trust management can be applied to control unwanted traffic. Trust management is concerned with: collecting the information required to make a trust relationship decision; evaluating the criteria related to the trust relationship as well as monitoring and re-evaluating existing trust relationships; and automating the process (Grandison & Sloman, 2000). An extension of this definition is, however, needed to automatically ensure a dynamically changed trust relationship towards autonomic trust management (Yan & Prehofer, 2011). In the case of unwanted traffic control, autonomic trust management aims to control or filter traffic automatically based on the trust relationship between the traffic source and its destination.

A number of solutions were proposed to control unwanted traffic via trust and reputation mechanisms. Most existing unwanted traffic control systems based on trust and reputation mechanisms target on email spam.

A distributed architecture and protocol for establishing and maintaining trust between mail servers was proposed by McGibney and Botvich (2007). The architecture is a closed loop control system that can be used to adaptively improve spam filtering by automatically using trust information to tune the threshold of such filters. The design differs from our work in three folds: 1) a distributed trust management framework could cause extra traffic and processing loads with regard to trust information request and propagation. Our system adopts a global trust operator to manage trust in order to reduce such a cost; 2) trust information is used to tune filter threshold, while we directly use the global trust to indicate if a traffic from a source should be controlled; 3) we apply the detection trust to tailor the considerations of evidence collected from different entities for global trust evaluation in order to overcome a number of potential attacks (Sun, Han & Liu, 2008).

Some existing spam control solutions cannot provide personalized traffic control and overcome malicious attacks on the proposed system. For example, a layered trust management framework was proposed in order to help email receivers eliminate their unwitting trust and provide them with accountability support (Liu, Aggarwal & Duan, 2009). This framework deters misuses and addresses wrongdoings. It applies an evolved trust management scheme to incorporate full accountability into the Internet email system. This scheme explicitly establishes, uses, and updates the trust relationships between email receivers and senders. By improving the accountability in email and solving its misuse problem, it improves the security of email systems. IPGroupRep clusters the senders into different groups based on their IP addresses and computes the reputation value of each group according to the feedback of email receivers on the messages sent from the group (Zhang, Duan, Liu & Wu, 2009). The reputation value can be used to indicate whether an incoming message is spam or not. However, the above solutions cannot provide personalized control and overcome such attacks as wrong/malicious feedbacks. They cannot provide counter measures in both a defensive and offensive way.

Other spam control solutions adopt different system structure or mechanisms from the proposed solution, although some features are similar to ours. MailTrust filters out dishonest feedbacks to obtain an accurate trust value of each mail server (Zhang, Xu, Peng & Xu, 2010). The credibility-based reputation generation is similar to the detection trust in the proposed solution. But MailTrust is a distributed reputation system, while ours is based on GTO, but also supports distributed intrusion defense. The behavior of email senders was analyzed in order to figure out spammers by Tang, Krasser, He, Yang and Alperovitch (2008). This method is a predictive approach based on static statistical analysis, which cannot be applied into an unwanted traffic control system at runtime, like ours. It is not efficient to control fast spreading Botnets. A multi-level reputation-based greylisting solution was proposed to improve the efficiency of traditional greylisting anti-spam methods by significantly reducing the transfer delay of messages caused by the additional greylisting level (Janecek, Gansterer & Kumar, 2008). Comparing to the above work, the trust evaluation in the proposed solution is not only based on the detection reports of each host, the traffic and behavior analysis at hosts, but also the monitored behavior of unwanted traffic source at ISP. Particularly, the control can be personalized according to the correlation of past detection reporting behaviors.

A reporter-based reputation system for spam filtering was proposed to filter spam (Zheleva, Kolcz & Getoor, 2008). It is a reactive spam-filtering system, based on reporter reputation to complement existing spam-filtering techniques. This work aims to reduce the response time of spam reaction—that is, recognizing a spam campaign at an earlier stage, thus reducing the costs that users and systems incur. In this system, the reports of reliable users are assigned a higher validity than those of other users. Therefore, a crucial element in the spam-filtering algorithm of the system is how to identify these trustworthy users. Ideally, a few reliable reports would be enough to flag a campaign as spam. However, such a criterion is vulnerable to malicious users who could gain trust only to abuse it later. In order to solve the above problem, this system applies a reputation maintenance mechanism and an assessment of its vulnerability to attacks by creating a simple model of the behavior of malicious users and generating a synthetic dataset to match the model. The system was extensively analyzed and evaluated using complaints received from a large population of real users and by simulating the proposed reputation system for spam filtering over a period of time. The evaluation dataset includes spam reports collected over several months from the users of a large email service provider. The evaluation results showed that it can effectively reduce campaign detection time and increases spam coverage of the existing spam filter. Particularly, this system includes a trust-maintenance component, in which users gain and lose reputation, depending on their spam-reporting patterns (accurate or inaccurate), which is similar to the detection trust in the proposed solution. The filtering component uses the reports of highly reputable reporters for spam removal, while in the proposed solution the traffic control is fine-grained and based on all collected reports with the detection trust as discount. The control is also personalized based on the correlation of reporting behaviors. This work focused on large quantities of highly similar spam (i.e., a campaign) that are sent within a relatively short period of time. It didn't evaluate the system performance under various system attacks, such as bad mouthing attack. The authors did not discuss its applicability on other types of unwanted traffic. Further study and analysis is needed to make a generic solution that is applicable for controlling various types of unwanted traffic over the Internet.

A number of algorithms attempted to overcome web page spam in a specific way. PageRank is an example (Page, Brin, Motwani & Winograd, 1998). Most link-based anti-spamming algorithms are based on observed features, in which spam pages are different from reputable ones (Zhang, Han & Liang, 2009). Some anti-spamming algorithms utilize the implicit or explicit feedback of users to assist the page ranking, such as BrowseRank (Liu, Gao, Liu, Zhang, Ma, He & Li, 2008). It is very helpful and precise to use user information to predict page reputation although browsing data is usually confidential, private and hard to obtain. However, the above solutions haven't considered potential attacks or threats on the proposed system. TrustRank and its variations firstly select a certain number of seeds for the manual evaluation of experts, and then propagate trust or distrust through links from the seed sets (Wu, Goel & Davison, 2006; Gyongyi, Garcia-Molina & Pedersen, 2004). These kinds of algorithms are simple and efficient, but their efficiency is greatly influenced by the quality and size of the seed set (Zhang, Han & Liang, 2009). Obviously, this mechanism for web page spam is not suitable for the control of other unwanted traffic. In the working scenario of our research, we consider various unwanted traffic types sourced from some host in the Internet. The unwanted traffic can be any type of contents (e.g., web page links, emails, etc.), which is unexpected by the receivers.

The solutions for Voice spamming, SPIT were generally specific, thus hard to be widely applied for controlling other types of unwanted traffic. Unlike spam in e-mail systems, VoIP spam calls have to be identified in real time, thus, many of the techniques devised for e-mail spam detection are not practical for SPIT. To overcome this challenge by blocking a spam call before telephone rings, Kolan and Dantu (2007) proposed a multi-stage, adaptive spam filter based on presence (location,

mood and time), trust, and reputation to detect spam in voice calls. They applied a closed-loop feedback control between different stages to decide whether an incoming call is spam. Voice-specific trust and reputation analysis adopts a human intuitive behavior to detect spam based on the direct and indirect relationships between the called party and the calling party. Obviously, this solution is hard to be widely applied into other scenarios. But this method can play as a specific detection tool for SPIT in the proposed system.

Some existing anti-SPIM solutions made use of social networking to generate trust and reputation. In the context of instant messaging (IM), a trust and reputation based anti-SPIM method was proposed by Bi, Wu and Zhang (2008). This method integrated trust and reputation with black-list/white-list techniques. Since the method is proposed for IM spam (i.e., SPIM), trust and reputation generation is based on IM social networking, which cannot be directly applied into other application scenarios.

In summary, literature still lacks a generic unwanted traffic control mechanism, which should be efficient, accurate, and robust enough to be flexibly embedded into the current Internet architecture to control various unwanted traffic in a personalized manner. Our solution proposed in this chapter aims to solve this issue.

3. SYSTEM STRUCTURE AND UNWANTED TRAFFIC CONTROL PROCEDURE

3.1. Assumptions and Requirements

The research holds a number of assumptions as described below:

- **Identity Assumption:** A source of unwanted traffic and its receiver in most cases can be identified with the accuracy of an IP address of the host or a NAT (network address translation) outbound IP address when a NAT hides the source host. The identity of the sender's ISP can be extracted from any of these addresses. Meanwhile, each traffic flow (i.e., a sequence of packets from a source to a destination) can be identified based on its hash code.

- **GTO Assumption:** A GTO behaves as an authorized trusted party to collect trust evidence and conduct global trust evaluation on different system entities. We assume that a secure and dependable communication channel is applied in the system for unwanted traffic reporting and controlling. Multiple GTOs could exist in the system, each supporting their own alliance of ISPs. The GTOs can collaborate together to exchange trust information and instruct unwanted traffic control by applying a trustworthy collaboration protocol (Yan, 2010). Herein, we treat all GTOs as one authorized trusted party and simplify it as one GTO in our presentation.
- **Traffic Assumption:** We assume that the unwanted traffic is sourced from a host and targets other hosts via other entities (e.g., ISPs) in the network.
- **Tracking Assumption:** The unwanted traffic sources can be tracked by analyzing traffic logs and applying a traffic identification solution in normal situations. For supporting scalability, we use trust management to adaptively control the logging. For detecting and blocking IP address spoofing, cooperative firewalls can be adopted to track the unwanted traffic sources (retrieved from http://www.re2ee.org/).
- **Privacy Assumption:** We assume that privacy is taken care of by the GTM system, i.e., the detection reports are kept confidentially at ISPs and GTO. Therefore, telling about intrusions won't cause damage to public reputation of any entity.

We recognize the key desirable properties of the trust management system for unwanted traffic control as below:

- Timely/efficient and accurate defense against unwanted traffic intrusion at hosts;
- Efficient recognition of unwanted traffic sources under traffic intrusions, such as Botnet intrusion and DDoS intrusion;
- Automatic maintenance of trust for each system entity;
- Robustness against attacks raised by malicious or indifferent hosts and ISPs.
- Personalized control on unwanted traffic.

3.2. Attack Models

We focus on evaluating the accuracy and efficiency of the system under two kinds of unwanted traffic intrusion models:

- **Botnet Infection:** a number of hosts are infected by unwanted traffic in the Internet, thus they further send the traffic to other hosts.
- **DDoS via Reflectors (Bossardt, Dubendorfer & Plattner, 2007):** unwanted traffic could intrude one victim host from a number of attacked innocent hosts (reflectors). The unwanted traffic could be the same or different from different reflectors.

We also pay attention to the robustness of the trust management system under malicious host attacks and ISP attack as described below:

- **Malicious Attacks of Hosts:** A malicious or indifferent host may report or hide the unwanted traffic information by applying a malicious pattern, e.g., (a) hide evidence attack: malicious hosts hide detection evidence by not reporting to their ISP; (b) bad mouthing attack: malicious hosts intentionally frame a good traffic as unwanted; (c) on-off bad mouthing attack: malicious hosts behave well or frame a good traffic alternatively, hoping that they can remain undetected while causing damage; d) on-off hide evidence and bad mouthing attack: malicious hosts behave well or hide evidence/frame a good traffic alternatively.

- **Malicious Attack of ISP:** An ISP could maliciously perform an attack on the designed system. It behaves well to get a high trust value. It then turns its resources against the system. The malicious ISP could conduct a hide evidence attack by blocking all detection reports of its hosts or run a bad mouthing attack by framing a good traffic source.

3.3. System Structure

Figure 1 shows the structure of the trust management system for unwanted traffic control. In the system, each host has a User Behavior Monitor (UBMo) to track the host behaviors with regard

to unwanted traffic processing. A Local Traffic Monitor (LTMo) is applied to monitor inbound traffic to detect potential intrusions. The host also embeds an Unwanted Traffic Detector (UnTD), which can analyze the input data from UBMo and LTMo, as well as any unwanted traffic detection toolkits for detecting different kinds of spam or intrusions. An Evidence Reporter (EvR) at the host reports the unwanted traffic detection results to its local ISP. It can link to unwanted traffic detection toolkits related to various types of unwanted traffic.

At ISP, an Evidence Collector (EvC) collects the reports. A trust manager (TM) contains a number of functional blocks in order to do unwanted traffic control. Concretely, a Local User Monitor (LUMo) is applied to monitor the traffic sourced from a local system entity. A Local Trust Manager (LTM) conducts analysis based on the evidence collected from local hosts and/or the input from LUMo. Both analysis results of the local ISP and GTO are used to trigger traffic monitoring at ISP (LUMo) and traffic similarity check. An ISP Trust Manager (IspTM) is respon-

Figure 1. System structure of hybrid trust management (Yan, Kantola & Shen, 2012)

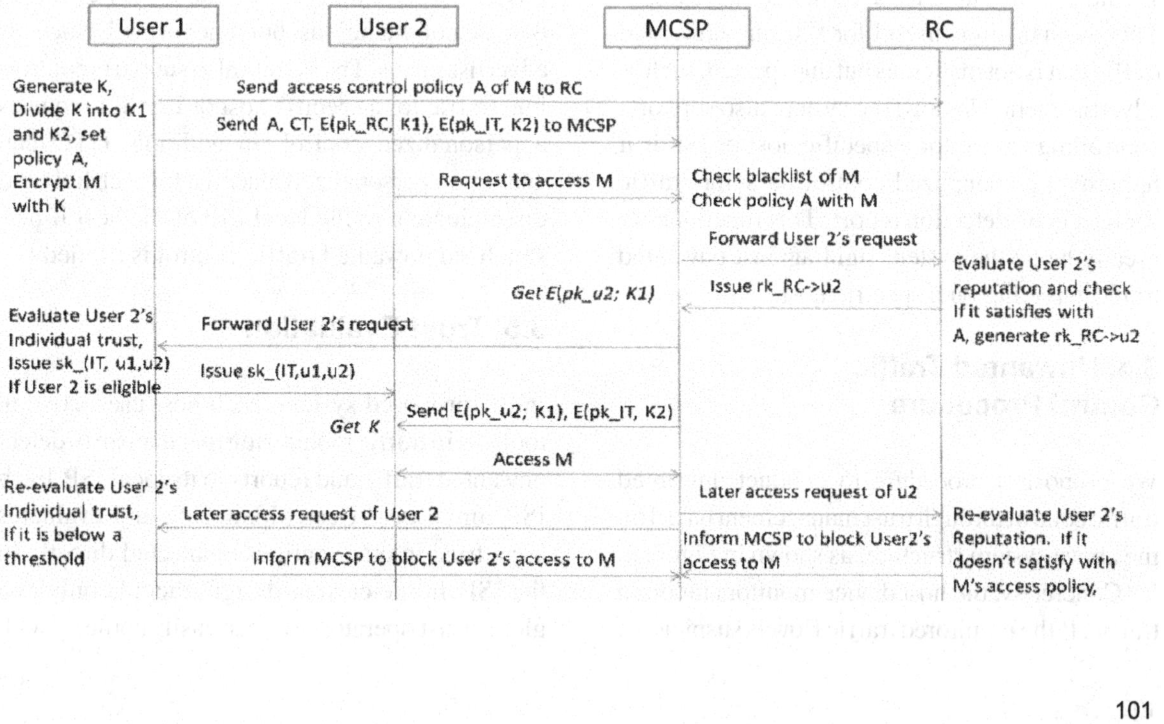

sible for transferring the results from LTM to GTO, requesting GTO for trust evaluation and unwanted traffic control, and receiving the trust value of the requested entity and a blacklist, as well as personalized traffic control decision from GTO.

At the GTO side, an Opinion Box is used to securely store trust evidence and information that are used to evaluate the global trust and detection trust of each entity and make an unwanted traffic control decision at an Aggregator. The Aggregator can also map a traffic source to its ISP. At GTO, a Distributor is applied to collect trust evidence and information, receive requests from ISPs and distribute the commands and decisions of GTO to ISPs.

The GTO collects the reports from ISPs all over the world. It aggregates all collected information and evaluates the global trust of each system entity (host or ISP) in order to detect the source of unwanted traffic and send blacklists to ISPs. Particularly, the proposed system can provide personalized unwanted traffic control. In this case, the ISP sends a request to the GTO if it discovers some traffic sourced from a host in the blacklist. Based on the past detection reporting behaviors, the GTO will decide if the traffic should be controlled for a particular destination. This mechanism is useful for filtering unwanted traffic that is not malicious but unexpected, such as advertisement. Notably, the system also supports controlling traffic for a specific host or ISP if it requests a personalized control on some traffic sources in its detection report. This functionality greatly helps the system fight against unwanted traffic targeting on a specific host.

3.4. Unwanted Traffic Control Procedure

We propose a procedure to conduct unwanted traffic control through trust management based on the above system structure, as shown in Figure 2.

Concretely, the host device monitors inbound traffic. If the monitored traffic flow is suspicious,

the unwanted traffic process behavior of the correspondent host is further tracked and inbound traffic similarity is calculated in order to generate an unwanted traffic detection report. The host also detects the unwanted traffic through installed commercial toolkits. The host reports to its local ISP if the detection is positive. The ISP collects the complaint reports from hosts and forwards them to GTO. If the complaint on a local host is serious or GTO triggers, ISP does traffic monitoring on the suspicious entities and checks content similarity. If the ISP checks are abnormal or suspicious, ISP sends its own check results to GTO. The GTO collects the reports from ISPs and hosts and then evaluates the global trust and detection trust of each system entity in order to detect the source of unwanted traffic and send a blacklist to ISPs. It requests to track the suspicious remote source of unwanted traffic by analyzing the reports from hosts and sends a command to the suspected attacker's local ISP to trigger traffic monitoring and similarity check. For personalized unwanted traffic control, the ISP sends a request to the GTO if it discovers some traffic sourced from a host in the blacklist. Based on the past detection reporting behaviors, the GTO will make a control decision for a particular destination. This mechanism is useful for filtering unwanted traffic that is not malicious but unexpected, such as advertisements. The system also supports controlling traffic for a specific host or ISP if it requests a personalized control. In addition, GTO can generate a personalized blacklist for each host and disseminate it to the local ISP of the host if personalized unwanted traffic control is needed.

3.5. Trust Evaluation

In the proposed system, each host uses existing tools and a traffic monitoring mechanism to detect unwanted traffic and reports to its local ISP. Each ISP runs Local User Monitoring and evaluates local trust in other entities connected directly to the ISP. In the current design, there is only one global trust operator, so it can easily come up with

Figure 2. An unwanted traffic control procedure (Yan, Kantola & Shen, 2012)

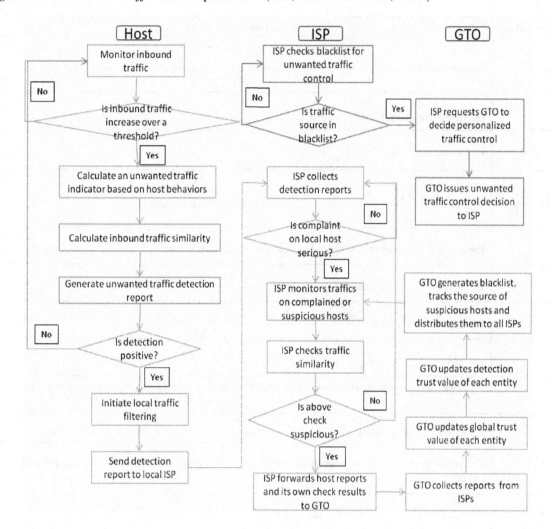

a unique trust value for each entity. The possibility of several collaborating global trust operators is also possible, which is left for future study.

The GTO is responsible for evaluating the global trust of each system entity, generating a blacklist accordingly and making a personalized unwanted traffic control decision. For generating a blacklist, each incident or piece of collected evidence is assigned a credibility or confidence value, which is the detection trust of its provider. Note that there are about 1800 ISPs in the Internet. Each ISP treats other ISPs as an entity. The GTO further aggregates the evidence and evaluates trust in hosts and ISPs.

The trust contains two parts: the global trust that indicates the probability (and nature) of unwanted traffic sourced from the entity and the detection trust that implies its unwanted traffic detection performance.

4. ALGORITHMS

Based on the above system design and the unwanted traffic control procedure, a number of algorithms are proposed to implement unwanted traffic control. For ease of reference, Table 1 summarizes the notations used in this section.

Table 1. Notations

Symbol	Description
$f(x)$	The Sigmoid function $f(x) = \dfrac{1}{1+e^{-x}}$; used to normalize a value into (0, 1);
U_k	The system entity, it can be either an ISP or a host;
$tr_k^{in}(t)$	The inbound traffic flow of host U_k at time t;
$d_t\{g(t)\}$	$d_t\{g(t)\} = \dfrac{g(t)-g(t-\tau)}{\tau}, (\tau \to 0)$; $g(t)$ is a function of variable t;
ϕ^k	The unwanted traffic indicator contributed by local traffic monitoring at host U_k;
e_i^k	The ith content received by host U_k ;
r_t^i	The receiving time of e_i^k at U_k ;
d_t^i	The deleting time of e_i^k at U_k ;
τ_i	The unwanted traffic indicator contributed by the unwanted traffic process behaviors of a host regarding the ith content;
T	The time window used to normalize the unwanted traffic process time;
$v_k^i(t)$	The probability of e_i^k being an unwanted content indicated by U_k at time t, i.e., the unwanted traffic intrusion indicator;
$s_i^k(t)$	The unwanted traffic detection result at time t by U_k about e_i^k ;
$s_i(t)$	The unwanted traffic detection result at time t about e_i^k ;
$sim\_in_i^k$	The similarity of inbound traffic correlated to e_i^k ;
sim_in^k	The similarity of U_k inbound traffic by considering all similar traffic received by U_k ;
$\theta(I)$	The Rayleigh cumulative distribution function $\theta(I) = \left\{1-\exp(\dfrac{-I^2}{2\sigma^2})\right\}$ to model the impact of integer number I , $\sigma = 100$ in our simulation;
$tr_k^o(t)$	The outbound traffic flow of U_k at time t;
ut_k^t	The global trust of U_k at time t;

continued on following page

Table 1. Continued

Symbol	Description
thr	The threshold of the host to report to ISP;
$thr0$	The threshold to trigger traffic monitoring at local ISP;
$thr1$	The threshold of ISP to report to GTO;
ϕ_{sp}^{k}	The unwanted traffic indicator contributed by the ISP traffic monitoring on U_k ;
$sim\_out_i^k$	The similarity of outbound traffic of U_k correlated to e_i^k ;
sim_out^k	The traffic similarity factor of U_k by considering all similar traffic sent by U_k ;
$sp_k^n(t)$	The unwanted traffic detection value about host U_k provided by the nth ISP SP_n at time t;
$rt_{k'}^t$	The contribution of reports from the hosts to the evaluation of $U_{k'}$'s global trust at time t;
$mt_{k'}^t$	The contribution of reports from the ISPs to the evaluation of $U_{k'}$'s global trust at time t;
dt_k^t	The detection trust value of U_k at time t;
y	The detection performance indicator;
δ	The parameter to control the adjustment of dt_k^t ;
γ	The warning flag to record the number of bad detections;
μ	The parameter to control bad detection punishment;
$thr2$	The threshold to put an entity into the blacklist at GTO;
$thr3$	The threshold to determine on-off or conflict behavior attack;
$thr4$	The threshold to determine dishonest ISP.

4.1. Unwanted Traffic Detection at Host

4.1.1. Local Traffic Monitoring

The purpose of monitoring the inbound traffic of a host U_k ($k = 1,......, K$) is to detect if the host has been intruded. The increase of inbound traffic of a node indicates the possibility of being intruded. An unwanted traffic indicator ϕ^k contributed by the local traffic monitoring can be described as below by using the Sigmoid function to normalize the traffic deviation into the interval of (0, 1):

$$\phi^k = \left| 1 - 2f \left\{ d_t \left[tr_k^{in}(t) \right] \right\} \right| \qquad (1)$$

The bigger ϕ^k is, the more probably U_k is intruded.

4.1.2. Traffic Process

The behaviors of a node in processing the received traffic imply its wants or dislikes. This information can be applied to indicate whether the traffic is wanted subjective to personal needs. If the receiving time of a content e_i^k is r_t^i and its discarding time (e.g., the time to move it to a spam folder or specify it as unwanted) is d_t^i, the interval between r_t^i and d_t^i implies user need. Thus, the unwanted traffic indicator τ_i contributed by the node content processing behavior can be described as:

$$\tau_i = 1 - \frac{d_t^i - r_t^i}{T},$$

when

$$d_t^i - r_t^i < T, \qquad (2)$$

where T is the time window used to normalize the content process time. The bigger τ_i is, the more possible e_i^k is unwanted by U_k. Note that if $d_t^i - r_t^i \geq T$, τ_i will not be counted and $\tau_i = 0$.

An average value of τ_i is

$$\tau = \frac{1}{I} \sum_{i=1}^{I} \left(1 - \frac{d_t^i - r_t^i}{T} \right).$$

4.1.3. Similarity Check

In most network intrusions, similar contents could be sent many times to the same hosts. Therefore,

we further check the similarity of contents received by U_k if $\phi^k \geq thr1$. For similar sized contents $E_k = \left\{ e_i^k \right\}$ $i = \left\{ 1, \ldots, I \right\}$ received by U_k within a time window ($w = \left[t - \frac{T}{2}, t + \frac{T}{2} \right]$), we calculate their similarity as:

$$sim\_in_i^k = \frac{\theta(I)}{I-1} \sum_{i' \neq i}^{I} \left(1 - \left| e_i^k - e_{i'}^k \right| \right), \qquad (3)$$

where $\left| e_i^k - e_{i'}^k \right|$ is the difference between e_i^k and $e_{i'}^k$. It can be calculated based on a semantic relevance measure (Wang et al., 2011). Obviously, U_k could receive multiple sets of similar traffic intrusion. The similarity of U_k inbound traffic by considering all similar contents is

$$sim\_in^k = \frac{1}{M'} \sum_{M'} \left[\frac{\theta(I)}{I-1} \sum_{i' \neq i}^{I} \left(1 - \left| e_i^k - e_{i'}^k \right| \right) \right], \qquad (4)$$

where M' is the number of the sets of similar contents. We note that the bigger the number of similar contents I in a set, the more possible that the similar content is unwanted. Thus in Formula 3 and 5.4, we model the influence of integer I using the Rayleigh cumulative distribution function $\theta(I)$.

4.1.4. Unwanted Traffic Reporting

A host could complain about unwanted traffic to its local ISP. The complaint is based on the host behavior in the content process and local traffic auto-monitoring, as well as traffic similarity check. Thereby, we describe the unwanted traffic detection value $v_k^i(t)$ at time t by U_k about traffic e_i^k as:

$$v_k^i(t) = sim\_in_i^k * \phi^k * \tau_i. \qquad (5)$$

The detection reports are aggregated at ISP in order to decide whether traffic monitoring and check at ISP is needed for a local traffic source. Aggregation is also conducted at GTO for a remote traffic source in order to decide whether traffic monitoring and check at its ISP is needed. The aggregation is based on Formula 6 by applying the global trust and detection trust of the host as the credibility of its complaint.

$$s_i(t) = \sum_k v_k^i(t) * ut_k^t * dt_k^t \bigg/ \sum_k ut_k^t * dt_k^t \quad (6)$$

An unwanted traffic detection report containing $v_k^i(t)$ is automatically sent to the local ISP of the host if $v_k^i(t) \geq thr$. Algorithm 1 is applied to detect and control unwanted traffic at a host.

4.2. Traffic Monitoring at ISP

The purpose of monitoring host U_k's traffic at its local ISP is to find the sources of unwanted traffic with such credibility that the ISP can either take administrative action or impose contractual penalties on the sources. This traffic monitoring is triggered by a condition $s_i(t) \geq thr0$ in order

Algorithm 1. Unwanted traffic detection and control at a host

---

1. Input:
2. - $tr_k^{in}(t)$, e_i^k, r_t^i, d_t^i ($i = 1, ..., I$).
3. Monitor U_k's inbound traffic to get ϕ^k if the traffic is increasing;
4. For each suspicious content e_i^k, do
5. Calculate τ_i;
6. If $\phi^k \geq thr1$, calculate $sim\_in^k(t)$ and $v_k^i(t)$;
7. If $v_k^i(t) \geq thr$,
8. Send $v_k^i(t)$ to the local ISP, initiate local traffic filtering;
9. Filter the contents identical or similar to e_i^k.
10. Output: $v_k^i(t)$, ($i = 1, ..., I_{U_k}$).

---

to save the running cost of the ISP. Particularly, it can detect an infected host that has become a source of unwanted traffic due to infection. U_k can be any entity that links to the ISP, thus its traffic can be monitored by the ISP. It is efficient for the ISP to monitor its own subscribers because it sees all traffic sourced from them while other ISP's subscribers are numerous and the ISP can only see a fraction of their traffic. Therefore, for scalability, monitoring of other ISP's subscribers should be very selective. Similar to Formula 1, an unwanted traffic indicator contributed by the ISP traffic monitoring on the outbound traffic of U_k is

$$\phi_{sp}^k(t) = \left| 1 - 2f\left\{ d_t\left[tr_k^o(t) \right] \right\} \right|. \quad (7)$$

Similar to Formula 4, the similarity of multiple M different unwanted contents sent from U_k can be designed as:

$$sim\_out^k = \frac{1}{M} \sum_M \left[\theta(I) \bigg/ I - 1 \sum_{i' \neq i}^I \left(1 - \left| e_i^k - e_{i'}^k \right| \right) \right]. \quad (8)$$

We calculate the unwanted traffic detection value about U_k provided by the nth ISP at time t using Formula 9 by monitoring the increase of out-bound traffic and checking content similarity.

$$sp_k^n(t) = \phi_{sp}^k(t) * sim\_out^k. \quad (9)$$

ISP reports $sp_k^n(t)$ to GTO if $sp_k^n(t) \geq thr1$. Algorithm 2 is applied to monitor the unwanted traffic at ISP.

4.3. Detection Trust: The Credibility of Detection

The credibility of detection reporting should be analyzed against malicious behaviors of reporters because of many reasons. For example, the com-

Algorithm 2. Unwanted Traffic Monitor at ISP

1. Input:
2. - $tr_k^o(t)$, $E_k = \{e_i^k\}$ $i = \{1, ..., I\}$;
3. - U_k ($k = 1, ..., K$).
4. For each complained U_k, do
5. Monitor U_k's traffic, calculate $\phi_{sp}^k(t)$;
6. Calculate sim_out^k and $sp_k^n(t)$;
7. if $sp_k^n(t) \geq thr1$
8. Report $sp_k^n(t)$ to GTO.
9. Output: $sp_k^n(t)$, $n = (1, ..., N)$.

plainer may be intruded; the host or ISP intentionally frames other hosts; the detection tools installed in the host are broken; the detection tools are poor and the detection is not qualified. Therefore, we apply the detection trust to indicate the quality of the reports since we can't ensure that the unwanted traffic detection is trustworthy. The detection trust is generated at GTO. If the detection reported by U_k doesn't match the final evaluation result, $y = -1$, and $\gamma + +$; If the detection matches the fact, $y = 1$ and γ is not changed; If no detection report is provided, $y = 0$ and γ is not changed. Good detection performance will cause an increase of dt_k^t, otherwise, dt_k^t will be decreased. The detection trust dt_k^t of U_k at time t is:

$$dt_k^t = \begin{cases} dt_k^t + \delta y & (\gamma < thr3) \\ dt_k^t + \delta y - \mu\gamma & (\gamma \geq thr3) \end{cases} = \begin{cases} 1 & (dt_k^t > 1) \\ 0 & (dt_k^t < 0) \end{cases},$$
(10)

where $\delta > 0$ is a parameter to control the change of dt_k^t. In order to detect on-off and conflict behavior of attackers (Yan, Zhang & Deng, 2012), we further introduce a warning flag γ to record the number of bad detections. The initial value of γ is 0. It is increased by 1 each time when a bad

detection happens. Parameter $thr3$ is a threshold to indicate the on-off and conflict behavior attacks. $\mu > 0$ is a parameter to control bad detection punishment. Yan, Zhang and Deng (2012) have proved that this design is effective in trust evaluation against a number of malicious behaviors (Sun, Han & Liu, 2008).

4.4. Unwanted Traffic Control at GTO

The GTO evaluates the trust of each entity based on the collected reports from the hosts and ISPs in order to find the sources of unwanted traffic. Obviously, U_k ($k = 1, ..., K1$) could report many times at different time t. Considering the time's influence and potential on-off and ballot stuffing attacks, we pay more attention to the recent reports. We use $e^{-|t-t_p|^2 / \rho}$ to decay $V_k^i(t)$, while t_p is the trust evaluation time, τ is a parameter to control the time decaying. We aggregate the reports $v_k^i(t)$ from K1 hosts who blamed $U_{k'}$ by considering both the global trust and the detection trust, as well as time decaying as below:

$$rt_{k'}^{t_p} = \sum_{k=1}^{K1} dt_k^{t_p} * ut_k^{t_p} * v_k^i(t) * e^{\frac{|t-t_p|^2}{\tau}} \Bigg/ \sum_{k=1}^{K1} dt_k^{t_p} * ut_k^{t_p} * e^{\frac{|t-t_p|^2}{\tau}}.$$
(11)

We further aggregate the reports from ISPs to calculate their contributions on $U_{k'}$'s global trust evaluation. Since ISP reporting will trigger the trust evaluation at the GTO, we don't apply time decaying in Formula 12.

$$mt_{k'}^{t_p} = \sum_{n=1}^{N} dt_n^{t_p} * ut_n^{t_p} * sp_{k'}^n(t_p) \Bigg/ \sum_{n=1}^{N} dt_n^{t_p} * ut_n^{t_p}.$$
(12)

The global trust value of the blamed entity k' can be calculated by deducting the original $ut_{k'}^{t_p}$ with $mt_{k'}^{t_p}$ and $rt_{k'}^{t_p}$. Meanwhile, we also consider the number of reporters by modeling its influence using the Rayleigh cumulative distribution function. Thus, the formula to update $ut_{k'}^{t_p}$ is designed as Formula 13. Algorithm 3 is used to conduct global trust evaluation.

$$ut_{k'}^{t_p} = ut_{k'}^{t_p} - \theta(K1) * rt_{k'}^{t_p} - \theta(N) * mt_{k'}^{t_p}. \quad (13)$$

4.5. Personalized Unwanted Traffic Control

The UTC can be personalized based on the correlation of detection reports. The past reporting behavior of a host implies its preference on received contents. In order to decide whether to control a traffic flow i' sourced from an entity in greylist for $U_{k'}$, we consider the past reporting correlation between $U_{k'}$ and U_k ($k = 1,...,K1$) who reported i' as unwanted. We set a personalized filtering indicator $fi_{k'}^{i'}$ for $U_{k'}$ as below for i' according to the past detection reports provided by both $U_{k'}$ and U_k:

$$fi_{k'}^{i'} = \left. \sum_{k=1}^{K1} v_k^{i'}(t) \middle/ K1 * K1 \sum_{k=1}^{K1}\left(1 - \frac{1}{I'}\sum_{i=1}^{I'}\left|v_k^i(t) - v_{k'}^i(t)\right|\right) \right., \quad (14)$$

Algorithm 3. Global Trust Evaluation at GTO

1. Input:
2. - $sp_k^n(t_p), v_k^i(t), (i = 1,......,I_{U_k})$.
3. For each blamed system entity k', do
4. Calculate $rt_{k'}^{t_p}, mt_{k'}^{t_p}$, and $ut_{k'}^{t_p}$ based on Formula 1-5.13;
5. If $ut_{k'}^{t_p} \le thr2$, put $U_{k'}$ into a greylist.
6. Output: greylist $\{U_{k'}\}$.

where I' is the total number of traffic flows reported by both $U_{k'}$ and U_k. $\left|v_k^i(t) - v_{k'}^i(t)\right|$ denotes the deviation of the detection reports between U_k and $U_{k'}$. Algorithm 4 is used to provide personalized unwanted traffic control.

This personalized filtering mechanism is a counter measure against the system vulnerability caused by malicious reporting behaviors that could make extra intrusions and unexpected filtering. For example, a malicious host u could report differently from other hosts, thus the unwanted traffic reported by these hosts may not be filtered for u due to the diverse behaviors. On the other hand, a good traffic flow reported as unwanted by other malicious hosts (collaborative bad mouthing users) could not be filtered for u. Thus, applying this mechanism can encourage good reporting behaviors and fight against collaborative bad mouthing attack.

5. EVALUATION AND ANALYSIS

5.1. Simulation Settings and Evaluation Measure

A number of simulations are designed to evaluate the feasibility and effectiveness of the proposed system with regard to accuracy, efficiency, ro-

Algorithm 4. Personalized UTC decided at GTO

1. Input:
2. - $v_k^i(t), v_{k'}^i(t), (i = 1,......,I'); v_k^{i'}(t),$ ($k = 1,...,K1$)
3. - $U_{k'}$: the destination host of traffic.
4. For each traffic flow i' sourced from a host in the greylist, do
5. For each destination host $U_{k'}$, do
6. Calculate $fi_{k'}^{i'}$ based on Formula 14;
7. If $fi_{k'}^{i'} \ge thr4$, filter the traffic flow i' for $U_{k'}$;
8. Output: $fi_{k'}^{i'}$.

bustness and personalization support. This is because real data based evaluation is not suitable for testing the system performance under various system attacks. In our simulations, we have a total of K=1000 hosts, N=5 ISPs. Each ISP has 200 hosts connected. There are L sources of unwanted traffic. All of them randomly select a number of hosts for intrusion within a time period. A good host that is not infected reports unwanted traffic honestly and timely. A malicious host or ISP may report the unwanted traffic by applying a malicious or indifferent pattern, e.g., (a) hide evidence attack; b) bad mouthing attack; c) on-off attack; d) the combination of above attacks; e) malicious attack of ISP. The traffic intrusion models tested are: a) Botnet intrusion with different infection rates; b) DDoS intrusion via reflectors.

In our simulations, we assume that the unwanted traffic from the same source is identical. The initial global trust value of each system entity is 1; the initial detection trust value of each entity is 0.5. We randomly select malicious hosts in our simulation. Table 2 provides the simulation settings of other system parameters.

We adopt commonly used metrics in information retrieval, Recall (R), Precision (P) and F measure (F) to describe the performance of unwanted traffic control. We denote the number of entities that are sources of unwanted traffic flows (SUT) and are indeed detected as SUT as x; the

Table 2. Simulation Settings of System Parameters

Symbol	Settings	Symbol	Settings
thr	0.8	σ	100
$thr0$	0.7	τ	2
$thr1$	0.8	δ	0.05
$thr2$	0.1	μ	0.1
$thr3$	5	$thr4$	0.1

number of entities that are not SUT but are added to SUT as y; the number of entities that are SUT but are not detected as SUT as z. With these data we do a precision-recall evaluation. We define:

$$R = \frac{x}{x+z}, \tag{15}$$

$$P = \frac{x}{x+y}, \tag{16}$$

$$F = \frac{2PR}{P+R}, \tag{17}$$

where $R, P, F \in [0,1]$. R indicates the performance of false negative detection (i.e., unwanted traffic goes unnoticed). P indicates the performance of false positive detection (i.e., the blame of innocent hosts). Good system performance requests both high recall R and high precision P. Thus, we make use of F measure to indicate the system performance. Obviously, high F measure is desirable for a good performance of the system.

5.2. Accuracy of Unwanted Traffic Detection

We design Experiment 1 to test the accuracy of the proposed system. In this experiment, we test the F measure under the following simulation conditions: there is no Botnet, only original independent (L=5, 10, 50, and 100) unwanted traffic sources and all system entities are good. Each source sends unwanted traffic to randomly selected destination hosts and this procedure continues until the unwanted traffic sources are detected. Figure 3 shows the experiment result. We observe that the system can accurately detect the unwanted traffic sources in an efficient way when they occupy no more than 10% of the system hosts (which is an extreme case in practice).

Figure 3. Accuracy of unwanted traffic source detection (Yan, Kantola & Shen, 2011)

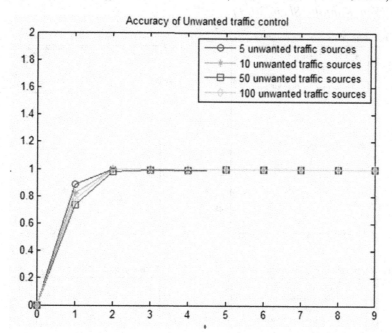

5.3. Efficiency of Unwanted Traffic Detection

We design Experiment 2 to test the efficiency of our system. Efficiency can be reflected by detection speed (number of time periods), i.e., how fast the system can detect the sources of unwanted traffic. In this experiment, we test the F measure in the following simulation settings: *every time 10% (15%, 20%, and 40%) destination hosts are infected and become Botnet, the infected hosts (if not detected) behave as the unwanted traffic sources and distribute the same traffic to randomly selected good hosts, and this procedure continues until the system detects all unwanted traffic sources.* Figure 4 shows the experiment result. We observe that the system can efficiently detect the unwanted traffic sources (F reaches 1 within 9 time periods) even when the infection rate is as high as 40% in the situation that the initial unwanted traffic sources occupy no more than 5% of the system hosts (which is a normal case in practice).

5.4. Robustness of Unwanted Traffic Control

Attacks could be intentionally designed to discredit our system by malicious hosts or the hosts attacked by hackers. We design Experiment 3 to test the robustness of our system. In this experiment, we test the F measure in the following simulation settings: *there is no Botnet, only a number of original independent unwanted traffic sources with attacks raised by a number of malicious hosts, who could be the destination hosts of unwanted traffic.* We test three malicious attacks:

1. **Hide Evidence Attack:** Indifferent hosts hide detection evidence. The simulation result is shown in Figure 5. The proportion of malicious hosts is 10%, 15%, 20%, and 40%, respectively. We observe that our system performs very well against the hide evidence attack. The F measure can reach 1 within 4 time periods in the situation that the unwanted traffic sources occupy no more than 5% of the system hosts.

Figure 4. Efficiency of unwanted traffic source detection with different infection rates: (a) 10%; (b) 15%; (c) 20%; (d) 40%. (Yan, Kantola, Shen, 2011)

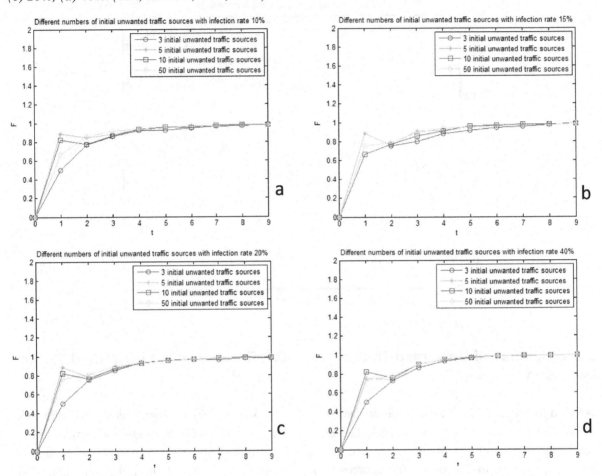

2. **Bad Mouthing Attack:** Malicious hosts intentionally frame a good traffic as unwanted. We simulate the same number of good traffic sources as the unwanted ones in the system and test the situations that the proportion of bad mouthing hosts is 10%, 15%, 20%, and 40%, respectively. Figure 6 shows the simulation result. We observe that our system performs well against the bad mouthing attack. The F measure can generally reach 1 within 9 time periods in the situation that the unwanted traffic sources occupy no more than 5% of the system hosts.

3. **On-Off Attack:** Malicious hosts behave well and badly alternatively, hoping that they can remain undetected while causing damage. In our simulation, we test three kinds of on-off attacks: i) on-off on hide evidence; ii) on-off on bad mouthing; iii) on-off on both hide evidence and bad mouthing. We simulate the same number of good traffic sources as the unwanted ones in the system and test the F measure in the situations that the proportions of hide evidence hosts and bad mouthing hosts are 10%, 15%, 20%, and 40%, respectively.

Figure 5. Robustness of unwanted traffic source detection under hide evidence attack: (a) 10% hide evidence hosts; (b) 15% hide evidence hosts; (c) 20% hide evidence hosts; (d) 40% hide evidence hosts. (Yan, Kantola, Shen, 2011)

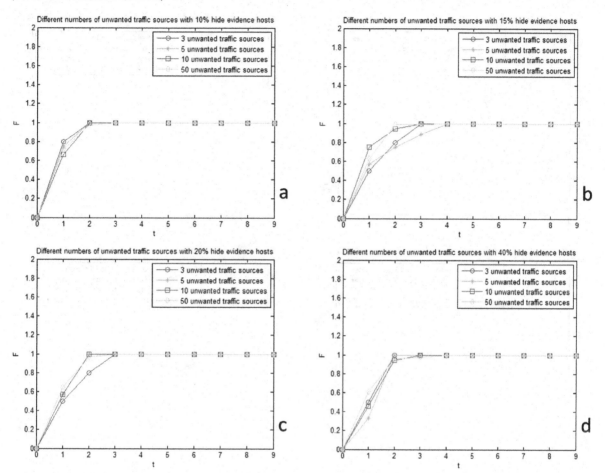

Figure 7 shows the simulation result under the on-off hide evidence attack. Figure 8 shows the result under the on-off bad mouthing attack. Figure 9 shows the result under the on-off hide evidence plus bad mouthing attack. We can see that the system performs well against these three kinds of attacks (either malicious or indifferent). The F measure can generally reach 1 in a short time period in the situation that the unwanted traffic sources occupy no more than 5% of the system hosts.

5.5. Efficiency and Robustness of Unwanted Traffic Detection

We design Experiment 4 to test both the efficiency and robustness of our system. In this experiment, we test the F measure in the following simulation settings: *every time 10% unwanted traffic destination hosts are infected and become Botnet and at the same time some attacks are raised by a number of malicious hosts.* We test five malicious attacks: 1) hide evidence attack; 2) bad mouthing attack; 3) on-off hide evidence attack; 4) on-off bad mouthing attack; and 5) on-off hide evidence plus bad mouthing attack.

Figure 6. Robustness of unwanted traffic source detection under bad mouthing attack: (a) 10% bad mouthing hosts; (b) 15% bad mouthing hosts; (c) 20% bad mouthing hosts; (d) 40% bad mouthing hosts. (Yan, Kantola, Shen, 2011)

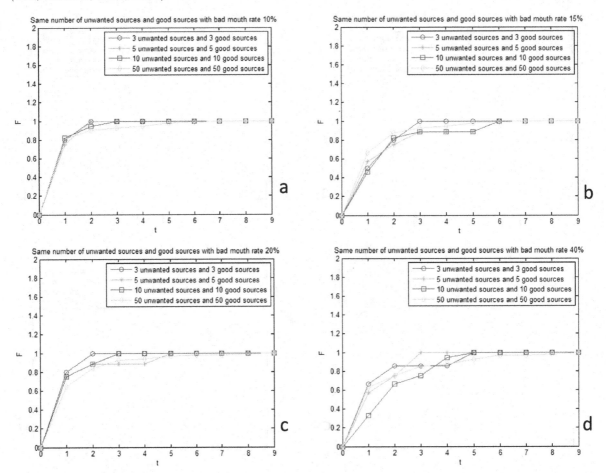

Figure 10, Figure 11, Figure 12, Figure 13, and Figure 14 show the experiment results. We observe that the system can efficiently detect the unwanted traffic sources (F reaches 1 within 9 time periods) under the attacks of hide evidence and on-off hide evidence (refer to Figure 10 and Figure 12), even when the proportion of malicious hosts is as high as 40% in the situation that the initial unwanted traffic sources occupy no more than 5% of the system hosts. We also tested and proved that the system performs very well when the infection rate is as high as 20% under the above two types of attacks. In the current simulation settings, the system performs well under the on-off

bad mouthing attack and on-off hide evidence plus bad mouthing attack when the proportions of hide evidence hosts and bad mouthing hosts are below 20% (refer to Figure 13 and Figure 14). In these cases, we also tested that the system can afford the infection rate as high as 20%. We noticed that the bad mouthing attack has the worst impact on the proposed system. But if the proportion of bad mouthing hosts is below 20%, the system can still perform effectively and robustly (refer to Figure 11).

Particularly, we also find that the value of P can reach 1 quickly in all above tests. It can reach 1 within 4 time periods in the worst case that the

Figure 7. Robustness of unwanted traffic source detection under on-off hide evidence attack: (a) 10% on-off hide evidence hosts; (b) 15% on-off hide evidence hosts; (c) 20% on-off hide evidence hosts; (d) 40% on-off hide evidence hosts.

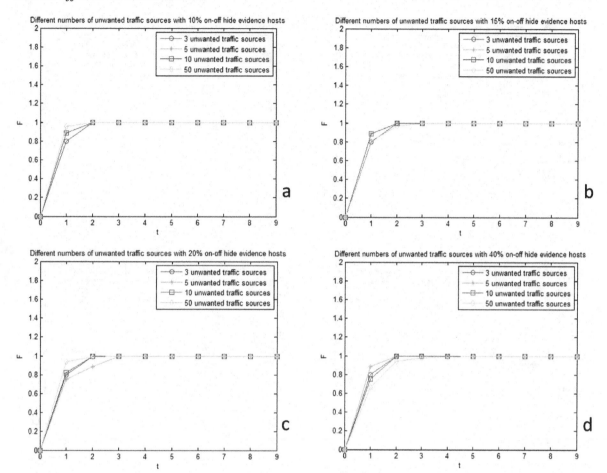

system is under bad mouthing attack and Botnet infection (with 10% Botnet infection rate and 40% bad mouthing hosts). This implies that the system performance of false positive detection is very good.

5.6. Efficiency and Robustness of Unwanted Traffic Detection

We tested the efficiency of unwanted traffic detection against an extreme Botnet infection: *800 hosts (Botnet) in 4 ISPs intrude 100 hosts in the 5th ISP, i.e., they send unwanted traffic to 100 hosts* *in the 5th ISP*. At each time slot, each of these 800 Botnet hosts randomly selects 100 hosts in the 5th ISP to intrude by sending the same content. We apply traffic function $tr_k^i\left(t\right) = \alpha t$, $\alpha = 10$, 10^2, 10^3, 10^4, or 10^5 in this test.

Efficiency can be reflected by detection speed/ performance, i.e., how fast the system can detect the sources of unwanted traffic. In this experiment, we test the F measure in the above simulation settings, and also show intrusion indication at the host device based on Algorithm 1.

Figure 15 shows the result. We observe that a host can detect this kind of intrusion immedi-

Figure 8. Robustness of unwanted traffic source detection under on-off bad mouthing attack: (a) 10% on-off bad mouthing hosts; (b) 15% on-off bad mouthing hosts; (c) 20% on-off bad mouthing hosts; (d) 40% on-off bad mouthing hosts.

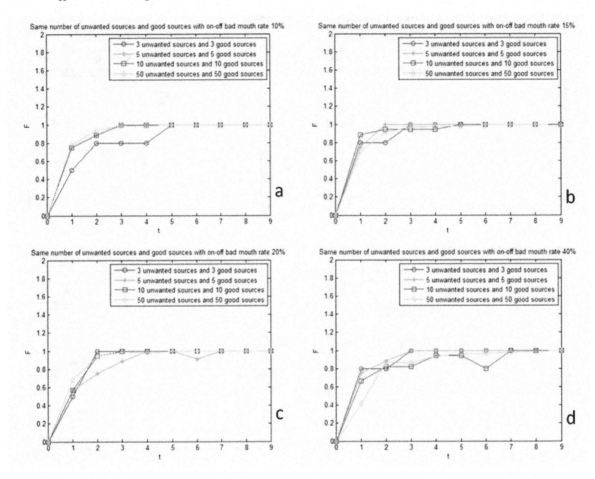

ately. In some time slots, $v_k^i(t) = 0$, indicating that the host is not intruded by the unwanted traffic at those slots. This is because the target hosts are randomly selected. We also observe that the system can detect all unwanted traffic sources efficiently. The bigger volume the traffic is, the faster the detection. Note that in this experiment the hosts do not bad mouth evidence.

5.7. Efficiency of Unwanted Traffic Source Detection under a Malicious Attack of ISP

In this experiment, we assume that the first ISP performs a malicious attack on the designed sys-

tem. It behaves well and gets a high trust value 1, then conduct a hide evidence attack by not forwarding any detection reports from its hosts to GTO at the 10th time slot. Meanwhile, it performs a bad mouthing attack by framing a good traffic source as unwanted one. We apply herein traffic function $tr_k^i(t) = \alpha t, \ \alpha = 10$.

Figure 16 shows the result. We observe from Figure 16 (a) that the detection trust value of this malicious ISP is initiated at 0.5, then increased to 1 due to good behaviors, but dropped to 0 sharply at the 10th time slot since it is very easy for GTO to find this malicious ISP. In addition, the system can find all unwanted traffic sources quickly even though the malicious ISP hides evidence provided

Figure 9. Robustness of unwanted traffic source detection under on-off hide evidence plus bad mouthing attack: (a) 10% hide evidence and 10% bad mouthing hosts; (b) 15% hide evidence and 15% bad mouthing hosts; (c) 20% hide evidence and 20% bad mouthing hosts; (d) 40% hide evidence and 40% bad mouthing hosts.

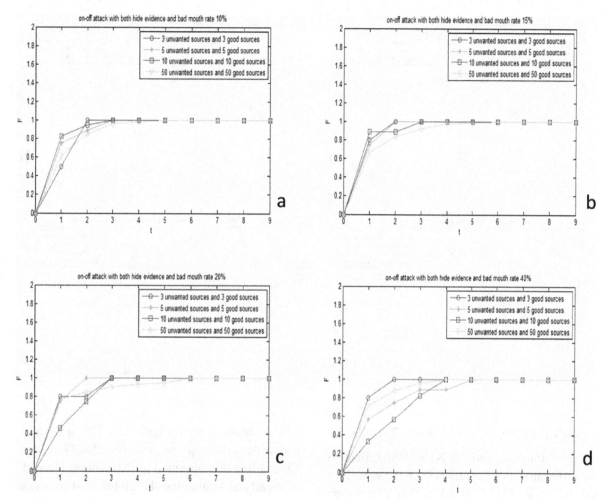

by its local hosts and conducts the bad mouthing attack at the 10th time slot (refer to Figure 16 (b)). The F measure is 0 at the 10th time slot because we clear the blacklist at that moment. But we notice that the system can immediately find all unwanted traffic sources even though one ISP becomes malicious. This result implies that the system can efficiently detect the malicious ISP and thus ignore its influence on the unwanted traffic control. Another test shows that performing only hide evidence attack by one ISP won't influence much on the system efficiency. Thereby, we conclude that the proposed system performs very well if some ISP suddenly turns into malicious.

5.8. Effectiveness Under DDoS Intrusion via Reflectors

We test two cases. In case 1, we randomly select N (N=100) hosts as reflectors that send the same contents to one target host. The simulation settings are: $T = 10$, $d_t^i - r_t^i = 1$, and $M' = 1$. We test two traffic flows: (1) $tr_k^i(t) = \alpha t$, $\alpha = 10, 10^2, 10^3$,

Figure 10. Efficiency and robustness of unwanted traffic source detection under hide evidence attack and Botnet infection: (a) 10% Botnet infection rate with 10% hide evidence hosts; (b) 10% Botnet infection rate with 15% hide evidence hosts; (c) 10% Botnet infection rate with 20%hide evidence hosts; (d) 10% Botnet infection rate with 40% hide evidence hosts.

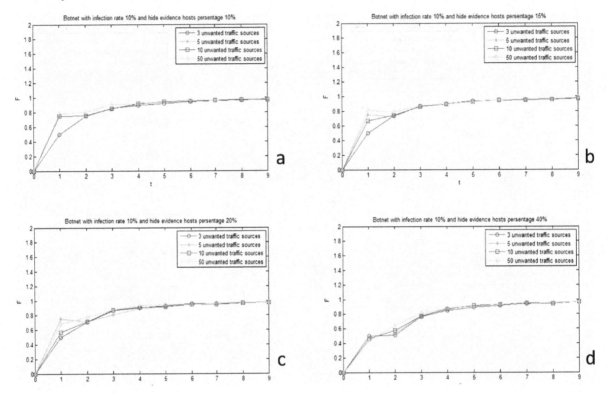

10^4, or 10^5; (2) $tr_k^i\left(t\right) = e^{\beta t}$, $\beta = 1, 2, 4, 8,$ or 16. In case 2, the contents from N (N=100) reflectors are different, but the contents from the same host are the same. That is M'=N. Other settings are the same as the case 1.

Figure 17 shows the result. We observe that the proposed system can detect all unwanted traffic sources within 9 time slots if all reflectors send the same contents to the target host. The system reacts slower in case 2 than case 1 when different reflectors send different contents to the target host, comparing Figure 17 (a) to Figure 17 (c) and Figure 17 (b) to Figure 17 (d). This is reasonable since the volume of one content is smaller in the second case. The system is more sensitive when the volume of traffic is bigger (refer to traffic

1-5 in each figure of Figure 17). This is because more detection reports are collected by GTO, thus it can find the unwanted traffic sources more efficiently by evaluating the global trust based on the detection reports.

In summary, the system performs accurate, efficient and robust in the situation that the unwanted traffic sources is below 10%, the Botnet infection rate is no more than 10%, and the percentage of malicious hosts is below 40%. Thus, we can set a reasonable deployment scenario for the system: 60% of hosts have trustworthy toolkits to detect and report unwanted traffic. Meanwhile, the system performs effectively under Botnet intrusion, DDoS intrusion via reflectors, and malicious ISP attack. The system performs better

Figure 11. Efficiency and robustness of unwanted traffic source detection under bad mouthing attack and Botnet infection: (a) 10% Botnet infection rate with 10% bad mouthing hosts; (b) 10% Botnet infection rate with 15% bad mouthing hosts; (c) 10% Botnet infection rate with 20% bad mouthing hosts; (d) 10% Botnet infection rate with 40% bad mouthing hosts.

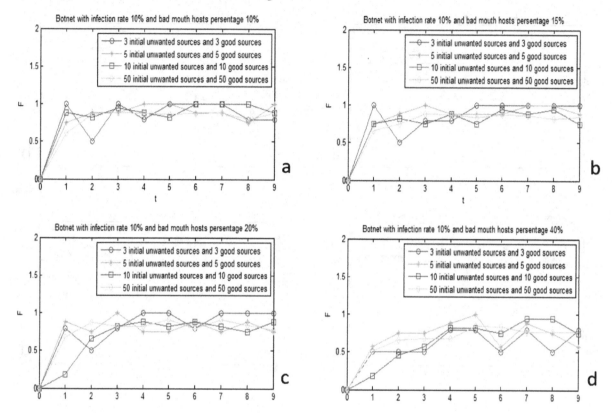

if the volume of traffic is big. It takes longer for the system to detect different unwanted contents than the same contents in the DDoS intrusion via reflectors.

5.9. Personalization of Unwanted Traffic Control

We design an experiment to prove that personalized unwanted traffic control can be provided by the proposed system. We simulate detection reporting behaviors of two hosts U_1 and U_2 regarding the traffic from the same host U in the blacklist. U_2 has similar past reporting behaviors to other hosts (U_3-U_{11}); while U_1 behaves dif-

ferently from others in the past detection reporting, as shown in Table 3 (which displays 5 slightly different cases of U_{11}). For a new coming traffic flow (flow No. 10) from host U, we try to find different decisions on unwanted traffic control by the system according to Algorithm 3. Figure 18 shows the filtering indicator in the five cases. We can see that the system will filter traffic No. 10 for U_2 and won't control this traffic for U_1. This is because the past detection reporting behavior of U_2 is similar to the nodes that mostly report flow No.10 as unwanted, while the past detection reporting behavior of U_1 is obviously different from these nodes (U_3-U_{11}).

Figure 12. Efficiency and robustness of unwanted traffic source detection under on-off hide evidence attack and Botnet infection: (a) 10% Botnet infection rate with 10% on-off hide evidence hosts; (b) 10% Botnet infection rate with 15% on-off hide evidence hosts; (c) 10% Botnet infection rate with 20% on-off hide evidence hosts; (d) 10% Botnet infection rate with 40% on-off hide evidence hosts.

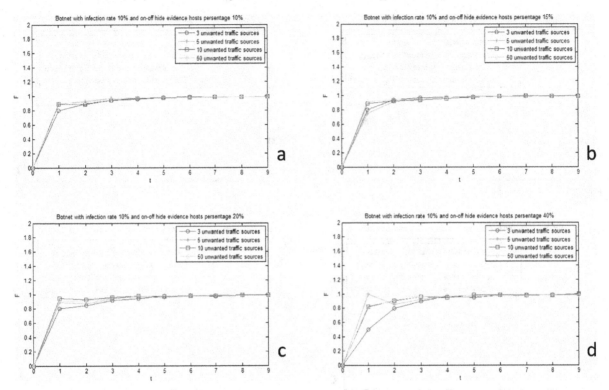

6. FURTHER DISCUSSIONS

6.1. Traffic Cost Based on Trust

We apply trust management to control unwanted traffic and propose to evolve the model of billing by taking into account the trust values of the entities. We aim to turn the cost from the unwanted traffic receivers to the sources in order to discourage unwanted traffic distribution, and thus achieve the objective of unwanted traffic control. Notably, the proposed system induces a new business model that determines traffic cost or issues communication bonus based on the trust values. This introduces an interesting study with regard to trust economy on the basis of the proposed trust management system. The proposed system encourages each host installing unwanted traffic detection software, which could benefit security software vendors.

Although the proposed system is verified accurate, robust and effective on unwanted traffic control, the success of system deployment in real practice greatly depends on the acceptance, adoption, and contribution of network entities (ISPs and hosts). In addition, the existence of selfish network entities makes network entities reluctant to contribute to the system (i.e., to cooperate with each other to control unwanted traffic), which creates a social dilemma. In another line of work, this problem is addressed by investigating the acceptance condition of the proposed system by applying a public goods based game. We considered the quality of network environment as public goods

Figure 13. Efficiency and robustness of unwanted traffic source detection under on-off bad mouthing attack and Botnet infection: (a) 10% Botnet infection rate with 10% on-off bad mouthing hosts; (b) 10% Botnet infection rate with 15% on-off bad mouthing hosts; (c) 10% Botnet infection rate with 20% on-off bad mouthing hosts; (d) 10% Botnet infection rate with 40% on-off bad mouthing hosts.

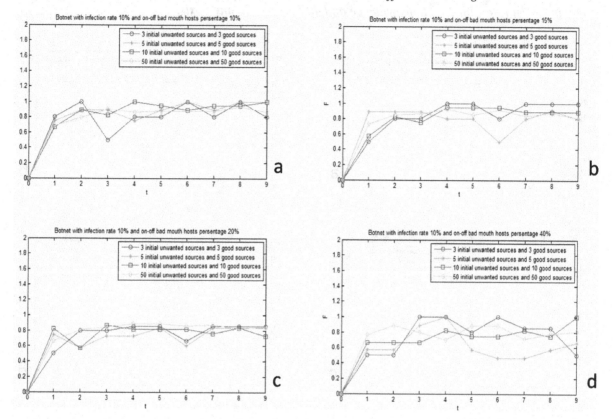

and formulated two games in both host layer and ISP layer for adoption analysis, respectively. To provide incentives for network entities to behave cooperatively, we further introduce a trust-based punishment mechanism to encourage cooperation behaviors of hosts and ISPs, which could play as a promising business model for deploying the proposed system. Based on our study, we also suggest an operating strategy for ISPs: to cooperate with antivirus vendors that free their toolkits in order to gain the maximum market share and benefit from this strategy from other business models. Our initial study shows a promising business potential of the proposed system for unwanted traffic control over the Internet.

6.2. Extra Communication Load

The extra traffic load caused by the system is reasonable since the detection reporting is triggered by a specific condition and the report only contains the following information:

- **From a Host to its ISP (Which can Be Forwarded to GTO by ISP):** Host ID, content IDs (with or without Sender IDs) and unwanted traffic detection values by the host;
- **From an ISP to GTO:** ISP ID, sender IDs and unwanted traffic detection values by the ISP.

Figure 14. Efficiency and robustness of unwanted traffic source detection under on-off hide evidence plus bad mouthing attack and Botnet infection: (a) 10% Botnet infection rate with 10% hide evidence and 10% bad mouthing hosts; (b) 10% Botnet infection rate with 15% hide evidence and 15% bad mouthing hosts; (c) 10% Botnet infection rate with 20% hide evidence and 20% bad mouthing hosts; (d) 10% Botnet infection rate with 40% hide evidence and 40% bad mouthing hosts.

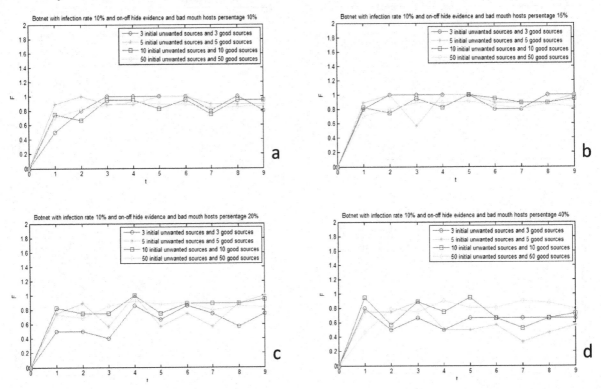

Figure 15. The efficiency of unwanted traffic detection in Botnet intrusion: a) unwanted traffic indication at a host; b) F-measure. (Yan, Kantola & Shen, 2012)

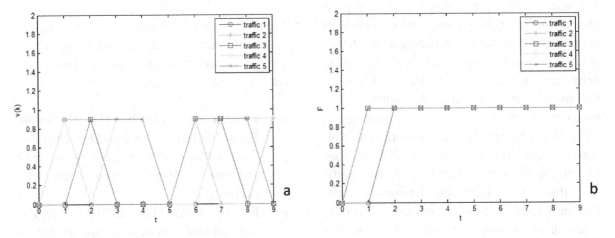

Figure 16. Unwanted traffic control performance under a malicious ISP attack: a) the detection trust of ISP; b) F measure. (Yan, Kantola & Shen, 2012)

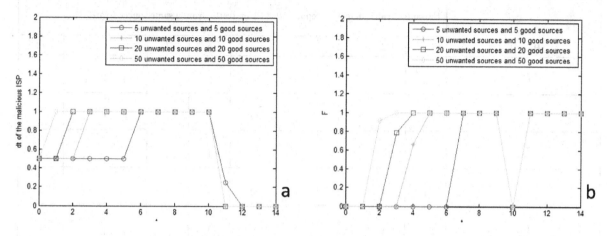

Figure 17. F measure of unwanted traffic detection in DDoS intrusion via reflectors: a) $tr_k^i\left(t\right) = \alpha t$, M'=1; b) $tr_k^i\left(t\right) = e^{\beta t}$, M'=1; c) $tr_k^i\left(t\right) = \alpha t$, M'=N; d) $tr_k^i\left(t\right) = e^{\beta t}$, M'=N. ($\alpha = 10$, 10^2, 10^3, 10^4, or 10^5; $\beta = 1$, 2, 4, 8, or 16) (Yan, Kantola & Shen, 2012)

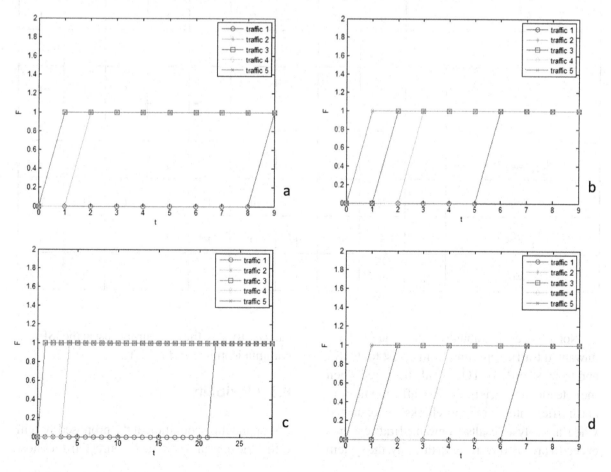

Table 3. Example Detection Reports

Host ID	Unwanted traffic detection reports $v_k^i(t)$ on traffic from a same source (traffic No.)									
	1	2	3	4	5	6	7	8	9	10
U_1	0	1	0	0	1	0	0	0	0	?
U_2	1	0	1	1	0	1	1	1	1	?
U_3	1	0	1	1	0	1	1	1	1	1
U_4	1	0	1	1	0	1	1	1	1	1
U_5	1	0	1	1	0	1	1	1	1	1
U_6	1	0	1	1	0	1	1	1	1	1
U_7	1	0	1	1	0	1	1	1	1	1
U_8	1	0	1	1	0	1	1	1	1	1
U_9	1	0	1	1	0	1	1	1	1	1
U_{10}	1	0	1	1	0	1	1	1	1	1
U_{11} (case1)	1	0	1	1	0	1	1	1	1	1
U_{11} (case 2)	1	1	1	1	0	1	1	1	1	1
U_{11} (case 3)	0	0	0	1	0	1	1	1	1	0
U_{11} (case 4)	0	1	0	1	0	1	1	1	1	1
U_{11} (case 5)	1	0	0	1	0	1	1	1	1	1

Notably, the communications requested for unwanted traffic reporting from a host to its ISP and from an ISP to GTO are only triggered when the detection/check is positive. Traffic monitoring and traffic content similarity checks are conducted when the analysis results of unwanted traffic source exceed a pre-set threshold. In this way, the system can greatly save the computing cost at the ISP and communication cost for UTC.

6.3. Flexibility

The application condition of the proposed system is that the unwanted traffic is sourced from a host

Figure 18: Personalized filtering indicator in five cases for two hosts with different past detection reporting behaviors

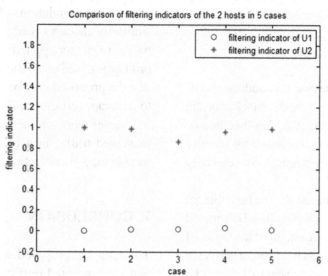

in the Internet and sent to other hosts through its local ISP. It is applicable to various unwanted traffic types, such as spam, spim, sipt, and so on. Automatic detection of web page spam remains a challenge. But if the web page or its link is sent in this way to other hosts, the system is still applicable.

6.4. Scalability

The scalability of the proposed system can be studied by either measuring or assuming a certain sending rate of evidence reports from each ISP, summing the rates at the GTO and assessing the required CPU cycles and memory needed to process all that evidence. In addition, the study needs to take into account the need to distribute the trust values of all entities as well as the black and grey lists to the ISPs. Scalability can be improved by capping the evidence sending rate by a local trust system to a maximum value irrespective of the level of hostile activity. By taking some time for local evidence aggregation and validation the

system can improve the quality of the evidence that is sent to the GTO. Based on the preliminary simulation study, the condition of the proposed system to work well is that the share of the Internet hosts that report detection honestly is above 60%.

The system improves the scalability of network based monitoring by making use of host based evidence collection and guiding the use of network based monitoring to the cases that are pointed by the aggregated evidence from hosts. The main role of network based monitoring is to collect conclusive evidence of malicious behaviors so that the ISP can act upon the host.

6.5. Privacy Preservation

One important and practical issue of the proposed system is related to privacy. Obviously, reporting intrusions to another party could cause bad influence on the system entities. Some hosts don't want other parties to know they are intruded since this could influence their reputation. Preserving the private information of hosts and ISP from GTO (i.e., their identity) and at the same time conducting unwanted traffic control is an interesting research topic.

6.6. Challenges

Under DDoS attack that uses source address spoofing, it is hard to put blame on the attacker or the source network of the attacker. Another line of work is needed to develop a solution for identity tracking, e.g., cooperative firewalls that can help with this problem.

By necessity in a simulator, the methods that are used for attack detection are simplified compared to the real network environment. The focus of simulation based evaluation has been in verifying that the trust management concept itself can be reasonably applied into the problem of unwanted traffic control. Future work is needed to integrate the trust processing algorithms with more realistic methods of intrusion detection.

6.7. Implementation

We have implemented a prototype system of the proposed system for SMS spam control in order to prove its concept design. The host functionalities were realized in Android mobile phones with Java. The ISP and GTO were implemented with Apache and PHP in a Windows 7 platform. The connection between the ISP, GTO and hosts is based on wireless LAN or cellular networks by applying the SSL security protocol. The communications between ISP and GTO are based on Internet with SSL. The implemented prototype system has three functional modules: Unwanted Traffic Control in host, Unwanted Traffic Control in ISP and Unwanted Traffic Control in GTO.

Practical test showed that the prototype can control SMS spam for mobile users. We further evaluated the system performance under a variety of intrusion and attacks and got similar results to those in simulation evaluation. Fortunately, we found that the prototype system performed much better under bad mouthing attack than the result achieved in simulations. This is because traffic similarity check worked in the prototype system, while it was not applied in the simulations. The prototype based evaluation results further proved that the proposed system is effective with regard to accuracy, efficiency and robustness. It is one of pioneer works in the literature for controlling unwanted traffic in a generic way by applying trust management technologies.

7. CONCLUSION

This chapter proposed a generic and comprehensive unwanted traffic control solution based on trust management by evaluating trust of each system entity at GTO and analyzing traffic and behaviors at hosts. We designed a number of algorithms for unwanted traffic detection and control at a host, unwanted traffic monitor at ISP, global trust evaluation at GTO and personalized unwanted traffic control decided at GTO. These algorithms can be adopted by the system to control unwanted traffic in both a distributed and centralized manner and in both a defensive and offensive way. The simulation results and prototype based evaluation show the effectiveness of the proposed system with regard to accuracy and efficiency for unwanted traffic control for Botnet intrusion and DDoS intrusion via reflectors, and robustness against system attacks raised by either hosts or ISPs, such as hide evidence attack, bad mouthing attack, on-off attack, malicious attack of ISP and the combinations of above, which play in conjunction with various traffic intrusions.

The research introduced in this chapter contributes to the literature in two folds: (1) it proposed an unwanted traffic control framework over the Internet or communication networks, which is more comprehensive and generic than previous work; (2) the proposed system is effective to control unwanted traffic under different intrusion models and robust against various system attacks caused by malicious or indifferent hosts or ISPs.

REFERENCES

Allman, E., Callas, J., Delany, M., Libbey, M., Fenton, J., & Thomas, M. (2007). *DomainKeys identified mail (DKIM) signatures*. RFC 4871 (Proposed Standard). Retrieved from http://www.ietf.org/rfc/rfc4871.txt

Bi, J., Wu, J., & Zhang, W. (2008). A trust and reputation based anti-spim method. [IEEE.]. *Proceedings - IEEE INFOCOM, 2008*, 2485–2493. doi:10.1109/INFOCOM.2008.319.

Bossardt, M., Dubendorfer, T., & Plattner, B. (2007). Enhanced Internet security by a distributed traffic control service based on traffic ownership. *Journal of Network and Computer Applications, 30*(3), 841–857. doi:10.1016/j.jnca.2005.07.006.

Grandison, T., & Sloman, M. (2000). A survey of trust in internet applications. *IEEE Communications and Survey, 3*(4), 2–16. doi:10.1109/COMST.2000.5340804.

Gyongyi, Z., Garcia-Molina, H., & Pedersen, J. (2004). Combating web spam with TrustRank. In *Proceedings of VLDB*, (pp. 576-587). VLDB.

Haskins, R., & Nielsen, D. (2004). *Slamming spam: A guide for system administrators*. Reading, MA: Addison-Wesley Professional.

Kolan, P., & Dantu, R. (2007). Socio-technical defense against voice spamming. *ACM Transactions on Autonomous and Adaptive Systems, 2*(1).

Liu, W., Aggarwal, S., & Duan, Z. (2009). Incorporating accountability into internet email. In *Proceedings of SAC '09*, (pp. 975-882). SAC.

Liu, Y. T., Gao, B., Liu, T. Y., Zhang, Y., Ma, Z. M., He, S. Y., & Li, H. (2008). BrowseRank: Letting web users vote for page importance. In *Proceedings of SIGIR*, (pp. 451-458). ACM. Janecek, A. G. K., Gansterer, W. N., & Kumar, K. A. (2008). Multi-level reputation-based greylisting. [ARES.]. *Proceedings of, ARES08*, 10–17.

McGibney, J., & Botvich, D. (2007). A trust overlay architecture and protocol for enhanced protection against spam. In *Proceedings of the Second International Conference on Availability, Reliability and Security* (ARES 2007), (pp. 749-756). ARES.

Meyer, T. A., & Whateley, B. (2004). Spambayes: Effective opensource, Bayesian based, email classification system. In *Proceedings of CEAS*. CEAS.

Page, L., Brin, S., Motwani, R., & Winograd, T. (1998). *The pagerank citation ranking: Bringing order to the web*. Palo Alto, CA: Stanford University.

Schwartz, A. (2004). *SpamAssassin*. Sebastopol, CA: O'Reilly Media, Inc..

Sun, Y., Han, Z., & Liu, K. J. R. (2008). Defense of trust management vulnerabilities in distributed networks. *IEEE Communications Magazine, 46*(2), 112–119. doi:10.1109/MCOM.2008.4473092.

Tang, Y., Krasser, S., He, Y., Yang, W., & Alperovitch, D. (2008). Support vector machines and random forests modeling for spam senders behavior analysis. In *Proceedings of IEEE GLOBECOM*, (pp. 1-5). IEEE.

Wang, J., Wang, F., Yan, Z., & Huang, B. (2011). Message receiver determination in multiple simultaneous IM conversations. *IEEE Intelligent Systems, 26*(3), 24–31. doi:10.1109/MIS.2010.33.

Wong, M., & Schlitt, W. (2006). *Sender policy framework (SPF) for authorizing use of domains in e-mail, version 1*. RFC 4408 (Experimental). Retrieved from http://www.ietf.org/rfc/rfc4408.txt

Wu, B., Goel, V., & Davison, B. D. (2006). Topical TrustRank: Using topicality to combat web spam. [IEEE.]. *Proceedings of WWW, 06*, 63–72.

Yan, Z. (2010). Security via trusted communications. In P. Stavroulakis, & M. Stamp (Eds.), *Handbook on Communications and Information Security* (pp. 719–746). Berlin: Springer. doi:10.1007/978-3-642-04117-4_33.

Yan, Z., Kantola, R., & Shen, Y. (2011). Unwanted traffic control via global trust management. [IEEE.]. *Proceedings of IEEE TrustCom, 2011*, 647–654.

Yan, Z., Kantola, R., & Shen, Y. (2012). Unwanted traffic control via hybrid trust management. [IEEE.]. *Proceedings of IEEE TrustCom, 2012*, 666–673.

Yan, Z., & Prehofer, C. (2011). Autonomic trust management for a component based software system. *IEEE Transactions on Dependable and Secure Computing, 8*(6), 810–823. doi:10.1109/TDSC.2010.47.

Yan, Z., Zhang, P., & Deng, R. H. (2012). TruBeRepec: A trust-behavior-based reputation and recommender system for mobile applications. *Journal of Personal and Ubiquitous Computing, 16*(5), 485–506. doi:10.1007/s00779-011-0420-2.

Zhang, H., Duan, H., Liu, W., & Wu, J. (2009). IPGroupRep: A novel reputation based system for anti-spam. In *Proceedings of the Symposia and Workshops on Ubiquitous, Autonomic and Trusted Computing*, (pp. 513-518). IEEE.

Zhang, J., Xu, W., Peng, Y., & Xu, J. (2010). MailTrust: A mail reputation mechanism based on improved TrustGuard. [CMC.]. *Proceedings of, CMC10*, 218–222.

Zhang, X., Han, B., & Liang, W. (2009). Automatic seed set expansion for trust propagation based anti-spamming algorithms. [WIDM.]. *Proceedings of WIDM, 09*, 31–38. doi:10.1145/1651587.1651596.

Zheleva, E., Kolcz, A., & Getoor, L. (2008). Trusting spam reporters: A reporter-based reputation system for email filtering. *ACM Transactions on Information Systems, 27*(1). doi:10.1145/1416950.1416953.

ENDNOTES

[1]   http://www.oecd.org/document/54/0,3746,en_2649_34225_38690102_1_1_1_1,00.html, referred Jan 25, 2012

APPENDIX

Questions and Exercises

1. Can you propose another method to conduct traffic intrusion detection at host, i.e., a mechanism to be applied at the host to detect its local intrusion?
2. Could you present your opinion on the influence of the trust management system for unwanted traffic control over the Internet, e.g., from telecommunication economy point of view?

Chapter 6
Trust Management for Pervasive Social Networking

ABSTRACT

Self-organized networks based on mobile devices (e.g., Mobile Ad Hoc Networks [MANET]) are becoming a practical platform for pervasive social networking. People, either familiar or strangers, communicate with each other via such a network for instant social activities. How to help mobile users to build up trust in pervasive social networking is becoming an important and interesting issue. Trust concerns not only security, but also privacy, as well as quality of social networking experiences. It relates to many properties that are essential for establishing a trust relationship in ephemeral and dynamically changed pervasive social environments. This chapter reviews the literature with regard to how to build up trust in pervasive social networking. The authors explore whether pervasive social networking is demanded, considering many existing popular Internet social networking services. Based on a need assessment survey, they propose a trust management framework that supports context-aware trust/reputation generation, trustworthy content recommendations, secure communications, unwanted traffic control, user privacy recommendations, and secure face-to-face pervasive social communications. Simulations, prototype implementation, and user experiments further prove the effectiveness of the proposed solutions.

1. INTRODUCTION

With the rapid growth of mobile computing and social networking technology, social network has extended its popularity from the Internet to mobile domain. Personal mobile devices (e.g., smart phones) could be self-organized and communicate with each other for social activities by forming a multi-hop radio network and maintaining connectivity in a decentralized manner. We call such kind of social networking based on mobile devices that supports instant and pervasive social activities as pervasive social networking (PSN). Nowadays, mobile ad hoc network (MANET) has become a practical platform for pervasive social networking and computing, playing as a valuable

DOI: 10.4018/978-1-4666-4765-7.ch006

Copyright © 2014, IGI Global. Copying or distributing in print or electronic forms without written permission of IGI Global is prohibited.

extension and complement of traditional Internet social networks. For example, a user could query people in vicinity using his/her mobile device about which shop is on sale, which movie is recommended to see, or which mobile application should be installed for tagging the locations of photos. The user neighbors can respond these queries by providing their recommendations via PSN. The user could also chat with people nearby via PSN with regard to sharing a taxi ride, or sharing the cost of a series of movie tickets. Moreover, they can seek services or aids from strangers in vicinity through PSN. People who are strangers but regularly in the same public places could want to make an instant appointment for a face-to-face meeting. This kind of social networking is very valuable for mobile users, especially when fixed networks (e.g., the Internet) or mobile networks are temporarily unavailable or costly to access.

Several research groups in academia have focused on social activities based on mobile ad hoc networks. Stanford MobiSocial Group has developed Junction, a mobile ad hoc and multiparty platform for MANET applications (retrieved from http://openjunction.org/). Micro-blog (retrieved from http://synrg.ee.duke.edu/microblog.html), developed by SyNRG in Duke University, helps users to post micro-blogs tagged by locations. AdSocial (Sarigöl et al., 2009), introduced by ETHz Systems Group, provides a pervasive social communication platform. Floating content concept was analyzed based on a theoretical framework to study the fundamental quantities of an ephemeral content sharing service in opportunistic networking, such as node encounter rate, mean contact times as a function of location, achievable transmission rates and transmission ranges (Hyytia et al, 2011; Ott et al, 2011). In a proposed floating content system, content is only shared within an anchor zone in a best-effort manner, i.e., copies are kept available within that zone while they are deleted outside the anchor zone.

In industry, quite a number of companies, such as Microsoft, Nokia and Intel have conducted

researches in the area of PSN. For example, Microsoft Research Asia developed EZSetup system in order to make a mobile user find services provided by his/her neighbors (retrieved from http://research.microsoft.com/en-us/groups/wn/mssn.aspx). The Nokia Instant Community (NIC) (retrieved from https://lausanne.nokiaresearch.com/nic/) developed by the Nokia Research Center provides an instant social networking platform to allow people in vicinity to communicate, get to know, and share information with each other (Ahtiainen et al, 2009). Similarly, Intel Berkeley Lab ran a project named Familiar Stranger based on mobile devices to extend our feelings and relationships with strangers that we regularly observe but do not interact with in public places (retrieved from http://www.paulos.net/research/intel/familiarstranger/index.htm). A familiar stranger is an individual who is recognized from regular activities, but with whom one does not interact. This concept was first identified by Stanley Milgram (Milgram, 1972). It has become an increasingly popular concept in research about social networks. Because group mobility is very common in modern life (Guo, Yan & Wang, 2010), PSN is becoming more and more valuable for mobile users, especially when they are familiar strangers and often appear in vicinity.

However, trust, security and privacy aspects in pervasive social networking have not seriously considered in existing projects. Traditional centralized social networking systems (e.g., facebook) have not taken user privacy into concern. They cannot satisfy instant social networking demands, especially when users do not have internet connection, but with location proximity. Issues on trust management for security assurance and privacy enhancement need serious research in order to deploy a practical pervasive social networking system that can be easily accepted by mobile users. More importantly, a number of crucial issues with regard to trust, security and privacy should be solved towards a trustworthy pervasive social networking.

First, key management for secure data access control in PSN should adapt to trust levels of users and social contexts. Due to the dynamic changes of PSN topology and user trust level, the encryption key used for securing social communications needs to be frequently changed and the decryption key should be distributed to each of the eligible users. This introduces a heavy traffic and processing load, which may cause a serious performance bottleneck. How to automatically control PSN data access in a secure and efficient way is a challenge. Most existing work in PSN didn't provide a solution to control social communication data access and effectively support user revocation. Past key management solutions didn't consider applying the trust level of users and context attributes as control conditions for data access (Bethencourt, Sahai & Waters, 2007; Goyal, Pandey, Sahai & Waters, 2006; Muller, Katzenbeisser & Eckert, 2008; Sahai & Waters, 2005; Wang, Liu & Wu, 2010). Thus they are not effective in practice.

Second, a practical privacy enhanced trust management system with context awareness and easy user acceptance is demanded in PSN. During pervasive social networking, how much should the user trust with each other in order to make a decision? On the other hand, users generally want to preserve personal privacy and avoid malicious tracking. Although there are a number of research activities about PSN in academia and industry, issues on usable and autonomic trust management for adaptive security assurance and privacy enhancement still need serious research. Herein, we define trust as the confidence, belief, and expectation regarding the reliability, integrity, ability, or character of an entity. Reputation is a measure derived from direct or indirect knowledge/experience on earlier interactions of entities and is used to assess the level of trust put into an entity.

Third, control unwanted traffic is another crucial issue in PSN. Herein, the unwanted content is defined as the content that is not expected by its destination or consumer. People communicate in different contexts for different purposes, various content information flows. Examples are a mobile application installation link, a URL of a service, a web page and a textual message typed by a user. However, at the time when mobile users expect useful and valuable contents via PSN, they may also receive unwanted or unexpected contents, for example, malware; a virus and Trojan; spammed emails, www pages, VoIP voice, Instant Messaging, short messages, and web contents; Denial of Service (DoS) and Distributed Denial of Service (DDoS) Attacks. The unwanted contents could intrude user devices, consume user time, occupy user device memory and irritate the users. How much should a user trust different contents received over the PSN? What contents are unwanted by the users, thus should be controlled? Controlling unwanted contents becomes a crucial issue in PSN.

Fourth, a context-aware recommender system for user privacy preservation is expected in PSN. For accessing services in PSN, a mobile user may be requested to share personal information and data (e.g., user profile and location information) with other node service providers. Privacy becomes a crucial issue in PSN because it is the ability of an entity to seclude itself or information about itself and thereby reveal itself selectively. However, it is normally difficult for a user to justify whether it is safe and proper to disclose personal data to others in different contexts. In addition, privacy is a subjective issue. Different users treat personal privacy differently even in the same situation. To solve all above problems, there is a demand to provide a context-aware recommender system for user privacy that could help the user make a decision on personal data sharing in PSN.

Finally, it is essential to provide an approach to let people who communicated before via pervasive social networking or other networks securely recognize with each other and physically meet in an easy way. Various instant social activities can be supported by PSN. For some social activities, after anonymous digital communications, people in proximity, but unfamiliar with each other would like to meet for further face-to-face contact. How to make unknown people to meet without mismatch and avoid troubles after digital communications? How to sustain their initially established trust through right recognition in crowds? How to preserve their privacy (e.g., still using nick names and hiding real names) but assure correct recognition in a secure and fashionable way? How to fight against malicious persons who may personate somebody for face-to-face contact? Obviously, an approach for secure recognition for pervasive face-to-face social communications is needed. However, literature still lacks an efficient, secure and convenient manner that allows strangers to recognize with each other in pervasive social communications.

This chapter explores whether pervasive social networking is demanded, considering many existing popular Internet social networking services. Based on a need assessment survey, we propose a hybrid trust management framework – PSN-Trust that supports context-aware trust/reputation generation, trustworthy recommendations, secure communications, unwanted traffic control, user privacy recommendation, and secure and fashionable recognition in PSN. We did a series of simulations, implemented a number of prototype systems and conducted user experiments to prove the effectiveness of the proposed solutions. In PSNTrust, we apply a trusted server (TS) who knows the node's real identity to calculate node trust, content reputations, a recommendation vector for privacy preservation based on historical PSN experiences and behaviors, aiming to support the social decisions of PSN nodes. The trusted server can also be applied to manage keys used for secure PSN data communications, playing in parallel with the key management processed by each PSN node.

The rest of the chapter is organized as follows. Section 2 reviews literature background and related work. We introduce the result of a need assessment survey to investigate how users consider and expect to cope with a reputation system for pervasive social networking in Section 3. Next, we describe the design of a trust management framework - PSNTrust for PSN in Section 4. Section 5 reports the main properties for trust that are supported by the framework. Simulation results, prototype implementation and the findings and implications of user experiments are presented in Section 6. In Section 7, we further discussion a number of interesting issues related to trust, security and privacy of PSN and conclude the whole chapter by discussing its contributions and suggesting future work. This chapter is based on the work presented by Yan et al. (2013).

2. THE STATE-OF-ART

2.1 Trust and Reputation Mechanism

Trust and reputation mechanisms have been widely studied in various fields of distributed systems, such as ad hoc networks, peer-to-peer (P2P) systems, Grid computing, pervasive computing and e-commerce (Yan, 2010). Many mechanisms have been developed for supporting trusted communications and collaborations among computing nodes (Sun, Yu, Han & Liu, 2006; Theodorakopoulos & Baras, 2006; Yan & Holtmanns, 2008). Examples are FuzzyTrust system (Song, Hwang, Zhou & Kwok, 2005), the eBay user feedback system (Resnick & Zeckhauser, 2002), PeerTrust model (Xiong & Liu, 2004), an objective trust management framework (OTMF) for MANET (Li, Li & Kato, 2008) and Credence - a robust and decentralized system for evaluating the reputation of files in a P2P system (Walsh & Sirer, 2005). Some work evaluates trust based on social relationships (Trifunovic, Legendre & Anastasiades, 2010). In these researches, trust can be modeled, calculated and thus expressed using a value. However, none of the above studies consider how to evaluate trust and reputation based on social networking behaviors and experiences, especially in the context of pervasive social networking.

None of them support user privacy. Some factors influencing trust in PSN are never considered in the previous work. Moreover, only little work in the literature develops a reputation system driven by the concern of users (Yan & Niemi, 2009). A reputation rating system based on past behavior of evaluators was proposed by Kujimura and Nishihara (2003). Trust in the evaluator indexes its impact on the rating system. The trust value is dynamically adjusted based on past estimation performance. In PSNTrust, the user reputation is adjusted based on his/her past social performance. It is evaluated by each individual node and the TS based on ephemeral and historical experiences, respectively.

The existing recommendation based trust/reputation mechanisms aim to support secure node collaboration for the purpose of routing and networking. Seldom, they concern trust, security and privacy issues in applications and services by applying MANET as a social networking and computing platform (Zouridaki, Mark, Hejmo & Thomas, 2006).

2.2 Trust and Reputation System Architecture

Jøsang et al. classified trust/reputation system architecture into two main types: centralized and distributed (Jøsang, Ismail & Boyd, 2007). The system architecture determines how ratings and reputation scores are communicated between participants in a reputation system. In the literature, distributed trust evaluations have been studied in MANET, but seldom the solutions support node privacy (Sun, Yu, Han & Liu, 2006; Theodora-kopoulos & Baras, 2006; Raya, Papadimitratos, Gligory & Hubaux, 2008). This could cause potential attacks such as bad mouthing attack or unfair rating attack targeting at a specific node (Sun, Han & Liu, 2008). Most existing systems maintain a statistical representation of reputation by borrowing tools from the realms of game theory (Buchegger & Boudec, 2002; Michiardi &

Molva, 2002) and Bayesian analytics (Buchegger & Boudec, 2003). These systems try to counter selfish routing misbehavior of nodes by enforcing nodes to cooperate with each other and counter any arbitrary misbehavior of nodes. However, little attention has been paid to the content and social communication reputation issue in MANET with node privacy as a main concern. On the other hand, practical reputation systems generally apply a centralized server to collect feedback for reputation generation, e.g., eBay (Resnick & Zeckhauser, 2002), Yahoo auctions (Resnick, Kuwabara, Zeckhauser & Friedman, 2000), and Internet-based systems such as Keynote (Blaze, Feigenbaum & Lacy, 1996). However, many existing systems (e.g., Amazon and eBay) lack considerations on the credibility of a user's rating. This greatly influences the quality of produced reputations. The usage of pseudonym and the ease of its change additionally complicate the picture by allowing participants to effectively erase their prior history. PSNTrust adopts a hybrid trust management system architecture in PSN to overcome the weakness of the above two types of architecture, where reputation is evaluated in a distributed way, but with the support of a centralized TS.

Recently, a number of reputation systems have been proposed in the context of digital contents and social networking. For example, Adler and Alfaro proposed a content driven reputation system for Wikipedia authors solely on the basis of content evolution; but not on user-to-user comments or ratings (Adler & Alfaro, 2007). The concept of data centric trust in volatile environments, such as ad hoc networks, was introduced by Raya, Papadimitratos, Gligory and Hubaux (2008) to evaluate the node trust through the data reported by it. Gupta, et al. proposed a partially distributed reputation system for P2P systems by introducing a reputation computation agent (RCA) (Gupta, Judge & Ammar, 2003). But this system does not concern the challenges caused by privacy enhancement and context awareness. In addition, the RCA is applied only for calculating peer's reputation based on its contributions to the system. This is not suitable for the PSN scenario. For managing the trust in PSN, the TS is applied to update the node user reputation on the basis of long-term historical social behaviors.

2.3 Problems of Trust and Reputation Management

In most reputation systems in the ad hoc networks, the reputation of a node is shared globally in the network. The purpose is to make the reputation of a node known to all other nodes and decrease the detection time. Thus maintaining and disseminating indirect reputation information incur overhead at both the individual node and the network. OCEAN discounts second-hand reputation exchange and only utilizes local reputation based on direct observations in order to achieve a reasonable performance (Bansal & Baker, 2003). PSNTrust concerns both local-aware and global-aware reputations by aggregating local experiences and global experiences together. By deploying the TS, the overhead of reputation maintenance and dissemination is eliminated among PSN nodes.

Inconsistent reputation problem (i.e. different nodes may have different reputation values for the same node) often occurs in the ad hoc networks due to subjective reason and/or different local experiences. This makes it hard to distinguish correct reputation ratings from reputation voting messages. LARS (Locally Aware Reputation System) (Hu & Burmester, 2006) was proposed to deal with selfish behaviors and malicious behaviors (e.g., packet dropping and unfair rating). In LARS, the reputation of a node is derived from direct observation and exchange of second hand reputation information is disallowed. PSNTrust applies the TS to unify node reputation based on local experiences reported by nodes. This reputation information is issued to the node by the TS. Serving as the initial value of reputation, it is further evolved based on experiences newly collected at the individual node. In addition, the

above process is iterated. Thereby, we avoid the inconsistent reputation problem and eliminate user reputation inaccuracy caused by multi-hop reputation dissemination. Reputation generation is based on first-hand experiences and direct votes no matter at the TS or the node.

Nowadays, reputation systems may face the problem of unfair ratings by artificially inflating or deflating reputations (Resnick & Zeckhauser, 2002; Resnick, Kuwabara, Zeckhauser & Friedman, 2000; Corritore, Kracher & Wiedenbeck, 2003; Yang, Sun, Kay & Yang, 2009). They are vulnerable to a number of potential attacks, such as Sybil attack, on-off attack, independent/collaborative bad mouthing attack, and conflict behavior attack, ballot stuffing attack, and new-comer attack (Douceur, 2002; Liu, Yau, Peng & Yin, 2008). The usage of pseudonyms introduces new challenges since it makes hard to trace malicious behaviors. It also influences the accuracy of reputation. Sun et al. proposed a number of schemes to overcome some of the above attacks, but they did not consider the additional challenges caused by privacy preservation and context awareness (Sun, Han & Liu, 2008; Sun, Han, Yu & Liu, 2006). PSNTrust aims to overcome the above traditional attacks and challenges in the trust management of PSN.

2.4 Projects of Pervasive Social Networking

Several research groups have focused on social activities based on mobile ad-hoc networks. Stanford MobiSocial Group has developed Junction, a mobile ad hoc and multiparty platform for MANET applications. Micro-blog, developed by SyNRG in Duke University, helps users to post micro-blogs tagged by locations and viewed by others. It supports query, chatting and recommendation in ad-hoc networks. Posts about different contents are floating on the map of the application user interface. Whenever a user travels, posts about the location are floated to the user. If there is no enough information, users can query in ad-hoc networks, and replies could be added to the current location. It can be applied in many application areas such as tourism, advertisement, emergent alerts and so on. AdSocial, introduced by ETHz Systems Group, is a pervasive social communication platform based on MANET. Important functions include Presence Detector, Buddy Search and chatting, VoIP calls, video calls and ad-hoc games. It supports real time communication with friends. Example use cases are chatting in a bar or on a train. Besides that, AdSocial supports multiple message exchange methods, e.g., through Wifi and Bluetooth. However, trust and reputation in social networking are not concerned in these projects. In addition, secure recognition for face-to-face meeting between strangers after pervasive social networking is not considered at all. On the other hand, traditional centralized social networking systems (e.g., Facebook) have not taken the above issues into account. They cannot support instant social face-to-face meeting in a secure, easy and fashionable way, especially when users do not have Internet connection, but with location proximity.

2.5 Recommendation Services

Advogato (retrieved from http://www.advogato.org/) is an online service to provide a platform for free software developers to advocate software and promote research. One significant impact of Advogato is its trust metrics behind the service, which is the basis of many research projects (retrieved from http://www.advogato.org/trust-metric.html). Advogato trust metric stimulates users to contribute quality ensured software and protects against attacks. However, Advogato only applies a centralized architecture for reputation generation, whilst PSNTrust adopts hybrid reputation system architecture.

Netflix prize (retrieved from http://www.netflixprize.com/) is a competition to encourage the design of best movie recommendation algorithms. However, privacy is becoming a concern for Netflix algorithms since 2007 (retrieved from http://

en.wikipedia.org/wiki/Netflix_Prize). PSNTrust enhances privacy through frequent change of pseudonyms in PSN, but at the same time keeping track of user reputation information by applying a centralized TS that can map the user's pseudonyms to his/her real identity.

MovieLens (retrieved from http://www.movielens.org/login) is a movie sharing and recommendation website developed by GroupLens Research (retrieved from http://www.grouplens.org/) at the University of Minnesota. While MovieLens focuses on movie (content) reputation, PSNTrust can provide node reputation and content reputation for the purpose of content recommendation based on social behaviors in PSN.

2.6 User Interface Trust

A lot of work has been conducted regarding user interface design in order to improve user trust, mainly for web sites and in the context of e-commerce. Still, prior art left rooms for further studies on the effects of trust information on social networking and, in particular, on how to provide trust information for mobile users. PSNTrust uses a reputation indicator to indicate each user's local reputation during pervasive social networking and provide detailed information about local reputation generation and global reputation. They are interface design elements that provide the cue of trust information in pervasive social services. Particularly, a user's local reputation could play as the credibility of a user's voting on other users. But few previous researches investigated visualizing reputation's effects on mobile users in the context of pervasive social networking. It is an indispensible issue that should be considered for usable trust management.

2.7 Unwanted Content Control based on Trust Management

A number of anti-spam solutions were proposed based on trust/reputation management. Examples are MailTrust (Zhang, Xu, Peng & Xu, 2010) and IRGroupRep (Zhang, Duan, Liu & Wu, 2009) based on user feedback, a reporter-based reputation system for email filtering (Zheleva, Kolcz & Getoor, 2008), SpimRank for Instant Messaging according to user history tracks (Bi, Wu & Zhang, 2008). Tang, et al. (2008) proposed a solution based on spam sender behavior analysis. A few of studies are focusing on web spam control, such as TrustRank, Topical TrustRank, PageRank, etc. (Wu, Goel & Davison, 2006; Zhang, Han & Liang, 2009; Becchetti et al, 2006). Kolan and Dantu (2007) proposed a spam filter based on presence (location, mood and time), trust, reputation, voice specific trust and reputation analysis. It is a specific unwanted traffic control mechanism used to filter voice spam via VoIP. Based on our knowledge, few existing studies try to solve the issue of unwanted content control in social networking, particularly in pervasive social networking, which, however, is a crucial issue for the success of services based on PSN.

2.8 Recommendation for Privacy Preservation

Recommender systems generally apply information filtering technique that attempts to recommend information items (e.g., films, books, web pages, music, etc.) that are likely to be of interest to users (Resnick & Varian, 1997). Typically, a recommender system compares a user profile to some reference characteristics, and seeks to predict the 'rating' that a user would give to an item they had not yet experienced (Hancock, Toma & Ellison, 2007). These characteristics may be from an information item (a content-based approach) or a user's social environment (a collaborative filtering approach) (Su & Khoshgoftaar, 2009). O'Donovan & Smyth (2005) introduced using trust as both weighting and filtering in recommendations. The recommendation partners should have similar tastes of preferences and they should be trustworthy with a history of making reliable

recommendations. This trust information can be incorporated into the recommendation process. But to our knowledge, most characteristics used for recommendations are not based on users' private data sharing behaviors, which however is an important clue to imply users' preferences on privacy. In PSNTrust, we consider both recommender's trust and service provider's trust in the generation of recommendations. Little exiting work provides recommendations on user data privacy preservation, especially in pervasive/instant social services with context-awareness (Resnick & Varian, 1997; Luo, Le & Chen, 2009). Although some recommender systems concerns privacy preservation, seldom they support mobile social services (Polat & Du, 2005; Luo, Le & Chen, 2009; Li, Gao & Du, 2009; Bilge & Polat, 2010; Ahn & Amatriain, 2010; Tada, Kikuchi & Puntheeranurak, 2010; Kikuchi, Kizawa & Tada, 2009; Katzenbeisser & Petkovic, 2008).

Privacy preservation has been considered in a number of existing recommender systems. A scheme for binary rating-based top-N recommendation on horizontally partitioned data was proposed by Polat and Du (2005). In this scheme, two parties own disjoint sets of users' ratings for the same items to preserve data owners' privacy. A recommender system applies a privacy-preserving agent that adopts a k-anonymity technique to prevent the data circulated in the system from attackers' access by reasoning, statistic analysis and data mining (Luo, Le & Chen, 2009). Some work improves the collaborative filtering (CF) approach in order to preserve privacy, e.g., a privacy-preserving CF algorithm based on non-negative matrix factorization (NMF) and random perturbation techniques (Li, Gao & Du, 2009), a naive Bayesian classifier-based privacy-preserving recommender system by utilizing pre-processing (Bilge & Polat, 2010), expert collaborative filtering (Ahn & Amatriain, 2010), a CF protocol based on similarity between items, instead of similarity between users (Tada, Kikuchi & Puntheeranurak, 2010). Another classic solution for privacy preservation is applying cryptographic privacy enhancing protocols. However, large overhead in performing cryptographic operations is a practical issue, especially in a mobile domain. A couple of efficient schemes were proposed to reduce the preference matrix of the sets of items and users in order to improve the efficiency of cryptographic operations (Kikuchi, Kizawa & Tada, 2009). Current research focuses on preserving user data provided for generating recommendations without leaking the private information of users to service providers, not on recommendations for the purpose of user data privacy, which is the focus of PSNTrust. Meanwhile, PSNTrust adopts TS to support the frequent change of node pseudonyms in order to avoid potential privacy tracking.

We can find a number of solutions for context-aware or personalized recommendations (Yu et al, 2006; Yap, Tan & Pang, 2007; Wang, Kodama, Takada & Li, 2010; Zhang & Yu, 2007; Chuong, Torabi & Loke, 2009; Liiv, Tammet, Ruotsalo & Kuusik, 2009; Liu, Meng & Chen, 2008; Xiao, Zou, Ng & Nigul, 2010; Seetharam & Ramakrishnan, 2008; Berkovsky, De Luca & Said, 2010). However, none of them provide recommendations on user data privacy preservation. Most of them, e.g., CoMeR (Yu et al, 2006) and SCAMREF (Zhang & Yu, 2007), apply client-server architecture, while PSNTrust supports both centralized and distributed recommendation generation at TS and in PSN nodes. Yu et al. proposed a hybrid media recommendation approach CoMeR by integrating content-based approach, Bayesian-classifier approach and rule-based approach together to support context awareness (Yu et al, 2006). Yap et al. presented a recommender system based on Bayesian networks (BNs) that minimizes context acquisition. Their context model is trimmed until it contains the minimal set of context parameters that are important to a user (Yap, Tan & Pang, 2007). A novel sequential pattern mining algorithm was proposed to mine the group patterns of context (Wang, Kodama, Takada & Li, 2010). PSNTrust uses a context ID to identify a context that is de-

scribed with context parameters and their values. It supports context awareness by recommending a private data sharing strategy on different types of data in different contexts.

3. NEED ASSESSMENT

A usable trust management methodology was applied in the design of PSNTrust (Yan & Niemi, 2009). For the details of this methodology for usable trust management, refer to Chapter 9. The purpose is to consider the preference and expectation of users as early as possible thus effectively saving the cost of the system development and enhancing user acceptance. Following this method, a need assessment survey was conducted in order to explore the potential usefulness and significance to develop a trust management system for PSN, and the preference of users with regard to reputation visualization. A 5-point Likert scale was applied in the survey.

3.1 Design

The survey contains two parts. The first part evaluates the potential significance of developing trust/reputation management for PSN based on three PSN scenarios:

Scenario 1: sharing the cost of ´buy 3 pay 2´ goods in a shopping mall: Right now you are at a shopping center, and a product you want is on sale with a condition that ´buy 3 pay 2´. However, you only need one. You want to ask strangers nearby, via your mobile phone, whether they want to share the discount with you.

Scenario 2: sharing the price of a packet of 5 movie tickets in front of a movie theater: After shopping, you want to watch Avatar in a movie theater. The ticket price is 13.8e. However, if you buy a packet of 5 tickets, it will be 8.6e for each. You want to share the ticket packet with strangers nearby. You discuss with them whether they want to share the discount with you via your mobile phone.

Scenario 3: sharing a taxi ride after movie: After the movie, a lot of people are leaving the theatre. You want to watch a figure skating competition quite far away. You would like to take a taxi and think about sharing a ride. You discuss with people nearby via your mobile phone whether they want to share the ride with you.

The participants were asked to express their opinions on the usefulness of a reputation system in the above pervasive social scenarios.

The second part attempts to study the user preference on reputation visualization. We proposed 4 visualization methods, as illustrated in Table 1: UI1 – reputation is indicated based on the font size of an input chatting message; UI2 – reputation is indicated by the number of stars; UI3 – reputation is indicated through a growing process of a cartoon character; UI4 – reputation is indicated through a role in a community, which can be customized by a user. We asked the participants to mark their preferences. Note that UI2 is a traditional reputation visualization method applied by Amazon and eBay.

3.2 Participants and Results

We conducted the survey in Finland and China and collected the survey response via email. A small gift was awarded to each participant. We got a total of 107 valid responses; among them 83 were university students, 68 (63.6%) male and 39 (36.4%) female, most participants were between 21-28 years old. All of them had Internet social networking experiences, 84.1% had mobile social networking experiences, and 18.7% had experience on MANET based pervasive social networking.

The survey result and its implication are summarized as below:

Table 1. Reputation visualization methods (Yan, Chen & Shen, 2013)

1. The average rating scales regarding the potential usefulness of a reputation system in three pervasive social networking scenarios were 3.74 (SD=1.08), 3.90 (SD=.98) and 4.00 (SD=1.00), respectively. All of them are over 3.5. This implies that a reputation system for PSN (e.g., pervasive social chatting) is thought as useful in some scenarios. Therefore, it is a significant contribution to design and develop such a system.

2. Most participants preferred the traditional reputation visualization style UI2 (with

an average value 4.07), but they were also interested in the new styles UI3 and UI4 proposed by us (UI3-3.32 and UI4-3.21). However, the font size based reputation indication was disliked (UI1-2.50). Some participants commented that UI4 design is very interesting and expect an implementation for optional selection. In addition, other schemes of UI2 design (e.g., the number of crowns or diamonds) were also preferred by the participants. Thus, personalized reputation visualization is suggested in practice.

This need assessment gave us confidence to develop PSNTrust for managing trust in the context of PSN. Meanwhile, we found that PSNTrust should provide personalized reputation visualization to its users.

4. PSNTRUST: A TRUST MANAGEMENT FRAMEWORK

We design PSNTrust, a trust management framework for pervasive social networking. This framework can provide context-aware trust management for different PSN scenarios and support key management, secure data communications, unwanted content control, privacy preservation and secure face-to-face recognition.

4.1 System Design Requirements

A number of constraints and requirements are raised in the practical deployment of such a framework. We summarize them as basic requirements of PSNTrust design.

First, the framework is expected to support user privacy. Node real identity should be hidden in PSN. Node pseudonym could be frequently changed in order to enhance privacy and avoid potential tracking; whilst the node real identity can be registered at a trusted party.

Second, the nodes can connect to the trusted server periodically (e.g., 1 time per day) although real time connection is not always available.

Third, a small amount of transferring data is preferred among PSN node-to-node communications in order to achieve effective power consumption (Ahtiainen et al, 2009). However, there is no such strict constraint with regard to message length for the node and TS communications.

Forth, PSNTrust aims at overcoming potential system attacks. Especially, PSNTrust can fight against the attacks on itself, such as bad-mouthing attack, collaborative bad-mouthing attack, on-off attack, conflict behavior attack, etc.

Fifth, the system provides a mechanism to allow each node to control/filter traffic sourced from a distrusted node. It has capability to identify a malicious node and filter messages from it based on reputation evaluation.

Sixth, the information or message communicated between the TS and PSNTrust nodes should be protected to avoid malicious attacks; the confidentiality of PSN communications should be protected in a certain level in order to achieve expected efficiency.

Finally, PSNTrust should support various mobile social services and provide trust and reputation information according to the context of social behaviors. That is PSNTrust supports scalability, flexibility and context-awareness.

4.2 Reasons to Introduce a Centralized Trusted Server

Introducing the centralized TS into the hybrid trust management framework of PSNTrust has a number of practical merits. First, this design can support privacy preservation by frequently changing the pseudonyms of nodes and avoid inconsistent reputation problem. It can support accurate node reputation/trust evaluation based on the registered unique node ID even though the node pseudonyms could be changed. Second, this design provides an economic approach to collect useful data from pervasive social networking that can further support other promising services, e.g., location based content recommendation services. Thereby, the design can potentially support new business models. Finally and more importantly, this design is flexible to provide the reputation information no matter the TS is available or not. PSNTrust can generate reputation in either a distributed or centralized manner or both.

In PSNTrust, we assume that TS is trustworthy enough to preserve the private data of nodes. A potential weakness is that each party should trust TS, thus the TS could be the target of attackers. Notably, PSNTrust can also work in a distributed way based on the node pseudonyms when TS is not available.

4.3 PSNTrust System Structure

We can find both distributed and centralized reputation architecture in the literature. Both have advantages and disadvantages (Jøsang, Ismail & Boyd, 2007). We attempt to utilize their advantages in the PSNTrust design. Figure 1 illustrates the structure of PSNTrust. It is a hybrid trust management infrastructure. At each node device, a User Behavior Observer records node communications (e.g., chatting) to generate real user behavior based trust cue (Yan, Zhang & Deng, 2012). A PSN UI (i.e., a set of PSN applications, e.g., TWIN, GhostTalk, Facebook/Linkedin friends) provides a user interface for the node user to do social networking. Communication Reporter and Voter report the communication records and lo-

Figure 1. PSNTrust system structure

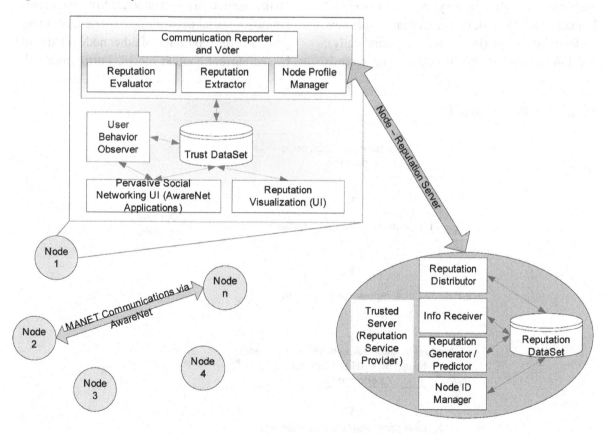

cal reputation information to the TS. Meanwhile, the user can also vote other nodes through it to the TS. A Reputation Evaluator evaluates node reputation and provides the results to the user via a Reputation Visualization UI. A Reputation Extractor receives the reputation tokens (containing the node reputation value) issued by the TS. Trust DataSet stores all data related to the above functional blocks in the node in a secure measure. In addition, a Node Profile Manager is used to maintain the personal information of node. It can communicate with the TS to register the node into the PSNTrust system and update the node pseudonym and reputation token.

At the Trusted Server, a Reputation Generator/Predictor calculates the node reputation values; meanwhile it identifies malicious nodes. A Reputation Distributor distributes the reputation tokens (containing the node reputation value) to each node periodically or by request. A Node ID Manager handles node registration and issues new node pseudonyms (by request or periodically). An Information Receiver collects the records

reported by the nodes and saves them into Reputation DataSet, which also saves the reputation token of each node and its real ID and pseudonyms.

4.4 PSNTrust Model

The way to calculate trust is often called the trust model (Yang, Sun, Kay & Yang, 2009). Based on the above system design, we propose a hybrid trust model – PSNTrust model to generate node user reputation, as shown in Figure 2. This information is evolved at both node side based on ephemeral local experience and TS side according to collected historical PSN information.

In PSNTrust, TS generates/predicts node reputation according to the context model and issues a reputation token to the node. The reputation token contains node reputation values, context IDs, pseudonym, and token expired time. Based on the reputation token attached to each node and pervasive social networking experiences, a node generates the reputation of other nodes instructed by the current context model. Furthermore, the

Figure 2. PSNTrust model

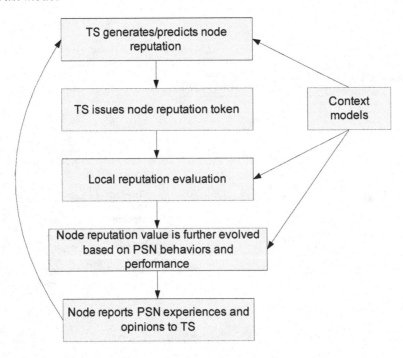

node updates other nodes' reputation values based on their social networking behaviors and performance (according to the context model). Particularly, the node reports pervasive social networking experiences and opinions to TS (e.g., reporting past chatting records or vote other users who chatted with him/her). After collecting additional pervasive social networking records, the TS updates the reputation of each node according to his/her performance in different contexts. The evaluation of node reputation is iterative at both the node and TS based on newly accumulated experiences and information.

In order to preserve privacy, PSNTrust applies the TS to issue and manage the pseudonyms of nodes. The TS can identify the real identities of nodes. It could frequently or periodically issue a new pseudonym to the node. Thus, local social experiences are accumulated only based on valid pseudonyms. For example, Node A would assume Node B as a different node once Node B uses a new pseudonym, even though they had interaction with each other before. Historical evaluation on the node reputation can be only conducted at the TS by considering all social networking behaviors in different contexts related to a specific node that possibly has used multiple pseudonyms. Notably, a new reputation token is always issued when the node pseudonym is changed. However, the node may only request the TS to update the reputation value by issuing a new reputation token without changing its pseudonym.

The pseudonym can be the node ID expressed by its MAC address and/or network layer address. This ID could be frequently changed in order to enhance node privacy. The system supports the node pseudonym is selected from a pre-prepared list stored at both the TS and the node. Thus the server knows 'who is who' after getting the reports from the nodes, even though the node could change the pseudonym without contacting the server.

Particularly, the TS also collects direct votes on nodes and the statistical data of node interaction for the purpose of evaluating the node reputation.

The node reputation token is issued by the TS with non-repudiation. Due to the usage of pseudonyms, only the TS can evaluate the node reputation in an accurate way based on historical pervasive social networking behaviors. Thus, introducing the TS can greatly improve the precision of reputation evaluation (Yan & Chen, 2010). Optionally, TS is also responsible for issuing the blacklist of malicious nodes and the favorite list of honest nodes to the PSNTrust nodes if needed in practice. For example, the blacklist can be used to filter or control contents from disreputable nodes.

The context model is the way to describe the situations that need assistance from PSNTrust and specify the way to adopt a suitable reputation evaluation algorithm. Applying the context models, PSNTrust can support various applications that need PSNTrust assistance, thus provide sound system flexibility and scalability.

The example of context model for MANET chatting is shown in Algorithm 1.

Based on the context model, the PSNTrust system knows which algorithm should be applied in which context based on the context ID and operation name. We have prototyped two demo systems supported by PSNTrust, one is ad hoc content recommendation service ("AdContRep") (Yan & Chen, 2010) and the other is ad hoc chatting service ("AdChatRep") (Yan & Chen, 2011). Additional MANET social services can be supported by PSNTrust by adding new context models into the system.

It is important to note that the node reputation values generated in different contexts can be further combined to get a single value that represents the general node reputation. In addition, the reputation generated in other contexts can play as an important reference for decision making in a new context if the reputation value linked to the underlying context is not available. PSNTrust supports multiple contexts. It can evaluate node reputation for multiple instances or events in different contexts. The algorithms used in different contexts could be different in Reputation Evalu-

Algorithm 1.

```
<?xml version="1.0" encoding="UTF-8"?>
<contextIdentity='PSNTrust_chatting'>
  <contextDescription>
      <name> chatting service in MANET </name>
  </contextDescription >
  <operationRequest>
      <operation>
          <name> On-Chat reputation evaluation at node </name>
          <host> node side </host>
          <algorithm> PSNTrust_algo1 </algorithm>
      </operation>
      <operation>
          <name> Reputation generation at the Trusted Server (TS) </name>
          <host> TS side </host>
          <algorithm> PSNTrust_algo2 </algorithm>
      </operation>
      <operation>
          <name> Personal reputation prediction </name>
          <host> TS side </host>
          <algorithm> PSNTrust_algo3 </algorithm>
      </operation>
    </operationRequest>
A simple example of context model for MANET content recommendation is:
<?xml version="1.0" encoding="UTF-8"?>
<contextIdentity='PSNTrust_contentRecommendation'>
  <contextDescription>
      <name> content recommendation service in MANET </name>
  </contextDescription >
  <operationRequest>
      <operation>
          <name> Trust/Reputation Evaluation at a Query Node </name>
          <host> node side </host>
          <algorithm> PSNTrust_algoA </algorithm>
      </operation>
      <operation>
          <name> Trust/Reputation Evaluation at the Trusted Server (TS) </
name>
          <host> TS side </host>
          <algorithm> PSNTrust_algoB </algorithm>
      </operation>
    </operationRequest>
```

ator. The Reputation Evaluator has capability to evaluate and maintain the reputation values in various contexts with the help of Trust DataSet.

5. PROPERTIES FOR TRUST

PSNTrust supports a number of key system properties for achieving trust in pervasive social networking. This section introduces some key properties for trust, such as context-aware trust/reputation generation, trustworthy content recommendations, secure data communications, unwanted traffic control, user privacy recommendation, and secure face-to-face recognition.

5.1 Trust/Reputation Generation for PSN Chatting

To generate the local reputation of a node $R(i \to j)$ (i.e., node j's local reputation evaluated by node i), we apply Formula 1 to aggregate three trust impact aspects together (Yan & Chen, 2011). The trust impact factors considered herein are explored in a user survey (Yan, Chen & Shen, 2013). The first part is the sum of previous local reputation (or personalized reputation if available) and the general reputation, which serves as the initial reputation of current chatting. The second part is the reputation generated on the basis of current chatting experience. Since there could be multiple on-chat votes during chatting, we integrate them together by averaging the product of on-chat votes and the depth of chatting at the vote that impacts the preciseness of the opinion of a user. Furthermore, this part is weighted by $is(i, j)$, the interest similarity between node i and j and $cl(i)$, the crucial level of chatting topic from the view of node i, which are other two on-chat factors influencing trust, as we explored in the user survey (Yan & Chen, 2011; Yan, Chen & Shen, 2013). This is because $is(i, j)$ and $cl(i)$ impacts the extent of node i's opinion on node j. The third part is generated based on the on-chat

votes on node j provided by other nodes except i, which is certified by an opinion deviation factor as described in Formula 2. This part should be considered in the calculation of $R(i \to j)$ because other nodes' opinions on node j could also influence the opinion of node i. The opinion deviation factor indicates the opinion deviation of two nodes on a target node by considering their on-chat votes and the depth of chatting during the votes. Applying this factor makes it easy to figure out the nodes that hold different opinions from the reputation evaluating node. Thus applying this opinion deviation factor in reputation generation can avoid the negative influence of bad mouthing attack and collaborative bad mouthing attack, as verified by Yan, Chen and Shen (2013).

$$R(i \to j) = f \begin{pmatrix} \alpha \left(R'(i \to j) + R(j) \right) \\ + \beta \sum_{l=1}^{L} \left\{ cv(i \to j)_l * dc(i, j)_l \right\} \\ * is(i, j) * cl(i) \\ + \gamma \sum_{k \neq i} \sum_{l=1}^{L'} \left\{ cv(k \to j)_l \right\} * od(i \leftrightarrow k, j) \end{pmatrix} \tag{1}$$

$$od(i \leftrightarrow k, j)$$
$$= 1 - 2 * \left| f \left\{ \begin{array}{c} \sum_{l=1}^{L} cv(i \to j)_l * dc(i, j)_l \\ - \sum_{l=1}^{L'} cv(k \to j)_l * dc(k, j)_l \end{array} \right\} - \frac{1}{2} \right| \tag{2}$$

where $R(i \to j)$ is the reputation of node j locally evaluated by node i. $R'(i \to j)$ denotes the personalized reputation predicted and issued by TS, or the reputation previously evaluated by node i on j. $R(j)$ is the general reputation of node j issued by TS. $cv(i \to j)_l$ is the lth on-chat voting by node i on the message of node j. $is(i, j)$ is the number of common communities shared by node i and j, which indicates their common interests. $cl(i)$ is the crucial level of chatting topic. $dc(i, j)_l$ is the depth of chatting between node i and j at the time of the *l*th voting of node *j*. It is the minimum number of messages input by node *i* and *j* at the time of the voting. For example, if node *j* has input 4 messages and node *i* has input 6 ones at the time of the *l*th voting of node *j* on *i*, we set $dc(i,j)_l = 4$. $f(x) = \dfrac{1}{1+e^{-x}}$ is the Sigmoid function used to normalize an arbitrary value into $(0,1)$. We use it to normalize $R(i \rightarrow j)$ into $(0,1)$. L denotes the total number of on-chat votes by node *i* on *j*. L' denotes the total number of on-chat votes by node *k* on *j*. Parameters α, β, γ indicate the weights of different contributions. Note that $\alpha + \beta + \gamma = 1$. $od(i \leftrightarrow k, j)$ is the opinion deviation factor that indicates the difference of opinions between node *k* and *j* on the chatting messages input by node *i* in the same chat. Again, we applied the Sigmoid function in Formula 2 to normalize $od(i \leftrightarrow k, j)$ into $(0,1)$. The bigger the value of $od(i \leftrightarrow k, j)$, the more close the opinions between node *k* and *i*. Formula 1 is suitable to be applied if a PSNTrust node would like to use its own opinion to measure the trustworthiness of other nodes in the pervasive social chatting.

Based on the vote after PSN social interaction (named afterwards voting) and local reputation, two types of node reputation are generated at TS: personalized reputation and general reputation. We apply weighted aggregation using local reputation $R(i \rightarrow j)$ as credibility to overcome unfair rating attack. Meanwhile, we also consider time influence on the afterwards voting in order to overcome on-off and conflict behavior attacks (Sun, Han & Liu, 2008).

Formula 3 is applied to generate the personalized reputation of node *j*, $\overline{R(i \rightarrow j)}$, evaluated by node *i* by considering afterwards voting and time decaying. The afterwards voting is the vote on a party after chatting based on interaction experiences.

$$\overline{R(i \rightarrow j)} = \frac{1}{O} \sum_m R(i \rightarrow j)^{t_m} * V_i^{j(t_m)} e^{\frac{|t-t_m|^2}{\tau}} \quad (3)$$

where

$$O = \sum_m R(i \rightarrow j)^{t_m} * e^{-\frac{|t-t_m|^2}{\tau}};$$

$V_i^{j(t_m)}$ is the afterwards voting of node *i* on node *j* at time t_m; t is the calculation time of node reputation; parameter τ is used to control time decaying. $R(i \rightarrow j)^{t_m}$ is the local reputation of node *j* reported by node *i* at time t_m, with afterwards voting $V_i^{j(t_m)}$ attached in the report. If $V_i^{j(t_m)}$ is not provided by the node, we set $V_i^{j(t_m)} = 0.5$. Note that $V_i^{j(t_m)} \in [0,1]$ and $R(i \rightarrow j)^{t_m} \in [0,1]$.

The general reputation of node *j*, denoted $R(j)$, should be aggregated based on the evaluation of all nodes $\overline{R(i \rightarrow j)}$, as designed in Formula 4. The aggregation is weighted by the general reputation $R(i)$ as the credibility of $\overline{R(i \rightarrow j)}$, i.e. the personal reputation value of node *j* with regard to *i*. Meanwhile, we also consider the influence of the number of reputation contributors on the general reputation generation with the Rayleigh cumulative distribution function, since the more contributors, the more convinced the generation result is.

$$R(j) = \frac{f(K)}{W} \sum_{i=1}^{K} R(i) * \overline{R(i \rightarrow j)} \quad (i \neq j) \quad (4)$$

where, K is the total number of nodes who have direct experiences with node *j*. $W = \sum_{i=1}^{K} R(i)$ is the total sum of the general reputation values of those nodes.

$$f(K) = \left\{ 1 - \exp\left(\frac{-K^2}{2(\sigma + \varepsilon)^2}\right) \right\}$$

is the Rayleigh cumulative distribution function to model the impact of K on node reputation, $\varepsilon = -K/K'$, is a factor to indicate sociability of node j, which is the radio of the number of nodes that socially interact with node j and the total number of nodes registered in the system (denoted K').

5.2 Trustworthy Content Recommendations

Figure 3 illustrates the process for generating trustworthy recommendations in PSN (Yan & Chen, 2010). As shown in Figure 6.3, the query node processes query response about content recommendations. The trust evaluator calculates the content reputation based on the votes provided by recommender nodes, the number of collected recommendations (i.e., content popularity) and the recommender node trust values certified by the TS. The node trust issued by TS is further evolved based on recommendation performance at the query node. The

evaluated content reputation will be displayed to help the node user make a selection decision. The query node will report its pervasive social activities to the TS. Thus the TS can generate content reputation by aggregating all content recommendations and precisely evaluate node trust based on node real IDs. The TS can issue the trust token that contains the node trust and update the content reputation periodically or by request. Herein, the trust value of a recommender node partially serves as the credibility of its recommendation. This trust value contains two parts: one is provided by the TS by assessing historical node recommendation behaviors. The other is the query node evaluation on the recommender node based on locally accumulated experiences. The local evaluation is evolved on the basis of the trust value issued by the TS. Notably, credibility provides a reason to trust.

Figure 3. Process of generating trustworthy content recommendations in PSN

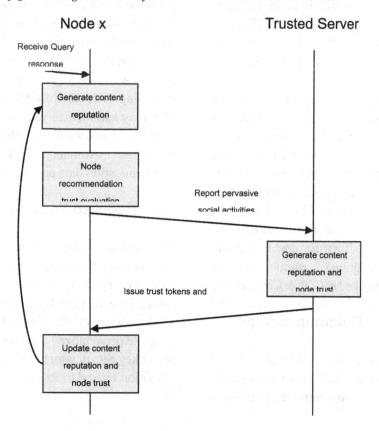

Recommendation credibility is essential for generating a reliable reputation value.

In order to preserve privacy, PSNTrust applies the TS to issue and manage the pseudonyms of nodes. The TS can identify the real identities of nodes. It could frequently or periodically issue a new pseudonym to the node. Thus, the local experiences are accumulated only based on valid pseudonyms. Historical evaluation on the node recommendation trust can only be conducted at the TS by considering all recommendation behaviors related to a concrete node who possibly have applied multiple pseudonyms.

Particularly, the TS also collects direct votes on different contents and the statistical data of node interaction for the purpose of evaluating the node trust and content reputation. The node trust token (containing the node recommendation trust value) is issued by the TS with non-repudiation. Due to the usage of pseudonyms, only the TS can evaluate the node trust in an accurate way based on historical recommendation behaviors. Thus, introducing the TS can greatly improve the precision of trust/reputation evaluation. The TS is also responsible for issuing the blacklist of malicious nodes and the favorite list of honest nodes to the PSN nodes.

Meanwhile, the TS can generate the reputation of various contents based on the feedback and recommendation records reported by the query nodes. A content recommendation service based on content reputation can be provided. The evaluation of node trust and content reputation is iterative at both the node and TS based on newly accumulated experiences and information. The detailed algorithms used for trust/reputation evaluation and recommendation generation at a query node and TS are described in (Yan & Chen, 2010).

5.3 Secure Data Communications

PSNTrust uses either a local trust level evaluated by the PSN node or a general trust level evaluated by the TS or both to control data access in PSN communications. Any PSN node can select other nodes with at least a minimum level of local and/or general trust for secure communications. The nodes with a lower trust level cannot access the data.

In the case that the TS is available and the node would like to control data access only based on the general trust level, the general trust level controlled access keys (i.e., encryption public keys and personalized secret keys) are generated and issued by the TS. In case that the TS is not available, each node generates the encryption public key and corresponding personalized secret keys based on the local trust level for decryption. It issues the secret keys to those nodes that satisfy access conditions. Then, it broadcasts the encrypted messages to nearby nodes. In case that the local trust levels of some nodes change, the node will regenerate suitable keys for encrypting and decrypting later communication data and resend new secret keys to eligible users.

In the case that the trusted server is available, the node could control communication data access with both the general trust level and the local trust level. Based on periodically issued keys from the server, the node further controls the access of its data with newly generated public/secret keys according to local trust levels. With this way, PSNTrust automatically secures data communications based on trust relationships. It is one way of autonomic trust management for the purpose of communication data access control.

5.3.1 Required Keys and System Setup

During system setup, a public master key PK and a secret master key MK are generated; PK is available to every entity in the system, whereas MK is only known to the TS. Every node u maintains a public user key PK_u, which is used by TS to generate personalized secret attribute keys, and a secret key SK_u, which is used in the decryption operation related to PK_u.

Generation and distribution of PK_u and SK_u is the task of the TS, who is also required to verify the unique identity of the nodes before these two keys are generated and issued during node registration into the system. The keys SK_u and PK_u of node u are bound to the unique identity of the node by the TS. This binding is crucial for the verification of node attributes.

The TS maintains a secret key SK_gt which is used to issue secret attribute keys to nodes based on the general trust (GT) level. We denote the public representation of this attribute as GT. An attribute is consisting of an identifier describing the attribute itself (an arbitrary string). Each node maintains a secret key SK_u that is used to issue secret attribute keys to nodes based on general trust level and/or local trust level. It is also used to generate the public key of attribute, e.g., local trust (LT) of node u. We denote the public representation of the attribute of local trust as LT. For the attribute with representation GT there is a public key, denoted PK_GT, which is issued by the TS and is used to encrypt communication data in order to control access based on the general trust level. For the attribute with representation (LT, u) there is a public key, denoted PK_(LT,

u), which is generated by the node u and is used to encrypt communication data of u, aiming to control access based on the local trust level evaluated by u. The corresponding secret attribute keys of PK_GT, personalized for eligible users, are issued by the TS to the eligible users. To prevent collusion, every node gets a different secret attribute key personalized for each node. A secret attribute key of an attribute GT, issued for node u is denoted SK_(GT, u). A secret attribute key of the attribute LT, issued for an eligible node u' by node u is denoted SK_(LT, u, u'). We call the set of secret keys that the node u' has (i.e., the key SK_u' and all keys SK_(GT, u'), SK_(LT, u, u')) as its key ring.

5.3.2 Schemes

A number of fundamental algorithms are designed to realize secure data communications in PSN that is controlled by general trust and/or local trust. These algorithms are: Setup, InitiateUser, IssueGeneralTrustPK, IssueGeneralTrustSK, CreateLocalTrustPK, IssueLocalTrustSK, Encrypt and Decrypt. The details of the eight algorithms are described as follows.

Table 2. Summaries of the keys used in secure data communications

Key	Description	Usage
PK	The global key	The input for all operations
MK	The master key	For creation of user keys
PK_u	The public key of node u	The unique ID of node and the key for verification of the node's attributes. It is used for personalized secret attribute key generation
SK_u	The secret key of node u	For decryption (to get personalized secret attribute keys)
SK_gt	The secret key of TS w.r.t. general trust attribute	For creation of attribute keys about general trust
PK_GT	The public key of attribute general trust	For encryption (of PSN communication data)
SK_(GT, u)	The secret key of attribute general trust for node u	For decryption (of PSN communication data)
PK_(LT, u)	The public key of attribute local trust generated by node u	For encryption (of PSN communication data of node u)
SK_(LT, u, u')	The secret key of attribute local trust for node u' issued by u	For decryption (of PSN communication data of node u)

Setup. The Setup algorithm takes as input the implicit security parameter 1^k. It outputs the public key PK and the master key MK. It also generates a secret key SK_gt for TS for the purpose of general trust attribute related operations in PSN. This process is conducted at TS.

InitiateUser(PK, MK, u). The InitiateUser algorithm takes as input the public key PK, the master key MK, and a node identity u (generally a unique node identifier). It outputs a public node key PK_u, that will be used by TS to issue secret attribute keys for u, and a secret node key SK_u, used for the decryption of ciphertexts. This process is also conducted at TS when the node registers into the system.

IssueGeneralTrustPK(PK, GT, SK_gt). The IssueGeneralTrustPK algorithm is automatically executed by the TS whenever it is time to issue a public attribute key by checking the validity period of previous issue. The algorithm checks the policies related to GT. If this is the case, the algorithm outputs a public attribute key for GT, denoted PK_GT, otherwise NULL. This operation is executed at TS automatically by checking a clock and the validity period of the previously issued key.

IssueGeneralTrustSK(PK, GT, SK_gt, u, PK_u). The IssueGeneralTrustSK algorithm is automatically executed by the TS whenever it is time to issue a secret attribute GT key by checking the validity period of previous issue. The algorithm checks whether the node u with public key PK_u is eligible of the attribute GT (i.e., the node u's general trust level is equal or above an indicated level). If this is the case, IssueGeneralTrustSK outputs a secret attribute key SK_(GT, u) for the eligible node u. Otherwise, the algorithm outputs NULL. This process is executed at TS automatically by checking a clock and the validity period of the previously issued keys.

CreateLocalTrustPK(PK, LT, SK_u). The CreateLocalTrustPK algorithm is executed by the node u whenever the node would like to double control the access of its data (e.g., PSN chatting messages). The algorithm checks the LT related policies. If this is the case, the algorithm outputs a public attribute key for the LT of node u, denoted PK_(LT, u), otherwise NULL.

IssueLocalTrustSK(PK, LT, SK_u, u', PK_u'). The IssueLocalTrustSK algorithm is executed by the node u by checking the eligibility of u'. The algorithm checks whether the node u' with public key PK_u' is eligible of the attribute LT (i.e., the local trust level of u' is equal or above an indicated level). If this is the case, IssueLocalTrustSK outputs a secret attribute key SK_(LT, u, u') for the node u'. Otherwise, the algorithm outputs NULL. This process is executed by the node u based on the request from u'.

Encrypt(PK, M, A, PK_GT, PK_(LT, u)). The Encrypt algorithm takes as input the public key PK, a PSN communication message M, an access policy A and the public keys PK_GT, PK_(LT,u) corresponding to the general trust and local trust occurring in the policy A. The algorithm encrypts M with the policy A and outputs ciphertext CT. This process is conducted at a node to protect its PSN communication message. Note that either PK_GT or PK_(LT, u), or both can appear in the Encrypt algorithm, which depends on the access control policy defined in A. Concretely, if the node would like to control data access only based on the general trust level, the Encrypt algorithm is simplified as Encrypt(PK, M, A, PK_GT). If the user would like to control data access only based on the local trust level, the Encrypt algorithm is simplified as Encrypt(PK, M, A, PK_(LT, u)). If the data access is controlled by both the general trust level and the local trust level, the Encrypt algorithm is kept as its original.

For example, one node would like other nodes with general trust level over 4 and local trust level over 4 to access his data. He encrypts his data with a policy A1: GT_u>=4, and A2: LT_u>=4 to encrypt the data.

Note that a policy should be described in Disjunctive Normal Form (DNF). The policy in DNF can be written as

$$AA = \bigvee_{j=1}^{n} \left(\bigwedge_{A \in S_j} A \right) \qquad (5)$$

where n (not pairwise disjoint) sets $S_1, \ldots, S_n$ denote attributes that occur in the j-th conjunction of AA. The encryption algorithm iterates over all $j = 1, \ldots, n$ and constructs CT_j corresponding to each S_j. The ciphertext CT is obtained as tuple CT:= <CT_1, CT_2, ..., CT_n>

Decrypt(PK, CT, A, SK_u', SK_(GT, u'), SK_(LT, u, u')). The Decrypt algorithm takes as input a ciphertext produced by the Encrypt algorithm, an access policy A, under which CT was encrypted, and a key ring SK_u', SK_(GT, u'), SK_(LU, u, u') for node u'. The algorithm Decrypt decrypts the ciphertext CT and outputs the corresponding plaintext M if the attributes were sufficient to satisfy A; otherwise it outputs NULL. This process is executed when a node receives a PSN message. It firstly checks the encryption policy A, then conducts decryption with the key rings issued by TS or node u or both.

Note that either SK_(GT, u') or, SK_(LT, u, u') or both can appear in the Decrypt, which depends on the access control policy defined in A. Concretely, if a node would like to control data access only based on the general trust level, the Decrypt algorithm is simplified as Decrypt(PK, CT, A, SK_u', SK_(GT, u')). If the node would like to control data access only based on the local trust level, the Decrypt algorithm is simplified as Decrypt(PK, CT, A, SK_u', SK_(LT, u, u')). If the data access is controlled by both the general trust level and the local trust level, the Decrypt algorithm is kept as its original.

5.3.3 Procedures

We illustrate the procedures of flexibly securing pervasive social networking based on 2-dimensional trust levels in three cases.

In the case that the data access is only controlled by the general trust level. The general trust level

controlled access keys (i.e., encryption public keys and personalized secret keys) are generated and issued by the TS (e.g., periodically). The procedure is shown in Figure 4.

- **Issue Keys:** TS evaluates the general trust level of nodes; it generates encryption public keys and personalized decryption secret keys of attributes and then issues the proper keys (both the public encryption keys and personalized secret keys) to eligible nodes.
- **Secure PSN Communications:** The node encrypts its message based on personal access policies using corresponding public keys and broadcast the message to nearby nodes. Other nodes check the encryption policy and use their personalized secret keys to decrypt the messages if eligible to access.
- **Quit from PSN:** Some node may quit from the PSN at any time by sending a request to TS. The TS confirms it by not sending any new keys to this node after its current keys are expired.
- **Re-issue Keys:** TS checks the clock frequently. If the validity period of current keys will be expired, it will re-evaluate the general trust level; then re-generate encryption public keys and personalized decryption secret keys, set their validity period and re-issue the new keys to the eligible nodes. The PSN nodes continue secure communications with the new keys when their validity period starts.

In the case that the server is not available, each node generates the encryption key and corresponding personalized secret keys based on the local trust level for decryption. It issues the secret keys to those nodes that satisfy the decryption conditions. Then, it broadcasts the encrypted messages to nearby nodes. In case that the local trust levels of some node change, the node will regenerate suitable keys for encrypting and decrypting later communication data and then re-send new secret

Figure 4. Control PSN data access based on general trust

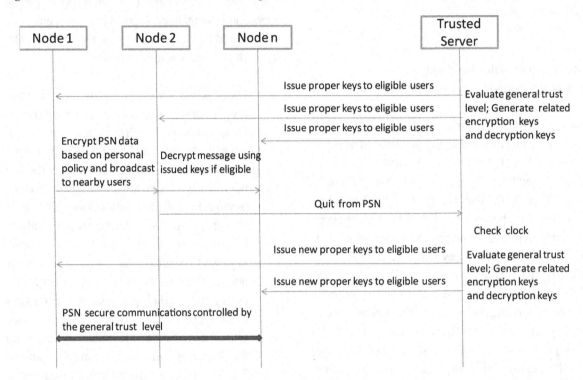

Figure 5. Control PSN data access based on local trust

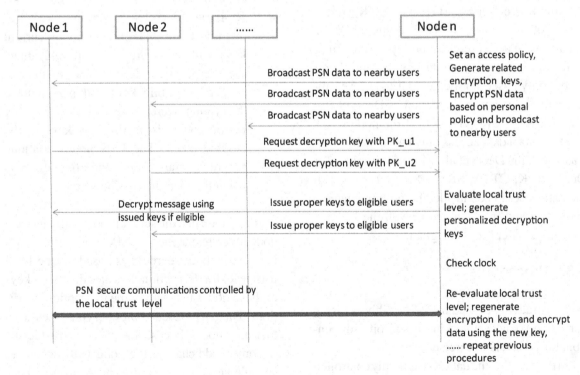

keys to eligible nodes. The procedure is shown in Figure 5.

- **Protect PSN Data:** A node u sets an access policy, generates related encryption keys, encrypts its data in PSN based on the personal policy and broadcast to nearby users. After detecting the broadcast message from this node, other nodes check the local trust value of the node and decide if communicate with it. If the decision is positive, the other nodes send a key request to the node u with their identities. The node u evaluates the local trust levels of requesting nodes; it generates personalized decryption secret keys of local trust and issues the proper keys (personalized secret keys) to eligible nodes.

- **Secure PSN Communications:** The eligible node u' decrypts the message of the node u based on personal access policies using corresponding secret keys.
- **Re-generate Keys:** The node u checks the clock frequently. If it is time to re-evaluate the local trust, the node re-evaluates the local trust of other users. If the results have a big difference, the node u will regenerate encryption keys based on a new access policy. It will adopt the new keys to protect later PSN communication data.

In the case that the trusted server is available and the node would like to control communication data access based on both the general trust level and the local trust level. Based on periodically issued keys from the server, the node further controls the access of its data with the server issued keys and

Figure 6. Control PSN data access based on both general trust and local trust

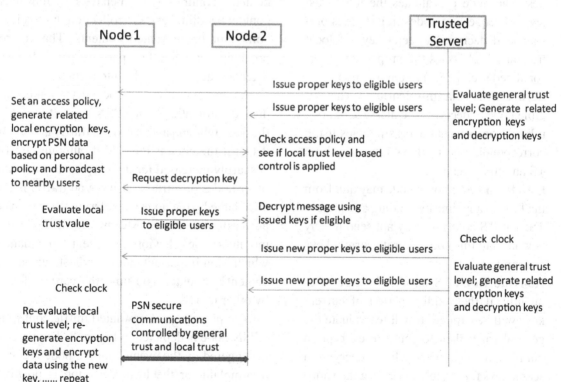

its own issued keys. The procedure is illustrated in Figure 6.

- **Issue Keys:** TS evaluates the general trust of nodes; it generates encryption public keys and personalized decryption secret keys of attributes and then issues the proper keys (both public encryption keys and personalized decryption keys) to eligible nodes.

- **Protect PSN Data:** A node u sets an access policy, generate related encryption keys, encrypt its data based on the personal policy using corresponding public keys (issued by both TS and itself) and broadcast to nearby nodes. After detecting the broadcast message from the node, other nodes check the local trust value of the node and decide if communicating with it. If the decision is positive, the other nodes send a key request to the node u with their identities. The node u evaluates the local trust level of requesting nodes; it generates personalized decryption secret keys of local trust and then issues the proper keys (personalized secret keys) to eligible nodes.

- **Secure PSN Communications:** The eligible node u' decrypts the message of node u based on personal access policies using corresponding secret keys issued by both TS and the node u.

- **Quit from PSN:** Some node may quit from the PSN at any time by sending a request to TS. The TS confirms it by not sending any new keys to this node after its current keys are expired.

- **Re-issue Keys:** TS checks the clock frequently, if the validity period of current keys will be expired, it will re-evaluate the general trust; then re-generate encryption public keys and personalized decryption secret keys for eligible nodes, set the valid-

ity period of new keys and re-issue the new keys to the eligible nodes.

- **Re-generate Keys by Nodes:** The node u checks the clock frequently. If it is time to re-evaluate the local trust, the node re-evaluates the local trust of other nodes. If the results have a big difference from previous local trust, the node u will regenerate encryption keys based on a new access policy. It will use the new keys to protect later PSN communication data.

The PSN nodes continue secure communications with the new keys when their validity period starts. The communication data are protected based on both the general trust and the local trust.

5.4 Unwanted Content Control

The unwanted content control at the mobile device in pervasive social networking is based on content monitoring, the behavior of unwanted content handling, and the collection of broadcast complaint on unwanted contents. The control procedure contains two parts in parallel: local detection and unwanted content control.

As shown in Figure 7, local detection is conducted automatically in a PSN node. It monitors the node inbound and outbound traffic in order to detect if the node is infected if outbound traffic is sharply increased for the purpose of intruding other nodes or intruded if inbound traffic is unaffordable by the node considering the remained power of node device. Meanwhile, the node also monitors node behaviors on content maintenance, which is an important clue to indicate unwanted content by a content consumer that can be referred by other nodes.

The procedure of unwanted traffic control in a PSN node is depicted in Figure 8. The process is triggered by the events that the node receives a complaint or the local detection is positive.

Figure 7. Procedure of local unwanted content detection

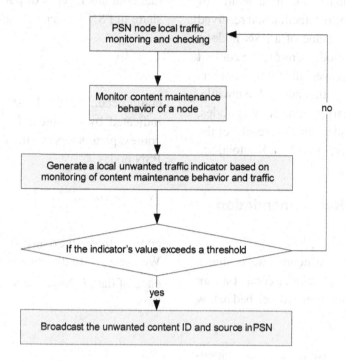

Figure 8. Procedure of unwanted content control at the PSN node

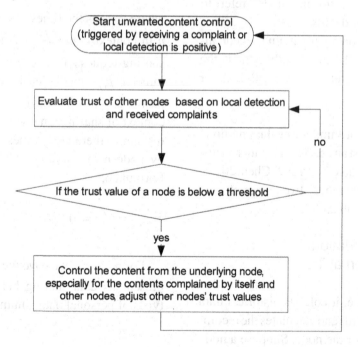

Firstly, the node evaluates the trust values of other nodes based on local detection and received complaints. If the trust value of a PSN node is below a threshold, the node controls the content from that node in PSN, especially for the contents that were complained by other nodes. Meanwhile, it also adjusts the local trust value of other nodes. Detailed algorithms and evaluation results of the above solution are reported in (Yan, Kantola, Shi & Zhang, 2013).

5.5 User Privacy Recommendation and Preservation

Based on the PSNTrust structure, we design a number of algorithms for generating context-aware user privacy recommendation as described below (Yan & Zhang, 2011):

- When TS is accessible, the recommendation vector is calculated at the TS and provided to a requesting node, refer to Algorithm 1 for details.
- Recommendation vector is fine-tuned/calculated and at the node with/without the input from TS, refer to Algorithm 2 for details.

Note that the algorithms for evaluating node recommendation trust and service provider's trust are proposed and evaluated in (Yan & Chen, 2010). Herein, we assume that these two pieces of trust information are available.

5.5.1 Recommendation Vector Calculation at TS

When TS is available, it collects historical data communication records and calculates the recommendation vectors for the node. Suppose a node has a data set

$$I = \left\{ i_1, i_2, \ldots\ldots, i_L \right\}$$

that contains L types of personal data needed to share in PSN services. A number M of contexts

$$C = \left\{ c_1, c_2, \ldots\ldots, c_M \right\}$$

could occur. In PSNTrust, a specific context is indicated by a context ID and described with context parameters and their values. There are K PSN nodes

$$N = \left\{ n_1, n_2, \ldots\ldots, n_K \right\}$$

contributing to the data privacy recommendation. We use $p_{i,n,c}$ to denote the probability or preference of data i shared by node n in context c, we have

$$p_{i,n,c} = \frac{s_{i,n,c}}{S_{i,n,c} + 1} \tag{6}$$

where $s_{i,n,c}$ is the times of data i shared by node n in context c and $S_{i,n,c}$ is the total number of sharing requests of data i in context c. The parameter $p_{i,n,c}$ can be easily calculated based on past data sharing behaviors. For example, in the context of sharing a name to reserve a table in a restaurant there are 7 times of sharing provided by node n in a total of 10 requests. Based on Formula 6,

$$p_{i,n,c} = \frac{7}{11} = 0.636$$

For node n_k, we have the following matrix to present its data sharing behaviors regarding L types of personal data a number of M contexts.

$$D(n_k) = \left\{ \begin{bmatrix} p_{i_1,n_k,c_1} \\ p_{i_2,n_k,c_1} \\ \\ p_{i_L,n_k,c_1} \end{bmatrix} \cdots\cdots\cdots \begin{bmatrix} p_{i_1,n_k,c_M} \\ p_{i_2,n_k,c_M} \\ \\ p_{i_L,n_k,c_M} \end{bmatrix} \right\} \quad (7)$$

The matrix that represents the data sharing behaviors of all nodes in PSN is expressed below:

$$D(N) = \left\{ \begin{array}{c} \begin{bmatrix} p_{i_1,n_1,c_1} \\ p_{i_2,n_1,c_1} \\ \\ p_{i_L,n_1,c_1} \end{bmatrix} \cdots\cdots\cdots \begin{bmatrix} p_{i_1,n_1,c_M} \\ p_{i_2,n_1,c_M} \\ \\ p_{i_L,n_1,c_M} \end{bmatrix} \\ \cdots \\ \cdots \\ \begin{bmatrix} p_{i_1,n_K,c_1} \\ p_{i_2,n_K,c_1} \\ \\ p_{i_L,n_K,c_1} \end{bmatrix} \cdots\cdots\cdots \begin{bmatrix} p_{i_1,n_K,c_M} \\ p_{i_2,n_K,c_M} \\ \\ p_{i_L,n_K,c_M} \end{bmatrix} \end{array} \right\} \quad (8)$$

According to the similarity of past data sharing behaviors, a personalized recommendation vector $R^p_{n_k,c_m}$ can be pre-calculated for node n_k regarding context c_m at the TS based on Formula 6.9 based on past personal data sharing behaviors.

$$R^p_{n_k,c_m} = \frac{\sum_{k'=1}^{K} \left(p_{n_{k'},c_m} * \mathrm{Re}\, l\left(n_k, n_{k'}\right) \right)}{\sum_{k'=1}^{K} \mathrm{Re}\, l\left(n_k, n_{k'}\right)}, \quad (9)$$

where

$$\mathrm{Re}\, l(n_k, n_{k'})$$
$$= \frac{1}{M-1} \sum_{m \neq m', m'=1}^{M} \left(1 - \sqrt{\frac{\sum_{l=1}^{L} \left(p_{i_l,n_k,c_m} - p_{i_l,n_{k'},c_m} \right)^2}{L}} \right), \quad (10)$$

$k' = 1, ..., K$, $p_{n_{k'},c_m}$ is a vector that denotes the probability of data set I shared by node $n_{k'}$ in context c_m. Herein, $k' \neq k$; $\mathrm{Re}\, l(n_k, n_{k'})$ is applied to calculate the correlation of data sharing behaviors, which is reflected by the average deviation of data sharing probabilities of two nodes by considering both contexts and data types.

Based on a user study conducted in both Finland and China, we found that users show more trust in an item if more people would like to recommend it (Yan, Liu, Niemi & Yu, 2009). Considering the influence of the number of recommenders (i.e., service popularity), we set

$$N_p = 1 - \exp\left(\frac{-K^2}{2\sigma^2} \right) \quad (11)$$

where $\sigma > 0$, is a parameter that inversely controls how fast the number of recommenders impacts recommendation. It increases as K increases. The parameter σ can be set from 0 to theoretically ∞, to capture the characteristics of different scenarios. We use N_p to adjust the recommendation vector $R^p_{n_k,c_m}$, where N_p plays as the credibility of recommendation contributed by the service popularity.

Particularly, the recommendations from trustworthy recommenders should be weighted higher than those from distrusted ones. This could benefit PSNTrust against a number of attacks. Similarly, the trust of destination party should also be considered in data sharing. In addition, the recommendations from the members in the same community with similar interests and/or having interaction experiences should be paid more attention than those from other communities. If $T_{n_{k'}}$ denotes the trust value of recommender node $n_{k'}$ and T_d denotes the trust value of the destination party d, PSNTrust considers a comprehensive number of factors, such as service popularity, community information, and the influence of both $T_{n_{k'}}$ and T_d in the generation of user privacy recommendation. Thus, the recommendation vector R_{n_k,c_m} for node n_k in context c_m can be tailored as

$$R_{n_k,c_m} = \frac{\sum_{k'=1}^{K}\left(p_{n_{k'},c_m} * \mathrm{Re}\, l\left(n_k,n_{k'}\right) * \lambda T_{n_{k'}}\right)}{\sum_{k'=1}^{K}\left(\mathrm{Re}\, l\left(n_k,n_{k'}\right)\right)} * N_p * T_d \tag{12}$$

where λ is a community factor, $\lambda = \omega$ if n_k and $n_{k'}$ are in the same community (e.g., with common shopping interests) and $\lambda = \omega'$ if n_k and $n_{k'}$ are in different communities; and $\omega > \omega'$. The algorithm used for recommendation vector calculation at TS is described in Algorithm 2.

Algorithm 2. Recommendation vector calculation at TS

1. Input:
2. - $D(n_k)$, $D(n_{k'})$, ($k' = 1, ..., K; k \neq k'$): the matrix of data sharing behaviors;
3. - $T_{n_{k'}}$ ($k' = 1, ..., K$): the trust value of node $n_{k'}$;
4. - T_d : the trust value of destination party with whom to share private data;
5. - K : the total number of recommenders; λ ;
6. - n_k : the recommendee node;
7. - c_m : a specific context for recommendation.
8. Generate R_{n_k,c_m} based on Formula 9-12).
9. Output: R_{n_k,c_m} .

5.5.2 Recommendation Vector Calculation at PSN Nodes

Similarly, a recommendation vector R'_{n_k,c_m} can be generated at the node n_k based on locally collected data $D'(n_k)$ according to Formula 13,

$$R'_{n_k,c_m} = \frac{\sum_{k'=1}^{K}\left(p_{n_{k'},c_m} * \mathrm{Re}\, l\left(n_k,n_{k'}\right) * \lambda T'_{n_{k'}}\right)}{\sum_{k'=1}^{K}\left(\mathrm{Re}\, l\left(n_k,n_{k'}\right)\right)} * N_p * T'_d \tag{13}$$

where $T'_{n_{k'}}$ and T'_d are trust values of node $n_{k'}$ and destination party d, generated based on the locally accumulated experiences at n_k (Yan & Chen, 2010).

Considering the recommendation vector generated at TS, we have the final recommendation vector as described below:

$$R^f_{n_k,c_m} = \alpha R'_{n_k,c_m} + (1-\alpha)R_{n_k,c_m} \tag{14}$$

where $0 \leq \alpha \leq 1$, it is a parameter used to weight R'_{n_k,c_m} and R_{n_k,c_m} .

Algorithm 3. Recommendation vector calculation at node n_k

1. Input:
2. - $D'(n_k)$, $D'(n_{k'})$, ($k' = 1, ..., K; k \neq k'$): the matrix of data sharing behaviors collected by node n_k;
3. - $T'_{n_{k'}}$ ($k' = 1, ..., K$): the trust value of node $n_{k'}$ at n_k;
4. - T'_d : the trust value of destination party d evaluated by n_k;
5. - K : the total number of recommenders; λ ; α ;
6. - R_{n_k,c_m} got from TS if any
7. Generate R'_{n_k,c_m} based on Formula 6.13;
8. Aggregate R'_{n_k,c_m} and R_{n_k,c_m} based on Formula 6.14 if R_{n_k,c_m} is input.
9. Output: $R^f_{n_k,c_m}$.

The algorithm used to calculate the recommendation vector at a PSN node is described in Algorithm 3.

5.6 Secure Face-to-Face Recognition

A novel approach was proposed to realize secure and fashionable recognition for pervasive face-to-face social communications based on PSN, local connectivity and fashionable technology (Yan, Chen & Zhang, 2012; Chen & Yan, 2012). It is an inter-disciplinary technology and could open up a new research horizon on fashionable security. Concretely, a fashionable wearable device (FWD) (e.g., embedded into handbags, garments, accessories or jewelries) is applied with the assistance of its wearer's mobile device (e.g., a mobile phone) to provide a secure and fashionable way to recognize strangers for face-to-face social communications. The FWD is decorated with some displaying elements, e.g., Light Emitting Diode (LED) lights. The status of the LED lights is controlled by a corresponding mobile FWD application (MFA) executed in the FWD wearer's mobile device. The communication between the FWD and the MFA is securely paired, thus the information displayed or illustrated by the FWD can be controlled by the MFA. For example, the control signal between the FWD and MFA is transmitted through Bluetooth or other local connection methods.

For secure and fashionable recognition, we use the FWD to illustrate a pre-defined recognition protocol among strangers. The FWD plays as a displaying platform, in order to make short distance pervasive social communications obvious and attractive. The protocol could contain one or several rounds of 'argot' (i.e., a kind of code word) interaction in order to securely make the strangers recognize with each other in crowds. The successful execution of the recognition protocol is coordinated by the mobile devices based on PSN. That is the display of FWDs can be coordinated based on the control and communications of their corresponding MFAs.

The recognition protocol is designed by PSN node users through their mobile devices during the pervasive social networking. If needed, those people unknown with each other can use their mobile devices to define how to recognize with each other if a face-to-face meeting is needed. Note that photo or video sharing may not be preferred by some users who would like to keep their privacy by hiding any tracking clues and personal information. The protocol can be designed via MFA by indicating the identity and type of FWD for mobile device local pairing and the 'argots' used in each step of the recognition protocol, as well as their displaying style. The MFA provides a user interface to help users easily fulfill this function.

6. SIMULATIONS, PROTOTYPES AND USER STUDIES

6.1 A Reputation System Prototype for PSN Chatting and User Study

6.1.1 Prototype

The reputation system for PSN chatting is implemented by extending the functions of Twin application developed by Tempere University of Technology (Chen, Yan & Niemi, 2011). The Twin application is an ad-hoc chatting application based on Nokia Instant Community platform - an energy-efficient and fully distributed pervasive social networking platform developed by the Nokia Research Center, Helsinki (Ahtiainen, et al, 2009). We develop PSN nodes using Nokia N900 with Python and GTK binding. The PSN communications are based on wireless LAN. The TS is implemented with Apache and PHP in Linux platform (Ubuntu 9.04). The connection between the TS and nodes is also based on wireless LAN, which could also be extended to cellular networks (Chen, 2010).

The implemented prototype system has three modules: mobile social chatting, reputation man-

Figure 9. Create a chatting community (Yan, Chen & Shen, 2013)

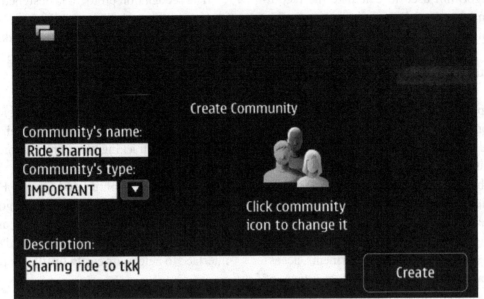

agement and privacy/identity management. The system supports both node-to-node chatting and community chatting. Any user can create a community by indicating the community name and its importance (i.e., the crucial level of chatting topic) through the UI as shown in Figure 9. After creating a community, other people in vicinity can find the community in their device and join the community chatting. PSNTrust allows on-chat voting and reputation visualization during chatting. Figure 10 shows a community chatting UI with personalized reputation visualization and on-chat voting with comments (e.g., "You DOWN Node 3: Too expensive" and "You UP Node 3: Good".). Particularly, a PSNTrust user can select a preferred visualization scheme and activate or deactivate it.

Figure 10. Community chatting UI and on-chat voting (Yan, Chen & Shen, 2013)

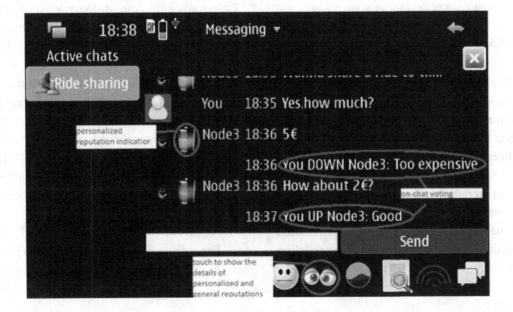

In Figure 10, a reputation visualization scheme is shown with battery volume. PSNTrust also provides detailed information of personalized and general reputations by touching the 'eyes' icon and the user photos in Figure 10.

6.1.2 User Experiment

We performed a between-subject study to investigate the impacts of this prototype on mobile users. We selected 2 groups of participants from two student villages (each had 7 persons). All participants were university students aging between 23 and 28 years old. Among 7 participants in each group, 3 of them were female and 4 were male. They didn't know with each other. All of them had Internet chatting experiences, but none of them had experience on PSN chatting. Group 1 used this system during chatting whilst Group 2 did not (i.e., turned off reputation visualization).

The experiment was designed in a board game style in order to organize the study and make the results of two tests comparable. The participants were asked to simulate three chatting scenarios as described in our survey. Before the experiment, each participant got a card that indicates his/her roles and tasks in chat. The participants tried to make a decision with regard to their chatting purpose. For each scenario, they chatted in a community. During the tests, the chatting information, such as chatting time, contents, length, on-chat voting, and afterwards voting were automatically logged for future analysis.

Additionally, an interview was conducted after the experiment to evaluate the perceived usefulness, perceived ease of use, interface, playfulness and user attitude in terms of PSN chatting. Our interview was designed based on the TAM model (Technology Acceptance Model) and its extension, which indicates that usefulness, ease of use and playfulness lead to user acceptance (Davis, 1989; Venkatesh & Bala, 2008). This theory also indicates that good interface leads to better perceived usefulness and ease of use; playfulness

causes better acceptance (attitude). Finally, we randomly talked to some participants in order to get their additional comments. After the test, each participant was awarded a movie ticket.

6.1.3 Experiment Implications

Investigating the chatting time and length, we observed that displaying reputation information could encourage participants to chat more and become more social (refer to chatting record length), and help them chat in a more efficient way (i.e., chatting time was shorter) than the situation without displaying reputation. We also noted that participants became more serious and took longer time to make a decision in a more crucial chatting scenario (e.g., Scenario 3 - car riding), when the reputation value is visualized (refer to chatting time).

The prototype system has satisfactory evaluation scores with regard to perceived ease of use, perceived usefulness, interface, playfulness and user attitude. In terms of perceived ease of use, we notify that visualizing reputation in PSN chatting made participants easier to select a person they like from many candidates during chatting than without reputation visualization. The result showed that the prototyped system is a very useful and interesting (playful) application that can aid user decision in PSN chatting. Its UI (especially reputation visualization) got good feedback from the participants. They liked using it. Based on the TAM, we can conclude that the prototype system was well accepted by the participants.

6.2 A Prototype of PSN Content Recommendation

We have implemented a prototype system using Nokia N810 tablets as the PSN nodes and an Apache server playing as the TS for PSN content recommendations. We developed the mobile node part on Nokia N810 using Python with GTK binding and server part on Linux

(Ubuntu 9.04) together with Apache, MySql and PHP. PSN communication is based on Wireless LAN. There is no guarantee for PSN nodes to connect to TS. The implementation satisfies all requirements as specified in Section 4.1. We attempt to achieve efficient power consumption by controlling the message length of node communication within 100 bytes and applying an awareness ad hoc networking platform developed in by the Nokia Research Center. This is because the message length of node communications will greatly influence power consumption. The

Figure 11. User interface of node query for content recommendations

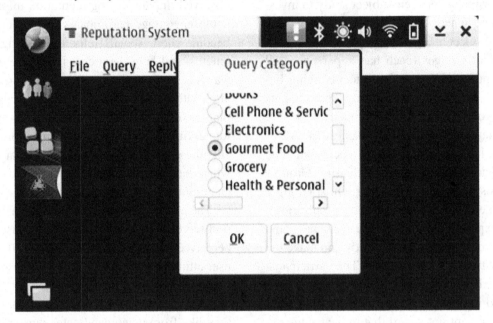

Figure 12. User interface of query response for content recommendations

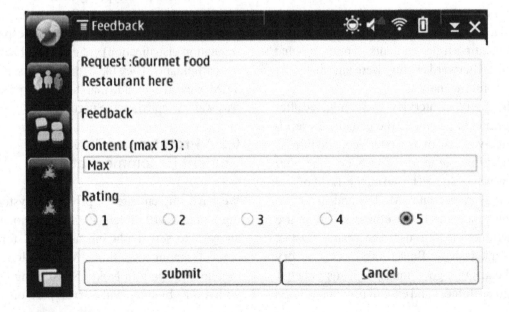

longer the length, the more power will be consumed (Ahtiainen, et al, 2009). The prototype system provides essential security protection on node-server communications with Open SSL and node-node communications by utilizing a community symmetric key. The user interfaces of query and query response are shown in Figure 11 and Figure 12.

6.3 Simulations

We also conducted a series of simulations to evaluate the accuracy, efficiency and robustness of the designed algorithms for PSN trust/reputation generation, trustworthy content recommendations, unwanted traffic control, and user privacy recommendations. Detailed simulation results are presented in (Yan & Chen, 2010; Yan & Chen, 2011; Yan, Kantola, Shi & Zhang, 2013; Yan & Zhang, 2011).

Table 3. Scenarios

Scenarios
1. Right now you are at a shopping center alone, and a product you want is on sale under a condition that ´buy 3 pay 2´. However, you only need one. You want to ask your neighbor(s), whom you don't know, via your mobile phone whether he/she wants to share the discount with you. You would like to meet somebody face-to-face you are unknown for concrete discussions about purchase share after MANET chat. Do you think the proposed system is helpful for you in this scenario?
2. After shopping, you want to watch Avatar in a movie theater. The ticket price is 13.8e. However, if you buy a packet of 5 tickets, it will be 8.6e for each. You want to share the ticket packet cost with your neighbor(s) whom you don't know. You inquire and discuss whether he/she wants to share the discount with you via your mobile phone After MANET based instant social chatting, you think it is necessary to meet some guys you preferred to share a packet ticket cost. Do you think the proposed system is helpful for you in this scenario?
3. After the movie, a lot of people are leaving the theatre. You want to watch a figure skating competition quite far away. You would like to take a taxi and think about sharing a ride. You discuss with your neighbors nearby via your mobile phone whether he/she wants to share the ride with you. Of course, you need to meet some guys you preferred to share a ride face-to-face for further discussion or call a taxi together. Do you think the proposed system is helpful for you in this scenario?

6.4 Pilot Study on Secure Face-to-Face Recognition

We performed a small-scale user study on the social acceptance of the system with the proposed secure face-to-face recognition approach. We showed the low fidelity prototypes to a total of 23 university students (47.8% female). The participants ranged in age from 21-24 years. We showed the participants the system design, its user interface design and the design for recognition protocol generation. We then asked them to provide their feedback on whether this system is useful in a number of scenarios as described in Table 3.

Additionally, we conducted a survey to evaluate the perceived usefulness, perceived ease of use, interface, playfulness and user attitude in terms of the proposed system. The participants were asked to express their agreement on the statements listed in Table 4. A 5-point Likert scale was applied. Our interview was also designed based on the TAM model (Technology Acceptance Model) and its extension (Davis, 1989; Venkatesh & Bala, 2008). Finally, we interviewed the participants in order to get their additional comments. After the test, each participant was awarded a small gift.

The result in Figure 13 showed that the proposed system is a very helpful application that can aid unknown people to recognize with each other for physical face-to-face contact after digital communications in a number of PSN scenarios. The system has satisfactory evaluation scores (over 4) with regard to perceived ease of use, perceived usefulness, interface, playfulness and user attitude, shown in Figure 14. We got the highest average scores (>4.4) in terms of playfulness. We notify that the participants thought the proposed system is an interesting, exciting and joyful application for secure social communications. Based on the TAM, we can conclude that this system was well accepted by the participants.

Table 4. Interview Statements

Purpose	Interview Statements
Perceived ease of use	Q1: I think it is easy for me to recognize a person I don't know with the help of the proposed system.
	Q2: I think It is easy for me to use the proposed system to design a recognition protocol for pervasive social communications.
	Q3: I think it is convenient for me using the proposed system to recognize a person I preferred to meet although I don't know him or her before.
Perceived Usefulness	Q4: The proposed system can help me design my preferred recognition way for face-to-face meetings.
	Q5: The proposed system assists me to find a person in crowds in a safe way.
	Q6: The proposed system is a useful and helpful application.
Interface	Q7: LED display provides a fashionable and attractive way for meeting recognition.
	Q8: The proposed system has a good design on LED display.
	Q9: The proposed system provides a good user interface for recognition protocol design.
Playfulness	Q10: The proposed system is an interesting application.
	Q11: The proposed system is an exciting application.
	Q12: The proposed system provides a joyful way for secure social communications.
Attitude	Q13: I would like to use the proposed system.
	Q14: The proposed system is very cool.
	Q15: The proposed system offers me a way of outstanding in crowds.

Figure 13. Helpfulness

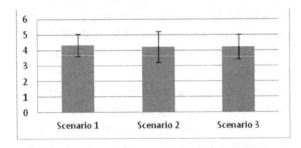

Figure 14. Feedback of interview statements

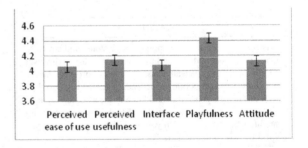

The feedback regarding user interface design is not as good as other items. We will further improve it by applying easily accepted technologies such as voice-control to guide MFA execution and improve user experience.

In addition, the user interview after user survey provided us interesting implications: a) We found other potential use cases such as dating, making friends, healthcare support for the elder, and customer pick-up at the airport that need a secure face-to-face meeting; b) The system should be improved for a better user experience on multi-person recognition. Some participants thought recognizing more than one person could be difficult at the same time; c) Some participants thought that the system has a big potential market. It can be extended for other purposes, such as on-body blogging, on-body advertisement and assisting the arrangement of a social party.

7. FURTHER DISCUSSIONS

Nowadays, social networking is changing the style of people's social life. With the rapid growth and usage of mobile devices, pervasive social networking will play an important role of social activities in the future. Trust, security and privacy have become extremely important and relevant in pervasive social networks. This section further discusses additional issues related to trust, security and privacy in PSN, and concludes the whole chapter.

7.1 Additional Issues

We try to answer the following questions based on our research experiences. The opinions presented below only represent the personal views of the author.

1. How can we infer trust based on social relationships?

Pervasive social networking has a characteristic as pervasive. People who are mostly strangers would like to communication in a pervasive and private way in order to pursue instant reciprocal benefits. In this case, trust is hard to be inferred based on existing social relationships. On the other hand, pervasive social networking can play as an important complement for Internet social networks by extending our daily feelings and relationships with strangers that we may regularly observe but do not interact with in public places. In addition, strangers could become acquaintances later on with the support of pervasive social networking. In this case, PSNTrust can be applied to share PSN experiences by reporting PSN activities to TS and then it is possible to plug in new social relationships into the Internet social networking if users would like to.

2. Can privacy be accomplished based on social groups so only those people who were within the pervasive social network can only access that content?

It is hard to ensure user data privacy based on social groups. It is obvious that any malicious social group members could disclose confidential contents shared within a social group. Thus additional control should be provided. Cryptographic solutions will play an important role to solve this issue. PSNTrust offers flexible PSN data access based on two-dimensional trust levels of different nodes based on attribute-based encryption. Thus, it can protect user data privacy in a flexible manner.

3. Are the issues in PSN different than in regular online social networks, or are extensions?

The issues of trust, security and privacy in PSN are different from those in regular online Internet social networks. The reason is obvious since PSN is based on self-organized mobile networks, not the Internet or mobile Internet. The issues related to trust, security and privacy should be mostly solved in a distributed manner, not a centralized way. The framework for trust, security and privacy should follow the system structure of PSN, supporting the mobility of each PSN nodes. PSNTrust is a hybrid trust management framework that can support PSN trust in a distributed way with the support of a centralized trusted server. It brings convenience to merge pervasive social networking into the Internet social networking.

4. Do we need new models for this?

New models are needed to support the new system structure of PSN, which is obviously different from the traditional Internet based online social networks. This could open a new research area of trust, security and privacy in pervasive social networking.

7.2 Future Research Trend

This chapter only discussed some issues of trust, security and privacy and provided a limited number of solutions based on past work. Towards real trustworthy pervasive social networking, more issues and challenges should be considered and overcome. Herein, we simply list a number of challenges for the readers who are interested in researching this area:

- Efficient private data preservation in a distributed manner in PSN;
- The integration of PSN with online social networks with privacy preservation;
- Anonymous trust evaluation that can hide user identity privacy;
- Sound user experience support for trustworthy PSN;
- The extension of PSN for trustworthy physical social networking based on PSN experiences;
- New applications and services based on PSN.

7.3 Conclusion

This chapter discussed trust management in pervasive social networking. Based on a brief literature review, we proposed PSNTrust, a trust management framework that supports context-aware trust/reputation generation, trustworthy content recommendations, secure communications, unwanted traffic control, user privacy recommendation and preservation, and secure face-to-face recognition. Simulations, prototype implementation and user experiments further prove the effectiveness of our proposed solutions with regard to their accuracy, efficiency, robustness, and usability, as well as social acceptance. Obviously, pervasive social networking is a new application area that plays a significant complement for the Internet social networking. In PSN, trust, security and privacy are the most crucial issues that influence its future

success. Nowadays, academia and industry have initiated a number of research and development activities in this area. But there are still many unsolved issues worth our further investigation. We believe more work should be conducted in order to achieve trustworthy pervasive social networking and assist its real success.

REFERENCES

Adler, B. T., & Alfaro, L. (2007). A content driven reputation system for the Wikipedia. In *Proceedings of WWW*, (pp. 261-270). IEEE.

Ahn, J., & Amatriain, X. (2010). Towards fully distributed and privacy-preserving recommendations via expert collaborative filtering and RESTful linked data. [WI-IAT.]. *Proceedings of WI-IAT, 10*, 66–73.

Ahtiainen, A. et al. (2009). Awareness networking in wireless environments: Means of exchanging information. *IEEE Vehicular Technology Magazine, 4*(3), 48–54. doi:10.1109/MVT.2009.933475.

Bansal, S., & Baker, M. (2003). *Observation-based cooperation enforcement in ad hoc networks*. Palo Alto, CA: Stanford University.

Becchetti, L., Castillo, C., Donatol, D., Leonardi, S., & Baeza-Yates, R. (2006). Using rank propagation and probabilistic counting for link-based spam detection. In Proceedings of WebKDD. WebKDD.

Bethencourt, J., Sahai, A., & Waters, B. (2007). Ciphertext-policy attribute based encryption. In *Proceedings of the 2007 IEEE Symposium on Security and Privacy*, (pp. 321–334). IEEE.

Bi, J., Wu, J., & Zhang, W. (2008). A trust and reputation based anti-SPIM method. In *Proceedings of IEEE INFOCOM* (pp. 2485–2493). IEEE. doi:10.1109/INFOCOM.2008.319.

Bilge, A., & Polat, H. (2010). Improving privacy-preserving NBC-based recommendations by preprocessing. [WI-IAT.]. *Proceedings of WI-IAT, 2010*, 143–147.

Blaze, M., Feigenbaum, J., & Lacy, J. (1996). Decentralized trust management. In *Proceedings of the IEEE Conference on Security and Privacy*, (pp. 164-173). IEEE.

Buchegger, S., & Boudec, J. L. (2002). Performance analysis of the confidant protocol. In *Proceedings of the ACM International Symposium on Mobile Ad Hoc Networking and Computing (MobiHoc)*, (pp. 226-236). ACM.

Buchegger, S., & Boudec, J. Y. L. (2003). The effect of rumor spreading in reputation systems for mobile ad-hoc networks. In *Proceedings of WiOpt Modeling and Optimization in Mobile, Ad Hoc and Wireless Networks*. IEEE.

Chen, Y. (2010). *A privacy-enhanced reputation system for mobile ad hoc services*. (Master Thesis). Aalto University, Espoo, Finland.

Chen, Y., & Yan, Z. (2012). Gemini: A handbag for pervasive social communications. In *Proceedings of IEEE TrustID 2012*. IEEE.

Chen, Y., Yan, Z., & Niemi, V. (2011). Implementation of a reputation system for pervasive social networking. [IEEE.]. *Proceedings of IEEE TrustID, 2011*, 857–862.

Chuong, C., Torabi, T., & Loke, S. W. (2009). Towards context-aware task recommendation. [JCPC.]. *Proceedings of JCPC, 09*, 289–292.

Corritore, C. L., Kracher, B., & Wiedenbeck, S. (2003). On-line trust: Concepts, evolving themes, a model. *International Journal of Human-Computer Studies. Trust and Technology, 58*(6), 737–758.

Davis, F. D. (1989). Perceived usefulness, perceived ease of use, and user acceptance of information technology. *Management Information Systems Quarterly, 13*(3), 319–340. doi:10.2307/249008.

Douceur, J. R. (2002). The sybil attack. [LNCS]. *Proceedings of IPTPS, 2429*, 251–260.

Goyal, V., Pandey, O., Sahai, A., & Waters, B. (2006). Attribute-based encryption for fine-grained access control of encrypted data. In *Proceedings of the 13th ACM Conference on Computer and Communications Security*, (pp. 89–98). ACM.

Guo, Z., Yan, Z., & Wang, F. (2010). A methodology to predicate human-being's movement based on movement group. In *Proceedings of ACM/IEEE CPSCom*, (pp. 612-619). ACM/IEEE.

Gupta, M., Judge, P., & Ammar, M. (2003). A reputation system for peer-to-peer networks. In *Proceedings of the 13th international workshop on Network and Operating Systems Support for Digital Audio and Video (NOSSDAV '03)*. ACM.

Hancock, J. T., Toma, C., & Ellison, N. (2007). The truth about lying in online dating profiles. In *Proceedings of the ACM CHI*, (pp. 449–452). ACM.

Hu, J., & Burmester, M. (2006). LARS: A locally aware reputation system for mobile ad hoc networks. In *Proceedings of the 44th ACM Annual Southeast Regional Conference*, (pp. 119-123). ACM.

Hyytia, E., Virtamo, J., Lassila, P., Kangasharju, J., & Ott, J. (2011). When does content float? Characterizing availability of anchored information in opportunistic content sharing. [IEEE.]. *Proceedings - IEEE INFOCOM, 2011*, 3137–3145. doi:10.1109/INFCOM.2011.5935160.

Jøsang, A., Ismail, R., & Boyd, C. (2007). A survey of trust and reputation systems for online service provision. *Decision Support Systems, 43*(2), 618–644. doi:10.1016/j.dss.2005.05.019.

Katzenbeisser, S., & Petkovic, M. (2008). Privacy-preserving recommendation systems for consumer healthcare services. [ARES.]. *Proceedings of ARES, 08*, 889–895.

Kikuchi, H., Kizawa, H., & Tada, M. (2009). Privacy-preserving collaborative filtering schemes. [ARES.]. *Proceedings of ARES, 09*, 911–916.

Kolan, P., & Dantu, R. (2007). Socio-technical defense against voice spamming. *ACM Transactions on Autonomous and Adaptive Systems, 2*(1).

Kujimura, K., & Nishihara, T. (2003). Reputation rating system based on past behavior of evaluators. In *Proceedings of the 4th ACM Conference on Electronic Commerce*, (pp. 246–247). ACM.

Li, J., Li, R., & Kato, J. (2008). Future trust management framework for mobile ad hoc networks. *IEEE Communications Magazine, 46*(4), 108–115. doi:10.1109/MCOM.2008.4481349.

Li, T., Gao, C., & Du, J. (2009). A NMF-based privacy-preserving recommendation algorithm. [ICISE.]. *Proceedings of ICISE, 09*, 754–757.

Liiv, I., Tammet, T., Ruotsalo, T., & Kuusik, A. (2009). Personalized context-aware recommendations in SMARTMUSEUM: Combining semantics with statistics. [SEMAPRO.]. *Proceedings of SEMAPRO, 09*, 50–55.

Liu, D., Meng, X., & Chen, J. (2008). A framework for context-aware service recommendation. [ICACT.]. *Proceedings of ICACT, 08*, 2131–2134.

Liu, Z., Yau, S. S., Peng, D., & Yin, Y. (2008). A flexible trust model for distributed service infrastructures. In *Proceedings of 11th IEEE Symposium on Object Oriented Real-Time Distributed Computing*, (pp. 108-115). IEEE.

Luo, Y., Le, J., & Chen, H. (2009). A privacy-preserving book recommendation model based on multi-agent. [WCSE.]. *Proceedings of WCSE, 09*, 323–327.

Michiardi, P., & Molva, R. (2002). Core: A collaborative reputation mechanism to enforce node cooperation in mobile ad hoc networks. [LNCS]. *Proceedings of Advanced Communications and Multimedia Security, 2828*, 107–121. doi:10.1007/978-0-387-35612-9_9.

Milgram, S. (1972). The familiar stranger: An aspect of urban anonymity. In *The Individual in a Social World* (pp. 51–53). Reading, MA: Addison-Wesley.

Muller, S., Katzenbeisser, S., & Eckert, C. (2008). Distributed attribute-based encryption. In *Proceedings of the 11th Annual International Conference on Information Security and Cryptology*, (pp. 20–36). IEEE.

O'Donovan, J., & Smyth, B. (2005). Trust in recommender systems. In *Proceedings of IUI'05*, (pp. 167-174). IUI.

Ott, J., Hyytiä, E., Lassila, P. E., Kangasharju, J., & Santra, S. (2011). Floating content for probabilistic information sharing. *Pervasive and Mobile Computing, 7*(6), 671–689. doi:10.1016/j.pmcj.2011.09.001.

Polat, H., & Du, W. L. (2005). Privacy-preserving top-n recommendation on horizontally partitioned data. In *Proceedings of the 2005 IEEE/WIC/ACM International Conference on Web Intelligence*, (pp. 725-731). IEEE.

Raya, M., Papadimitratos, P., Gligory, V. D., & Hubaux, J. P. (2008). On data-centric trust establishment in ephemeral ad hoc networks. In *Proceedings of IEEE INFOCOM* (pp. 1912–1920). IEEE. doi:10.1109/INFOCOM.2008.180.

Resnick, P., Kuwabara, K., Zeckhauser, R., & Friedman, E. (2000). Reputation systems. *Communications of the ACM, 43*(12), 45–48. doi:10.1145/355112.355122.

Resnick, P., & Varian, H. R. (1997). Recommender systems. *Communications of the ACM, 40*(3), 56–58. doi:10.1145/245108.245121.

Resnick, P., & Zeckhauser, R. (2002). Trust among strangers in Internet transactions: Empirical analysis of eBay's reputation system. In M. Baye (Ed.), *Advances in Applied Microeconomics: The Economics of the Internet and E-Commerce* (Vol. 11, pp. 127–157). London: Elsevier. doi:10.1016/S0278-0984(02)11030-3.

Sahai, A., & Waters, B. (2005). Fuzzy identity-based encryption. In *Proceedings of 24th International Conference on the Theory and Application of Cryptographic Techniques*, (pp. 457–473). IEEE.

Sarigöl, E., Riva, O., Stuedi, P., & Alonso, G. (2009). Enabling social networking in ad hoc networks of mobile phones. *Proceedings of VLDB Endow.*, 9(2), 1634–1637.

Seetharam, A., & Ramakrishnan, R. (2008). A context sensitive, yet private experience towards a contextually apt recommendation of service. [IMSAA.]. *Proceedings of IMSAA, 2008*, 1–6.

Song, S., Hwang, K., Zhou, R., & Kwok, Y. K. (2005). Trusted P2P transactions with fuzzy reputation aggregation. *IEEE Internet Computing*, 9(6), 24–34. doi:10.1109/MIC.2005.136.

Stuedi, P., Riva, O., & Alonso, G. (n.d.). *Demo abstract ad hoc social networking using MAND*. Retrieved from: http://www.iks.inf.ethz.ch/publications/files/mobicom08_demo.pdf

Su, X., & Khoshgoftaar, T. M. (2009). A survey of collaborative filtering techniques. *Advances in Artificial Intelligence*. doi:10.1155/2009/421425.

Sun, Y., Han, Z., & Liu, K. J. R. (2008). Defense of trust management vulnerabilities in distributed networks. *IEEE Communications Magazine*, 46(2), 112–119. doi:10.1109/MCOM.2008.4473092.

Sun, Y., Han, Z., Yu, W., & Liu, K. J. R. (2006). A trust evaluation framework in distributed networks: Vulnerability analysis and defense against attacks. In *Proceedings of IEEE INFOCOM* (pp. 1–13). IEEE. doi:10.1109/INFOCOM.2006.154.

Sun, Y., Yu, W., Han, Z., & Liu, K. J. R. (2006). Information theoretic framework of trust modeling and evaluation for ad hoc networks. *IEEE Journal on Selected Areas in Communications*, 24(2), 305–317. doi:10.1109/JSAC.2005.861389.

Tada, M., Kikuchi, H., & Puntheeranurak, S. (2010). Privacy-preserving collaborative filtering protocol based on similarity between items. [AINA.]. *Proceedings of AINA, 10*, 573–578.

Tang, Y., Krasser, S., He, Y., Yang, W. I., & Alperovitch, D. (2008). Support vector machines and random forests modeling for spam senders behavior analysis. In *Proceedings of IEEE GLOBECOM*, (pp. 1-5). IEEE.

Theodorakopoulos, G., & Baras, J. S. (2006). On trust models and trust evaluation metrics for ad hoc networks. *IEEE Journal on Selected Areas in Communications*, 24(2), 318–328. doi:10.1109/JSAC.2005.861390.

Trifunovic, S., Legendre, F., & Anastasiades, C. (2010). Social trust in opportunistic networks. In *Proceedings of IEEE INFOCOM Workshops*, (pp. 1-6). IEEE.

Venkatesh, V., & Bala, H. (2008). Technology acceptance model 3 and a research agenda on interventions. *Decision Sciences*, 39(2), 273–315. doi:10.1111/j.1540-5915.2008.00192.x.

Walsh, K., & Sirer, E. G. (2005). Fighting peer-to-peer SPAM and decoys with object reputation. In Proceedings of P2PECON, (pp. 138-143). P2PECON.

Wang, G., Liu, Q., & Wu, J. (2010). Hierarchical attribute-based encryption for fine-grained access control in cloud storage services. In *Proceedings of the 17th ACM Conference on Computer and Communications Security*, (pp. 735–737). ACM.

Wang, J., Kodama, E., Takada, T., & Li, J. (2010). Mining context-related sequential patterns for recommendation systems. [CAMP.]. *Proceedings of CAMP*, *10*, 270–275.

Wu, B., Goel, V., & Davison, B. D. (2006). Topical TrustRank: Using topicality to combat web spam. In *Proceedings of the 15th international conference on World Wide Web*, (pp. 63-72). IEEE.

Xiao, H., Zou, Y., Ng, J., & Nigul, L. (2010). An approach for context-aware service discovery and recommendation. [IEEE.]. *Proceedings of IEEE ICWS*, *10*, 163–170.

Xiong, L., & Liu, L. (2004). PeerTrust: Supporting reputation-based trust for peer-to-peer electronic communities. *IEEE Transactions on Knowledge and Data Engineering*, *16*(7), 843–857. doi:10.1109/TKDE.2004.1318566.

Z. Yan (Ed.). (2010). *Trust modeling and management in digital environments: From social concept to system development*. Hershey, PA: IGI Global. doi:10.4018/978-1-61520-682-7.

Yan, Z., & Chen, Y. (2010). AdContRep: A privacy enhanced reputation system for MANET content services. In *Proceedings of UIC 2010* (LNCS), (vol. 6406, pp. 414-429). Berlin: Springer.

Yan, Z., & Chen, Y. (2011). AdChatRep: A reputation system for MANET chatting. In *Proceedings of SCI2011 in UbiComp2011*, (pp. 43-48). ACM.

Yan, Z., Chen, Y., & Shen, Y. (2013). A practical reputation system for pervasive social chatting. *Journal of Computer and System Sciences*, *79*(5), 556–572. doi:10.1016/j.jcss.2012.11.003.

Yan, Z., Chen, Y., & Zhang, P. (2012). An approach of secure and fashionable recognition for pervasive face-to-face social communications. [IEEE.]. *Proceedings of IEEE WiMob*, *2012*, 853–860.

Yan, Z., & Holtmanns, S. (2008). Trust modeling and management: from social trust to digital trust. In R. Subramanian (Ed.), *Computer Security, Privacy and Politics: Current Issues, Challenges and Solutions*. Hershey, PA: Idea Group Inc. doi:10.4018/978-1-59904-804-8.ch013.

Yan, Z., Kantoal, R., Shi, G., & Zhang, P. (2013). Unwanted content control via trust management in pervasive social networking. In *Proceedings of IEEE TrustCom2013*. Melbourne, Australia: IEEE.

Yan, Z., Kantola, R., & Shen, Y. (2012). Unwanted traffic control via hybrid trust management. In *Proceedings of IEEE TrustCom 2012*. Liverpool, UK: IEEE.

Yan, Z., Liu, C., Niemi, V., & Yu, G. (2009). *Trust information indication: Effects of displaying trust information on mobile application usage*. Retrieved from http://research.nokia.com/files/ NRCTR2009004.pdf.

Yan, Z., & Niemi, V. (2009). A methodology towards usable trust management. In *Proceedings of ATC'09* (LNCS), (vol. 5586, pp. 179-193). Berlin: Springer.

Yan, Z., Niemi, V., Chen, Y., Zhang, P., & Kantola, R. (2013). Towards trustworthy mobile social networking. In *Mobile Social Networking: An Innovative Approach*. Berlin: Springer.

Yan, Z., & Zhang, P. (2011). AdPriRec: A context-aware recommender system for user privacy in MANET services. In *Proceedings of UIC2011* (LNCS), (vol. 6905, pp. 295-309). Berlin: Springer.

Yan, Z., Zhang, P., & Deng, R. H. (2012). TruBeRepec: A trust-behavior-based reputation and recommender system for mobile applications. *Journal of Personal and Ubiquitous Computing, Springer*, *16*(5), 485–506. doi:10.1007/s00779-011-0420-2.

Yang, Y., & Sun, Y. Kay, S., & Yang, Q. (2009). Defending online reputation systems against collaborative unfair raters through signal modeling and trust. In *Proceedings of SAC'09*, (pp. 1308-1315). SAC.

Yap, G., Tan, A., & Pang, H. (2007). Discovering and exploiting causal dependencies for robust mobile context-aware recommenders. *IEEE Transactions on Knowledge and Data Engineering, 19*(7), 977–992. doi:10.1109/TKDE.2007.1065.

Yu, Z., Zhou, X., Zhang, D., Chin, C., Wang, X., & Men, J. (2006). Supporting context-aware media recommendations for smart phones. *IEEE Pervasive Computing / IEEE Computer Society [and] IEEE Communications Society, 5*(3), 68–75. doi:10.1109/MPRV.2006.61.

Zhang, D., & Yu, Z. (2007). Spontaneous and context-aware media recommendation in heterogeneous spaces. [IEEE.]. *Proceedings of the IEEE VTC, 07*, 267–271.

Zhang, H., Duan, H., Liu, W., & Wu, J. (2009). IPGroupRep: A novel reputation based system for anti-spam. In *Proceedings of the Symposia and Workshops on Ubiquitous, Autonomic and Trusted Computing*, (pp. 513-518). ACM.

Zhang, J., Xu, W., Peng, Y., & Xu, J. (2010). MailTrust: A mail reputation mechanism based on improved TrustGuard. In *Proceedings of the International Conference on Communications and Mobile Computing* (CMC), (pp. 218-222). CMC.

Zhang, X., Han, B., & Liang, W. (2009). Automatic seed set expansion for trust propagation based auti-spamming algorithms. In *Proceedings of the Eleventh International Workshop on Web Information and Data Management*, (pp. 31-38). IEEE.

Zheleva, E., Kolcz, A., & Getoor, L. (2008). Trusting spam reporters: a reporter-based reputation system for email filtering. *ACM Transactions on Information Systems, 27*(1). doi:10.1145/1416950.1416953.

Zouridaki, C., Mark, B. L., Hejmo, M., & Thomas, K. R. (2006). Robust cooperative trust establishment for MANETs. In *Proceedings of the Fourth ACM Workshop on Security of Ad Hoc and Sensor Networks*, (pp. 23-34). ACM.

APPENDIX

Questions and Exercises

1. Please summarize the research methods applied in the evaluation of proposed trust solutions in this chapter.

2. Could you please propose a comprehensive research method that can be applied to evaluate the trustworthiness of a trust management system in pervasive social networking?

Section 3

Autonomic and Usable Trust Management in Mobile Environments

Chapter 7
User Trust and Human–Computer Trust Interaction

ABSTRACT

Trust plays an important role in human-computer interaction. It helps people overcome risk and uncertainty during the usage of a digital computing system. With the rapid growth of computer, communication, and networking technology, human-computer trust has been paid attention to, especially for human and mobile device interaction. This chapter investigates the factors that influence the trust in human-computer interaction (i.e., the construct of Human-Computer Trust Interaction [HCTI]). Based on a literature survey, a research model of human-computer trust interaction is explored. This model contains three root constructs: interaction intention, computer system trust, and communication trust. They are further delineated into 15 sub-constructs. Based on this model, the authors propose a number of instructions to improve user trust for human-computer interaction.

1. INTRODUCTION

Trust is firstly a social phenomenon. It is a multidimensional, multidisciplinary and multifaceted concept (Yan, 2007). Trust has been defined by researchers in many different ways, which often reflect the paradigms of particular academic disciplines. Common to these definitions are the notions of confidence, belief and expectation on the reliability, integrity, ability, etc. or characters of an entity (Yan, 2007). With the rapid growth of computer, communication and networking technology, human-computer trust has been paid attention to.

Trust is an integral component in many kinds of human interaction, allowing people to act under uncertainty and with the risk of negative consequences (Artz & Gil, 2007). Recently, researchers in Human-Computer Interaction (HCI) and human factors have studied trust in an on-line context.

DOI: 10.4018/978-1-4666-4765-7.ch007

Copyright © 2014, IGI Global. Copying or distributing in print or electronic forms without written permission of IGI Global is prohibited.

The realization that design can affect the trust of a user has had implications for user interface design, web sites and interactivity in general (Nielsen, 1999). Some researchers examined the cues that may affect trust. These cues range from design and interface elements, to perceived website credibility, to the extent to which the technology is perceived and responded to as a social actor (e.g., photographs and other indicators of social presence) (Corritore, Kracher & Wiedenbeck, 2003). Research focuses on the cues that convey trustworthiness to users. Interface design can give a cue of trust or signal trustworthiness (Corritore, Kracher & Wiedenbeck, 2003; Riegelsberger, Sasse & McCarthy, 2005a). On the other hand, Lee and Chung (2009) found that computer system quality and the quality of information provided by the computer influence trust and satisfaction of users.

Theory of Reasoned Action (TRA) posits that beliefs lead to attitudes, which lead to behavioral intentions, which lead to the behavior itself (Fishbein & Ajzen, 1975). Numerous researchers have conceptualized trust as a behavior, which has been validated in work collaboration and social communications (Deutsch, 1973; Fox, 1974; Anderson & Narus, 1990). Prior research has also confirmed a strong correlation between behavioral intentions and an actual behavior, especially for software system usage (Sheppard, Hartwick & Warshaw, 1988; Venkatesh & Davis, 2000; Venkatesh et al., 2003). Muir found a positive correlation between trust and use (Muir, 1994; Muir & Moray, 1996). The relationship between trust and interaction behavior is obvious since usage through human-computer interaction implies trust. Lee and Moray found that trust in a system partially explained system use, but other factors (such as the user's own ability to provide manual control) also influenced the system use (Lee & Moray, 1992). However, existing researches did not study or investigate a comprehensive construct of human-computer trust interaction. Thus, it lacks a generic guideline for building up trust interaction between human-beings and computers.

This chapter studies the factors that influence the trust in human-computer interaction, i.e., the construct of human-computer trust interaction (HCTI). HCTI plays an indispensible role in achieving usable trust management in digital computing, communication and networking environments. Based on a literature survey about system trust solutions, we explore a research model of HCTI and propose instructions to improve user trust for human-computer interaction. This chapter is based on the work presented by Yan, Kantola & Zhang (2011).

2. SYSTEM TRUST SOLUTIONS

In this section, we survey the work in the literature about system trust solutions. Trust in human-computer interaction can be enhanced by a number of technologies: a) user interface (UI) design for trust; b) trust information notification and visualization; c) trust management for computer systems and computer communications.

3.1 UI Design for Trust

Trust allows people to live in a risky and uncertain situation by providing the means to decrease complexity. It is the key to decision making and engaging in usage. It has been well realized that the design of computer user interface can affect the trust of a user (Nielsen, 1999).

Some researchers are examining the cues that may affect trust. These cues range from design and interface elements, to perceived website credibility, to the extent to which the technology is perceived and responded to as a social actor (Corritore, Kracher & Wiedenbeck, 2003). Wang and Emurian (2005) identified the types of trust cues that include interface design features, structure design (e.g., the look and feel of a web site), content design (e.g., inclusion of security and privacy policy seals of approval or third party certificates) (Jensen, Potts & Jensen, 2005) and social cue design (e.g., photographs and other indicators of social presence). In addition, trust is influenced by perceived integrity and expertise, predictability or familiarity of content and reputation (e.g., Bhattacherjee, 2002; Briggs et al., 2002; McKnight & Chervany, 2001).

Work on trust cues focuses on the cues that convey trustworthiness to users. Aspects of the interface design can give cues for trustworthiness (Corritore, Kracher & Wiedenbeck, 2003), or signal trustworthiness (Riegelsberger, Sasse & McCarthy, 2005b). Cues that have been found to have a positive impact on trustworthiness perceptions include ease of navigation or ease of access (Nielsen et al., 2000), good use of visual design elements (Kim & Moon, 1997), the presence or absence of visual anchors, interpersonal cues or prominent features such as a photograph, video/audio, avatar or trust seal (Riegelsberger et al., 2003; Riegelsberger et al., 2005a; Fogg, 2002; Olson et al., 2002; Sillence et al., 2006), but which strongly depends on context variables, as well as individual differences and personality (Riegelsberger, 2003; Riegelsberger & Sasse, 2001; Steinbrück et al., 2002; Lumsden & MacKay, 2006), freedom from small grammatical and typographical errors (Nielsen et al., 2000; Fogg et al., 2001b), an overall attractiveness and professional look (Nielsen et al., 2000; Fogg et al., 2001b, Fogg et al., 2002; Stanford et al., 2002; Kim & Moon, 1998; Sillence et al., 2006; Araujo & Araujo, 2003), ease of searching (Nielsen et al., 2000), professional images of products (Nielsen et al., 2000) and ease of carrying out transactions (Lohse & Spiller, 1998; Nielsen et al., 2000; Corritore et al., 2003). But the value of third-party trust logos and seals of approval is not clear (Corritore, Kracher & Wiedenbeck, 2003; Schechter et al., 2007). Users appeared to not notice or care about them (Nielsen et al., 2000; Schechter et al., 2007).

Particularly, social cues are important in the design of trustworthy websites or user interface. Appropriate graphics and photographs can add to a sense of social presence and inclusion whilst inappropriate mission statements or alienating language can have an opposite effect (Wang & Emurian, 2005; Sillence et al., 2006). However, research on the use of images of website personnel is contradictory: some studies found such images were a positive cue (Nielsen et al., 2000; Fogg et al., 2001a; Steinbrück et al., 2002), and others found them to be neutral or negative (Riegelsberger & Sasse, 2001). Social dialogue, an implementation in an embodied conversation agent was demonstrated to have an effect on trust for users with a disposition to be extroverts (Bickmore & Cassell, 2001). Real-time interactivity, but not through voice, also increased the judgments of friendliness and the trustworthiness of an on-line salesperson (Basso et al., 2001). Online word-of-mouth systems could affect user trust in e-commerce, where users can rate the products offered for sale (Awad & Ragowsky, 2008).

Information content also provides trust cues (Corritore et al., 2003). Providing content that is appropriate and useful to the target audience has been identified as a strong cue to trustworthiness (Shelat & Egger, 2002). On the other hand, conveying expertise, providing comprehensive information, and projecting honesty, lack of bias and shared values between the website and the user provide positive cues (Lee et al., 2000; Nielsen et al., 2000; Fogg et al., 2001b). In electronic commerce, company information, range of merchandise, branding, promotions, security, fulfillment and customer service affect user trust (Lohse & Spiller, 1998; Nielsen et al., 2000; Fogg et al., 2001b; Riegelsberger & Sasse, 2001; Corritore et al., 2003). Herlocker, Konstan and Riedl (2000) studied the influence of explanation on the user's acceptance of Automated Collaborative Filtering (ACF) systems. Cramer et al. (2008) showed that explaining to a user why a recommendation was made increased acceptance of the recommendation. Recent research has suggested that trust in an automated recommender can be increased by a conversational interface and disclosure of what the recommender system knows about its users (Zimmerman & Kurapati, 2002; Corritore et al., 2003).

3.2 Trust Information Notification and Visualization

Trust information notification and visualization provides useful information for trust. Notification systems attempt to efficiently and effectively deliver current and important information to users without causing unwanted distraction to ongoing tasks (McCrickard, Czerwinski & Bartram, 2003). However, some issues remain unexplored in this area. McCrickard et al. commented that the effects of incoming notifications on ongoing computing tasks have been relatively unexplored (McCrickard, Czerwinski & Bartram, 2003). Notification without usage interruption still lacks investigation, especially for mobile and ubiquitous devices that include a small display element. Antifakos et al. conducted experiments to show that displaying confidence information increases user trust in a system in various contexts classified by criticalness (Antifakos, Kern, Schiele & Schwaninger, 2005). Rukzio et al. (2006), however, proved that the user needs slightly more time and produces slightly more errors when the system confidence is visualized. The contradictory results implied that the visualization of system confidence seems questionable or works differently in different situations.

Yan et al. (2010) found that visualizing trust information could leverage usage behavior and decisions on mobile application usage. They explored the impact of trust information visualization on mobile application usage with a three-stage experiment conducted in both Finland and China (1) by studying user opinions on the importance of mobile applications, (2) by evaluating the

impact of a trust indicator on mobile application usage and (3) by evaluating the impact of a trust/reputation indicator on mobile application usage. Although the results achieved in this study in Finland and China showed small differences on usage willingness and remarkable difference on trust information check willingness, both countries indicated that visualizing the reputation value of an application and/or the individual trust value of a user can assist in mobile application usage with different importance rates.

3.3 Trust Management

Rather than identifying specific interface elements that are perceived as signals for trustworthiness (Riegelsberger, Sasse, & McCarthy, 2005b), research on trust management play an important role to enhance the trustworthiness of a computing, communication or networking system. Trust management is the technology to collect information to make a trust decision; evaluate the criteria related to trust; monitor and reevaluate existing trust relationships; and further ensure the dynamically changed trust relationships and automate the above processes.

Recently, trust management has been emerging as a promising technology to facilitate collaboration among entities in a digital environment where traditional security paradigms cannot be enforced due to lack of centralized control and incomplete knowledge of the environment. Trust management deals with security policies, credentials, and trust relationships (Blaze, Feigenbaum & Lacy, 1996). It has been applied in various areas to enhance system trust and user trust in a computing, communication or networking system (Yan, 2010). It is also applied to support e-commerce and web services.

Various trust management systems have been described in the literature, as described in Chapter 3. Basically, there are three categories of trust management systems. The first is security enhanced trust management solutions, e.g., trusted computing technology based solutions. This kind of solutions applies sound security technologies in order to ensure a computer system's trustworthiness. It deals with root trust module, security policies, credentials, privacy and trust relationships. The second is trust evaluation based solutions, e.g., reputation systems. Trust evaluation is a technical approach to calculate trust value for the purpose of trust management. The third is a hybrid trust management solution by adopting both of above technologies.

Trust and reputation mechanisms have been proposed in various fields of distributed systems, such as ad hoc networks, peer-to-peer (P2P) systems, Grid computing, pervasive computing, social networking, cloud computing and e-commerce (Yan, 2010), as well as computing platforms and Internet architecture (Yan, 2007; Yan & Prehofer, 2010; Yan, Kantola & Shen, 2011). Recently, many mechanisms have been developed for supporting trusted communications and collaborations among computing nodes in the distributed system (Sun et al., 2006; Zhang et al., 2005; Theodorakopoulos & Baras, 2006; Lin et al., 2004). Notably, other technologies, such as identity management, risk management and privacy enhancement, are also essential to support sound trust management.

3. RESEARCH MODEL

We theorize that three root constructs will play a significant role as direct determinants of HCTI: interaction intention, computer system trust and communication trust. Each root construct is consistent of a number of sub-constructs. The labels used for the constructs describe the essence of the construct and are meant to be independent of any particular theoretical perspective. In the remainder of this section, we define each of the determinants, specify the role of factors and provide the theoretical justification for hypotheses. Figure 1 presents our research model. The

definitions of constructs and measurement scale items are described in Table 1. Most items in the measurement scale are adapted from prior related research, and are modified to fit this research context. The items on personal motivations and perceived usefulness are designed based on the definitions in TAM (Venkatesh & Davis, 2000; Davis, Bagozzi & Warshaw, 1989). The items about social factors, perceived ease of use, and relative advantage are the same as the design in Venkatesh et al. (2003). The items about reputation/brand and personality are designed on the basis of the theoretic results achieved in (Corritore et al., 2003; Grabner-Kräuter & Kaluscha, 2003; Yan, Dong, Niemi & Yu, 2011; Yan, Kantola & Zhang, 2011).

3.1 Interaction Intention (II)

Interaction intention is the degree of willingness or disposition to interact a computing, communication or networking system. Trust is seen as an intervening variable that mediates user behavior with computers (Muir, 1994). The theory of reasoned action (TRA) posits that beliefs lead to attitudes, which lead to behavioral intentions, which lead to the behavior itself (Fishbein & Ajzen, 1975). Additionally, numerous researchers have conceptualized trust as a behavior (Anderson & Narus, 1990; Fox, 1974; Deutsch, 1973). Prior research has also confirmed a strong correlation between behavioral intentions and actual behavior, especially for human - software system interaction (Sheppard, Hartwick, & Warshaw, 1988; Venkatesh & Davis, 2000). Grounded on the effort of TRA, theory of planned behavior (TPB) was proposed to eliminate the limitations of the original model in dealing with the behavior over which people have incomplete volitional control (Ajzen, 1991).

One important issue that contributes to whether the users would like to use a new product or system is how much they trust it. Muir is one of the first

Figure 1. A research model

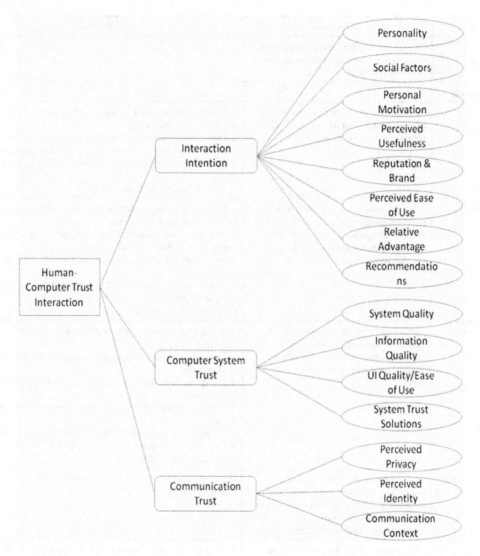

researchers to look at a decision process between supervisors and automated systems. She verifies the hypothesis proposed by Sheridan (1980) that the supervisor's intervention behavior is based upon his/her trust in automation. A positive correlation between trust and use has been proved (Muir, 1994; Muir & Moray, 1996). The relationship between trust and interaction behavior is obvious.

Thus, we expect that the influence of human-computer trust interaction will be moderated by human's interaction intention.

Personality (P)

Personality is the particular combination of emotional, attitudinal, and behavioral response patterns of an individual. Personality was one of the important factors that might affect usage decision and usage behavior. Different personalities attribute different importance levels to each of accepted trust cues in HCI (such as branding, third party security seals, clearly stated policies, vendor information and professional user interface

Table 1. Constructs and Definitions and Scales

Constructs	Definitions	Scales
II: Interaction Intention (root construct)	The degree of willingness or disposition to interact a computing, communication or networking system;	
Sub-Construct		
Personality (P)	Personality is the particular combination of emotional, attitudinal, and behavioral response patterns of an individual;	1. I believe the computer system I used will be continuously improving and upgrading. 2. I have confidence on the future of computer systems. 3. I think the computer system I used is liked by most people. 4. I think the computer systems benefit my life and work very much. (Yan, Dong, Niemi & Yu, 2009)
Social Factors (SF)	The individual's internalization of the reference group's subjective culture, and specific interpersonal agreements that the individual has made with others, in specific social situations;	1. I use the computer system because of the proportion of coworkers who use the system. 2. The senior management of this business has been helpful in the use of the computer system. 3. My supervisor is very supportive of the use of the computer system for my job. 4. In general, the organization has supported the use of the computer system. (Venkatesh et al., 2003)
Perceived Usefulness (PU)	The degree to which a person believes that using a particular computing, communication or networking system would enhance his or her benefits or profits;	1. Using the computer system would enable me to accomplish tasks more quickly. 2. Using the computer system would improve my working performance. 3. Using the computer system in my job would increase my productivity. 4. Using the computer system would enhance my effectiveness on the job. 5. Using the computer system would make it easier to do my job. 6. I would find the computer system useful in my job. (Venkatesh et al., 2003)
Personal Motivation (PM)	The perception that interaction of a computing, communication or networking system will achieve valued outcomes that are distinct from the activity itself, such as improved performance, benefits or profits;	the same items as perceived usefulness from TAM (items 1 through 6 below).
Reputation & Brand	The perspective that the public opinion of a computing, communication or networking system and its vendor influences the intension of HCI;	1. I like the computer system developed by a famous vendor. 2. I like using a computer system with a popular brand. 3. I would like to select using a computer system recommended by many people and with good feedback. (Yan, Dong, Niemi & Yu, 2009)
Perceived Ease of Use (ES)	The degree to which a person believes that using a system would be free of effort;	1. Learning to operate the computer system would be easy for me. 2. I would find it easy to get the computer system to do what I want it to do. 3. My interaction with the computer system would be clear and understandable. 4. I would find the computer system to be flexible to interact with. 5. It would be easy for me to become skillful at using the computer system. 6. I would find the computer system easy to use. (Venkatesh et al., 2003)

continued on followig page

Table 1. Continued

Constructs	Definitions	Scales
Relative Advantage (RA)	The degree to which using a computing, communication or networking system is perceived as being better than using its precursor or other similarly functioned systems;	1. Using the computer system enables me to accomplish tasks more quickly. 2. Using the computer system improves the quality of the work I do. 3. Using the computer system makes it easier to do my job. 4. Using the computer system enhances my effectiveness on the job. 5. Using the computer system increases my productivity. (Venkatesh et al., 2003)
Recommendation (R)	The information provided to suggest a behavior;	1. I would like to recommend a computer system that I have good usage experiences. 2. High recommendations on a computer system would encourage me to use it. 3. The more people recommend a computer system, the easier for me to select using it.
ST: Computer System Trust (root construct)	The degree of trustworthiness of a computing, communication or networking system;	
Sub-Construct		
System Quality (SQ)	The degree to which the system can perform with regard to a number of concerned quality attributes;	1. I like using the computer system if it performs well as my expectation. 2. I like continuously using the computer system if my previous usage experience is good. 3. I like the computer system if it performs efficiently. 4. I like the computer system if it is secure and dependable.
Information Quality (IQ)	The reliability and correctness of the information or contents provided by the computing, communication or networking system;	1. I like using the computer system if it can provide accurate information to me. 2. I like using the computer system if it can provide contents efficiently. 3. I use the computer system since it provides me sufficient information. 4. I use the computer system because I can find the contents I need.
UI Quality (UQ)	The feeling of use, the feeling of interaction trust and the ease of use;	1. I use the computer system because its user interface is attractive for me. 2. I use the computer system because its user interface is easy for me to follow. 3. I use the computer system because interacting with it is full of fun.
System Trust Solution (TS)	The mechanisms or technologies applied by the computing, communication or networking system in order to enhance its own trustworthiness, such as security, privacy, dependability and usability, and make its users feel trust during system usage;	1. I use the computer system because it is designed with sound security solution. 2. I use the computer system because it can preserve my privacy very well. 3. I use the computer system because it is reliable and free of problem. 4. I use the computer system because it obviously provides good solution to make me away from risk. 5. I use the computer system because I feel safe using it.
CT: Communication Trust (root construct)	The degree of trustworthiness in communications	

continued on followig page

Table 1. Continued

Constructs	Definitions	Scales
Sub-Construct		
Perceived Privacy (PP)	The degree to which a person believes that using a system would be free of concerned private information disclosure;	1. Using the computer system would enable me to protect my private data that I care. 2. Using the computer system would keep my private information in a better way than other systems. 3. Using the computer system would guarantee my privacy. 5. Using the computer system would make me care little about my privacy.
Perceived Identity (PI)	The degree to which a person believes that a computing, communication or networking system would reliably recognize entities for communications;	1. Using the computer system would enable me to identify other communication entities. 2. Using the computer system would help me to identify other people in a good way. 3. The computer system would guarantee correct identity. 4. The computer system would provide right and sufficient identity information.
Communication Context (CC)	Any information that can be used to characterize the situation of communication.	1. A secure communication channel makes me feel safe when using the computer system. 2. Communications in a computer system via the Internet can't guarantee everything I concerned. 3. I am open to make social communications via social networking.

design, etc). Extroversion and openness to experience lead to a high disposition to trust. However, neuroticism and conscientiousness lead to a low disposition to trust (Lumsden & Mackay, 2006; Tan & Sutherland, 2004). Deutsch (1960) found a significant correlation between trust and personal pre-disposition. Emotion and mood could also influence trust judgment (Dunn & Schweitzer, 2005). Thus, we believe that the property of human is an influential factor of the trust in human-computer interaction.

Social Factors (SF)

Social factors are defined as the individual's internalization of the reference group's subjective culture, and specific interpersonal agreements that the individual has made with others, in specific social situations (Venkatesh et al., 2003).

Cultural factors are important variables affecting trust and its development (Baba et al., 1996).

Yamagishi and Yamagishi (1994) found that compared with American, Japanese have a generally low level of trust. Karvonen (2001) compared trust of consumers from Finland, Sweden and Iceland in e-commerce. She found that Finnish consumers are the most cautious and Icelandic consumers are the most trusting. Cultural deviation influenced trust in an on-line environment (Karvonen, 2001). More generally, the level of social trust varied substantially among countries (Huang, Keser, Leland & Shachat, 2002). The culture-dependent nature of trust suggests that trust in human-computer interaction may need to be verified when they are extrapolated from one culture to another. Zuboff (1988) found that the culture associated with people who had been exposed to computer led to greater trust and acceptance of automation. Thus, we propose that social factors (e.g., culture) will influence trust when a human-being is interacting with a computing, communication or networking system.

Personal Motivation (PM) and Perceived Usefulness (PU)

Personal motivation is the perception that interaction of a computing, communication or networking system will achieve valued outcomes that are distinct from the activity itself, such as improved performance, benefits or profits. It is the intrinsic reason of a human-being to initiate his/her intention to interact a computer system (Davis et al. 1992; McKnight et al., 2002; Yan, Dong, Niemi & Yu, 2009). Thereby, we propose personal motivation's influence on HCTI.

Perceived usefulness is the degree to which a person believes that using a particular computing, communication or networking system would enhance his or her benefits or profits (Venkatesh et al., 2003). Davis et al. (1989) studied the positive influence of perceived usefulness on the acceptance of information technology, which includes computer systems. Thus, we think that perceived usefulness will positively influence interaction intension.

Reputation and Brand

Reputation & brand indicate the perspective that the public opinion on a computing, communication or networking system and its vendor with regard to the intension of HCI. Reputation is public trust derived from direct and indirect knowledge or experiences (Yan, Liu, Niemi & Yu, 2010). It is widely accepted that trust is influenced by brand and reputations (Corritore et al. 2003; Grabner-Kräuter & Kaluscha, 2003; Kim et al., 2008; Yan, 2010). Thus, we expect that reputation and brand will influence the interaction intension of human-beings with a computing, communication or networking system.

Perceived Ease of Use (EU)

Perceived ease of use is defined as the degree to which a person believes that using a system would

be free of effort (Venkatesh et al., 2003). It was indicated by the previous researches that ease of use is one of important variables that are good predictors for behavior intention to use on-line shopping (David et al., 1989; Wu & Chen, 2005). Thus, we propose that perceived ease of use will positively influence interaction intension.

Relative Advantage (RA)

Relative advantage is defined as the degree to which using a computing, communication or networking system is perceived as being better than using its precursor or other similarly functioned systems. Yan et al. studied trust behaviors of mobile application usage (Yan, Dong, Niemi, Yu, 2009; Yan, Zhang & Deng, 2012). One of the trust behaviors is correlation behavior, which is the usage behaviors correlated to mobile applications with similar functionalities. They found that more usage of one application than other similar ones implies more trust. Thus, through comparison, we can find a cue of human-computer trust interaction. Thereby, we propose that relative advantage will positively influence interaction intention and imply trust in the usage of a computing, communication or networking system.

Recommendations (R)

Recommendation is the information provided to suggest a behavior. Recommender systems generally apply information filtering technique that attempts to recommend items (e.g., a computer system, web pages, etc.) that are likely to be of interest to users (Resnick & Varian, 1997). Typically, a recommender system compares a user profile to some reference characteristics, and seeks to predict the 'rating' that a user would give to an item they had not yet considered or experienced (Hancock, Toma & Ellison, 2007). These characteristics may be from the item (a content-based approach) or the user's social environment (a collaborative filtering approach) (Su & Khoshgoftaar, 2009). Obviously, recommendations imply the popularity and quality of a recommended item, which is statistically tailored based on the taste of a recommendee. Thereby, we propose that recommendations to use a computing, communication or networking system will have positive influence on the human-computer interaction intension.

3.2 Computer System Trust

Computer system trust is defined as the degree of trustworthiness of a computing, communication or networking system, which concerns system security and dependability; information quality provided by the system; UI quality such as ease of use and its intrinsic trust solutions.

System Quality (SQ) and Information Quality (IF)

System quality is defined as the degree to which the system can perform with regard to a number of concerned quality attributes. Avizienis, Laprie, Randell & Landwehr (2004) summarized the quality attributes that should be considered in trusted computing. The quality attributes consist of availability, reliability, integrity, safety, maintainability, and confidentiality. Of which, the first listed five attributes are related to dependability, while availability, integrity, and confidentiality are related to security. The quality of used computer systems could be an essential (but not sufficient) condition of human-computer interaction trust (Kim & Prabhakar, 2004; Pavlou, 2003). Muir and Moray (1996) argued that trust in automated machines is based mostly on the perceptions of users of the expertise of the machine, i.e., the extent to which the automation performs its function properly. Lee and Chung (2009) found that system quality and the quality of information provided by the computer influence user trust and satisfaction. Information quality is defined as the reliability and correctness of the information or contents provided by the computer system. Thereby, we

propose that system quality and the quality of information provided by the system will influence the human-computer trust interaction.

UI Quality (UQ)

UI quality is defined as the feeling of use, the feeling of interaction trust and the ease of use. Particularly, ease of use is the degree to which using a computer system is perceived as being difficult (Moore & Benbasat, 1991). Based on the survey in Section II, it is obvious that UI design and its quality can influence trust. Thus, we propose that UI quality will influence the human-computer trust interaction.

System Trust Solutions (TS)

System trust solutions are the mechanisms or technologies applied by the computing, communication or networking system in order to enhance its own trustworthiness, such as security, privacy, dependability and usability, and make its users feel trust during system usage. Three trust solutions are applied in the literature: a) UI design for trust; b) trust information notification and visualization; c) trust management for computing, communication or networking systems. All of these solutions could be applied to improve the trustworthiness of the system. Thus, we propose the positive influence of system trust solutions on human-computer trust interaction.

3.3 Communication Trust

Nowadays, computers are generally connected through various networks, e.g., the Internet and mobile networks. They help users remotely communicate with each other. Computer communication plays an important role in people's digital life. Particularly, the computer could be a smart phone and the human-computer interaction could be for the purpose of a telephone call. Thus, communication trust becomes an impact factor of HCTI. That is the degree of trustworthiness in communications, which concerns the perceived identities of communication parties, perceived privacy and communication context. All these factors relate to communication trust that happen before or during "interaction". For emphasizing the importance of computer communications, we define the communication trust as one of the root constructs of HCTI.

Perceived Privacy (PP)

Perceived privacy is defined as the degree to which a person believes that using a system would be free of concerned private information disclosure. Posting privacy policy is considered good business practice and allows consumers to make informed decisions about using the site and disclosing their information (Culnan, 1999). However, few people actually read the privacy policy. A 2002 report by Jupiter Media Metrix (CyberAtlas, 2002) found that only 40% of Web users read the privacy policies of sites on which they plan to make a purchase. Kim and Moon (1998) found that visual design factors of user interface can affect perceptions of privacy. The prominence of privacy policy links had a significant effect on preference (Resnick & Montania, 2003). On the other hand, perceived privacy was mediated by trust. Low concerned privacy compensates high trust, and vice versa (Joinson, Reips, Buchanan & Schofield, 2010). Obviously, a computer system with better privacy enhancement solution and higher level of privacy policy compliance can achieve more trust. Thus, we propose that perceived privacy of a computer system will influence the human-computer trust interaction.

Perceived Identity (PI)

Perceived identity is the degree to which a person believes that a computing, communication or networking system would reliably recognize entities for computing, communications or networking. Identity authentication is the basis of trust establishment. The researchers in SECURE project held such an opinion that the ability to reliably recognize another entity is sufficient to establish trust in that entity based on past experiences, and entity recognition provides a local reference for trust (Cahill et al., 2003). Identity management is the foundation of trust management, especially for evaluating the trust relationships among system entities and ensuring the relationships. Meanwhile, identity management also plays a crucial role to support authentication, authorization, access control, policy management, and key management, as well as personalized services. Without the proper support of identity management, trust management cannot be practically deployed in a real system. Thus, we propose that perceived identity will influence the human-computer trust interaction.

Communication Context (CC)

Communication context contains any information that can be used to characterize the situation of communication. It is one of the important factors that influence communication trust (Yan & Prehofer, 2010). For example, communication trust would be obviously much higher in a Virtual Private Network (VPN) than the open Internet and social networks. Therefore, trust interaction between a human and a computer in VPN can be better ensured. Herein, we assume that communication context will influence the human-computer trust interaction.

4. DESIGN GUIDELINES

This section proposes a generic guideline for building up trust interaction between human-beings and computers.

4.1 Initial Trust Establishment

For establishing initial trust in a computing, communication or networking system, we should pay attention to the following:

1. Apply suitable user interface design (e.g., visualizing brand logo) in order to attract user initial trust;
2. Get user's feedback on the ease of use of the system for improvement;
3. Consider the target user groups of the system to provide a flexibility to personalize user interface to satisfy different preferences;
4. Ensure the quality of the system by reducing system errors or bugs caused by carelessness and mistakes during the system development;
5. Provide latest reputation information (e.g., the feedback or comments of existing users);

4.2 User Trust Maintenance

For maintaining and sustaining initially built trust in a computing, communication or networking system during later usage, we should:

6. Adopt proper technologies that can sustain user trust in a computing, communication or networking system even though in a dynamically changed environment;
7. Properly improve system user interface based on collected user comments for improving usage experience and user acceptance by upgrading with a new package;
8. Efficiently maintain the system by fixing bugs and problems in time;
9. Provide an essential feature to inform users proper information that can ensure their trust during usage;

10. Adopt trustworthy and reputable resources in order to provide timely, true and qualified information and contents via the system to the users.
11. Adopt efficient user privacy enhancement technologies in order to preserve user privacy if needed;
12. Provide essential identity information to users in order to release their confusion during communications;
13. Adopt adaptive solutions to achieve context-aware trust management;
14. Provide proper trust information to users in a usable way in order to positively steer or instruct system usage behaviors.

5. CONCLUSION

In this chapter, we surveyed the trust solutions that have been studied in the literature to improve or enhance the trustworthiness of a computing, communication or networking system. We further proposed a research model that summarizes the factors influencing HCTI. This model contains three root constructs: interaction intention, computer system trust and communication trust. We theorize that three root constructs will play a significant role as direct determinants of HCTI and each root construct is consistent of a number of sub-constructs. The root construct of interaction intention comprises personality, social factors, perceived usefulness, personal motivation, reputation & brand, perceived ease of use, relative advantage and recommendation. The computer system trust concerns system quality, information quality, UI quality, and system trust solutions. The communication trust is positively affected by perceived privacy, perceived identity and communication context. Based on this model, we propose instructions to improve user trust for human-computer interaction.

REFERENCES

Aberer, K., & Despotovic, Z. (2001). Managing trust in a peer-to-peer information system. In *Proceedings of the ACM Conference on Information and Knowledge Management (CIKM)*, (pp. 310-317). ACM.

Ajzen, I. (1991). The theory of planned behavior. *Organizational Behavior and Human Decision Processes*, *50*, 179–211. doi:10.1016/0749-5978(91)90020-T.

Anderson, J. C., & Narus, J. A. (1990). A model of distributor firm and manufacturer firm working partnerships. *Marketing*, *54*(1), 42–58. doi:10.2307/1252172.

Antifakos, S., Kern, N., Schiele, B., & Schwaninger, A. (2005). Towards improving trust in context-aware systems by displaying system confidence. In *Proceedings of the 7th International Conference on Human Computer Interaction with Mobile Devices & Services*. ACM Press.

Araujo, I., & Araujo, I. (2003). Developing trust in internet commerce. In *Proceedings of the 2003 Conference of the Centre for Advanced Studies on Collaborative Research*, (pp. 1-15). IEEE.

Artz, D., & Gil, Y. (2007). A survey of trust in computer science and the semantic web. *Web Semantics: Science, Services, and Agents on the World Wide Web*, *5*(2), 58–71. doi:10.1016/j.websem.2007.03.002.

Avizienis, A., Laprie, J. C., Randell, B., & Landwehr, C. (2004). Basic concepts and taxonomy of dependable and secure computing. *IEEE Transactions on Dependable and Secure Computing*, *1*(1), 11–33. doi:10.1109/TDSC.2004.2.

Awad, N., & Ragowsky, A. (2008). Establishing trust in electronic commerce through online word of mouth: An examination across genders. *Journal of Management Information Systems*, *24*(4), 101–121. doi:10.2753/MIS0742-1222240404.

Baba, M. L., Falkenburg, D. R., & Hill, D. H. (1996). Technology management and American culture: Implications for business process redesign. *Research Technology Management*, *39*(6), 44–54.

Barber, B. (1983). *The logic and limits of trust*. New Brunswick, NJ: Rutgers University Press.

Basso, A., Goldberg, D., Greenspan, S., & Weimer, D. (2001). Emotional and cognitive factors underlying judgments of trust e-commerce. In *Proceedings 3rd ACM Conference on Electronic Commerce*. ACM Press.

Bhattacherjee, A. (2002). Individual trust in online firms: Scale development and initial test. *Journal of Management Information Systems*, *19*(1), 211–241.

Bickmore, T., & Cassell, J. (2001). Relational agents: A model and implementation of building user trust. In *Proceedings of the SIGCHI Conference on Human Factors in Computing Systems*, (pp. 396-403). ACM.

Blaze, M., Feigenbaum, J., & Lacy, J. (1996). Decentralized trust management. In *Proceedings of IEEE Symposium on Security and Privacy*, (pp. 164-173). IEEE.

Boon, S., & Holmes, J. (1991). The dynamics of interpersonal trust: Resolving uncertainty in the face of risk. In R. Hinde, & J. Groebel (Eds.), *Cooperation and Prosocial Behavior*. Cambridge, UK: Cambridge University Press.

Briggs, P., Burford, B., De Angeli, A., & Lynch, P. (2002). Trust in online advice. *Social Science Computer Review*, *20*(3), 321–332.

Cahill, V. et al. (2003). Using trust for secure collaboration in uncertain environments. *IEEE Pervasive Computing / IEEE Computer Society [and] IEEE Communications Society, 2*(3), 52–61. doi:10.1109/MPRV.2003.1228527.

Corritore, C. L., Kracher, B., & Wiedenbeck, S. (2003). On-line trust: Concepts, evolving themes, a model. *International Journal of Human-Computer Studies. Trust and Technology, 58*(6), 737–758.

Cramer, H., Evers, V., Ramlal, S., Someren, M., Rutledge, L., & Stash, N. et al. (2008). The effects of transparency on trust in and acceptance of a content-based art recommender. *User Modeling and User-Adapted Interaction, 18*(5), 455–496. doi:10.1007/s11257-008-9051-3.

Creed, W. E. D., & Miles, R. E. (1996). Trust in organizations: A conceptual framework linking organizational forms, managerial philosophies, and the opportunity costs of controls. In *Trust in Organizations: Frontiers of Theory and Research*. London: Sage Publications. doi:10.4135/9781452243610.n2.

Culnan, M. (1999). *Georgetown internet privacy policy study: Privacy online in 1999: A report to the federal trade commission*. Washington, DC: Georgetown University.

CyberAtlas. (2002). *Privacy worries plague Ebiz*. Retrieved July 5, 2002 from http://cyberatlas.internet.com/markets/retailing/article/06061_1183061,00.html

Davis, F. D. (1989). Perceived usefulness, perceived ease of use, and user acceptance of information technology. *Management Information Systems Quarterly, 13*(3), 319–339. doi:10.2307/249008.

Davis, F. D., Bagozzi, R. P., & Warshaw, P. R. (1989). User acceptance of computer technology: A comparison of two theoretical models. *Management Science, 35*, 982–1002. doi:10.1287/mnsc.35.8.982.

Davis, F. D., Bagozzi, R. P., & Warshaw, P. R. (1992). Extrinsic and intrinsic motivation to use computers in the workplace. *Journal of Applied Social Psychology, 22*(14), 1111–1132. doi:10.1111/j.1559-1816.1992.tb00945.x.

Denning, D. E. (1993). A new paradigm for trusted systems. In *Proceedings of the IEEE New Paradigms Workshop*, (pp. 36-41). IEEE.

Deutsch, M. (1960). Trust, trustworthiness, and the f scale. *Journal of Abnormal and Social Psychology, 61*(1), 138–140. doi:10.1037/h0046501 PMID:13816271.

Deutsch, M. (1962). Cooperation and trust: Some theoretical notes. *Nebraska Symposium on Motivation. Nebraska Symposium on Motivation, 10*, 275–318.

Deutsch, M. (1973). *The resolution of conflict: Constructive and destructive processes*. New Haven, CT: Yale University Press. doi:10.1177/000276427301700206.

Douceur, J. R. (2002). The sybil attack. [LNCS]. *Proceedings of IPTPS, 2429*, 251–260.

Dunn, J. R., & Schweitzer, M. E. (2005). Feeling and believing: the influence of emotion on trust. *Journal of Personality and Social Psychology, 88*(5), 736–748. doi:10.1037/0022-3514.88.5.736 PMID:15898872.

Fishbein, M., & Ajzen, I. (1975). *Beliefs, attitude, intention and behavior: An introduction to theory and research*. Reading, MA: Addison-Wesley.

Fogg, B. J. (2002). *Persuasive technology: Using computers to change what we think and do*. San Francisco, CA: Morgan Kaufman. doi:10.1145/764008.763957.

Fogg, B.J., Kameda, T., Boyd, J., Marchall, J., Sethi, R., Sockol, M., & Trowbridge, T. (2002). *Stanford-Makovsky web credibility study: Investigating what makes web sites credible today*. A Research Report by the Stanford Persuasive Technology Lab.

Fogg, B. J., Marshall, J., Kameda, T., Solomon, J., Rangnekar, A., Boyd, J., & Brown, B. (2001a). Web credibility research: A method for online experiments and early study results. In *Proceedings of the Conference on Human Factors in Computing Systems CHI 2001*. ACM Press.

Fogg, B. J., Marshall, J., Laraki, O., Osipovich, A., Varma, C., Fang, N., et al. (2001b). What makes web sites credible? A report on a large quantitative study. In *Proceedings of the Conference on Human Factors in Computing Systems CHI 2001*. ACM Press.

Fogg, B. J., & Tseng, H. (1999). The elements of computer credibility. In *Proceedings of the CHI '99*. ACM Press.

Fox, A. (1974). *Beyond contract: Work, power, and trust relations*. London: Faber.

Gambetta, D. (2000). Can we trust trust? In *Trust: Making and Breaking Cooperative Relations*. Retrieved from http://www.sociology.ox.ac.uk/papers/gambetta213-237.pdf

Gefen, D., Karahanna, E., & Straub, D. (2003). Trust and TAM in online shopping: An integrated model. *Management Information Systems Quarterly*, *27*(1), 51–90.

Grabner-Kräuter, S., & Kaluscha, E. A. (2003). Empirical research in on-line trust: A review and critical assessment. *International Journal of Human-Computer Studies*, *58*(6), 783–812. doi:10.1016/S1071-5819(03)00043-0.

Grandison, T., & Sloman, M. (2000). A survey of trust in internet applications. *IEEE Communications and Survey*, *3*(4), 2–16. doi:10.1109/COMST.2000.5340804.

Granovetter, M. S. (1985). Economic action and social structure. *American Journal of Sociology*, *91*, 481–510. doi:10.1086/228311.

Guha, R., & Kumar, R. (2004). Propagation of trust and distrust. In *Proceedings of the 13th International Conference on World Wide Web*, (pp. 403-412). IEEE.

Hancock, J. T., Toma, C., & Ellison, N. (2007). The truth about lying in online dating profiles. In *Proceedings of the ACM Conference on Human Factors in Computing Systems* (CHI 2007). ACM.

Herlocker, J. L., Konstan, J. A., & Riedl, J. (2000). Explaining collaborative filtering recommendations. In *Proceedings of the 2000 ACM Conference on Computer Supported Cooperative Work*. ACM Press.

Herrmann, P. (2001). Trust-based procurement support for software components. In *Proceedings of the 4th International Conference of Electronic Commerce Research* (ICECR04), (pp. 505-514). IEEE.

Jensen, C., Potts, C., & Jensen, C. (2005). Privacy practices of Internet users: Self-reports versus observed behavior. *International Journal of Human-Computer Studies*, *63*(1-2), 203–227. doi:10.1016/j.ijhcs.2005.04.019.

Joinson, A. N., Reips, U., Buchanan, T., & Schofield, C. B. P. (2010). Privacy, trust, and self-disclosure online. *Human-Computer Interaction*, *25*(1), 1–24. doi:10.1080/07370020903586662.

Kamvar, S., Scholsser, M., & Garcia-Molina, H. (2003). The EigenTrust algorithm for reputation management in P2P networks. In *Proceedings of 12th International Conference of World Wide Web*. ACM.

Karvonen, K. (2001). Designing trust for a universal audience: A multicultural study on the formation of trust in the internet in the Nordic countries. In C. Stephanidis (Ed.), *First International Conference on Universal Access in Human-Computer Interaction*, (vol. 3, pp. 1078-1082). Mahwah, NJ: Erlbaum.

Kim, J., & Moon, J. Y. (1998). Designing towards emotional usability in customer interfaces-trustworthiness of cyber-banking system interfaces. *Interacting with Computers, 10*, 1–29. doi:10.1016/S0953-5438(97)00037-4.

Koehn, D. (1996). Should we trust in trust? *American Business Law Journal, 34*(2), 183–203. doi:10.1111/j.1744-1714.1996.tb00695.x.

Lee, J., Kim, J., & Moon, J. Y. (2000). What makes Internet users visit cyber stores again? Key design factors for customer loyalty. In *Proceedings of the Conference on Human Factors in Computing Systems CHI 2000*. ACM.

Lee, J., & Moray, N. (1992). Trust, control strategies and allocation of function in human-machine systems. *Ergonomics, 35*(10), 1243–1270. doi:10.1080/00140139208967392 PMID:1516577.

Lee, K. C., & Chung, N. (2009). Understanding factors affecting trust in and satisfaction with mobile banking in Korea: A modified DeLone and McLean's model perspective. *Interacting with Computers, 21*(5-6), 385–392. doi:10.1016/j.intcom.2009.06.004.

Lee, S., Sherwood, R., & Bhattacharjee, B. (2003). Cooperative peer groups in NICE. In *Proceedings of IEEE Conference on Computer Communications* (INFOCOM 03). IEEE CS Press.

Lewicki, R. J., & Bunker, B. (1995). Trust in relationships: A model of trust development and decline. In *Conflict, Cooperation and Justice*. San Francisco, CA: Jossey-Bass.

Lewis, D., & Weigert, A. (1985). Trust as a social reality. *Social Forces, 63*(4), 967–985.

Liang, Z., & Shi, W. (2005). PET: A personalized trust model with reputation and risk evaluation for P2P resource sharing. In *Proceedings of the 38th Annual Hawaii International Conference on System Sciences*. IEEE.

Lin, C., Varadharajan, V., Wang, Y., & Pruthi, V. (2004). Enhancing grid security with trust management. In *Proceedings of IEEE International Conf. on Services Computing*, (pp. 303-310). IEEE.

Liu, Z., Joy, A. W., & Thompson, R. A. (2004). A dynamic trust model for mobile ad hoc networks. In *Proceedings of the 10th IEEE International Workshop on Future Trends of Distributed Computing Systems* (FTDCS 2004), (pp. 80-85). IEEE.

Liu, Z., Yau, S. S., Peng, D., & Yin, Y. (2008). A flexible trust model for distributed service infrastructures. In *Proceedings of the 2008 11th IEEE Symposium on Object Oriented Real-Time Distributed Computing*, (pp. 108-115). IEEE.

Lohse, G. L., & Spiller, P. (1998). Electronic shopping. *Communications of the ACM, 41*(7), 81–87. doi:10.1145/278476.278491.

Luhmann, N. (1979). *Trust and power*. Chichester, UK: Wiley.

Lumsden, J., & MacKay, L. (2006). How does personality affect trust in B2C e-commerce? In *Proceedings of 8th International Conference on Electronic Commerce: The New e-Commerce: Innovations for Conquering Current Barriers, Obstacles and Limitations to Conducting Successful Business on the Internet*. ACM Press.

Mayer, R. C., Davis, J. H., & Schoorman, F. D. (1995). An integrative model of organizational trust. *Academy of Management Review, 20*(3), 709–734.

McCrickard, D. S., Czerwinski, M., & Bartram, L. (2003). Introduction: Design and evaluation of notification user interfaces. *International Journal of Human-Computer Studies*, *58*(5), 509–514. doi:10.1016/S1071-5819(03)00025-9.

McKnight, D. H., & Chervany, N. L. (2000). What is trust? A conceptual analysis and an interdisciplinary model. In *Proceedings of the 2000 Americas Conference on Information Systems* (AMCI2000). Long Beach, CA: AIS.

McKnight, D. H., & Chervany, N. L. (2001). Trust and distrust definitions: One bite at a time. In *Trust in Cyber-Societies*. Berlin: Springer. doi:10.1007/3-540-45547-7_3.

McKnight, D. H., & Chervany, N. L. (2003). *The meanings of trust*. UMN University Report. Retrieved December 2006, from http://misrc.umn.edu/wpaper/WorkingPapers/9604.pdf

McKnight, D. H., Choudhury, V., & Kacmar, C. (2002). Developing and validating trust measures for e-commerce: An integrative typology. *Information Systems Research*, *13*(3), 334–359. doi:10.1287/isre.13.3.334.81.

Misztal, B. A. (1996). *Trust in modern societies: The search for the bases of social order*. New York: Polity Press.

Moore, G. C., & Benbasat, I. (1991). Development of an instrument to measure the perceptions of adopting an information technology innovation. *Information Systems Research*, *2*(3), 192–222. doi:10.1287/isre.2.3.192.

Mui, L. (2003). *Computational models of trust and reputation: Agents, evolutionary games, and social networks*. (Doctoral dissertation). Massachusetts Institute of Technology, Cambridge, MA.

Muir, B. M. (1987). Trust between humans and machines, and the design of decision aids. *International Journal of Man-Machine Systems*, *27*, 527–539. doi:10.1016/S0020-7373(87)80013-5.

Muir, B. M. (1994). Trust in automation part I: Theoretical issues in the study of trust and human intervention in automated systems. *Ergonomics*, *37*(11), 1905–1922. doi:10.1080/00140139408964957.

Muir, B. M., & Moray, N. (1996). Trust in automation part II: Experimental studies of trust and human intervention in a process control simulation. *Ergonomics*, *39*(3), 429–469. doi:10.1080/00140139608964474 PMID:8849495.

Nielsen, J. (1999). *Trust or bust: Communicating trustworthiness in web design*. Retrieved from http://www.useit.com/alertbox/990307.html

Nielsen, J., Molich, R., Snyder, S., & Farrell, C. (2000). *E-commerce user experience: Trust*. New York: Nielsen Norman Group.

Olson, J. S., Zheng, J., Bos, N., Olson, G. M., & Veinott, E. (2002). Trust without touch: Jumpstarting long-distance trust with initial social activities. [ACM.]. *Proceedings of, CHI2002*, 141–146.

Pu, P., & Chen, L. (2007). Trust-inspiring explanation interfaces for recommender systems. *Knowledge-Based Systems*, *20*(6), 542–556. doi:10.1016/j.knosys.2007.04.004.

Putnam, R. D. (1995). Bowling alone: America's declining social capital. *Journal of Democracy*, *6*(1), 3–10. doi:10.1353/jod.1995.0002.

Resnick, M. L., & Montania, R. (2003). Perceptions of customer service, information privacy, and product quality from semiotic design features in an online web store. *International Journal of Human-Computer Interaction*, *16*(2), 211–234. doi:10.1207/S15327590IJHC1602_05.

Resnick, P., Kuwabara, K., Zeckhauser, R., & Friedman, E. (2000). Reputation systems. *Communications of the ACM*, *43*(12), 45–48. doi:10.1145/355112.355122.

Resnick, P., & Varian, H. R. (1997). Recommender systems. *Communications of the ACM, 40*(3), 56–58. doi:10.1145/245108.245121.

Resnick, P., & Zeckhauser, R. (2001). *Trust among strangers in Internet transactions: Empirical analysis of eBay's reputation system.* Retrieved from http://www.si.umich.edu/Bpresnick

Resnick, P., & Zeckhauser, R. (2002). Trust among strangers in Internet transactions: Empirical analysis of eBay's reputation system. In M. Baye (Ed.), *Advances in Applied Microeconomics: The Economics of the Internet and E-Commerce* (Vol. 11, pp. 127–157). London: Elsevier. doi:10.1016/S0278-0984(02)11030-3.

Riegelsberger, J. (2003). Interpersonal cues and consumer trust in e-commerce. In *Proceedings of the Conference on Human Factors in Computing Systems* (CHI'03). New York: ACM.

Riegelsberger, J., Angela Sasse, M., & McCarthy, J. D. (2005a). Do people trust their eyes more than ears? Media bias in detecting cues of expertise. In *Proceedings of the Conference on Human Factors in Computing Systems* (CHI'05). New York: ACM.

Riegelsberger, J., Sasse, A. M., & McCarthy, J. D. (2005b). The mechanics of trust: A framework for research and design. *International Journal of Human-Computer Studies, 62*(3), 381–422. doi:10.1016/j.ijhcs.2005.01.001.

Riegelsberger, J., & Sasse, M. A. (2001). Trust builders and trustbusters: The role of trust cues in interfaces to e-commerce applications. In *Towards the E-Society: Proceedings of the First IFIP Conference on E-Commerce, E-Society, and E-Government.* London: Kluwer.

Rotter, J. B. (1967). A new scale for the measurement of interpersonal trust. *Journal of Personality, 35*, 651–665. doi:10.1111/j.1467-6494.1967.tb01454.x PMID:4865583.

Rotter, J. B. (1971). Generalized expectancies for interpersonal trust. *The American Psychologist, 26*, 443–452. doi:10.1037/h0031464.

Rukzio, E., Hamard, J., Noda, C., & Luca, A. D. (2006). Visualization of uncertainty in context aware mobile applications. In *Proceedings of Mobile HCI.* ACM Press. doi:10.1145/1152215.1152267.

Schechter, S. E., Dhamija, R., Ozment, A., & Fischer, I. (2007). The emperor's new security indicators. In *Proceedings of 2007 IEEE Symposium on Security and Privacy*, (pp. 51-65). IEEE.

Shelat, B., & Egger, F. N. (2002). What makes people trust online gambling sites? In *Proceedings of Conference on Human Factors in Computing Systems* (CHI 2002). ACM Press.

Sheppard, B. H., Hartwick, J., & Warshaw, P. R. (1988). The theory of reasoned action: A meta analysis of past research with recommendations for modifications in future research. *Consumer Res., 15*(3), 325–343. doi:10.1086/209170.

Sheridan, T. (1980). Computer control and human alienation. *Technology Review*, 61–73.

Sillence, E., Briggs, P., Harris, P., & Fishwick, L. (2006). A framework for understanding trust factors in web-based health advice. *International Journal of Human-Computer Studies, 64*(8), 697–713. doi:10.1016/j.ijhcs.2006.02.007.

Singh, A., & Liu, L. (2003). TrustMe: Anonymous management of trust relationships in decentralized P2P systems. In *Proceedings of IEEE International Conference on Peer-to-Peer Computing*, (pp. 142-149). IEEE.

Song, S., Hwang, K., Zhou, R., & Kwok, Y. K. (2005). Trusted P2P transactions with fuzzy reputation aggregation. *IEEE Internet Computing, 9*(6), 24–34. doi:10.1109/MIC.2005.136.

Stanford, J., Tauber, E., Fogg, B. J., & Marable, L. (2002). *Experts vs. online consumers: A comparative credibility study of health and finance web sites*. Retrieved from http://www.consumerwebwatch.org/news/report3_credibilityresearch/slicedbread_abstract.htm

Steinbrück, U., Schaumburg, H., Duda, S., & Kruger, T. (2002). A picture says more than a thousand words—Photographs as trust builders in e-commerce websites. In *Proceedings of Conference on Human Factors in Computing Systems CHI 2002*. ACM Press.

Su, X., & Khoshgoftaar, T. M. (2009). A survey of collaborative filtering techniques. *Advances in Artificial Intelligence*. doi:10.1155/2009/421425.

Sun, Y., Yu, W., Han, Z., & Liu, K. J. R. (2006). Information theoretic framework of trust modeling and evaluation for ad hoc networks. *IEEE Journal on Selected Areas in Communications*, *24*(2), 305–317. doi:10.1109/JSAC.2005.861389.

Theodorakopoulos, G., & Baras, J. S. (2006). On trust models and trust evaluation metrics for ad hoc networks. *IEEE Journal on Selected Areas in Communications*, *24*(2), 318–328. doi:10.1109/JSAC.2005.861390.

Venkatesh, V., & Davis, F. D. (2000). A theoretical extension of the technology acceptance model: Four longitudinal field studies. *Management Science*, *46*(2), 186–204. doi:10.1287/mnsc.46.2.186.11926.

Venkatesh, V., Morris, M. G., Davis, G. B., & Davis, F. D. (2003). User acceptance of information technology: Toward a unified view. *Management Information Systems Quarterly*, *27*(3), 425–478.

Walsh, K., & Sirer, E. G. (2005). Fighting peer-to-peer SPAM and decoys with object reputation. In *Proceedings of the Third Workshop on the Economics of Peer-to-Peer Systems* (P2PECON), (pp. 138-143). P2PECON.

Wang, Y. D., & Emurian, H. H. (2005). An overview of online trust: Concepts, elements and implications. *Computers in Human Behavior*, *21*, 105–125. doi:10.1016/j.chb.2003.11.008.

Williamson, O. E. (1993). Calculativeness, trust and economic organization. *The Journal of Law & Economics*, *30*, 131–145.

Wrightsman, L. S. (1991). *Assumptions about human nature: Implications for researchers and practitioners*. Newbury Park, CA: Sage.

Wu, I., & Chen, J. (2005). An extension of trust and TAM model with TPB in the initial adoption of on-line tax: An empirical study. *International Journal of Human-Computer Studies*, *62*(6), 784–808. doi:10.1016/j.ijhcs.2005.03.003.

Xiong, L., & Liu, L. (2004). PeerTrust: Supporting reputation-based trust for peer-to-peer electronic communities. *IEEE Transactions on Knowledge and Data Engineering*, *16*(7), 843–857. doi:10.1109/TKDE.2004.1318566.

Yamagishi, T., & Yamagishi, M. (1994). Trust and commitment in the United States and Japan. *Motivation and Emotion*, *18*, 129–166. doi:10.1007/BF02249397.

Yan, Z. (2007). *Trust management for mobile computing platforms*. (Doctoral dissertation). Helsinki Univ. of Technology, Helsinki, Finland.

Z. Yan (Ed.). (2010). *Trust modeling and management in digital environments: From social concept to system development*. Hershey, PA: IGI Global. doi:10.4018/978-1-61520-682-7.

Yan, Z., Dong, Y., Niemi, V., & Yu, G. (2009). Exploring trust of mobile applications based on user behaviours. In *Proceedings of InTrust 2009 (LNCS)* (Vol. 6163, pp. 212–226). Berlin: Springer.

Yan, Z., Dong, Y., Niemi, V., & Yu, G. (2011). Exploring trust of mobile applications based on user behaviors: An empirical study. *Journal of Applied Social Psychology*.

Yan, Z., & Holtmanns, S. (2008). Trust modeling and management: From social trust to digital trust. In R. Subramanian (Ed.), *Computer Security, Privacy and Politics: Current Issues, Challenges and Solutions*. Hershey, PA: IGI Global. doi:10.4018/978-1-59904-804-8.ch013.

Yan, Z., Kantola, R., & Shen, Y. (2011). Unwanted traffic control via global trust management. [IEEE.]. *Proceedings of IEEE TrustCom, 2011*, 647–654.

Yan, Z., Kantola, R., & Zhang, P. (2011). A research model for human-computer trust interaction. [IEEE.]. *Proceedings of IEEE TrustCom, 2011*, 274–281.

Yan, Z., Liu, C., Niemi, V., & Yu, G. (2010). Effects of displaying trust information on mobile application usage. In *Proceedings of ATC'10* (LNCS), (vol. 6407, pp. 107-121). Berlin: Springer.

Yan, Z., & Niemi, V. Dong, Y., & Yu, G. (2008). A user behavior based trust model for mobile applications. In Proceedings of Autonomic and Trusted Computing ATC08 (LNCS), (vol. 5060, pp. 455-469). Berlin: Springer.

Yan, Z., & Niemi, V. (2009). A methodology towards usable trust management. In *Proceedings of Autonomic and Trusted Computing ATC09 (LNCS)* (Vol. 5586, pp. 179–193). Berlin: Springer. doi:10.1007/978-3-642-02704-8_14.

Yan, Z., & Prehofer, C. (2011). Autonomic trust management for a component based software system. *IEEE Transactions on Dependable and Secure Computing, 8*(6), 810–823. doi:10.1109/TDSC.2010.47.

Yan, Z., & Yan, R. (2009). Formalizing trust based on usage behaviours for mobile applications. In *Proceedings of Autonomic and Trusted Computing ATC09 (LNCS)* (Vol. 5586, pp. 194–208). Berlin: Springer. doi:10.1007/978-3-642-02704-8_15.

Yan, Z., Zhang, P., & Deng, R. H. (2012). TruBeRepec: A trust-behavior-based reputation and recommender system for mobile applications. *Journal of Personal and Ubiquitous Computing, 16*(5), 485–506. doi:10.1007/s00779-011-0420-2.

Zhang, Z., Wang, X., & Wang, Y. (2005). A P2P global trust model based on recommendation. In *Proceedings of 2005 International Conf. on Machine Learning and Cybernetics*, (vol. 7, pp. 3975-3980). IEEE.

Zimmerman, J., & Kurapati, K. (2002). Exposing profiles to build trust in a recommender. In *Proceedings of the Conference on Human Factors in Computing Systems CHI 2001*. ACM Press.

Zucker, L. G. (1986). Production of trust: institutional sources of economic structure, 1840–1920. *Research in Organizational Behavior, 8*, 53–111.

APPENDIX

Questions and Exercises

1.   Are there any other factors that could influence user trust in human-computer interaction?
2.   Please summarize the positive UI design manners that can improve user trust in a system.

Chapter 8
Autonomic Trust Management in Mobile Environments

ABSTRACT

Autonomic trust management is the technology to automatically evaluate, establish, maintain, reevaluate, reestablish, and sustain dynamically changed trust relationships to adapt various contexts or situations. This chapter introduces an autonomic trust management solution in mobile environments by applying both trusted computing and trust evaluation technologies. The authors apply this solution to a number of mobile application scenarios in order to illustrate its applicability.

1. INTRODUCTION

1.1. Autonomic Trust Management

Autonomic Trust management is the technology to automatically evaluate, establish, maintain, and reevaluate, reestablish and sustain dynamically changed trust relationships to adapt various contexts or situations in order to continuously provide system trustworthiness (Yan & Prehofer, 2011). Yan and MacLaverty (2006) proposed that autonomic trust management includes the following four aspects and these four aspects are processed in an automatic way:

- **Trust establishment:** The process for establishing a trust relationship between a trustor and a trustee;
- **Trust monitoring:** The trustor or its delegate monitors the performance or behaviour of the trustee. The monitoring process aims to collect useful evidence for trust assessment of the trustee;
- **Trust assessment:** The process for evaluating the trustworthiness of the trustee by the trustor or its delegate. The trustor assesses the current trust relationship and decides if this relationship is changed;

DOI: 10.4018/978-1-4666-4765-7.ch008

Copyright © 2014, IGI Global. Copying or distributing in print or electronic forms without written permission of IGI Global is prohibited.

- **Trust control and re-establishment:** If the trust relationship will be broken/changed or is broken/changed, the trustor will take corresponding measures to control or re-establish the trust relationship.

As we can see from the above, autonomic trust management can be achieved through trust modeling and evaluation.

Various trust modeling and management mechanisms are described in the literature for different systems, such as P2P systems (Kamvar, Scholsser & Garcia-Molina, 2003; Lee, Sherwood & Bhattacharjee, 2003; Liang & Shi, 2005; Singh & Liu, 2003; Song, Hwang, Zhou & Kwok, 2005; Walsh & Sirer, 2005; Xiong & Liu, 2004), e-commerce (Guha, Kumar, Raghavan & Tomkins, 2004), and web services (Resnick & Zeckhauser, 2002). It is widely accepted that trust is influenced by reputation (i.e., public evidence on the trustee), recommendations (i.e., a group of entities' evidence on the trustee), the trustor's past experience, and context. Most work focuses on trust evaluation (i.e., trust assessment), but does not consider how to ensure or sustain trust for the fulfillment of an intended purpose. It still lacks comprehensive discussions with regard to how to automatically take an essential action according to a trust value. Although a number of trust models consider the dynamic nature of trust and context's influence, current literature does not adequately address context-aware adaptation of trust in some domains, such as services, component software, mobile applications, cloud computing and so on (Hall, Heimbigner, Van Der Hoek & Wolf, 1997; Herrmann, 2001; Herrmann, 2003; Malek, Esfahani, Menasce, Sousa & Gomaa, 2009; Mikic-Rakic, Malek & Medvidovic, 2008; Suryanarayana, Diallo, Erenkrantz & Taylor, 2006; Theodorakopoulos & Baras, 2006; Xiong & Liu, 2004; Zhou, Jiao & Mei, 2005; Zhou, Mei & Zhang, 2005). Most of existing solutions focus on a specific system that could be very different with each other. Particularly, due to the complexity and difference of context in different systems, a trust management solution, especially an autonomic trust management solution for one system could become inappropriate for another system. Recently, many solutions were developed for supporting trusted communications and collaborations among computing nodes in a distributed system, e.g., a P2P system (Zhang, Wang & Wang, 2005), an ad hoc network (Sun, Yu, Han & Liu, 2006; Theodorakopoulos & Baras, 2006) and a GRID computing system (Lin, Varadharajan, Wang & Pruthi, 2004). We found, however, that these methods are not feasible for supporting autonomic trust management, since most of them only concern trust assessment and evaluation. Current solutions generally ignore trust control and re-establishment by adapting dynamically changed environments and trust relationships, thus they cannot support or provide autonomic trust management.

The dynamic characteristic of trust is pushing trust management to become autonomic. This requires that trust management should handle the context's influence adaptively and intelligently. In addition, the trust model itself should be adaptively adjusted to reflect the real situation of a system. Context-aware trust management is a developing research topic and adaptive trust model optimization is an emerging research opportunity.

1.2. Research Issues

Nowadays, trust management for mobile computing platforms is becoming an important issue in mobile computing environments. Firstly, mobile commerce and mobile services hold the yet unfulfilled promise to revolutionize the way we conduct our personal, organizational and public business. Some attribute the problem to the lack of a mobile computing platform that all the players may trust enough. However, it is very hard to build up a long-term trust relationship among manufactures, service/application providers and mobile users. This could be the main reason that retards the further development of mobile applications and services.

On the other hand, new mobile networking is raising with the fast development of mobile ad hoc networks (MANET) and local wireless communication technology. It is more convenient for mobile users to communicate in their proximity to exchange digital information in various circumstances. However, the special characteristics of the new mobile networking paradigms introduce additional challenges on trust, security and privacy. This introduces special requirements for the mobile computing platform to embed trust management mechanisms for supporting trustworthy mobile communications.

However, due to the subjective characteristic of trust, trust management needs to take the trustor's criteria into consideration. For a mobile system, it is essential for a user's device to understand the user's trust criteria in order to behave as her/his agent for trust management. However, most of existing digital systems are not designed to be configured by the users with regard to their trust criteria. Generally, it is not good to require a user to make a lot of trust related decisions because that would destroy usability. Also, the user may not be informed enough to make sound decisions. Thus, establishing trust is quite a complex task with many optional actions to take. Trust should rather be managed automatically following a high level policy established by the trustor or auto-sensed by the device. In addition, the growing importance of the third party software in the domain of component software platforms introduces special requirements on trust. Particularly, the system's trustworthiness is varied due to component joining and leaving. How to manage trust in such a platform is crucial for an embedded device, such as a mobile phone.

Nowadays, cloud computing is seen as the future of mobile (Perez, 2009). Cloud computing virtualizes physical and software resources and provides generic services, e.g., Infrastructure as a Service (IaaS), Platform as a Service (PaaS), Software as a Service (SaaS), etc. It offers a number of advantages such as scalability, agility and economy efficiency, in comparison of traditional Information Technology (IT) infrastructure (Armbrust, 2009). Meanwhile, contributed by the rapid deployment of broadband wireless networks and fast growth of smart phones, more and more users are using mobile devices to access Internet services. However, cloud computing still faces a number of challenges, one of which is trust, i.e., how a cloud service provider can ensure trust for its services (Dillon, Wu & Chang, 2010). Herein, trust refers to a set of properties including objective ones (e.g., expected transmission rate, delay variance, packet loss, and cost) and subjective ones (user experience, privacy concern and satisfaction degree). There are some existing works on trust assurance for cloud computing, e.g., QoS framework and various QoS mechanisms (Dillon, Wu & Chang, 2010; Lodi, Panzieri, Rossi & Turrini, (2007; Stantchev & Schrofer, 2009; Wang, Du, Liu, Xie & Jia, 2010; Ye, Jain, Xia, Joshi, Yen, Bastani, Cureton & Bowler, 2010; Li, Hao, Xiao & Li, 2009; Xiao, Lin, Jiang, Chu & Shen, 2010). However, there still lacks a comprehensive study on trust for mobile cloud services. Notably, mobile cloud services are often affected by many specific factors, e.g., hardware and software limitations of mobile devices, signal strength of mobile networks, mobility of mobile users, etc. Thus, providing trust assurance, which includes QoS assurance for mobile cloud services requires a more advanced infrastructure and more effective mechanisms than traditional cloud services, e.g., based on mobile personal computers and devices.

All of the above problems influence the further development of mobile applications and services targeting at different areas, such as mobile enterprise, mobile networking, mobile terminal software and mobile computing. The key reason is that we lack a trust management solution for mobile computing platforms. This chapter presents an autonomic trust management solution for the mobile computing platforms, which is based on the trusted computing technology and an adaptive trust control model. This solution supports autonomic trust control on the basis of the trustor device's specification, which is ensured by a Root Trust module at the trustee device's computing platform. We also assume several trust control modes, each of which contains a number of control mechanisms or operations, e.g. encryption, authentication, hash code based integrity check, access control mechanisms, etc. A control mode can be treated as a specific configuration of trust management that can be provided by the trustee device. Based on a runtime trust assessment, the rest objective of autonomic trust management is to ensure that a suitable set of control modes are applied in the trustee device in order to provide a trustworthy service. As we have to balance several trust properties in this model, we make use of a Fuzzy Cognitive Map to model the factors related to trust for control mode prediction and selection. Particularly, we use the trust assessment result as a feedback to autonomously adapt weights in the adaptive trust control model in order to find a suitable set of control modes in a specific mobile computing context.

1.3. Chapter Organization

Providing a trustworthy mobile computing platform is crucial for mobile communications, services and applications. This chapter contributes a concrete autonomic trust management solution to the literature regarding the above research issues by making use of both trusted computing and trust evaluation technologies. It studies methodologies and mechanisms of providing a trustworthy computing platform for mobile devices. In addition, solutions to support trusted communications and collaboration among those platforms are proposed in a distributed and dynamic manner. Section 2 of this chapter specifies a mechanism for trust sustainability among the mobile computing

platforms based on the trusted computing technology. It plays as the first level of autonomic trust management. Section 3 describes an adaptive trust control model. The trust management mechanism based on this model plays as the second level of the proposed autonomic trust management solution. We demonstrate how the above two mechanisms can cooperate together to provide a comprehensive autonomic trust management solution in Section 4. Section 5 further discusses other related issues, such as standardization and implementation strategies. Finally, conclusions and future work are presented in the last section.

2. AUTONOMIC TRUST MANAGEMENT BASED ON TRUSTED COMPUTING PLATFORM

We propose a mechanism based on a Trusted Computing platform for trust sustainability among computing platforms. This mechanism can be further applied into P2P systems and ad hoc networks to achieve trust collaboration among mobile computing platforms. We also show how to use this mechanism to realize trust management in mobile enterprise networking.

2.1. Trust Form

This mechanism uses the following trust form: "Trustor A trusts trustee B for purpose P under condition C based on root trust R" (Yan & Cofta, 2004). The element C is defined by A to identify the rules or policies for sustaining or autonomic managing trust for purpose P, the conditions and methods to get the signal of distrust behaviors, as well as the mechanism to restrict any changes at B that may influence the trust relationship. It can also contain trust policies used for trust assessment and autonomic trust management at service runtime. The root trust R is the foundation of A's trust on B and its sustaining. Since A trusts B based on R, it is rational for A to sustain its trust on B based on R controlled by the conditions decided by A. The R is an existing component trusted by the trustor device. Thus, it can be used to ensure a long term trust relationship among the computing platforms. This form makes it possible to extend one-moment or short-term trust over a longer period of time.

2.2. Root Trust Module

The mechanism is based on a Root Trust (RT) module that is also the basis of the Trusted Computing (TC) platform (TCG, 2003). The RT module could be an independent module embedded in the computing platform. It could be also a build-in feature in the current Trusted Platform Module (TPM) of TC platform and its related software.

The RT module at the trustee is most possibly a hardware-based security module. It has capability to register, protect and manage the conditions for trust sustaining and self-regulating. It can also monitor any changes of computing platform including any alteration or operation on hardware, software and their configurations. The RT module is responsible for checking changes and

restricting them based on the trust conditions, as well as notifying the trustor accordingly. Figure 1 illustrates the basic structure of this module. It contains a number of secure registers that can register the record of platform trusted booting and the platform configurations. Meanwhile, it can be used to save the conditions for trust sustaining and self-regulating. The conditions are registered into the root trust module at the remote attestation among computing platforms. The RT contains a Monitor that monitors the changes of the platform hardware and software by calculating their hash codes and comparing them with the registered ones. It also receives change requests from platform components (hardware or software). By checking with the conditions for trust sustaining and self-regulating, a Controller in the RT controls the platform changes by allowing or rejecting change requests or reporting the trustor platform a signal of distrust through a Reporter.

There are two ways to know the platform changes. One is an active method, that is, the platform hardware and software notify the RT module about any changes for confirmation. The other way is a passive method, that is, the RT

Figure 1. Root trust module (Yan & Cofta, 2004)

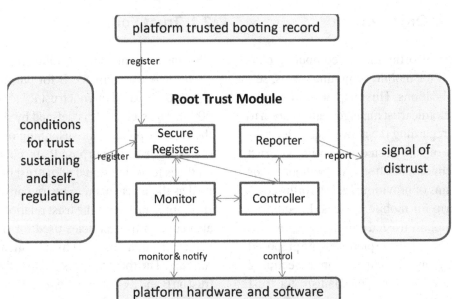

module monitors the changes at the hardware and the software. At the booting time and software installation, the RT module registers the hash codes of each part of platform hardware and software. That is the configurations of the platform are registered at the RT module. It also periodically calculates the run-time values of platform configurations and checks if they are the same as those registered and expected. If there is any change, the RT module will check with the registered trust conditions and decide which measure should be taken.

2.3. Protocol

As postulated, the trust relationship is controlled through the conditions defined by the trustor, which are executed by the RT module at the

trustee on which the trustor is willing to depend. The reasons for the trustor to depend on the RT module at the trustee can be various. Herein, we assume that the RT module at the trustee can be verified by the trustor as its expectation for some intended purpose and cannot be compromised by the trustee or other malicious entities later on. This assumption is based on the advance of current trusted computing technology and the work done in industry and in academy (TCG, 2003; Vaughan-Nichols, 2003; England, Lampson, Manferdelli, Peinado & Willman, 2003).

As shown in Figure 2, the proposed mechanism comprises the following procedures:

- Root trust challenge and attestation to ensure the trustor's basic trust dependence at the trustee device in steps 1-2; (Note that if

Figure 2. Protocol of trust sustainability

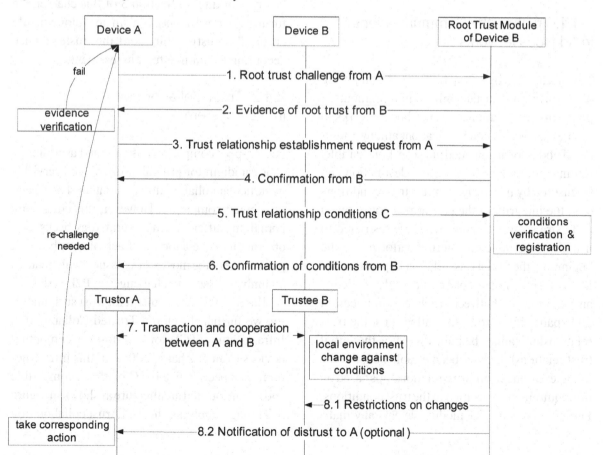

the attestation in this step is not successful, the trust relationship between device A and B cannot be established);

- Trust establishment by specifying the trust conditions and registering them at the trustee's RT module for trust sustaining in steps 3-6;
- Sustaining the trust relationship through the monitor and control by the RT module in steps 7-8;
- Re-challenge the trust relationship if necessary when any changes against trust conditions are reported.

2.4. Example Applications

In this sub-section, we present three use cases to illustrate how this mechanism can be applied to solve trust issues in ad hot networks, P2P systems and mobile enterprise networking.

2.4.1. Trustworthy Communications in Ad Hoc Networks

The mechanism based on the Trusted Computing platform for trust sustainability among computing platforms can be applied into ad hoc networks to ensure trustworthy communications among a number of nodes for an intended purpose. For example, routing from a source node to a destination can be ensured by imposing identical trust conditions (e.g. the integrity of the platform is not changed and extra software applications are restricted to install) in the node computing platforms. At the beginning, the initial trust relationships are established based on the Root Trust module challenge and attestation between each communication node pairs. If the trust attestation fails, the trust relationship cannot be built up. After the initial trust relationships have been established, the RT module can ensure the trust relationships based on the requirements specified in the trust conditions. Particularly, if the RT module detects any mali-

cious behaviors or software at the trustee device, it will reject or block it. If the RT module finds that the node platform is attacked, it will notify the trustor node platform. In addition, a trust evaluation mechanism can be embedded into the RT module or its protected components in the node computing platform in order to evaluate the trustworthiness of other nodes based on statistical experiences, the reputation of the evaluated node, node policies, an intruded node list and transformed data value. Any decision related to security (e.g., a secure route selection) should be based on trust analysis and evaluation among network nodes. Detailed discussion about this 'soft trust' solution is provided in the literature, e.g., a mechanism proposed by Yan, Zhang and Virtanen (2003). In particular, the trust evaluation results can greatly help in designing suitable trust conditions for trust sustainability during node communications. It could also help in selecting the most trustworthy node in the ad hoc networking. In Section 3 of this chapter, we further propose a mechanism to automatically ensure the trustworthiness of the trustee device according to runtime trust assessment.

2.4.2. Trust Collaboration in P2P Systems

Peer-to-peer computing has emerged as a significant paradigm for providing distributed services, in particular collaboration for content sharing and distributed computing. However, this computing paradigm suffers from several drawbacks that obstruct its wide adoption. Lack of trust between peers is one of the most serious issues, which causes a number of security challenges in P2P systems.

Based on the mechanism for trust sustainability, we further develop a Trusted Collaboration Infrastructure (TCI) for peer-to-peer computing devices (Yan & Zhang, 2006). In this infrastructure, each peer device is TC platform compatible and has an internal architecture as shown in Figure 3. Through applying the TCI, trust collaboration

Figure 3. Architecture of P2P peer device in TCI

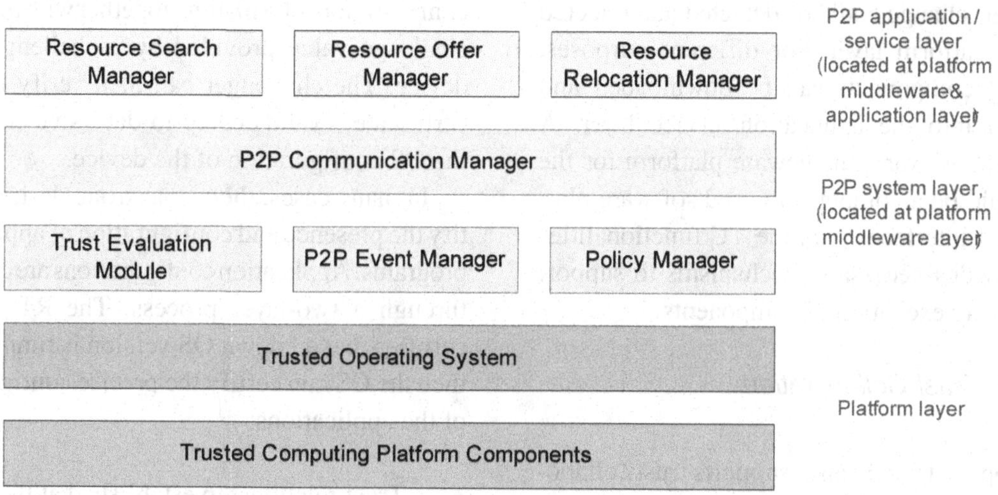

can be established among distributed peers through the control of the TC platform components.

There are three layers in the TCI. A platform layer contains TC platform components specified in TCG, 2003 (e.g., TPM) and an operating system that is booted and executed in a trusted status, which is attested and ensured by the TC platform components.

A P2P system layer contains common components required for trusted P2P communications. Those components are installed over the platform layer and ensured to be run in a trusted status. This is realized through trusted component installation and alteration-detection mechanism supported by the platform layer. A communication manager is responsible for various P2P communications (e.g., the communications needed for the P2P system joining and leaving). A trust evaluation module is applied to evaluate the trust relationship with any other peer before any security related decision is made. The trust evaluation module cooperates with a policy manager and an event manager in order to work out a proper trust evaluation result. The policy manager registers various local device policies regarding P2P applications and services. It also maintains subjective policies for trust evaluation. The event manager handles different P2P

events and cooperates with the trust evaluation module in order to process properly.

A P2P application/service layer contains components for P2P services. Taking resource sharing as an example, this layer should contain components such as a resource-search manager, a resource-offer manager and a resource-relocation manager. The resource-search manager is responsible for searching demanded resources in the P2P system. The resource-offer manager provides shared resources according to their copyright and usage rights. The offered resources could be encapsulated through the encryption service of the TC platform, refer to Chapter 3. The encryption service allows data to be encrypted in such a secure way that it can be decrypted only by a certain machine, and only if that machine is in a certain configuration. The encryption offered by the encryption service is attached to some special configurations as mandatory requirements for decryption. The resource-relocation manager handles remote resource accessing and downloading. The downloaded resources are firstly checked with no potential risk, and then stored at the local device.

Like the system layer, all the components in this layer are attested by the platform layer (e.g., by a trusted OS) as trusted for execution. Any malicious change could be detected and rejected by the platform layer. For different purposes, different components can be downloaded and installed into the application/service layer. A preferred software middleware platform for the TCI could be a component-based software platform that interfaces with the TC functionalities and provides necessary mechanisms to support trustworthy execution of components.

2.4.2.1. Trust Collaboration

The proposed mechanism supports trust collaboration among P2P peers. Trust collaboration is defined as interaction; communication and cooperation are conducted according to the expectation of involved entities. For example, the shared contents in the P2P systems should be consumed and used following the expectation of the content originators or right-holders without violating any copyrights. In peer-to-peer systems, the trust collaboration requires autonomous control on resources at any peer. The trust collaboration in the proposed P2P system infrastructure fulfills the following trust properties:

- Each peer device can verify that another peer device is working in its expected status.

Building up on the TC platform technology, each peer device with the underlying architecture can ensure that every component on the device is working in a trusted status. It can also challenge any other device and attest that it is working in its expected status, as shown in Figure 2 (step 1 and 2). This is done through digitally certifying the device configurations.

Two levels of certifying are provided: certifying OS configurations and certifying the applications running on the OS. For certifying the OS, the system uses a private key only known by the

RT module to sign a certificate that contains the configuration information, together with a random challenge value provided by a challenger peer device. The challenger can then verify that the certificate is valid and up-to-date, so it can know the OS configuration of the device.

In many cases, there is a strong desire to certify the presence and configuration of application programs. Application configurations are certified through a two-layer process. The RT module certifies that a known OS version is running and then the OS can certify the precise configuration of the applications:

- Trust relationship established at the beginning of the collaboration between peers can be sustained until the collaboration is fulfilled for an intended purpose based on trust conditions.

As shown in Figure 2, the trust relationship can be established between a trustor device and a trustee device based on the trust platform attestation (step 1-2) and the registration of trust conditions at the TC platform components of the trustee device, e.g., the RT module (step 3-4). Through applying the mechanism described above, a trustee device can ensure the trust sustainability according to pre-defined conditions (step 5-6). The conditions are approved by both the trustor device and the trustee device at the time of trust establishment. They can be further enforced through the use of the pre-attested TC platform components at the trustee device until the intended collaboration is fulfilled.

One example of the trust conditions could specify that a) upgrading of P2P applications is only allowed for applications certified by a Trusted Third Party; b) the changes of any hardware components in the computing platform is disallowed; and c) any changes for the rest of software in the computing platform are disallowed. All of above conditions can be ensured by the Root Trust module and the secure software installation mechanism that can verify the certificate of a software application before the installation.

The proposed mechanism for autonomic trust management based on trusted computing platform provides a way to automatically control the remote environment as trusted. Optionally, it is also possible to inform the trustor peer about any distrust behavior of the trustee according to pre-defined conditions (refer to step 7). Therefore, it is feasible for the trustor peer to take corresponding measures to confront any changes that may affect the continuation of trust for the purpose of a successful P2P service:

- Each peer can manage the trust relationship with other peers and therefore it can make the best decision on security issues in order to reduce potential risks.

Based on the trust evaluation mechanisms (e.g., Yan, Zhang & Virtanen, 2003; Fenkam, et al., 2002; Kortuem, et al., 2001; Jøsang, Ismail & Boyd, 2005; Lin, Varadharajan, Wang & Pruthi, 2004) embedded in the trust evaluation module, each peer can anticipate potential risks and make the best decision on any security related issues in the P2P communications and collaboration. The trust evaluation helps generating feasible conditions for sustaining the trust relationship. In particular, the trust evaluation is conducted in the expected trust environment, thus the evaluation results are generated with protection. This mechanism is very helpful in fighting against attacks raised by malicious peers that hold a correct platform certificate and valid data for trusted platform attestation:

- Resources are offered under expected policies.

This feature includes two aspects. One is that the resources are provided based on copyright restrictions. The contents that cannot be shared should not be disclosed to other peers. The other is that the resources are provided with limitations defined by the provider. The encryption services offered by the TC platform can cooperate with the resource-offer manager to provide protected resources and ensure copyrights and usage rights (TCG, 2003; Yan & Zhang, 2006a):

- Resources are relocated safely and consumed as the provider expects.

The trust attestation mechanism offered by the TC platform can support the resource-relocation manager to attest that the downloaded contents are not malicious code. In addition, the resources are used in an expected way, which is specified according to either copyrights or pre-defined usage restrictions. This can be ensured by the TC platform encryption mechanism before and during content consuming:

- Personal information of each peer is accessed under expected control.

The resource-offer manager in the proposed architecture can cooperate with the TC platform components to encapsulate the personal information based on the policies managed by the policy manager. Only trusted resource-search manager can access it. The trusted resource-search manager is an expected P2P application component that can process the encapsulated personal information according to the pre-defined requirements specified by the personal information owner.

With the TC platform components in the TCI, any P2P device component can only execute as expected and process resources in an expected way.

Furthermore, with the support of trust evaluation and trust sustainability, the peers could collaborate in the most trustworthy way.

2.4.3. Trust Management in Mobile Enterprise Networking

How to manage trust in mobile enterprise networking among various mobile devices is problematic for companies using mobile enterprise solutions. First, current Virtual Private Networks (VPN) lack the means to enable trust among mobile computing platforms from different manufactures. For example, an application can be trusted by Manufacture A's devices but may not be recognized by Manufacture B's devices. Moreover, from a VPN management point of view, it is difficult to manage the security of a large number of computing platforms. This problem is more serious in mobile security markets. Since different mobile device vendors provide different security solutions, it is difficult or impossible for mobile enterprise operators to manage the security of diverse devices in order to successfully run security-related services.

Second, no existing VPN system ensures that the data or components on a remote user device can only be controlled according to the security requirements of the enterprise VPN operator, during both VPN connection and disconnection. The VPN server is unaware as to whether the user device platform can be trusted or not although user verification is successful. Especially, after the connection is established, the device could be compromised, which could open a door for attacks. Particularly, data accessed and downloaded from the VPN can be further copied and forwarded to other devices after the VPN connection has been terminated. The VPN client user could conduct illegal operations using various ways, e.g. disk copy of confidential files and sending emails with confidential attachment to other people. Nowadays, the VPN operators depend on the loyalty of the VPN client users to address this potential security problem. In addition, a malicious applica-

tion or a thief that stole the device could also try to compromise the integrity of the device.

Regarding the problems described above, no good solutions can be found in the literature. Related work did not consider the solutions of the problems described above (Herscovitz, 1999; Wood, Stoss, Chan-Lizardo, Papacostas & Stinson, 1988; Regan, 2003; Cheung & Misic, 2002). For example, a trust management solution based on KeyNote for IPSec proposed by Blaze, Ioannidis and Keromytis (2002) could ensure trust during VPN connection in the network-layer. A security policy transmission model was presented to solve security policy conflicts in large-scale VPN (Shan, Li, Wang & Li, 2003). But the proposal could not help in solving the trust sustainability after the VPN connection and disconnection. Prior work focused on securing network connection, not paying much attention to the necessity to control VPN terminal devices (Hamed, Al-Shaer & Marrero, 2005). In addition, security or trust policies of the VPN operator should be different regarding different VPN client devices. This fact raises additional challenges for trust management in enterprise networking.

A solution for enhancing trust in a mobile VPN system can be provided based on the mechanism for trust sustainability among computing platforms. We aim to support confidential content management and overcome the diversity support of security in different devices manufactured by different vendors. In this case, a VPN trust management server is the trustor, while a VPN client device is the trustee. A trust relationship could be established between them. The VPN trust management server identifies the client device and specifies the trust conditions for that type of device at the VPN connection. Thereby, the VPN client device could behave as the VPN operator expects. Additional trust conditions could be also embedded into the client device in order to control VPN-originated resources (e.g. software components or digital information originated from the VPN). Therefore, those resources could be managed later on as the

VPN operator expects even if the device connection with the VPN is terminated. Even though the VPN client device is not RT module based, the trust management server can attest it and apply corresponding trust policies in order to restrict its access to confidential information and operations (Yan & Zhang, 2006b).

A simple example of trust conditions for trust management in a mobile enterprise networking could specify that a) printing and forwarding files achieved from the enterprise Intranet are disallowed when the device disconnects the Intranet; b) the changes for any hardware components in the computing platform are disallowed; and c) the changes by the device owner on any software in the computing platform are disallowed, too. All of above conditions can be ensured through the Root Trust module based trusted computing technology.

3. AUTONOMIC TRUST MANAGEMENT BASED ON AN ADAPTIVE TRUST CONTROL MODEL

In this section, we further introduce an adaptive trust control model via applying the theory of Fuzzy Cognitive Map (FCM) in order to conduct autonomic trust management based on trust assessment. This model illustrates the relationships among trust, its influence factors, the control modes used for managing trust, and the trustor's policies. It supports predicting trustworthiness to select proper trust control modes to ensure trust by adapting to current context. We illustrate how to manage trust adaptively in a middleware component software platform and for mobile cloud services by applying this method.

3.1. Adaptive Trust Control Model

The trustworthiness of a service or a combination of services provided by a device is influenced by a number of quality-attributes $QA_i (i = 1, ..., n)$. These quality attributes are ensured or controlled through a number of control modes $C_j (j = 1, ..., m)$. A control mode contains a number of control mechanisms or operations that can be provided by the device. We assume that the control modes are exclusive and that combinations of different modes are used.

The adaptive trust control model can be described as a graphical illustration using a FCM, as shown in Figure 4. It is a signed directed graph with feedback, consisting of nodes and weighted arcs. Nodes of the graph are connected by signed and weighted arcs representing the causal relationships that exist between the nodes. There are three layers of nodes in the graph. The node in the top layer is the trustworthiness of a service. The nodes located in the middle layer are its quality attributes, which have direct influence on the service's trustworthiness. The nodes at the bottom layer are control modes that could be supported and applied by the device. These control modes can control and thus improve the quality attributes. Therefore, they have indirect influence on the trustworthiness of the service. The value of each node is influenced by the values of the connected nodes with the appropriate weights and by its previous value. Thus, we apply an addition operation to take both into account.

Note that $V_{QA_i}, V_{C_j}, T \in [0,1]$, $w_i \in [0,1]$, and $cw_{ji} \in [-1,1]$. T^{old}, $V_{QA_i}^{old}$ and $V_{C_j}^{old}$ are old value of T, V_{QA_i}, and V_{C_j}, respectively. $\Delta T = T - T^{old}$ stands for the change of trustworthiness value. B_{C_j} reflects the current device configurations about which control modes are applied. The trustworthiness value can be described as:

$$T = f\left(\sum_{i=1}^{n} w_i V_{QA_i} + T^{old} \right) \quad (1)$$

such that $\sum_{i=1}^{n} w_i = 1$. Where w_i is a weight that indicates the importance rate of the quality attribute QA_i regarding how much this quality at-

Figure 4. Graphical modeling of trust control (Yan & Prehofer, 2011)

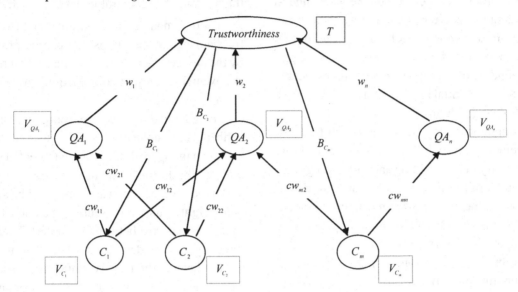

tribute is considered at the trust decision or assessment. w_i can be decided based on the trustor's policies. We apply the Sigmoid function $f(x) = \dfrac{1}{1 + e^{-\alpha x}}$ (e.g., $\alpha = 2$), to map node values V_{QA_i}, V_{C_j}, T into [0, 1]. The value of the quality attribute is denoted by V_{QA_i}. It can be calculated according to the following formula based on Figure 4:

$$V_{QA_i} = f\left(\sum_{j=1}^{m} cw_{ji} V_{C_j} B_{C_j} + V_{QA_i}^{old}\right) \qquad (2)$$

where cw_{ji} is the influence factor of control mode C_j to QA_i, cw_{ji} is set based on the impact of C_j on QA_i. Positive cw_{ji} means a positive influence of C_j on QA_i. Negative cw_{ji} implies a negative influence of C_j on QA_i. Zero implies no influence of C_j on QA_i. Null means no any relationship between C_j and QA_i. B_{C_j} is the selection factor of the control mode C_j, which can be either

1 if C_j is applied or 0 if C_j is not applied. Based on Figure 4, the value of the control mode can be calculated using:

$$V_{C_j} = f\left(T \cdot B_{C_j} + V_{C_j}^{old}\right) \qquad (3)$$

3.2. Procedure

Based on the above understanding, we propose a procedure to conduct autonomic trust management in a computing platform targeting at a trustee entity specified by a trustor entity, as shown in Figure 5. The entity could be a service or a combination of services or an application. Herein, we apply several trust control modes, each of which contains a number of control mechanisms or operations. The trust control mode can be treated as a special configuration of trust management that can be provided by the platform or system. In this procedure, trust control mode prediction is a mechanism to anticipate the performance or feasibility of applying some control modes before taking a concrete action. It predicts the trust value supposed that some control modes are applied

Figure 5. An autonomic trust management procedure (Yan & Prehofer, 2011)

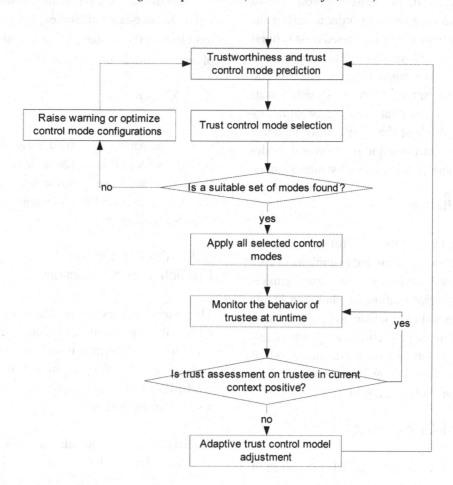

before the decision to initiate them is made. Trust control mode selection is a mechanism to select the most suitable trust control modes based on the prediction results. Trust assessment is conducted based on the subjective criteria of the trustor through evaluating the quality attributes of the trustee entity. It is also influenced by the platform context. Particularly, the quality attributes of the entity can be controlled or improved via applying a number of trust control modes, especially at system runtime. In this autonomic trust management solution, we consider such factors that impact trust as the trustee's objective factors (i.e., quality attributes), the trustor's objective factors (i.e., the

policies of trustor regarding a trust decision, e.g., the importance rates of QA, performance criteria and trust threshold).

For a trustor, the trustworthiness of its specified trustee can be predicted regarding various control modes supported by the system. Based on the prediction results, a suitable set of control modes could be selected to establish the trust relationship between the trustor and the trustee. Further, a runtime trust assessment mechanism is triggered to evaluate the trustworthiness of the trustee through monitoring its behavior based on the instruction of the trustor's criteria. According to the runtime trust assessment results in the underlying context, the system conducts trust control model adjustment in order to reflect the real system situation if the assessed trust value is below an expected threshold. This threshold is generally set by the trustor to express its expectation on the assessment. Then, the system repeats the procedure. The context-aware or situation-aware adaptability of the trust control model is crucial to re-select suitable trust control modes in order to conduct autonomic trust management.

3.3. Algorithms

Based on the adaptive trust control model, a number of algorithms are designed to implement each step of the procedure for autonomic trust management at the service runtime, as shown in Figure 5. These algorithms include trust assessment, trust control mode prediction and selection, and adaptive trust control model adjustment, which were evaluated in (Yan & Prehofer, 2007; Yan, 2008a; Yan & Prehofer, 2011).

3.3.1. Trust Assessment

We conduct trust assessment based on observation. At the trustee service runtime, the performance observer monitors its performance with respect to specified quality attributes. For each quality attribute, if the monitored performance is better than the criteria of the trustor, the positive point (p) of that attribute is increased by 1. If the monitored result is worse than the criteria, the negative point (n) of that attribute is increased by 1. For evaluating trust at system runtime, we suggest not considering recommendations in the algorithm because the evidence achieved through runtime monitoring is determinate. The trust opinion of each quality attribute can be generated based on an opinion generator, e.g.:

$$\theta = p / (p + n + r), r \geq 1 \tag{4}$$

In addition, based on the importance rates (ir) of different quality attributes, a combined opinion (θ_T) on the trustee can be calculated by applying weighted summation:

$$\theta_T = \sum_i ir_i \theta_i \tag{5}$$

By comparing to a trust threshold opinion (to), the system can decide if the trustee is still trusted or not. The runtime trust assessment results play as a feedback to trigger trust control and re-establishment.

3.3.2. Control Mode Prediction and Selection

The control modes are predicted by evaluating all possible modes and their compositions using a prediction algorithm based on Formula 1, 2 and 3. We then select the most suitable control modes based on the above prediction results using a selection algorithm:

Algorithm 1: Trustworthiness prediction is used to anticipate the performance or feasibility of all possibly applied trust control modes. Note that a constant δ is the accepted ΔT that controls the iteration of the prediction;

Algorithm 1. Trustworthiness prediction

```
- For every composition of control
modes, i.e.,
```
$\forall S_k (k = 1, ..., K)$, while
$\Delta T_k = T_k - T_k^{old} \geq \delta$, do

$$V_{C_j,k} = f\left(T_k \cdot B_{C_j,k} + V_{C_j,k}^{old}\right)$$

$$V_{QA_i,k} = f\left(\sum_{j=1}^{m} cw_{ji} V_{C_j,k} B_{C_j,k} + V_{QA_i,k}^{old}\right)$$

$$T_k = f\left(\sum_{i=1}^{n} w_i V_{QA_i,k} + T_k^{old}\right)$$

Algorithm 2: Control mode selection is applied to select a set of suitable trust control modes based on the control mode prediction results.

3.3.3. Adaptive Trust Control Model Adjustment

It is important for the trust control model to be dynamically maintained and optimized in order to precisely adapt to the real system situation and context. The influence factors of each control mode should sensitively indicate the influence of each control mode on different quality attributes in a dynamically changed environment. For example, when some malicious behaviors or attacks happen, the currently applied control modes can be found not feasible based on trust assessment. In this case, the influence factors of the applied control modes should be adjusted in order to reflect this situation. Then, the device can automatically re-predict and re-select a set of new control modes in order to ensure the trustworthiness. In this way, the device can avoid using the attacked or useless trust control modes in the underlying context. Therefore, it is crucial to make the trust control model context-adaptive in order to support autonomic trust management.

We apply two schemes to adjust the influence factors cw_{ji} of the trust control model in order to make it reflect the real system situation. We use $V_{QA_i}\_m$ and $V_{QA_i}\_p$ to stand for V_{QA_i} generated based on real system observation (i.e., the trust assessment result) and by prediction, respectively. In the schemes, ω is a unit deduction factor and σ is the accepted deviation between $V_{QA_i}\_m$ and $V_{QA_i}\_p$. We suppose C_j with cw_{ji} is currently applied. The first scheme (Algorithm 3) is an equal adjustment scheme, which holds a strategy that each control mode has the same impact on the deviation between $V_{QA_i}\_m$ and $V_{QA_i}\_p$. The second one (Algorithm 4) is an unequal adjustment scheme. It holds a strategy that the control mode with the biggest absolute influence factor always impacts more on the deviation between $V_{QA_i}\_m$ and $V_{QA_i}\_p$.

3.4. Autonomic Trust Management for Component Software Platform

The mobile computing platform generally consists of a layered architecture with three layers: an application layer that provides features to the user; a component-based middleware layer that

Algorithm 2. Control mode selection

- Calculate selection threshold $thr = \sum_{k=1}^{K} T_k / K$;
- Compare $V_{QA_i,k}$ and T_k of S_k to thr, set selection factor $SF_{S_k} = 1$ if $\forall V_{QA_i,k} \geq thr \wedge T_k \geq thr$; set $SF_{S_k} = -1$ if $\exists V_{QA_i,k} < thr \vee \exists T_k < thr$;
- For $\forall SF_{S_k} = 1$, calculate the distance of $V_{QA_i,k}$ and T_k to thr as $d_k = \min\{|V_{QA_i,k} - thr|, |T_k - thr|\}$; For $\forall SF_{S_k} = -1$, calculate the distance of $V_{QA_i,k}$ and T_k to thr as $d_k = \max\{|V_{QA_i,k} - thr|, |T_k - thr|\}$ only when $V_{QA_i,k} < thr$ and $T_k < thr$;
- If $\exists SF_{S_k} = 1$, select the best winner with the biggest d_k ; else $\exists SF_{S_k} = -1$, select the best loser with the smallest d_k .

Algorithm 3. An equal adjustment scheme

- While $\left| V_{QA_i}\_m - V_{QA_i}\_p \right| > \sigma$, do

a) If $V_{QA_i}\_m < V_{QA_i}\_p$, for $\forall cw_{ji}$,

$cw_{ji} = cw_{ji} - \omega$, if $cw_{ji} < -1, cw_{ji} = -1$
;

Else, for $\forall cw_{ji}$,

$cw_{ji} = cw_{ji} + \omega$, if $cw_{ji} > 1, cw_{ji} = 1$

b) Run Algorithms 1 - Trustworthiness Prediction.

Algorithm 4. An unequal adjustment scheme

- While $\left| V_{QA_i}\_m - V_{QA_i}\_p \right| > \sigma$, do

a) If $V_{QA_i}\_m < V_{QA_i}\_p$, for

$\max\left(\left| cw_{ji} \right| \right)$,

$cw_{ji} = cw_{ji} - \omega$, if $cw_{ji} < -1, cw_{ji} = -1$
(warning);

Else, $cw_{ji} = cw_{ji} + \omega$, if

$cw_{ji} > 1, cw_{ji} = 1$ (warning);

b) Run Algorithms 1 - Trustworthiness Prediction.

provides functionality to applications; and, the fundamental platform layer that provides access to lower-level hardware. Using components to construct the middleware layer divides this layer into two sub-layers: a component sub-layer that contains a number of executable components and a runtime environment (RE) sub-layer that supports component development.

We introduce a trust management framework that implements the above described mechanism into the RE sub-layer of the platform middleware. Placing trust management inside this architecture means linking the trust management framework with other frameworks responsible for component management (including download), security management, system management and resource management. Figure 6 describes interactions among different functional-blocks inside the RE sub-layer. The trust management framework is responsible for the assessment of trust relationships and trust management operations, system monitoring and autonomic trust management. The download framework requests the trust framework for trust assessment of a component to decide whether to download the component and which kind of mechanisms should be applied to this component. When a component service needs cooperation with other components' services, the execution framework will be involved, but the execution framework will firstly request the trust management framework for decision. The system framework takes care of system configurations related to the components. The trust management framework is located at the core of the runtime environment sub-layer. It monitors the system performance and instructs the resource framework to assign suitable resources to different processes. The trust management framework can shutdown any misbehaving component and gather evidence on the trustworthiness of a system entity. Meanwhile, it also controls the security framework, to ensure that it applies essential security mechanisms to maintain a trusted system. In short, the trust management framework acts like a critical system manager, ensuring that the system conforms to its trust policies. This architecture supports the implementation of both the 'hard trust' solution and the 'soft trust' solution.

3.4.1. Trust Management Framework

Figure 7 illustrates the structure of the trust management framework. In Figure 7, the trust manager is responsible for trust assessment and trust related decision-making, it closely collaborates with the security framework to offer security related management. The trust manager is composed of a number of functional blocks. The trust policy base saves the trust policy regarding making trust assessments and decisions. The recommendation

Figure 6. Relationships among trust management framework and other frameworks (Yan & Prehofer, 2011)

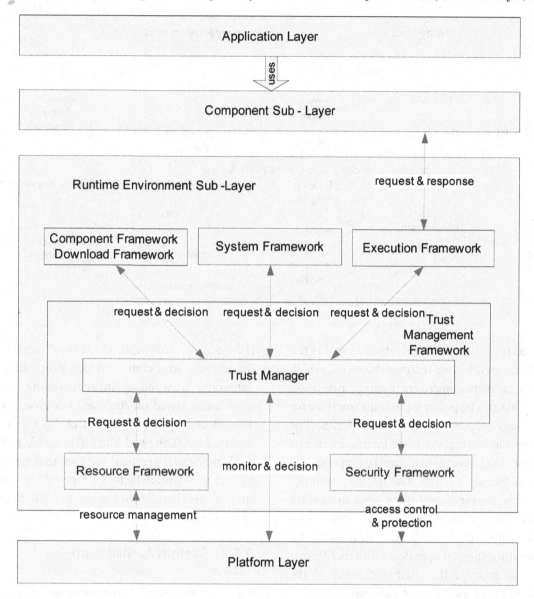

base saves various recommendations. The experience base saves the evidence collected from the component software platform itself in various contexts. The decision/reason engine is used to make trust decision when receiving requests from other frameworks (e.g., the download framework and the execution framework). It combines information from the experience base, the recommendation base and the policy base to conduct the trust assessment. It is also used to identify the reasons of trust problems. The mechanism base registers a number of mechanisms for trust control and establishment that are supported by the platform. It is also used to store the trust control models as described above. The selection engine is used to predict and select suitable mechanisms to ensure the platform trustworthiness in a specific context. It also conducts adaptive adjustments on the trust control model. The selected mechanisms are executed by the RE.

Figure 7. The structure of trust management framework

Figure 7. The structure of trust management framework

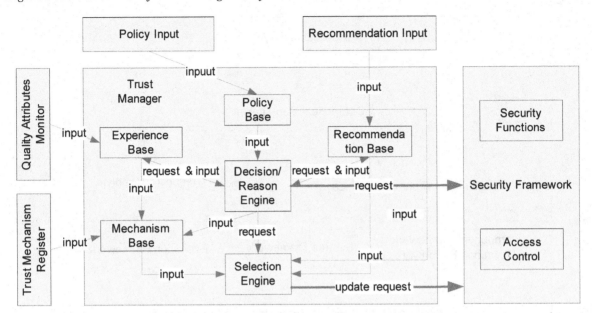

In addition, the recommendation input is the interface for collecting recommendations, which are useful to make component installation decision (Yan, 2008a). The policy input is the interface for the system entities to input their policies. The trust mechanism register is the interface to register trust mechanisms that can be applied and supported in the system. The quality attributes monitor is the functional block used to monitor the performance of specified system entity with regard to those attributes that may influence trust. The trust manager cooperates with other frameworks to manage the trustworthiness of the middleware component software platform.

3.5. Autonomic Trust Management for Mobile Cloud Services

Trust management is a crucial issue for mobile cloud services. This section proposes an autonomic trust management system for mobile cloud computing based on the adaptive trust control model. This solution facilitates trust prediction, establishment, assessment and assurance. We introduce the influence of QoS (Quality of Service) properties

(i.e., quality attributes) and service modes into the adaptive trust control model, which supports autonomic trust management according to trust assessment based on runtime QoS observation. The effectiveness and benefits of this solution is reported by Zhang and Yan (2011). This method contributes to a practical solution that can react against trust unsatisfactory adaptively at service runtime and handle trust requests with different QoS criteria.

3.5.1. System Architecture

Figure 8 shows trust management architecture based on QoS observation for mobile cloud services. In a mobile device, a QoS agent monitors QoS status at run time, e.g., percentage of memory and CPU consumption, connection speed, remaining battery percentage and packet loss rate, etc. The QoS status will be reported to a trust management center in cloud side. The trust management center aggregates and analyzes the huge set of QoS data at a data analyzer, and dynamically adjusts resources at a resource controller to meet trust requirements of each mobile cloud service.

Figure 8. Trust management architecture for mobile cloud services (Zhang & Yan, 2011)

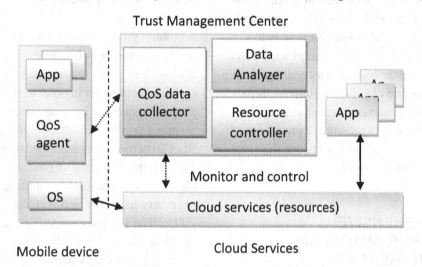

Based on the above trust management architecture and the adaptive trust control model, we apply several modes of mobile cloud services. Each mode contains multiple services, mechanisms and resource configuration schemes. A cloud service mode is a specific configuration to guarantee the trust requirements for a cloud service. Notably, the mobile cloud computing platform (offered by a mobile cloud service provider) can provide multiple similarly functioned services that can satisfy the demand of an integrated service. Especially, the trust requirements of a service can be assured by selecting suitable service modes. Herein, the data analyzer is applied to implement trust assessment based on the collected QoS data, while the resource controller is designed to conduct trustworthiness prediction, cloud service selection, control model adjustment and service/resource arrangement. The trust management center is responsible for autonomic trust management of cloud services for mobile devices based on the QoS observation reports from the devices.

In order to ensure the reliability of QoS observation reports from the mobile devices, we can apply the mechanisms introduced in Section 2 of this chapter to ensure the trustworthiness of the QoS agent running in the mobile device. Concretely, the QoS data collector at the cloud service side can remotely attest and ensure the trust of mobile device before and during the execution of cloud services.

3.5.2. Autonomic Trust Management Process

The process of autonomic trust management for mobile cloud services follows the procedure of Figure 5. In this case, trust predication is a mechanism to predict the performance of a set of cloud service modes before selecting a suitable one. Mode selection is a mechanism to select the best service mode based on previous prediction results. Trust assessment is a mechanism to monitor and assess the QoS status according to the trust requirements of a user. For the trust requirements on a service, the trust values can be predicted by assuming a service mode is selected. Based on prediction results, a service mode can be selected and set as the configuration of cloud services. The trust assessment mechanism evaluates the QoS status by collecting the QoS performance data of the cloud service from the mobile device. According to the assessment results, the system adjusts the parameters of the adaptive trust control model to reflect real status. The adjustment happens when the evaluation result is below a threshold defined by the user. The process runs over to achieve the autonomic trust management in a dynamic mobile cloud environment. In particular, the trust management supports context awareness by adaptively selecting a proper set of service modes that can always ensure the trust and quality of cloud services.

4. A COMPREHENSIVE SOLUTION FOR AUTONOMIC TRUST MANAGEMENT

An integrated solution can be further proposed by integrating the above two mechanisms together (Yan, 2008b). The trustworthiness of all kinds of mobile systems can be ensured by applying this solution. Taking a mobile pervasive system as an example, we demonstrate how trust can be automatically managed and the effectiveness of our solution.

4.1. A System Model

A mobile system is described in Figure 9. It is composed of a number of mobile computing devices. The devices offer various services. They could collaborate together in order to fulfill an intended purpose requested by a mobile system user. We assumed that the mobile computing device has a Root Trust module as described in Section 2, which supports the mechanism to sustain trust. This module locates at a trusted computing platform with necessary hardware and software support (TCG, 2003). The trusted computing platform protects the Operating System (OS) that runs a number of services (offered by various software components or applications) and a performance observer that monitors the performance of the running services. The service or device could behave as either a trustor or a trustee in the system. Particularly, an autonomic trust management framework (ATMF) is also contained in the trusted computing platform with the support of the RT module. The ATMF is responsible for managing the trustworthiness of the services.

Figure 9. Model of a pervasive system (Yan, 2008b)

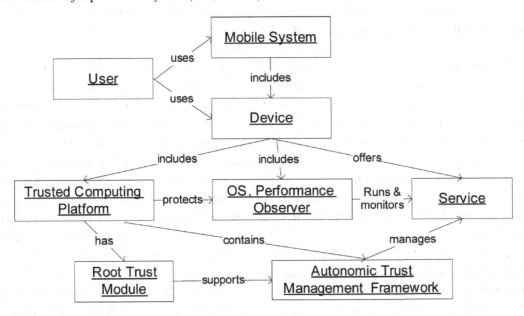

216

4.2. Autonomic Trust Management Framework (ATMF)

The ATMF is applied to manage the trustworthiness of a trustee service by configuring its trust properties or switching on/off the trust control mechanisms, i.e., selecting a suitable set of control modes. Its structure is shown in Figure 10.

The framework contains a number of secure storages, such as an experience base, a policy base and a mechanism base. The experience base is used to store the monitoring results of service performance regarding a number of quality attributes. The experience data could be accumulated locally or contain recommendations of other devices. The policy base registers the trustor's policies for trust assessment. The mechanism base registers the trust control modes that can be supported by the device in order to ensure the trustworthiness of the services. The ATMF located at the platform layer has secure access to the RT module in order to extract the policies into

the policy base for trust assessment if necessary (e.g., if a remote service is the trustor). In addition, an evaluation, decision and selection engine (EDS engine) is applied to conduct trust assessment, make trust decision and select suitable trust control modes.

4.3. A Procedure of Comprehensive Autonomic Trust Management

Based on the above design, we propose a procedure to conduct autonomic trust management targeting at a trustee service specified by a trustor service in the mobile system, as shown in Figure 11.

The device that locates the trustor service firstly checks whether remote service collaboration is required. If so, it applies the mechanism for trust sustaining to ensure that the remote service device will work as its expectation during the service collaboration. The trust conditions about the trustee device can be protected and realized with its RT module. Meanwhile, the trust

Figure 10. Autonomic trust management framework (Yan, 2008b)

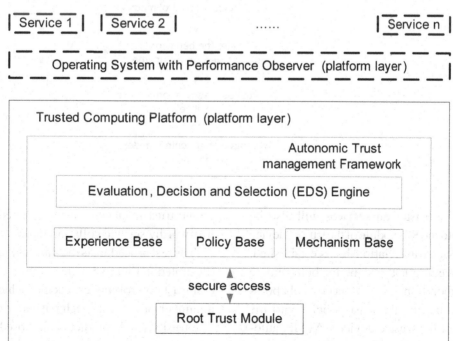

Figure 11. A comprehensive autonomic trust management procedure (Yan, 2008b)

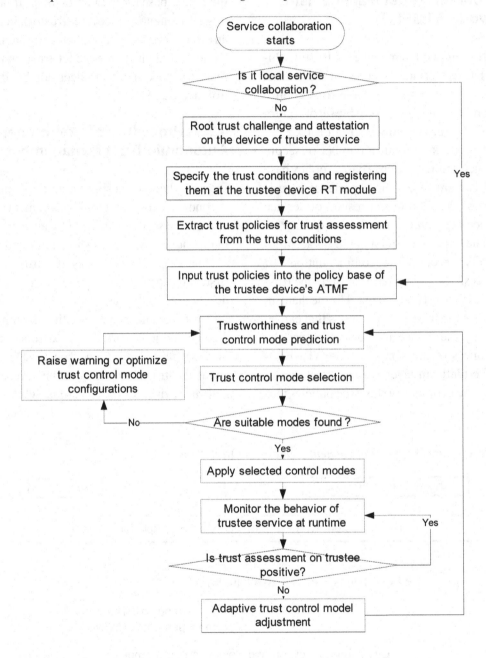

policies of the trustor on services will also be embedded into the RT module of the trustee device when the device trust relationship is established. The rest procedure is the same for both remote service collaboration and local service collaboration. After inputting the trust policies into the policy base of the trustee device's ATMF, auto-

nomic trust management is triggered to ensure trustworthy service collaboration.

The rest procedure is the same as the procedure illustrated in Figure 5. Concretely, we apply several trust control modes, each of which contains a number of control mechanisms or operations. The trust value is predicted supposed that some control modes are applied before the decision to initiate those modes is made. The most suitable trust control modes can be selected based on the prediction results. Trust assessment is then conducted based on the trustor's subjective policies by evaluating the trustee entity's quality attributes which are influenced by the system context. According to the runtime trust assessment results in the underlying context, the trustee device conducts trust control model adjustment in order to reflect the real system situation if the assessed trustworthiness value is below an expected threshold. The quality attributes of the entity can be controlled or improved via applying a number of trust control modes, especially at the service runtime. The context-aware or situation-aware adaptability of the trust control model is crucial to re-select a suitable set of trust control modes in order to conduct autonomic trust management.

4.4. An Application Example

This section takes a simple example to show how autonomic trust management is realized based on the cooperation of both the trust sustaining mechanism and the adaptive trust control model. The proof of applied algorithms has been reported in (Yan & MacLaverty, 2006; Yan, 2008a; Yan & Prehofer, 2007; Yan & Prehofer, 2011).

We take a mobile pervasive healthcare system as a concrete example. It is composed of a number of services located at different devices. For example, a health sensor locates at a potable mobile device, which can monitor a user's health status; a healthcare client service in the same device provides multiple ways to transfer health data to other devices and receive health guidelines. A healthcare consultant service locates at a healthcare centre, which provides health guidelines to the user according to the health data reported. It can also inform a hospital service at a hospital server if necessary. The trustworthiness of the healthcare application depends on not only the trustworthiness of each device and service, but

also the cooperation of all related devices and services. It is important to ensure that they can cooperate well in order to satisfy trust requirements with each other and their user. For concrete examples, the healthcare client service needs to provide a secure network connection and communication as required by the user. It also needs to respond to the request from the health sensor within expected time and performs reliably without any break in case of an urgent health information transmission. Particularly, if the system deploys additional services that could share resources with the healthcare client service, the mobile healthcare application should be still capable of providing qualified services to its users.

In order to provide a trustworthy healthcare application, the trustworthy collaboration among the mobile device, the healthcare centre and the hospital server is required. In addition, all related services should cooperate together in a trustworthy way. Our example application scenario is the user's health is monitored by a mobile device that reports his/her health data to the healthcare centre in a secure and efficient way. In this case, the hospital service should be efficiently informed since the user's health needs to be treated by the hospital immediately. Meanwhile, the consultant service also provides essential health guidelines to the user. Deploying our solution, the autonomic trust management mechanisms used to ensure the trustworthiness of the above scenario are summarized in Table 1 based on a number of example trust conditions and policies. Taking the first example in the Table 1, the trust policies include the requirements on different quality attributes: confidentiality, integrity, availability and reliability in order to ensure the trustworthiness of health data collection in the mobile device.

5. FURTHER DISCUSSIONS

The proposed solution supports autonomic trust management with two levels. The first level imple-

Table 1. Autonomic trust management for a healthcare application

Trustor	Trustee	Example Trust Requirements	Autonomic Trust Management Mechanisms
Health sensor	Healthcare client	Trust policies (data confidentiality: yes; data integrity: yes; service availability – response time: <3sec; service reliability – uptime: >10min)	Control mode prediction and selection, runtime trust assessment, trust control model adjustment and control mode re-selection to ensure the trustworthiness of health data collection;
Mobile device	Healthcare centre	Trust conditions (device and trust policies integrity: yes)	Trust sustaining mechanism to ensure the integrity of healthcare centre and trust policies for consultant service;
Healthcare client	Consultant service	Trust policies (authentication: yes; data confidentiality: yes; data integrity: yes; service availability – response time: <30sec; service reliability – uptime: >10hour)	Control mode prediction and selection, runtime trust assessment, trust control model adjustment and control mode re-selection to ensure the trustworthiness of health data reception;
Healthcare centre	Mobile device	Trust conditions (device and trust policies integrity: yes)	Trust sustaining mechanism to ensure the integrity of mobile device and trust policies for healthcare client service;
Consultant service	Healthcare client	Trust policies (authentication: yes; data confidentiality: yes; data integrity: yes; service availability – response time: <10sec; service reliability – uptime: >1hour)	Control mode prediction and selection, runtime trust assessment, trust control model adjustment and control mode re-selection to ensure the trustworthiness of guidelines reception;
Healthcare centre	Hospital server	Trust conditions (device and trust policies integrity: yes)	Trust sustaining mechanism to ensure the integrity of hospital server and trust policies for hospital service;
Consultant service	Hospital service	Trust policies (authentication: yes; data confidentiality: yes; data integrity: yes; service availability – response time: <10min; service reliability – uptime: >10hour)	Control mode prediction and selection, trust assessment, trust control model adjustment and control mode re-selection to ensure the hospital service's trustworthiness.

ments autonomic trust management among different system devices by applying the mechanism to sustain trust. On the basis of a trusted computing platform, this mechanism can also securely embed the trust policies into a remote trustee device for the purpose of trustworthy service collaboration. This mechanism is mainly implemented at the device platform layer. Regarding the second level, the trustworthiness of the service is automatically managed based on the adaptive trust control model at its runtime. This mechanism can be implemented in either the platform layer or the middleware layer (e.g., a component software middleware layer), depending on the concrete system requirements. Both levels of autonomic trust management can be conducted independently or cooperate together in order to ensure the trustworthiness of the entire mobile system. From this point of view, none of

the existing work reviewed in this book provides a similar solution. The proposed solution applied the trust sustaining mechanism to stop or restrict any potential risky activities. Thus, it is a more active approach than the existing solutions.

Trusted computing platform technology is developing in both industry and academia in order to provide more secure and better trust support for future digital devices. The technology aims to solve existing security problems by hardware trust. Although it may be vulnerable to some hardware attacks (Huang, 2002), it has advantages over many software-based solutions. It has potential advantages over other solutions as well; especially when the Trusted Computing Group standard (TCG, 2003) is deployed and more and more industry digital device vendors offer TCG-compatible hardware and software in the future. The proposed solution will have potential advantages when various digital device vendors produce TCG compatible products in the future.

The RT module can be designed and implemented inside a secure main chip in the mobile computing platform. The secure main chip provides a secure environment to offer security functions or services for the operating system (OS) and application software. It also has a number of security enforcement mechanisms (e.g., secure booting, integrity checking, privacy enhancement, and device authentication). Particularly, it provides cryptographic functions and secure storages. The RT module functionalities and the ATMF functionalities can be implemented by a number of protected applications. The protected applications are small applications dedicated to performing security critical operations inside a secure environment. They have strict size limitations and resemble function libraries. The protected applications can access any resource in the secure environment. They can also communicate with normal applications in order to offer security services. New protected applications can be added to the system at any time. The secure environment software controls loading and execution of the protected applications. Only signed protected applications are allowed to run. Notably, the secure registers in the RT module, the policy base, the execution base and the mechanism base could be implemented by a flexible and light secure storage mechanism supported by the trusted computing platform (Asokan & Ekberg, 2008).

6. CONCLUSION

This chapter elaborates the demand of autonomic trust management in mobile environments. We specify a number of research issues regarding mobile computing platforms in mobile environments. In order to solve these issues, we presented a comprehensive and generic autonomic trust management solution based on the trust sustaining mechanism and the adaptive trust control model. The main significance of this solution lies in the fact that it supports two levels of autonomic trust management: between devices as well as between services offered by the devices. This solution can also effectively avoid or reduce risks by stopping or restricting any potential risky activities based on the specification of the trustor. We demonstrated the effectiveness of this solution by applying it into a number of mobile systems, e.g., ad hoc networks, P2P systems, mobile enterprise networking, component software platform, mobile cloud services and mobile pervasive systems. We also discussed the advantages and implementation strategies of this solution.

Regarding future work direction, it is essential to analyze the performance of the proposed solution on the basis of a mobile trusted computing platform. Furthermore, how to automatically extract mobile the trust policies of mobile users based on machine learning through user-device interaction is also an interesting research topic. The usability of autonomic trust management is a crucial issue for the success of practical deployment.

REFERENCES

Armbrust, M. (2009). *Above the clouds: A Berkeley view of cloud.* Berkeley, CA: University of California.

Asokan, N., & Ekberg, J. (2008). A platform for OnBoard credentials. In *Financial Cryptography and Data Security (LNCS)* (Vol. 5143, pp. 318–320). Berlin: Springer. doi:10.1007/978-3-540-85230-8_31.

Blaze, M., Ioannidis, J., & Keromytis, A. D. (2002). Trust management for IPSEC. *ACM Transactions on Information and System Security, 5*(2), 95–118. doi:10.1145/505586.505587.

Cheung, K. H., & Misic, J. (2002). On virtual private network security design issues. *Computer Networks, 38*(2), 165–179. doi:10.1016/S1389-1286(01)00256-0.

Dillon, T., Wu, C., & Chang, E. (2010). Cloud computing: Issues and challenges. In *Proceedings of 24th IEEE International Conference on Advanced Information Networking and Applications*, (pp. 27-33). IEEE.

England, P., Lampson, B., Manferdelli, J., Peinado, M., & Willman, B. (2003). A trusted open platform. *IEEE Computer, 36*(7), 55–62. doi:10.1109/MC.2003.1212691.

Fenkam, P., Dustdar, S., Kirda, E., Reif, G., & Gall, H. (2002). Towards an access control system for mobile peer-to-peer collaborative environments. In *Proceedings of Eleventh IEEE International Workshops on Enabling Technologies: Infrastructure for Collaborative Enterprises*, (pp. 95-100). IEEE.

Grandison, T., & Sloman, M. (2000). A survey of trust in internet applications. *IEEE Communications and Survey, 3*(4), 2–16. doi:10.1109/COMST.2000.5340804.

Hall, R. S., Heimbigner, D., Van Der Hoek, A., & Wolf, A. L. (1997). An architecture for post-development configuration management in a wide-area network. In *Proceedings of the 17th Int'l Conf. Distributed Computing Systems*, (pp. 269-278). IEEE.

Hamed, H., Al-Shaer, E., & Marrero, W. (2005). Modeling and verification of IPSec and VPN security policies. In *Proceedings of 13th IEEE International Conference on Network Protocols*, (pp. 259 – 278). IEEE.

Herrmann, P. (2001). Trust-based procurement support for software components. In *Proceedings of the Fourth Int'l Conf. Electronic Commerce Research*, (pp. 505-514). IEEE.

Herrmann, P. (2003). Trust-based protection of software component users and designers. In *Proceedings of the First Int'l Conf. Trust Management*, (pp. 75-90). IEEE.

Herscovitz, E. (1999). Secure virtual private networks: The future of data communications. *International Journal of Network Management, 9*(4), 213–220. doi:10.1002/(SICI)1099-1190(199907/08)9:4<213::AID-NEM328>3.0.CO;2-E.

Huang, A. B. (2002). The trusted OC: Skin-deep security. *Computer, 35*(10), 103–105. doi:10.1109/MC.2002.1039525.

Jøsang, A., Ismail, R., & Boyd, C. (2005). A survey of trust and reputation systems for online service provision. *Decision Support Systems*, 618–644.

Kortuem, G., Schneider, J., Preuitt, D., Thompson, T. G. C., Fickas, S., & Segall, Z. (2001). When peer-to-peer comes face-to-face: Collaborative peer-to-peer computing in mobile ad hoc networks. In *Proceedings of the First International Conference on Peer-to-Peer Computing*, (pp. 75-91). IEEE.

Li, Q., Hao, Q., Xiao, L., & Li, Z. (2009). Adaptive management of virtualized resources in cloud computing using feedback control. In *Proceedings of 1st International Conference on Information Science and Engineering* (ICISE), (pp. 99-102). ICISE.

Lin, C., Varadharajan, V., Wang, Y., & Pruthi, V. (2004). Enhancing grid security with trust management. In *Proceedings of IEEE International Conference on Services Computing*, (pp. 303-310). IEEE.

Lodi, G., Panzieri, F., Rossi, D., & Turrini, E. (2007). SLA-driven clustering of QoS-aware application servers. *IEEE Transactions on Software Engineering, 33*(3), 186–197. doi:10.1109/TSE.2007.28.

Malek, S., Esfahani, N., Menasce, D., Sousa, J., & Gomaa, H. (2009). Self-architecting software systems (SASSY) from QoS-annotated activity models. In *Proceedings of the Int'l Conf. Software Eng. (ICSE) Workshop Principles of Eng. Service-Oriented Systems*, (pp. 62-69). ICSE.

Mikic-Rakic, M., Malek, S., & Medvidovic, N. (2008). Architecture-driven software mobility in support of QoS requirements. In *Proceedings of the First Int'l Workshop Software Architectures and Mobility*, (pp. 3-8). IEEE.

Perez, S. (2009). *Why cloud computing is the future of mobile*. Retrieved from http://www.readwriteweb.com/archives/why_cloud_computing_is_the_future_of_mobile.php

Regan, K. (2003). Secure VPN design considerations. *Network Security*, 5–10.

Shan, R., Li, S., Wang, M., & Li, J. (2003). Network security policy for large-scale VPN. In *Proceedings of International Conference on Communication Technology*, (pp. 217-220). IEEE.

Stantchev, V., & Schrofer, C. (2009). Negotiating and enforcing QoS and SLAs in grid and cloud computing. In *Proceedings of the 4th International Conference on Advances in Grid and Pervasive Computing* (LNCS), (vol. 5529, pp. 25-35). Berlin: Springer.

Suryanarayana, G., Diallo, M. H., Erenkrantz, J. R., & Taylor, R. N. (2006). Architectural support for trust models in decentralized applications. In *Proceedings of the 28th Int'l Conf. Software Eng.*, (pp. 52-61). IEEE.

TCG. (2003). TPM *specification* v1.2. Retrieved from https://www.trustedcomputinggroup.org/specs/TPM/

Theodorakopoulos, G., & Baras, J. S. (2006). On trust models and trust evaluation metrics for ad hoc networks. *IEEE Journal on Selected Areas in Communications*, 24(2), 318–328. doi:10.1109/JSAC.2005.861390.

Vaughan-Nichols, S. J. (2003). How trustworthy is trusted computing? *IEEE Computer*, 36(3), 18–20. doi:10.1109/MC.2003.1185209.

Wang, X., Du, Z., Liu, X., Xie, H., & Jia, X. (2010). An adaptive QoS management framework for VoD cloud service centers. In *Proceedings of 2010 International Conference on Computer Application and System Modeling* (ICCASM), (pp. 527-532). ICCASM.

Wood, D., Stoss, V., Chan-Lizardo, L., Papacostas, G. S., & Stinson, M. E. (1988). Virtual private networks. In *Proceedings of International Conference on Private Switching Systems and Networks*, (pp. 132-136). IEEE.

Xiao, Y., Lin, C., Jiang, Y., Chu, X., & Shen, X. (2010). Reputation-based QoS provisioning in cloud computing via dirichlet multinomial model. In *Proceedings of IEEE International Conference on Communications* (ICC), (pp. 1-5). IEEE.

Xiong, L., & Liu, L. (2004). PeerTrust: Supporting reputation-based trust for peer-to-peer electronic communities. *IEEE Transactions on Knowledge and Data Engineering*, 16(7), 843–857. doi:10.1109/TKDE.2004.1318566.

Yan, Z. (2008a). A comprehensive trust model for component software. [IEEE.]. *Proceedings of SecPerU, 08*, 1–6. doi:10.1145/1387329.1387330.

Yan, Z. (2008b). Autonomic trust management for a pervasive system. [IEEE.]. *Proceedings of Secypt, 08*, 491–500.

Yan, Z. (2010). Security via trusted communications. In P. Stavroulakis, & M. Stamp (Eds.), *Handbook on Communications and Information Security* (pp. 719–746). Berlin: Springer. doi:10.1007/978-3-642-04117-4_33.

Yan, Z., & Cofta, P. (2004). A mechanism for trust sustainability among trusted computing platforms. In *Proceedings of the First International Conference on Trust and Privacy in Digital Business* (TrustBus'04) (LNCS), (vol. 3184, pp. 11-19). Berlin: Springer.

Yan, Z., & MacLaverty, R. (2006). Autonomic trust management in a component based software system. In *Proceedings of ATC06* (LNCS), (vol. 4158, pp. 279-292). Berlin: Springer.

Yan, Z., & Prehofer, C. (2007). An adaptive trust control model for a trustworthy software component platform. In *Proceedings of the 4th International Conference on Autonomic and Trusted Computing* (LNCS), (vol. 4610, pp. 226-238). Berlin: Springer.

Yan, Z., & Prehofer, C. (2011). Autonomic trust management for a component based software system. *IEEE Transactions on Dependable and Secure Computing*, 8(6), 810–823. doi:10.1109/TDSC.2010.47.

Yan, Z., & Zhang, P. (2006a). Trust collaboration in P2P systems based on trusted computing platforms. *WSEAS Transactions on Information Science and Applications*, 2(3), 275–282.

Yan, Z., & Zhang, P. (2006b). A trust management system in mobile enterprise networking. *WSEAS Transactions on Communications*, 5(5), 854–861.

Yan, Z., Zhang, P., & Virtanen, T. (2003). Trust evaluation based security solution in ad hoc networks. In *Proceedings of the 7th Nordic Workshop on Secure IT Systems* (NordSec03). NordSec.

Ye, Y., Jain, N., Xia, L., Joshi, S., Yen, I.-L., Bastani, F., et al. (2010). A framework for QoS and power management in a service cloud environment with mobile devices. In *Proceedings of the Fifth IEEE International Symposium on Service Oriented System Engineering* (SOSE), (pp. 236-243). IEEE.

Zhang, P., & Yan, Z. (2011). Adaptive QoS management for mobile cloud services. *China Communications*, 10, 36–43.

Zhou, M., Jiao, W., & Mei, H. (2005). Customizable framework for managing trusted components deployed on middleware. In *Proceedings of 10th IEEE Int'l Conf. Eng. of Complex Computer Systems*, (pp. 283-291). IEEE.

Zhou, M., Mei, H., & Zhang, L. (2005). A multi-property trust model for reconfiguring component software. In *Proceedings of the Fifth International Conference on Quality Software* (QAIC2005), (pp. 142–149). QAIC.

APPENDIX

Questions and Exercises

1. What are the advantages and disadvantages of the comprehensive autonomic trust management solution presented in this chapter?
2. What are the characteristics of autonomic trust management?
3. What is the difference of autonomic trust management from normal trust management?

Chapter 9
Usable Trust Modeling and Management

ABSTRACT

Trust management has emerged as a promising technology to facilitate collaboration among entities in an environment where traditional security technologies cannot provide an effective solution. However, prior art generally lack considerations on usable means to gather and disseminate information for effective trust evaluation, as well as provide trust information to users in order to assist user decision. Current trust management solution could be hard to understand, use, and thus be accepted by the users. This chapter introduces a human-centric trust modeling and management method in order to design and develop a usable trust management solution that can be easily accepted by the users towards practical deployment. The authors illustrate how to apply this method into the design of a reputation system for mobile applications in order to demonstrate its effectiveness.

1. INTRODUCTION

Trust has two distinct characteristics. It is subjective, thus the level of trust considered sufficient is different for each individual in a certain situation. It is the subjective expectation of the trustor on the trustee that could influence the belief of the trustor. Trust is also dynamic as it is affected by many factors. It can further develop and evolve due to good experiences about the trustee. It is sensitive to be decayed caused by bad experiences.

Trust management has become a promising technology to facilitate collaboration among entities in a digital environment where traditional security technologies cannot provide an effective solution. Trust management is concerned with: collecting the information required to make a trust relationship decision; evaluating the criteria related to the trust relationship; monitoring and reevaluating existing trust relationships; as well as ensuring the dynamically changed trust relationships and automating the process (Grandison &

DOI: 10.4018/978-1-4666-4765-7.ch009

Copyright © 2014, IGI Global. Copying or distributing in print or electronic forms without written permission of IGI Global is prohibited.

Sloman, 2000; Yan & Prehofer, 2011). Various trust management systems have been described in the literature. One important category consists of reputation based trust management systems. Trust and reputation mechanisms have been proposed in various fields such as distributed computing, agent technology, GRID computing, and component software (Resnick & Zeckhauser, 2002; Xiong & Liu, 2004; Herrmann, 2001; Walsh & Sirer, 2005). Recently, many mechanisms have been developed for supporting trusted communications and collaborations among computing nodes in a distributed system (Sun, Yu, Han & Liu, 2006; Zhang, Wang & Wang, 2005; Theodorakopoulos & Baras, 2006; Lin, Varadharajan, Wang & Pruthi, 2004). These mechanisms are based on digital modeling of trust for trust evaluation and management.

Due to the subjective characteristic of trust, trust management needs to take the criteria of trustor into consideration. For a digital system, it is essential for the user device to understand the trust criteria of the user in order to behave as her/his agent for trust management. Generally, it is not good to require the user to make a lot of trust related decisions or interactions because that would destroy usability. Also, the user may not be informed enough to make sound decisions and act accordingly. Thus, establishing trust is quite a complicated task with many optional actions to take. Trust should rather be managed automatically following a high level policy established by the trustor (Yan & Prehofer, 2007; Yan & Prehofer, 2011). User-device interaction is needed if the device inquires trust criteria or feedback from the user in various contexts. This would require a friendly user interface to a) collect useful information for trust evaluation and management; b) present the evaluation results in a comprehensive and acceptable manner to the user; and c) disseminate individual experiences to other devices as recommendations or contribute to reputation generation. Or other novel approaches could be adopted to help us design a usable trust management system.

In this chapter, we introduce a human-centric trust modeling and management method in order to design and develop a usable trust management solution that can be easily accepted by the users towards practical deployment. Our focus is to manage trust between a user and a digital system, which is either a device or a digital system or service or a software application consumed by the user.

The rest of the chapter is organized as follows. Section 2 gives a brief overview of the literature background of social trust, computational trust and trust behavior studies. Section 3 introduces the method of human-centric trust modeling and management. In Section 4, we illustrate how to apply this method by taking the design and development of a reputation system for mobile applications as an example. We further discuss the advantages of our method in Section 5. Finally, conclusions and future work are presented in the last section.

2. BACKGROUND

This section briefly reviews two main divisions of trust management study. One is psychological and sociological study on trust. The other is the study on computational trust and trusted computing in information and computer technologies. Meanwhile, we also review the study on trust behavior that is an objective expression of subjective trust. We investigate different methods applied in the literature in order to propose a feasible approach that can be adopted in practice towards usable trust management.

2.1. Psychological and Sociological Study on a Trustworthy System

Basso et al. (2001) examined the early formation of trust and the likelihood that a shopper will return to a website for subsequent purchases. Two hypotheses were proposed in the study and corresponding experiments were conducted to prove them. The first hypothesis is that the presence of voice and interactivity should each lead to higher ratings on trustworthiness and other positive attributions. The second hypothesis assumed that trust in the reliability of a store and the UI ability to engage the shopper should significantly predict purchase intent. Based on the hypothesis, the authors studied shopper behaviors after first impression and after real experience based on initial trust. Results indicated that real-time interactivity, but not voice, increased judgments of friendliness and of the trustworthiness of the salesperson.

Lumsden and MacKay (2006) presented and discussed the results of a study which took an initial look at whether consumers with different personality types (a) are generally more trusting and (b) rely on different trust cues during their assessment of first impression vendor trustworthiness in B2C e-commerce. They developed a questionnaire to serve as an initial investigation into the effect of personality type on consumer trust and perception of importance of trust triggers. A five-point Likert scale was applied to let respondents respond their feedback of each questionnaire item. The applied research method is helpful to investigate the trust influencing factors and user opinions on human-computer interaction designs.

Herlocker, Konstan and Riedl (2000) studied the influence of explanation on user acceptance of ACF (Automated Collaborative Filtering) systems. They addressed explanation interfaces for ACF systems – how they should be implemented and why they should be implemented. A model for explanations based on a conceptual model of the recommendation process was proposed. User experimental results demonstrated what components of an explanation are the most compelling. To address why, experimental evidence was presented to show that providing explanations can improve the acceptance of ACF systems. It has been proved that user experiment study greatly help in designing a trustworthy system user interface.

Dimoka (2010) used functional neuroimaging tools to complement psychometric measures of trust and distrust by observing the location, tim-

ing, and level of brain activity that underlies trust and distrust and their underlying dimensions. He found that trust and distrust activate different brain areas and have different effects, helping explain why trust and distrust are distinct constructs associated with different neurological processes.

Riedl, Hubert and Kenning (2010) applied functional magnetic resonance imaging (fMRI) to capture the brain activity of 10 female and 10 male participants simultaneous to decisions on trustworthiness of eBay offers. They found that most of the brain areas that encode trustworthiness differ between women and men and women activated more brain areas than did men. This study also argued that future Information Science research investigating human behaviors should consider the role of biological factors that are a significant consideration for management, marketing, and engineering attempts to influence behavior.

Pu and Chen (2006) used a qualitative survey to find research focus – explanation interface and the related design issues. They further used pilot study and interview; post-survey discussion/interview; significant scale empirical study; paired samples t-test, and five-point Likert scale to conduct continuous research.

An integrated model of trust in electronic commerce was proposed by Kini and Choobineh (1998). This model serves as the theoretical foundation to study the impact of trust on the success of electronic commerce. The model was developed by studying existing research in diverse fields such as psychology, social psychology, relationship theory, and human machine interaction, then integrated all valuable results into a comprehensive model. This method is beneficial for us in order to propose a new method built upon the advantages of previous work.

Turel, Yuan and Connelly (2008) examined how justice and trust affect user acceptance of e-customer services by conducting an online experiment. The results suggested that trust in an e-customer service fully mediates the effects of trust in service providers and continuous usage of service; the effect of distributive justice on trust in the e-customer service was fully mediated by trust in the service provider; the effect of informational justice on user intentions to reuse the e-customer service was partially mediated by trust in the service provider and trust in the e-customer service.

Applying a measurement scale to conceptualize trust based on user studies is a generally adopted method for social trust study. This kind of research aims to prove the complicated relationships among trust and other multiple factors in different facets. Two typical examples are the initial trust model proposed by McKnight, Choudhury, and Kacmar (2002) that explained and predicted customer trust towards an e-vender in an e-commerce context, and the Technology Trust Formation Model (TTFM) studied by Li, Valacich, and Hess (2004) to explain and predict people trust towards a specific information system. For other examples, Gefen (2000) proved that familiarity builds trust; Pennington, Wilcox, and Grover (2004) tested that one trust mechanism, vendor guarantees, has direct influence on system trust; Bhattacherjee (2002) studied three key dimensions of trust: trustee's ability, benevolence and integrity; Pavlou and Gefen (2004) explained that institutional mechanisms engender buyer's trust in the community of online auction sellers. This measurement scale based study could help us work out a trust construct, which can be described in a graphic or linguistic way. The result could instruct the design of a trust management system. Unfortunately, it is impossible to apply the graphic or linguistic trust constructs directly for digital trust evaluation and management.

Zahedi and Song (2008) explored the process by which trust evolves over time (i.e., on-going trust study). The evolution of trust was investigated using the case of health infomediaries. The examination of the temporal changes in trust was carried out through two approaches-comparative statics and dynamic analyses. The results of analysis showed that the structure of trust changes over time and information quality becomes the single

most important antecedent in infomediary trust building in the later stages of use. Furthermore, it was also indicated that satisfaction plays an important role in changing Web customers' trust beliefs.

Psychological or sociological studies on trust can be structured into four aspects: nature and role of trust, moderators of trust, antecedents of trust, and empirical methods for examining trust (Gefen, Benbasat & Pavlou, 2008). Some of the above work aims to conceptualize trust based on user studies through a psychological or sociological approach. The trust models generated based on this approach are generally linguistic or graphic (Yan & Holtmanns, 2008). These models do not quantify trust for computer processing purposes. Therefore, the achieved results could only help people understanding trust more precisely. They generally work as guidelines or organizational policies for developing a trustworthy digital system or designing a trustworthy user interface. Although little work has been conducted to integrate psychological, sociological and computational theories together, we believe that the psychological and sociological study should play as a practical foundation of computational trust – modeling trust for a digital processing purpose.

2.2. Computational Trust

Computational trust is a technical approach applied to represent trust for the purpose of trust calculation and digital processing. Regarding computational trust, we found quite a number of studies in the literature (Yan, 2010). One of the earliest formalizations of trust in computing systems was done by Marsh (1994). In his approach, he integrated the various facets of trust from the disciplines of economics, psychology, philosophy and sociology. Since then, many trust models have been constructed for various computing paradigms such as ubiquitous computing, peer-to-peer (P2P) networks, and multi-agent systems. For example, Abdul-Rahman and Hailes (2000) used discrete integer numbers to describe the degree of trust in virtual communities. Then, simple mathematics, such as minimum, maximum, and weighted average, is used to calculate a trust value through concatenation and multi-path trust propagation. Buchegger and Le Boudec (2004) designed a distributed reputation system using a Bayesian approach for P2P and mobile ad-hoc networks, in which the second-hand reputation rating is accepted only when it is not incompatible with the primary rating. In almost all of these studies, trust is accepted as a subjective notion by all researchers, which brings us to a problem: how to measure trust? Translation of this subjective concept into a machine readable language becomes a main objective. However, most of above studies focus on computational trust expression and calculation. Some factors or subjective policies used in the models were generally hidden in the system without any confirmation by the users.

Sun, Yu, Han and Liu (2006) presented an information theoretic framework to quantitatively measure trust and model trust propagation in ad hoc networks. In the proposed framework, trust is a measure of uncertainty with its value represented by entropy. The authors develop four axioms that address the basic understanding of trust and the rules for trust propagation. Based on these axioms two trust models are introduced: an entropy-based model and a probability-based model, both satisfy all the axioms. The only doubt of this work is whether the fundamental axioms are accepted by normal users, which could be an issue in practical deployment.

Xiong and Liu (2004) presented five trust parameters used in PeerTrust, namely, feedback a peer receives from other peers, the total number of transactions a peer performs, the credibility of the feedback sources, a transaction context factor, and a community context factor. By formalizing these parameters, a general trust metric is presented. It combines these parameters in a coherent scheme. This model can be applied into a decentralized P2P environment. It is effective against dynamic

personality of peers and malicious behaviors of peers. This work did not consider the concern of P2P system users regarding all trust parameters and feedback distribution and collection. It applied a laboratory simulation to prove trust evaluation metric and its efficiency against malicious peers.

2.3. Trust Behavior Study

Trust provides the means to decrease complexity by reducing the number of options one has to consider in a given situation (Barber, 1983; Lewis & Weigert, 1985; Luhmann, 1979). It is the key to decision making. Previous research has examined how trust is established, maintained, lost and regained in human–computer systems (Corritore et al., 2003). Trust has been seen as an intervening variable that mediates user behavior with computers (Muir, 1994). It enables people to live in a risky and uncertain situation (Deutsch, 1962; Mayer et al., 1995).

Trust behaviors are a trusting subject's actions to depend on or make her/him vulnerable to a trusting object (McKnight et al., 2002). McKnight et al. (2002) proposed that consumer subjective probability of depending involves the projected intention to engage in three specific risky behaviors—provide the vendor personal information, engage in a purchase transaction, or act on vendor information (e.g., financial advice). McKnight et al. (2002) also pointed out a number of opportunities for future research. Some of them relate directly to overcoming the limitations of their study. One particular suggestion was to conduct a study in which the ultimate outcome of interest—trust behavior—is directly measured. They identified a handful of commonly discussed trust-related behaviors in e-commerce—there may be others. Because of the difficulty of asking subjects to undertake such behavior, they did not measure actual behavior in their study. Note that trust and trust behavior are different concepts: trust is the willingness to assume risk; trust behavior is the assuming of risk (Mayer et al., 1995, p. 724).

Whether or not the trustor will take a specific risk is influenced by trusting beliefs, trusting intentions and the perceived risk of the trust behavior (Grabner-Kräuter & Kaluscha, 2003). However, still very few studies examined trust from the view of trust behaviors [19]. Some work studies the trust behavior in e-banking (Grabner-Kräuter & Kaluscha, 2003). To our knowledge, no existing work explores trust behavior of mobile application usage, which is a different context from the previous research domains with regard to running environment and user interface. Due to the above differences and the challenges caused by small device interface, the design of reputation systems for mobile applications has additional challenges considering usability and performance.

The Theory of Reasoned Action (TRA) explains how people form initial trust in an unfamiliar entity (Fishbein & Ajzen, 1975). It posits that beliefs lead to attitudes, which lead to behavioral intentions, which lead to the behavior itself (Fishbein & Ajzen, 1975). Numerous researchers have conceptualized trust as a behavior. Validation has been done in the context of work collaboration and social communications (Anderson & Narus, 1990; Deutsch, 1973; Fox, 1974); software system usage (Sheppard et al., 1988; Venkatesh & Davis, 2000); e-banking and economy (Grabner-Kräuter & Kaluscha, 2003).

The Technology Acceptance model (TAM) (Gefen et al., 2003) has been well studied in on-line shopping and the results showed that understanding both the Internet technology and issues around trust is important in determining behavioral intention to use (Gefen et al., 2003; Wu & Chen, 2005). This model placed the use of on-line system into two system features: ease of use, usefulness and playfulness (Davis et al., 1989; Venkatesh & Bala, 2008), as well as trust in e-vendors. This theory also indicates that good interface leads to better perceived usefulness and ease of use; playfulness causes better acceptance (attitude). Existing research result indicated that

these variables are good predictors for behavior intention to use on-line shopping (Wu & Chen, 2005).

One important issue that contributes to whether the users would like to use a new product or system (e.g., a mobile application) is how much they trust it. Muir is one of the first researchers to look at a decision process between supervisors and automated systems. She verified the hypothesis proposed by Sheridan et al. that the supervisor's intervention behavior is based upon his/her trust in automation (Sheridan, 1980). A positive correlation between trust and use has been proved (Lee & Moray, 1994; Muir, 1994; Muir & Moray, 1996). Lee and Moray (1992) found that trust in a system partially explains system use, but other factors (such as the user's own ability to provide manual control) also influence the system use. Muir and Moray (1996) further argued that trust in automated machines is based mostly on users' perceptions on the expertise of the machine, i.e., the extent to which the automation performs its function properly. The relationship between trust and interaction behavior is obvious. Trust has a direct influence on behavioral intention to use (Bandura, 1986; Davis et al., 1989). Wu and Chen (2005) also pointed that trust is apparently an important antecedent of attitude toward the on-line transaction behavior. All above studies show that: a user's trust in a mobile application can be evaluated based on the user's trust behaviors.

Many studies have empirically examined the determinants of continued usage (continuance) (Hsu et al., 2006). These studies provided preliminary evidence that continued usage behaviors are determined by different factors. Most studies aimed to examine the change of users' cognitive beliefs and attitude from pre-usage stage to usage stage and how they influence users' intention to continue their usage, especially within the context of online shopping. For example, expectancy disconfirmation theory (EDT) (Oliver, 1980), which is a consumer behavior model, explained and predicted consumer satisfaction and repurchase intentions. Based on this theory, satisfied consumers form intentions to reuse a product or service in the future, while dissatisfied users discontinue subsequent use. Users would evaluate whether their initial cognition is consonant or dissonant with actual experience (Bhattacherjee & Premkumar, 2004). Continuance implies ongoing trust of a user based on actual experiences.

Grabner-Kräuter and Kaluscha (2003) reviewed 11 trust construct studies. Trusting intentions and their antecedents are examined in several studies (Bhattacherjee, 2002; Gefen, 2000; Gefen & Straub, 2003; Jarvenpaa et al., 1999, 2000), whereas trust-related behaviors are only investigated in two studies (in Kim & Prabhakar, 2004; Pavlou, 2003). In order to investigate trust behavior as a consequence of trust, the former has to be measured in terms of actual behavior, not willingness to engage in behavior (Mayer et al., 1995). In some of the past studies (e.g., Jarvenpaa et al., 1999, 2000; Pavlou, 2003; de Ruyter et al., 2001), company reputation was discussed and included, but none of the eleven studies explicitly investigated the interrelationship between trust and branding. Another largely unexplored factor is product quality. The interdependencies between consumer trust and product performance played as a basis for upcoming research (Shankar et al., 2002). Varying the trustor or trustee or context may result in different sets of antecedents and consequences trust. All of above offer additional directions for future research.

Existing studies focus on human trust in an automation and intelligent machine. A number of trust models have been proposed in the context of e-commerce. Little work has been done in the context of mobile environments although the significance of such study is obvious. Prior arts also lack study on the influence of recommendations, personality and usage context with regard to human-computer trust. With the rapid development of mobile computing technology, a mobile device has become a multi-application

system for multi-purpose and multi-usage. It is an open platform that allows deploying new or upgraded applications at anytime and anywhere through a network connection. It can access the Internet through various local and wireless connection techniques. Therefore, such a dynamically changed system, different from the previous research domains, introduces new challenges for human computer trust. We believe that research should go into depth in the newly thrived mobile domain and should pay special attention to usability issues.

2.4. Applied Methods

The study of a trustworthy system is wide. We briefly summarize a number of typical methods applied in the literature in Table 1. Herein, we do not involve some interesting researches due to its infancy, e.g., a trust model derived based on a bio-inspired approach. For more methods of trust modeling and management, refer to Chapter 2 and 3.

Obviously, a thorough understanding of both the psychological/sociological, behavioral and engineering aspects of trust is necessary in order to develop a usable trust management solution. However, the psychological and sociological trust study lacks a way towards digital trust management, while current engineering study lacks a basic sociological and psychological foundation in order to convince normal users for easy acceptance. Current computational trust study generally has no sociological and psychological support although trust is first a social concept. Therefore, it is hard to predict if a trust management system built upon it could be easily accepted and widely used by users. A gap exists between the two disciplines of trust research. On the other hand, the tight relationship between trust and behavior is also ignored in most of previous researches. The reason could be they are solving different research issues. But for developing a practical trust management system, we need to

Table 1. Research methods for establishing a trustworthy system

Examples	Research Methods
Basso, Goldberg, Greenspan and Weimer (2001)	Hypothesis based initial study; trust model design based on experimental results on users
Lumsden and MacKay (2006)	Questionnaire-based survey with five-point Likert measurement scale
McKnight, Choudhury, and Kacmar (2002); Li, Valacich and Hess (2004); Gefen (2000); Pennington, Wilcox, and Grover (2004); Bhattacherjee (2002); Pavlou and Gefen (2004)	A number of measurement scales developed to study trust constructs and trust relationships with other factors
Herlocker, Konstan and Riedl (2000)	Prove research hypothesis through user experimental study
Pu and Chen (2006)	Qualitative survey; pilot study and interview; post-survey discussion/interview; significant scale empirical study; paired samples t-test, and five-point Likert scale
Kini and Choobineh (1998)	Integration of previous research results
Abdul-Rahman and Hailes (2000)	A discrete trust model of virtual communities, which is based on experience and reputation. An example application was illustrated
Buchegger and Le Boudec (2004)	A continuous trust model based on a modified Bayesian estimation approach. Evaluation on its performance was conducted based on simulations
Sun, Yu, Han and Liu (2006)	Trust modeling and evaluation based on axioms with laboratory simulation based evaluation
Xiong and Liu (2004)	Laboratory simulation evaluation on the proposed trust metric

apply the advances of all related researches and make computational trust derived from social trust finally benefit the users.

3. A METHODOLOGY OF USABLE TRUST MANAGEMENT

This section introduces a human-centric trust modeling and management method. We aim to design and develop a usable trust management solution that can be easily accepted by the users towards practical deployment. Our focus is to support user-device and user-system trust. For low level trust management (e.g., trustworthy network routing) without any concern and involvement of users (in the areas such as wireless sensor networks), this method may not applicable since it only treats the cases with the user as the trustor. Herein, the term "human-centric" means that user is the core concern during the design and development of the system. We apply user study in every step of our

research in order to make the trust management system easily accepted by its users. Particularly, a user-driven computational trust model achieved through applying this method will play as the core of the trust management system. This trust model is different from either the traditional trust models in e-commerce based on psychological and sociological studies (McKnight, Choudhury & Kacmar, 2002; Li, Valacich & Hess, 2004) or the general computational trust models derived from information and computer technologies (Yan & Holtmanns, 2008). It is achieved by formalizing an empirical trust construct in a mathematical way. The trust model achieved with this method reflects user perspective and integrates the advantages of both computational trust and social trust studies. Essential evaluation is performed for optimizing the computation trust model in order to achieve good effectiveness, such as accuracy, robustness, efficiency and so on. Additional user experimental studies are also conducted for the purpose of providing a trustworthy human-computer interaction design required in the trust management system. Furthermore, real user data can be collected after prototyping the system in order to conduct additional research on trust, e.g., exploring trust behavior patterns. Figure 1 presents the methodology that contains four steps.

Step 1 aims to figure out a trust construct for computational trust modeling and study the demand and concern of users with regard to trust in a specific usage context and for a specific purpose. Firstly, we propose a research model based on a number of hypotheses according to literature theories and existing research results. We then design a measurement scale to conduct user experiments on a suitable number of users. We further apply a psychometric method to analyze the experimental data in order to find out the

constructs and sub-constructs of trust, as well as user need with regard to the investigated use cases and scenarios. The above procedure could be repeated in order to achieve a stable trust construct. For example, the user experiments should be conducted a couple of times in order to extract principle factors of trust construct, optimize the measurement scale and study the causal relationships among those factors (Yan, Dong, Niemi & Yu, 2009; Yan, Dong, Niemi & Yu, 2013). This is the psychological and sociological study of trust model. The result is a clear construct of trust based on experimental data collected. This step aims to study trust based on 'static' user data collected from a limited number of users. It has such a shortcoming that the reliability and accuracy of the trust construct could be influenced by the

Figure 1. A procedure of human-centric trust modeling and management

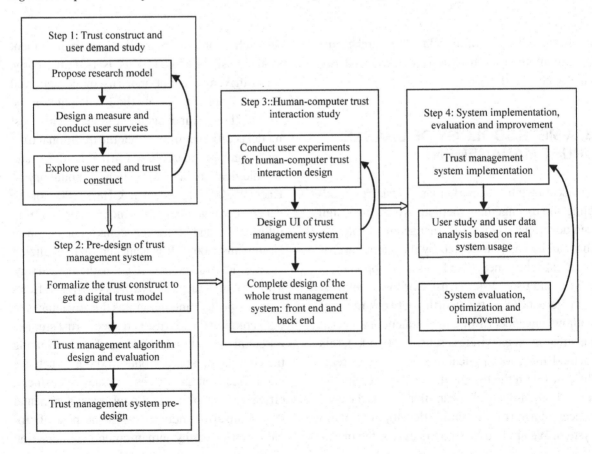

number of samples, the technical, regional and culture background of samples and other elements since it is not a complete-sample study. But conducting user experiments with a suitable number of participants that delegate various categories of users can overcome this weakness. Another weakness is the test is conducted in an assumed scenario, not a real usage context. This could influence the feedback and comments of experiment participants. Actually, the study in this step answers the question: what data or information should be collected in order to do trust/reputation evaluation. Thereby, it is an initial step to develop a usable trust management system.

Step 2 aims to work out a user driven trust model and the pre-design of trust management system. In the way towards digital management of trust, we should further work out a computational trust model on the basis of the trust construct achieved in the first step. One way is formalizing trust construct using a mathematic approach. The computational trust model should reflect the principle factors of trust construct and their causal relationships. Laboratory simulation based proof is essential in order to optimize the computational trust model since direct formalization of trust construct cannot ensure the model can overcome the weakness caused by a number of malicious behaviors or serious attacks. The computational trust model proposed based on the user study should be further improved and optimized according to the simulation results. We call what is achieved in this step as a user driven trust model. At this time, we can design all the algorithms used for trust management and pre-design the trust management system according to the achieved model.

In Step 3, we aim to research and design human-computer trust interaction strategy related to the trust management system. We conduct relevant user studies about the user interface design of the pre-designed trust management system. User feedback will be collected and analyzed. The user experiment could be mockup based and repeated several times in order to improve/optimize and pre-prove the user-device interaction design for trust management. After this, a complete trust management system design (i.e. both backend design and front end user interface design) can be achieved.

In Step 4, a prototype or a trial product is implemented. Real system usage experiences and feedback can be further collected from the users for system improvement. The improved system could be evaluated again for further optimization. By collecting real user data, additional investigation and exploration can be conducted to deeply study the trust patterns and trust behaviors using data mining techniques and statistical user data analysis. Real user data based study is more convinced than laboratory studies and the results can be applied for system improvement and new service/business development. Notably, this step studies trust based on 'dynamic' or 'real' user data that are automatically collected during usage without special user attention. It can overcome the weakness of Step 1. Thus, this study is valuable and essential since it provides a significant complement to the research in Step 1. All above four steps provide a comprehensive exploration method towards usable trust management.

It is important to note that some sub-steps listed above are iterative in order to achieve either a good model or a usable design. The purpose is to take user preference and expectation into the concern of system design and development as early as possible. Thereby, this method can effectively save the cost of the system development and greatly increase the trend of user acceptance.

4. APPLICABILITY STUDY: A TRUST BEHAVIOR BASED REPUTATION SYSTEM FOR MOBILE APPLICATIONS

In this section, we take the design of a mobile application reputation system as an example to illustrate how to apply the proposed method into practice. Mobile device has evolved into an open platform to execute various applications. Mobile applications are software packages that can be installed and executed in mobile devices, for example, a mobile email client to access emails in a mobile phone. Generally, mobile applications developed by various vendors can be downloaded for installation. The trustworthiness of a mobile application influences user purchase and usage and thus becomes a crucial issue that impacts its final success.

Trust is an internal 'state' of the user. A user's trust in a mobile application is highly subjective. It is hard to measure it directly. It is built up over time and changes with the use of the application due to the influence of many factors. The trustworthiness of mobile applications relates to their dependability, security, and usability (Avizienis, Laprie, Randell & Landwehr, 2004), as well as popularity (Yan, Dong, Niemi & Yu, 2013). Many reputation systems of applications evaluate application trust based on the number of download although it is not so accurate. Herein, we define a user's trust in a mobile application as his/her belief on the application that could fulfill a task as expectation. Reputation is public trust derived from direct and indirect knowledge or experiences. In our study, it is defined as the public belief on a mobile application that could fulfill a task according to many people's expectations. Obviously, trust plays an important role in application consumption and usage because it helps users overcome perceptions of uncertainty and risk and engages in trust behaviors to use mobile applications to fulfill important tasks.

Marsh reasoned that it might prove more suitable to model trust behavior rather than trust itself, removing the need to adhere to specific definitions (Marsh, 1994). Meanwhile, modeling trust behavior overcomes the challenges to measure a subjective concept by evaluating it through

objective trust behavior observation, which actually provides a concrete clue of trust. Regarding mobile application usage, we posit that credible information is gained only after a mobile user has both engaged in trust behaviors (e.g., acting on using a mobile application) and assessed the trustworthiness of the application by observing the consequences of its performance and depending on it in his/her routine life.

However, few existing trust models explore trust in the view of human trust behaviors (Yan & Holtmanns, 2008). Thus little work in the literature generates reputation and provides recommendations based on trust behaviors. In this section, we develop a trust-behavior-based reputation system for mobile applications following the methodology described in Section 3. We explore a model of trust behavior for mobile applications through a large scale user survey with more than 1500 participants. Its construct has been examined and proved with sound validity and reliability by principal components analysis, reliability analysis and confirmatory factor analysis (Yan, Dong, Niemi & Yu, 2009; Yan, Dong, Niemi & Yu, 2013). We further formalize this model in order to evaluate individual mobile user's trust in a mobile application through trust behavior observation (Yan & Yan, 2009). Thereafter, we design several algorithms to generate the reputation of an application by aggregating individual trust and provide application recommendations based on the correlation of trust behaviors (Yan, Zhang & Deng, 2012).

For human-computer trust interaction design, we further conducted a three stage user experiment to explore the question: Is it helpful for the users if trust information (i.e., trust and/or reputation values) is displayed in real time during the application usage or consumption? We aim to evaluate the impact of visualizing trust information on mobile application usage. We try to explore the following research questions:

- How important do people consider various mobile applications?
- How does individual trust information affect mobile application usage?
- How do the individual trust and public reputation affect mobile application usage?

The above mentioned system achieves auto-data collection for an individual user trust evaluation through trust behavior observation and provides application recommendations based on trust behavior correlation. It supports both user voting and non-voting. It has sound usability by releasing the need of human-computer interaction and at the same time providing a convinced explanation on trust, which can be easily accepted by users since the trust explanation follows the model achieved from a large scale user study. The reputation scheme of the system is robust against a number of malicious system attacks according to our simulation results (Yan, Zhang & Deng, 2012). It applies the device auto-generated individual trust as the credibility of user votes, thus overcomes the unfair rating attack. Meanwhile, the system adopts recommendation trust in reputation generation with the concern of recommendation quality and time decay in order to punish on-off attackers and conflict behavior attackers, as well as attackers on trust behaviors. The system also preserves user privacy since it does not require users to share and specify personal details, e.g., usage statistics and personal interests.

In what follows, we illustrate the design and development of the reputation system for mobile applications by applying the human-centric trust modeling and management method.

4.1. Trust Construct Analysis

In order to collect usage experiences of users in an easy and usable way for trust and reputation evaluation, we proposed a hypothesis: a user's trust in a mobile application can be reflected through his/her usage behaviors. Then, we designed a questionnaire with seven-point Likert measurement scale to conduct a user survey. We hypothesize several types of usage behaviors that reflect a user's trust: Using Behavior (UB) related to normal usage, Reflection Behavior (RB) about application performance reaction and Correlation Behavior (CB) with regard to the usage difference on applications with similar functions. All types of behaviors comprise the user's trust behaviors (i.e. a trustor's actions to depend on, or make her/him vulnerable to a trustee) related to a mobile application.

In order to achieve the trust behavior model, we design a questionnaire survey that asks for user opinion about trust behaviors regarding mobile application usage. Firstly, we conducted a pre-experiment with more than 300 participants and applied Exploratory Factor Analysis (i.e., Principal Component Analysis) in order to optimize the questionnaire (Yan, Niemi, Dong & Yu, 2008). Then, we ran a formal experiment with more than 1500 participants to figure out a rational trust behavior construct, a conceptual trust behavior model as shown in Figure 2. The construct of the model and the relations among all factors are analyzed and validated using Principal Component Analysis (PCA), Confirmatory Factor Analysis (CFA), correlation analysis and reliability analysis with positive psychometric properties and sound validity and reliability. The relationships of different components (i.e., the edge values in Figure 2) are set based on the correlation analysis with the values in the scope of [0, 1]. The model relates the trust behaviors to three types of usage behaviors: Using Behavior (UB), Reflection Behavior (RB) and Correlation Behavior (CB). These behaviors can be automatically monitored by a mobile device during application consumption. They also relate to a number of external factors: personal motivation, brand impact, perceived device quality and personality. They are further delineated into twelve measurable sub-constructs. Figure 3

Figure 2. Trust behavior construct of mobile applications (Yan, Zhang & Deng, 2012)

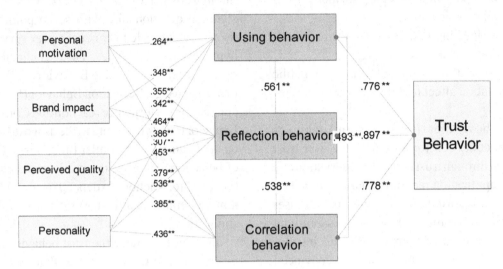

Figure 3. Internal relationships of (a) UB; (b) RB; and (c) CB (Yan, Zhang & Deng, 2012)

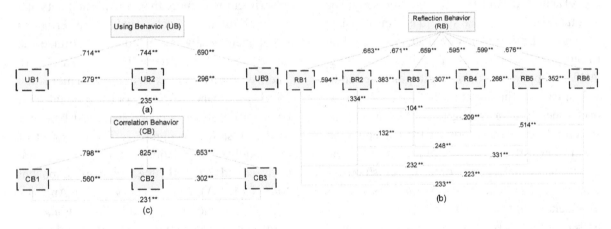

in Yan, Zhang & Deng, (2012) illustrates the sub-construct of the UB, RB and CB according to the PCA, CFA and correlation analysis.

Concretely, the first type of trust behavior - Using Behavior relates to normal application usage, which can be reflected mainly by elapsed usage time, number of usages and usage frequency. We found that trust is reflected by UB1, normal usage behavior. Meanwhile, usage context such as risk, importance and urgency could also influence the trust behavior (i.e., UB2: behaviors related to context). Generally, a mobile application provides a number of functionalities, i.e. features.

The more features experienced by the user, the more proficient he/she has in the application usage (i.e., UB3: feature related usage behavior). What is more, frequent usage can somehow indicate trust. This is also reflected from the user data collected in our survey (Yan, Dong, Niemi & Yu, 2009). Herein, we pay more attention to public trust, i.e., reputation, which aggregates many users' trust opinions on an application.

The second type of trust behavior is Reflection Behavior. It concerns the usage behaviors after the user confronts application problems/errors or has good/bad usage experiences. It contains six sub-constructs: RB1: bad performance reflection behavior; RB2: bad performance reflection behavior related to context; RB3: good performance reflection behavior; RB4: good performance reflection behavior related to context; RB5: bad experience reflection to context; RB6: good experience reflection to context. The difference of the reflection behavior and the using behavior lies in the fact that the first is a type of event-related behavior while the second is about general usage statistics. Their contributions to trust evaluation could be different. For example, one type of the reflection behavior is the usage behavior when the user confronts an application error, whether he/she would like to continue using the application or not in such a situation. The using behavior only reflects normal usage information, not indicates the change of usage.

Future mobile market could be very competitive. A number of similar functioned mobile applications developed by different vendors would be available at the same time for consumption. The third type of behavior is Correlation Behavior, which concerns the usage behaviors correlated to a number of similar functioned mobile applications. Since trust is obviously correlated to use (Muir, 1994; Muir, 1996; Lee & Moray, 1992), the usage could imply trust. Meanwhile, it is also influenced by various contexts (Marsh, 1994; Anderson & Narus, 1990). The Correlation Behavior has 3 sub-constructs: CB1: comparison of normal usage behavior; CB2: comparison related to context; CB3: recommendation behavior (i.e., a behavior to suggest other people using a mobile application).

We achieved the trust behavior construct (i.e., the trust behavior model) for mobile applications with sound reliability (UB: alpha=0.71; RB: alpha =0.85; CB: alpha=0.79; overall trust behavior: alpha=0.90). Reliability is reflected by alpha, a value between 0 and 1, with a larger value indicating better reliability. Generally, alpha above 0.7

implies sound reliability (Crocker & Algina, 1986). We found that UB, RB, and CB have significant correlation (as shown in Figure 2) with the trust behavior, which indicates that these three factors can represent it. We also found that these factors have lower correlations with each other than their correlations with the trust behavior. This indicates that these three factors can measure not only the general aspects but also the specific aspects of the trust behavior. Notably, their mutual correlations are around 0.5, which implies that these factors may influence or impact with each other. However, the assumed relationships cannot be well proved by internal nomological validity of our experiment and in literature theories. This means that these factors could be correspondingly in parallel, without any causal relationships. We also found the influence of a number of external variables (i.e. personal motivation, brand impact, perceived device quality and personality) on UB, RB, and CB; their correlations are shown in Figure 1. Note that ** indicates correlation is significant at the 0.01 level (2-tailed); * indicates correlation is significant at the 0.05 level (2-tailed). Herein, the level of correlation significance indicates the error probability of correlation. Thus, the lower the level, the more significant the correlation holds.

As can be seen from Figure 3, the correlation between each internal sub-factor (e.g. UB1, UB2, and UB3) and its corresponding principal factor (construct) (e.g., UB) is almost in the same level (except CB3's correlation with CB is a bit lower than CB1-CB's and CB2-CB's). This correlation is also higher than the correlations among the sub-factors. This indicates that the sub-factors belonging to a concrete principal factor can measure not only the general aspects but also the specific aspects of the represented type of trust behavior.

Those trust behaviors can be automatically monitored and thus recorded when the mobile user is using the application. Therefore, the mobile device can automatically collect useful information for trust/reputation evaluation in a natural and usable way, which at the same time plays a foundation for autonomic trust management.

4.2. Pre-Design of Trust Management System

A computational trust model can be further proposed based on the trust construct achieved from Step 1. It expresses the principle factors related to trust and their relationships in a mathematical method. This model was achieved by formalizing the trust behavior constructs (Yan & Yan, 2009; Yan, Zhang & Deng, 2012). Briefly, a general trust metric of mobile application i can be expressed as:

$$T(i) = T(i)_o + \alpha T(i)_{UB} + \beta T(i)_{RB} + \gamma T(i)_{CB} \tag{1}$$

where parameters α, β, γ denote the normalized weight factors for using behavior evaluation $T(i)_{UB}$, reflection behavior evaluation $T(i)_{RB}$, and correlation behavior evaluation $T(i)_{CB}$. $T(i)_o$ stands for an original trust value that may be influenced by some external variables, such as personality, brand, personal motivation and experienced device quality. $T(i)_o$ could also be a past trust value generated according to the past trust behaviors. Yan & Yan, (2009) provided the details for calculating $T(i)_{UB}$, $T(i)_{RB}$, and $T(i)_{CB}$.

We further proposed a number of algorithms to implement individual trust evaluation in a mobile device, and application reputation and recommendation generation (Yan, Zhang & Deng, 2012). Then we conducted a number of laboratory simulations to evaluate the accuracy, efficiency and robustness of the proposed algorithms in order to optimize and improve the computational model. Target is to evaluate the formalization with example usage models. For examining the robustness of the algorithms, we tested its performance against various malicious behaviors and attacks, such as on-off attack, bad mouthing/unfair rating attack, conflict behavior attack. This computational trust model can be used to calculate individual user trust in a mobile application. It can also be referred to achieve a reputation value of the mobile application based on a number of users' trust behaviors, as well as provide recommendations based on trust behavior correlation. On the basis of the above achieved model and the designed algorithms, a reputation system can be pre-designed.

A distributed client-server system structure was designed for implementing this reputation system, see Figure 4. Its client software 'Trust Manager' can be installed in a number of mobile devices (MD_k, k=1, ..., K). The Trust Manager contains a Trust Behavior Monitor that monitors trust behaviors and inputs statistical data about UB, RB and CB into a secure storage (Trust Data), which is located inside the device platform and has a secure channel to communicate with the behavior monitor and a Trust/Reputation Information Presenter. The statistical data can be accessed by a Data Interpreter for a) individual trust evaluation regarding a specific application by a Trust Evaluator; b) data dissemination to send local trust information and vote applications to a Reputation Service Provider (RSP) or other devices by a Trust Value Disseminator; c) reputation/recommendation extraction to get mobile applications reputation information and/or application recommendations from the RSP or other devices by a Reputation/Recommendation Extractor. Particularly, the Trust Evaluator can also generate application reputation and recommendation at the user device based on collected information from other mobile devices, e.g., through a mobile ad hoc network. The Data Interpreter is a secure mechanism to access usage statistical data from the Trust Data since these data are private information. We design the Data Interpreter based on the trusted computing technology (TCG, 2003).

Figure 4. Structure of a mobile application reputation system (Yan, Zhang & Deng, 2012)

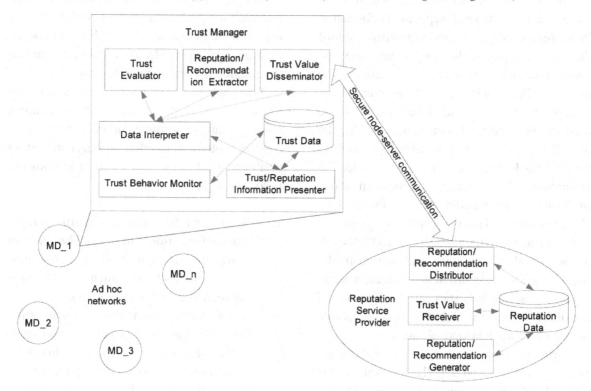

Only authorized data interpreter applications can access and unseal the protected usage information. The reputation/recommendation extraction can be tailored based on the mobile user's preference, either a reputation extraction policy or a recommendation extraction policy, or both. In addition, a Trust/Reputation Information Presenter is applied to show trust/reputation information to the user in order to aid his/her application usage (Yan, Liu, Niemi & Yu, 2010).

In the RSP, a Trust Value Receiver receives individual trust information and votes automatically or by request from the mobile devices. A Reputation/Recommendation Generator generates application reputations and recommendations for mobile users. Herein, the reputation could be generated based on the usage statistics of all users. But due to a privacy concern, we apply another approach to aggregate the individual trust values based on UB, RB, and CB (calculated in each mobile device). The reputation/recommendation

information about each mobile application is saved in a secure storage (Reputation Data) in the RSP. This information can be retrieved and distributed to the mobile devices through a Reputation/Recommendation Distributor, which receives reputation retrieve requests and provides application reputations and recommendations to the requestors.

Assuming a mobile application, a user receives a recommendation from the RSP that indicates its high public reputation and high personalized recommendation to install it since most people using it consume other applications in a similar way as he does regarding trust behaviors. Further initiated by some external factors (e.g., personal motivation, brand impact, perceived device quality and personality), the user installs the application and starts consuming it. The Trust Behavior Monitor monitors his trust behaviors regarding UB, RB and CB and inputs collected statistical data into the Trust Data. Based on these data, the Trust

Evaluator evaluates the user's individual trust in the application. The Trust/Reputation Information Presenter shows the user's individual trust value of the application, the application's reputation value and provides recommendation information to the user. Periodically or by request, the user sends local trust information (e.g., individual trust value, the trust values respectively contributed by UB, RB and CB) and/or the user's vote on the application) to the RSP. The RSP then re-generates the application reputation and re-provides the recommendations of the application based on newly collected data. If the re-calculated recommendation suggests the user not trusting in the application that he/she has already installed, the device could automatically inquire the user to uninstall it or initiate a warning at the application start-up. The user could configure his/her personal settings in the mobile device to handle this kind of situations.

Particularly, the user can recommend this application to his friend directly, for example via a mobile ad hoc network. In this case, the trust information is attached to the recommendation message. The device of his can generate the application reputations and recommendations at the Trust Evaluator based on the individual trust values of recommenders and their trust behavior correlations with regard to commonly consumed applications.

4.3. Human-Computer Trust Interaction Study

At this point, we were clear about what user-device interactions are needed in the underlying system pre-design. Clearly, data extraction for trust management can be conducted automatically with few user interactions (e.g., user confirmation to allow the device to share the individual trust information anonymously). What we need to study is why, how, what and when to show the trust/reputation information to the user and the corresponding design for trustworthy user-device interaction (e.g. how to make user feel convenient

to share his personal usage experiences and trust information). A practical strategy could be that the user is inquired to agree sharing his/her personal trust information in order to retrieve the reputation information of a mobile application.

For each required user-device interaction in the pre-designed system, we should conduct corresponding user studies in order to design an easily accepted user interface by fully considering user concern. In this case, we need to study the following issues:

1. Whether it is helpful to provide trust or reputation information to the users when they are using a mobile application. This study aims to solve the issue why such an interaction between user and device is needed;

2. How to display the trust/reputation information and what contents should be provided to the users and in which way. This study aims to solve the issues how to interact and what to be interacted;

3. At which moment the user-device interaction is required, (e.g., whether a user's confirmation is needed for sharing his usage history with others or a reputation service provider). This study aims to answer the question when interaction is required.

We developed an experiment toolkit and conducted a three-stage user study to investigate the above research questions in both China (CN) and Finland (FI) in 2008. We adopted 48 mobile applications and recorded their usage videos. The 48 mobile applications were selected from real products or prototypes, which provide a diverse sample of various mobile application scenarios and usage contexts. Examples include mobile enterprise solutions (e.g., corporate email checking); mobile personal business solutions (e.g., mobile payment, wallet, and safe box); mobile entertainment solutions (e.g., mobile TV, mobile video/audio/radio/music, gaming and camera); mobile life and social networking solutions (e.g., mobile search, location based services, maps, instant messaging and VoIP applications, travel aids, and mobile diary); mobile education solutions (e.g., e-book reader and multi-language translator); and integrated applications that provide an easy access to various mobile Internet services, e.g., Nokia WidSets; and Yahoo! Go.

In the first experiment we assessed the importance of mobile application scenarios. Using this result we selected a small set of 9 applications based on their importance rates (low, medium and high) and showed them in the later two experiments. In the second and the third experiments with different participants, the trust indicator (TI) or the trust/reputation indicator (TRI) shown in Figure 5 was displayed in one experiment block, while in the other block no information about trust was given. For each application usage scenario (showed as a video) we asked the participants to rate their willingness to continue consumption and check trust information. Thereby, the effects of three variables: the availability of trust information, trust information itself (either a trust value indicator or a trust/reputation values indicator), and the specific mobile application scenario (with different importance rates) were studied, respectively.

Meanwhile, the results achieved in both countries were also compared. Table 2 shows the design of Experiment 2(E2) and Experiment 3 (E3).

We conducted a mock up based user study to explore the item a) in both China and Finland with about 90 participants, respectively. The three stage user study results are described as below.

4.3.1. Result of Experiment 1: Mobile Application Importance

The importance rates (IR) of the 48 application scenarios varied between .224 and .777, with an average of .487 in Finland, and between .314 and .887, with an average of .553 in China, respectively. This showed that the applications adopted in the experiment covered the continuum of importance well.

We grouped and selected the applications based on the importance rate. As shown in Table 3, the results in Finland and China are different, implying that people's opinions on mobile applications' importance could be different in different regions. Surprisingly, one of the high important applications (i.e. mobile web browser) in Finland was treated unimportantly in China although its

Figure 5. Trust indicator and trust/reputation indicator (Yan & Niemi, 2009)

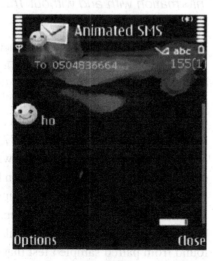

Trust Indicator

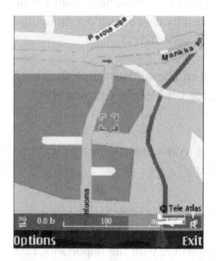

Trust/Reputation Indicator

Table 2. The design of experiment 2 and 3

	Experiment Variables	Block 1	Block 2
E2	Indicated trust value	Low, mid, high	Low, mid, high
	Indicator availability	No	Yes
	Application importance	Low, mid, high	Low, mid, high
	Region (test sites)	Finland & China	Finland & China
E3	Indicated (trust value) × (reputation value)	(low, mid, high) × (low, mid, high)	(low, mid, high) × (low, mid, high)
	Indicator availability	No	Yes
	Application importance	Low, mid, high	Low, mid, high
	Region (test sites)	Finland & China	Finland & China

Table 3. Experiment 2 ANOVA results on usage willingness

Factors	Effects in Finland (FI)	Effects in China (CN)
IR	$F(2,56)=30.447$, $p<0.005$	$F(2,50)=6.830$, $p=0.005$
TV	$F(2,56)=1035.187$, $p<0.001$	$F(2,50)=17.651$, $p<0.001$
IR × TV	$F(4,112)=0.183$, $p=0.941$	$F(4,100)=0.275$, $p=0.830$

usage experience rate is not low (73.9% in Finland and 49.2% in China). We further conducted paired samples t test to evaluate the validity of our grouping. The results showed that our groupings in both countries are valid.

4.3.2. Result of Experiment 2: Effects of Trust Indicator on Mobile Application Usage

4.3.2.1. Usage Willingness with and without Trust Indicator

An analysis of variance (ANOVA) was performed to test the effects of the trust indicator on the usage of mobile application, with the importance rate (high, medium, and low) and the trust indicator value (high, medium, and low) as within-subject factors, as reported in Table 3. We found significant main effects of the importance rate (IR) and the trust value (TV), indicating that the willingness of continuously using a mobile application increased from the importance rate low to high and from the trust value low to high. However, the interaction between IR and TV was not significant in both countries. This indicated that the effect of trust value did not differ over application scenarios with different importance rates.

4.3.2.2. Willingness of Checking Trust Information with and without Trust Indicator

We conducted a two-way (importance rate × trust value) repeated measure ANOVA to test the effects of the trust indicator on the user's willingness to check detailed information behind trust indication. We only found very significant effect of trust indicator [$F (2, 56) = 124.777$, $p < 0.000$] in Finland. This indicated that the willingness to check the detailed trust information behind trust indicator did not vary over the importance rate and the indicated trust value in China, but varied over the indicated trust value in Finland. We also found from paired sample t test that the trust indicator affects the check willingness according to its displayed values. But the effects are different in two countries. As shown in Table 4, the check willingness in both countries was lower with a high trust value indicator than that without TI. The check willingness is similar in Finland but lower in China with a medium trust value indicator to/than that without TI. The check willingness is higher in Finland but lower in China with a low trust value indicator than that without TI.

4.3.3. Result of Experiment 3: Effects of Trust/Reputation Indicator on Mobile Application Usage

4.3.3.1. Usage Willingness with and without Trust/Reputation Indicator

The usage willingness scale was subjected to an analysis of variance (ANOVA) with three within-subject factors: the importance rate (IR) (high, medium, and low), the indicated trust value (TV) (high, medium, and low), and the indicated reputation value (RV) (high, medium, and low), as reported in Table 5. We found significant main effects of IR, TV and RV, indicating that the willingness of continuous usage increased from the importance rate low to high, from the indicated trust value low to high, and from the indicated reputation value low to high in both countries. There was a significant interaction between IR and

Table 4. Paired-samples t test on trust information check willingness with and without a trust indicator

Pairs	Finland		China	
	t	*p*	*t*	*p*
NOTI - TV_L	-4.390	<.005	4.731	<.001
NOTI - TV_M	.862	.411	4.898	<.001
NOTI - TV_H	3.888	<.005	2.699	<.05

Table 5. Experiment 3 ANOVA results on usage willingness

Factors	Effects in Finland (FI)	Effects in China (CN)
IR	$F(2,48)=13.202$, $p<0.02$	$F(2,54)=4.629$, $p=0.05$
TV	$F(2,48)=707.86$, $p<0.000$	$F(2,54)=42.148$, $p<0.001$
RV	$F(2,48)=1009.887$, $p<0.000$	$F(2,54)=28.734$, $p<0.001$
IR × TV	$F(4,96)=0.951$, $p=0.483$	$F(4,108)=14.614$, $p<0.001$
IR × RV	$F(4,96)=1.513$, $p=0.286$	$F(4,108)=3.212$, $p=0.05$
TV × RV	$F(4,96)=8.317$, $p=0.006$	$F(4,108)=8.780$, $p=0.001$
IR × TV × RV	$F(8,192)=0.364$, $p=0.925$	$F(8,216)=2.388$, $p=0.05$

TV in China; but not significant in Finland. There was a significant interaction between IR and RV in China; but not significant in Finland. However, there was a significant interaction between TV and RV in both countries. The interaction effect among IR, TV and RV was significant in China; but not significant in Finland. This indicated that the effect of trust value and/or reputation value did not differ over application scenarios with different importance rates in Finland, but the situation is different in China. The effects of TV differ over RV significantly in both countries, and vice versa. The paired sample t test also indicated that the trust/reputation indicator has significant impact on the usage willingness according to its displayed values.

4.3.3.2. Willingness of Checking Trust Information with and without Trust/Reputation Indicator

We conducted a three-way (IR × TV × RV) repeated measure ANOVA to test the effect of the trust/reputation indicator on the user's willingness to check detailed trust information behind the indicator. We found a significant main effect of trust value (TV) [$F (2, 54) = 9.809$, $p < 0.01$ in China; $F (2, 48) = 13.840$, $p < 0.05$ in Finland]. The main effect of reputation value (RV) reached marginal significant level [$F (2, 54) = 3.293$, $p = 0.069$] in China and significant level [$F (2, 48) = 77.646$, $p < 0.005$] in Finland. No other main effects and interactions reached statistical significance in China. But in Finland, The main effect of IR reached marginal significant level [$F (2, 48) = 3.037$, $p = 0.158$]. In addition, there was a significant interaction between TV and RV [F

(4, 96) = 64.817$, $p < 0.000$] in Finland, implying that the effects of TV differ over RV significantly, and vice versa.

As shown in Table 6, the paired samples t test implied that the sharper difference between the trust value and the reputation value, the higher willingness is to check the detailed trust/reputation information in Finland. However, the check willingness is generally lower with the trust/reputation indicator than without any indicator in China. The results indicated that the trust/reputation indicator has positive impact on the check willingness according to its displayed values.

4.3.4. Result of Interview

For studying the items b) and c), we interviewed about 120 participants in both China and Finland to get their feedback about user interface design and trust/reputation indicator design. Based on the interview, the designed trust indicator and trust/reputation indicator are preferred and accepted by the participants, as shown in Figure 5. But some participants prefer that the indicator should be shown transparently at the usage beginning and then decaying gradually. We understood that it is applicable to provide a personalized trust information display solution in order to satisfy different users' preference. For the users who would like to keep their usage privacy, we could only show the trust indicator since the direct trust value can be calculated by their personal devices. Regarding the item c), most of participants think the usage information is private in both countries (73.3% in Finland and 90% in China), but most of them would like to share this information with privacy protection (70% in Finland and 60% in China). We found the necessity to apply suitable technologies to allow the users to control their usage information sharing with anonymous support. Regarding the detailed trust/reputation information (such as how the trust/reputation value is calculated and who certifies it), it is not conveniently to show it together with the indicator since it will ruin us-

Table 6. Paired-samples t test on trust information check willingness with and without a trust/reputation indicator

Pairs	Finland		China	
	t	*p*	*t*	*p*
CW_NOTRI - TRI_LL	4.061	.004	6.022	.000
CW_NOTRI - TRI_LM	4.275	.003	7.306	.000
CW_NOTRI - TRI_LH	-2.155	.063	3.166	.004
CW_NOTRI - TRI_ML	1.433	.190	4.966	.000
CW_NOTRI - TRI_MM	6.673	.000	6.086	.000
CW_NOTRI - TRI_MH	2.691	.027	3.371	.002
CW_NOTRI - TRI_HL	-2.113	.068	2.901	.007
CW_NOTRI - TRI_HM	3.536	.008	4.867	.000
CW_NOTRI - TRI_HH	7.314	.000	2.216	.035

ability and has negative effect on user experiences. People would like to check it when, for example, trust value and reputation value are quite different in Finland or the application scenario is very important in both Finland and China. In both countries, about half participants think menu is their preferred way to get the trust information details (50% in Finland and 60% in China). More participants like touching the indicator to access the detailed trust information in Finland (40%) than in China (3.3%). In both countries, some people prefer short-cut key access; the percentage is a bit higher in China (26.7%) than in Finland (10%). But this preference could be changed nowadays with the wide popularity of mobile phones with touch screens.

According to the above user study results, the system user interface design can be worked out to satisfy user preferences and considerations. Based on the guidelines summarized from our user studies, we then worked out a complete reputation system design for implementation.

4.4. System Implementation, Evaluation and Improvement

A prototype/product trial could now be implemented on the basis of the human-centric trust modeling and management system design. Based on the prototype or trial system, real system usage experiences and feedback can be collected from the users through survey, field study or focus group interview for further system improvement. We can also conduct user data analysis based on real system usage for more accurate trust behavior pattern extraction to further investigate trust behaviors with regard to mobile application usage and consumption. Based on newly achieved results, the system design, implementation and performance can be evaluated in a more accurate way. Thus it is possible for us to further optimize and improve the whole system.

5. DISCUSSIONS

We believe our method for usable trust management holds a number of advantages over existing methods. First, the human-centric trust model is proposed based on a wide user survey. Statistical data analysis and Structural Equation Modeling play as the foundation that could help us generate a trust model reflecting user concern, thus it could be easily accepted by the users (MacCallum & Austin, 2000). Therefore, the proposed method overcomes the weakness of current computational trust models that were built beyond any proof and acceptance of users.

Second, the computational trust model is proposed on the basis of trust constructs achieved from the user study. It is further improved and optimized based on laboratory experiments. This method compensates the problem of linguistic or graphic trust models generated purely from the user study and its difficulty to be directly applied into trust management for a digital system.

Third, sound usability can be easily achieved if applying our method. Based on the pre-design of the usable trust management system, we can study why, when, how and what should be interacted between the users and their devices. These user study results play as the design guidelines for developing a usable trust management system. In addition, the method itself can study the applicability of the design that aims to improve system usability and release the burden of user-computer interaction.

On the other hand, we also got a number of lessons from previous research and experiments. Firstly, we realized that it is important to seriously study the theories behind our hypothesis before conducting the trust construct study based on the user survey. However, the theoretical support was hard to find since the mobile application is a new area (unlike e-commerce on-line trust). Actually, trust behavior was rarely studied in the literature. The Exploratory Factor Analysis can indicate the problems of our questionnaire, but it is not enough to improve and optimize it (e.g., adding new items). An additional survey could be needed in order to achieve a more stable measure than the current one. Secondly, the human-centric trust model is formalized directly based on the trust construct. It could be incomprehensive and imprecise, unlike many existing computational trust models. How to overcome this weakness is a challenge if applying this methodology. Or we have to make some trade-off in the trust modeling in order to achieve both usability and efficiency. Finally, we found a special privacy concern during the user studies on human-computer interaction. We recognized that trust and privacy could conflict with each other. How to enhance privacy and at the same time achieve trust management is a practical challenge that motivates our future research.

In addition, we think real user data based user study is a valuable way to achieve deep understanding of users in order to provide real-time guidelines on usage decision. Meanwhile, it will provide a good evidence for further system improvement and optimization. The studies proposed in Step 4 in our method provide a future research direction.

6. CONCLUSION

In this chapter, we presented our motivations for developing a usable trust management solution. We briefly overviewed the existing research methods applied for establishing a trustworthy system. We found that it lacks a practical approach that could help us design and develop a usable trust management system. Furthermore, we proposed a method called human-centric trust modeling and management to overcome the weakness of the existing methods. We illustrated its applicability by applying it into the design and development of a reputation system for mobile applications. The methodology of usable trust management development contributes on two folds. Firstly, it motivated to drive trust modeling and management from the view of users towards practical system

deployment. Secondly, it proposed an applicable and inter-disciplinary method to design and develop a usable trust management system through integrating the advances of both social trust and computational trust studies.

At present, we are developing a reputation system for mobile application based on the achieved trust management system design driven by a series of user studies. Further proof and improvement of our method could be based on research experiences and the feedback collected from prototype users. Regarding the methodology proposed in this paper, we have attempted to apply it into the design and development of a reputation system for Nokia Instant Community (Yan & Chen, 2011; Chen, Yan & Niemi, 2011; Yan, Chen & Shen, 2013). We have achieved sound user feedback on the developed reputation system based on a user study with real prototype system usage.

REFERENCES

Abdul-Rahman, A., & Hailes, S. (2000). Supporting trust in virtual communities. In *Proceedings of the 33rd Hawaii International Conference on System Sciences*. IEEE.

Anderson, J. C., & Narus, J. A. (1990). A model of distributor firm and manufacturer firm working partnerships. *Marketing*, *54*(1), 42–58. doi:10.2307/1252172.

Avizienis, A., Laprie, J. C., Randell, B., & Landwehr, C. (2004). Basic concepts and taxonomy of dependable and secure computing. *IEEE Transactions on Dependable and Secure Computing*, *1*(1), 11–33. doi:10.1109/TDSC.2004.2.

Basso, A., Goldberg, D., Greenspan, S., & Weimer, D. (2001). Emotional and cognitive factors underlying judgments of trust e-commerce. In *Proceedings of the 3rd ACM Conference on Electronic Commerce EC '01*, (pp. 137-143). ACM.

Bhattacherjee, A. (2002). Individual trust in online firms: Scale development and initial test. *Journal of Management Information Systems, 19*(1), 211–241.

Buchegger, S., & Le Boudec, J. Y. (2004). A robust reputation system for P2P and mobile ad-hoc networks. In *Proceedings of the 2nd Workshop Economics of Peer-to-Peer Systems*. IEEE.

Chen, Y., Yan, Z., & Niemi, V. (2011). Implementation of a reputation system for pervasive social networking. [IEEE.]. *Proceedings of the IEEE TrustID, 2011*, 857–862.

Crocker, L., & Algina, J. (1986). *Introduction to classical and modern test theory*. Mason, OH: Thomson Leaning.

Dimoka, A. (2010). What does the brain tell us about trust and distrust? Evidence from a functional neuroimaging study. *Management Information Systems Quarterly, 34*(2), 373–396.

Gefen, D. (2000). E-commerce: The role of familiarity and trust. *Omega: Internet. J. Management Sci., 28*(6), 725–737.

Gefen, D., Benbasat, I., & Pavlou, P. (2008). A research agenda for trust in online environments. *Journal of Management Information Systems, 24*(4), 275–286. doi:10.2753/MIS0742-1222240411.

Grabner-Kräuter, S., & Kaluscha, E. A. (2003). Empirical research in on-line trust: A review and critical assessment. *International Journal of Human-Computer Studies, 58*(6), 783–812. doi:10.1016/S1071-5819(03)00043-0.

Grandison, T., & Sloman, M. (2000). A survey of trust in internet applications. *IEEE Communications and Survey, 3*(4), 2–16. doi:10.1109/COMST.2000.5340804.

Herlocker, J. L., Konstan, J. A., & Riedl, J. (2000). Explaining collaborative filtering recommendations. In *Proceedings of the 2000 ACM Conference on Computer Supported Cooperative Work CSCW '00*, (pp. 241-250). ACM.

Herrmann, P. (2001). Trust-based procurement support for software components. In *Proceedings of the 4th International Conference of Electronic Commerce Research* (ICECR04), (pp. 505-514). ICECR.

Kini, A., & Choobineh, J. (1998). Trust in electronic commerce: Definition and theoretical considerations. In *Proceedings of the 31st Hawaii International Conference on System Science*, (vol. 4, pp. 51-61). IEEE.

Lee, J., & Moray, N. (1992). Trust, control strategies and allocation of function in human-machine systems. *Ergonomics, 35*(10), 1243–1270. doi:10.1080/00140139208967392 PMID:1516577.

Li, X., Valacich, J. S., & Hess, T. J. (2004). Predicting user trust in information systems: A comparison of competing trust models. In *Proceedings of the 37th Annual Hawaii International Conference on System Sciences*. IEEE.

Lin, C., Varadharajan, V., Wang, Y., & Pruthi, V. (2004). Enhancing grid security with trust management. In *Proceedings of IEEE International Conf. on Services Computing*, (pp. 303-310). IEEE.

Lumsden, J., & MacKay, L. (2006). How does personality affect trust in B2C e-commerce? In *Proceedings of the 8th International Conference on Electronic Commerce: The New e-Commerce: Innovations for Conquering Current Barriers, Obstacles and Limitations to Conducting Successful Business on the Internet ICEC '06*, (pp. 471-481). ICEC.

MacCallum, R. C., & Austin, J. T. (2000). Applications of structural equation modeling in psychological research. *Annual Review of Psychology*, *51*, 201–226. doi:10.1146/annurev.psych.51.1.201 PMID:10751970.

Marsh, S. (1994). *Formalising trust as a computational concept*. (Doctoral dissertation). University of Stirling, Stirlingshire, UK.

McKnight, D. H., Choudhury, V., & Kacmar, C. (2002). Developing and validating trust measures for e-commerce: An integrative typology. *Information Systems Research*, *13*(3), 334–359. doi:10.1287/isre.13.3.334.81.

Muir, B. M. (1994). Trust in automation part I: Theoretical issues in the study of trust and human intervention in automated systems. *Ergonomics*, *37*(11), 1905–1922. doi:10.1080/00140139408964957.

Muir, B. M. (1996). Trust in automation part II: Experimental studies of trust and human intervention in a process control simulation. *Ergonomics*, *39*(3), 429–469. doi:10.1080/00140139608964474 PMID:8849495.

Pavlou, P., & Gefen, D. (2004). Building effective online marketplaces with institution-based trust. *Information Systems Research*, *15*(1), 37–59. doi:10.1287/isre.1040.0015.

Pennington, R., Wilcox, H. D., & Grover, V. (2004). The role of system trust in business-to-consumer transactions. *Journal of Management Information Systems*, *20*(3), 197–226.

Pu, P., & Chen, L. (2006). Trust building with explanation interfaces. In *Proceedings of the 11th International Conference on Intelligent User Interfaces IUI '06*, (pp. 93-100). IEEE.

Resnick, P., & Zeckhauser, R. (2002). Trust among strangers in internet transactions: Empirical analysis of eBay's reputation system. *Advances in Applied Microeconomics: The Economics of the Internet and E-Commerce*, *11*, 127–157. doi:10.1016/S0278-0984(02)11030-3.

Riedl, R., Hubert, M., & Kenning, P. (2010). Are there neural gender differences in online trust? An FMRi study on the perceived trustworthiness of eBay offer. *Management Information Systems Quarterly*, *34*(2), 397–428.

Sun, Y., Yu, W., Han, Z., & Liu, K. J. R. (2006). Information theoretic framework of trust modeling and evaluation for ad hoc networks. *IEEE Journal on Selected Areas in Communications*, *24*(2), 305–317. doi:10.1109/JSAC.2005.861389.

TCG. (2003). *TPM specification v1.2*. Retrieved from http://www.trustedcomputinggroup.org/resources/tpm_main_specification

Theodorakopoulos, G., & Baras, J. S. (2006). On trust models and trust evaluation metrics for ad hoc networks. *IEEE Journal on Selected Areas in Communications*, *24*(2), 318–328. doi:10.1109/JSAC.2005.861390.

Turel, O., Yuan, Y., & Connelly, C. (2008). In justice we trust: Predicting user acceptance of e-customer services. *Journal of Management Information Systems*, *24*(4), 123–151. doi:10.2753/MIS0742-1222240405.

Venkatesh, V., & Bala, H. (2008). Technology acceptance model 3 and a research agenda on interventions. *Decision Sciences*, *39*(2), 273–315. doi:10.1111/j.1540-5915.2008.00192.x.

Walsh, K., & Sirer, E. G. (2005). Fighting peer-to-peer SPAM and decoys with object reputation. In *Proceedings of the Third Workshop on the Economics of Peer-to-Peer Systems* (P2PECON), (pp. 138-143). P2PECON.

Xiong, L., & Liu, L. (2004). PeerTrust: Supporting reputation-based trust for peer-to-peer electronic communities. *IEEE Transactions on Knowledge and Data Engineering*, *16*(7), 843–857. doi:10.1109/TKDE.2004.1318566.

Z. Yan (Ed.). (2010). *Trust modeling and management in digital environments: From social concept to system development*. Hershey, PA: IGI Global. doi:10.4018/978-1-61520-682-7.

Yan, Z., & Chen, Y. (2011). AdChatRep: A reputation system for MANET chatting. In *Proceedings of SCI2011 in UbiComp2011*, (pp. 43-48). UbiComp.

Yan, Z., Chen, Y., & Shen, Y. (2013). A practical reputation system for pervasive social chatting. *Journal of Computer and System Sciences*, 79(5), 556–572. doi:10.1016/j.jcss.2012.11.003.

Yan, Z., Dong, Y., Niemi, V., & Yu, G. (2009). Exploring trust of mobile applications based on user eehaviors. In *Proceedings of InTrust 2009 (LNCS)* (Vol. 6163, pp. 212–226). Berlin: Springer.

Yan, Z., Dong, Y., Niemi, V., & Yu, G. (2013). Exploring trust of mobile applications based on user behaviors: An empirical study. *Journal of Applied Social Psychology*. doi:10.1111/j.1559-1816.2013.01044.x.

Yan, Z., & Holtmanns, S. (2008). Trust modeling and management: From social trust to digital trust. In R. Subramanian (Ed.), *Computer Security, Privacy and Politics: Current Issues, Challenges and Solutions*. Hershey, PA: IGI Global. doi:10.4018/978-1-59904-804-8.ch013.

Yan, Z., Liu, C., Niemi, V., & Yu, G. (2010). Effects of displaying trust information on mobile application usage. In *Proceedings of ATC'10* (LNCS), (vol. 6407, pp. 107-121). Berlin: Springer.

Yan, Z., Liu, C., Niemi, V., & Yu, G. (2010). *Trust information indication: Effects of displaying trust information on mobile application usage* (Technical Report NRC-TR-2009-004). Nokia Research Center. Retrieved from http://research.nokia.com/files/NRCTR2009004.pdf

Yan, Z., & Niemi, V. (2009). A methodology towards usable trust management. In *Proceedings of ATC2009* (LNCS), (vol. 5586, pp. 179-193). Berlin: Springer.

Yan, Z., Niemi, V., Dong, Y., & Yu, G. (2008). A user behavior based trust model for mobile applications. In *Proceedings of ATC'08* (LNCS), (vol. 5060, pp. 455-469). Berlin: Springer.

Yan, Z., & Prehofer, C. (2007). An adaptive trust control model for a trustworthy component software platform. In *Proceedings of ATC'07* (LNCS), (vol. 4610, pp. 226-238). Berlin: Springer.

Yan, Z., & Prehofer, C. (2011). Autonomic trust management for a component based software system. *IEEE Transactions on Dependable and Secure Computing*, 8(6), 810–823. doi:10.1109/TDSC.2010.47.

Yan, Z., & Yan, R. (2009). Formalizing trust based on usage behaviours for mobile applications. In *Proceedings of ATC09* (LNCS), (vol. 5586, pp. 194-208). Berlin: Springer.

Yan, Z., Zhang, P., & Deng, R. H. (2012). TruBeRepec: A trust-behavior-based reputation and recommender system for mobile applications. *Journal of Personal and Ubiquitous Computing*, 16(5), 485–506. doi:10.1007/s00779-011-0420-2.

Zahedi, F., & Song, J. (2008). Dynamics of trust revision: Using health infomediaries. *Journal of Management Information Systems*, 24(4), 225–248. doi:10.2753/MIS0742-1222240409.

Zhang, Z., Wang, X., & Wang, Y. (2005). A P2P global trust model based on recommendation. In *Proceedings of 2005 International Conf. on Machine Learning and Cybernetics*, (vol. 7, pp. 3975-3980). IEEE.

APPENDIX

Questions and Exercises

1. Please further illustrate how the proposed trust management system as described in Section 4 provides both autonomic and usable trust management.
2. Could you please propose a new application scenario to apply the proposed human-centric trust management method for usable and autonomic trust management?

Compilation of References

Abdul-Rahman, A., & Hailes, S. (2000). Supporting trust in virtual communities. In *Proceedings of the 33rd Hawaii International Conference on System Sciences*. IEEE.

Aberer, K., & Despotovic, Z. (2001). Managing trust in a peer-to-peer information system. In *Proceedings of the ACM Conference on Information and Knowledge Management* (CIKM), (pp. 310-317). ACM.

Adler, B. T., & Alfaro, L. (2007). A content driven reputation system for the Wikipedia. In *Proceedings of WWW*, (pp. 261-270). IEEE.

Ahn, J., & Amatriain, X. (2010). Towards fully distributed and privacy-preserving recommendations via expert collaborative filtering and RESTful linked data.[WI-IAT.]. *Proceedings of WI-IAT, 10*, 66–73.

Ahtiainen, A. et al. (2009). Awareness networking in wireless environments: Means of exchanging information. *IEEE Vehicular Technology Magazine, 4*(3), 48–54. doi:10.1109/MVT.2009.933475.

Ajzen, I. (1991). The theory of planned behavior. *Organizational Behavior and Human Decision Processes, 50*, 179–211. doi:10.1016/0749-5978(91)90020-T.

Allman, E., Callas, J., Delany, M., Libbey, M., Fenton, J., & Thomas, M. (2007). *DomainKeys identified mail (DKIM) signatures*. RFC 4871 (Proposed Standard). Retrieved from http://www.ietf.org/rfc/rfc4871.txt

Almutairi, A., Sarfraz, M., Basalamah, S., Aref, W., & Ghafoor, A. (2012). A distributed access control architecture for cloud computing. *IEEE Software, 29*(2), 36–44. doi:10.1109/MS.2011.153.

Amazon Web Services (AWS). (n.d.). Retrieved from http://aws.amazon.com

Anderson, J. C., & Narus, J. A. (1990). A model of distributor firm and manufacturer firm working partnerships. *Marketing, 54*(1), 42–58. doi:10.2307/1252172.

Angin, P., et al. (2010). An entity-centric approach for privacy and identity management in cloud computing. In *Proceedings of 29th IEEE Symposium on Reliable Distributed Systems*, (pp. 177-183). IEEE.

Antifakos, S., Kern, N., Schiele, B., & Schwaninger, A. (2005). Towards improving trust in context-aware systems by displaying system confidence. In *Proceedings of the 7th International Conference on Human Computer Interaction with Mobile Devices & Services*. ACM Press.

Araujo, I., & Araujo, I. (2003). Developing trust in internet commerce. In *Proceedings of the 2003 Conference of the Centre for Advanced Studies on Collaborative Research*, (pp. 1-15). IEEE.

Armbrust, M., et al. (2009). *Above the clouds: A Berkeley view of cloud computing* (Tech. Rep. USB-EECS-2009-28). Berkeley, CA: University of California.

Armbrust, M. (2009). *Above the clouds: A Berkeley view of cloud*. Berkeley, CA: University of California.

Artz, D., & Gil, Y. (2007). A survey of trust in computer science and the semantic web. *Web Semantics: Science, Services, and Agents on the World Wide Web, 5*(2), 58–71. doi:10.1016/j.websem.2007.03.002.

Asokan, N., & Ekberg, J. (2008). A platform for OnBoard credentials. In *Financial Cryptography and Data Security (LNCS)* (Vol. 5143, pp. 318–320). Berlin: Springer. doi:10.1007/978-3-540-85230-8_31.

Ateniese, G., Fu, K., Green, M., & Hohenberger, S. (2005). Improved proxy re-encryption schemes with applications to secure distributed storage. In *Proceedings of the 12th Annual Network and Distributed System Security Symposium*, (pp. 29–43). IEEE.

Avizienis, A., Laprie, J. C., Randell, B., & Landwehr, C. (2004). Basic concepts and taxonomy of dependable and secure computing. *IEEE Transactions on Dependable and Secure Computing*, 1(1), 11–33. doi:10.1109/TDSC.2004.2.

Awad, N., & Ragowsky, A. (2008). Establishing trust in electronic commerce through online word of mouth: An examination across genders. *Journal of Management Information Systems*, 24(4), 101–121. doi:10.2753/MIS0742-1222240404.

Baba, M. L., Falkenburg, D. R., & Hill, D. H. (1996). Technology management and American culture: Implications for business process redesign. *Research Technology Management*, 39(6), 44–54.

Balakrishnan, V., & Varadharajan, V. (2005). Designing secure wireless mobile ad hoc networks. In *Proceedings of the 19th International Conference on Advanced Information Networking and Applications* (AINA 2005), (vol. 2, pp. 5–8). AINA.

Banerjee, S., Mattmann, C. A., Medvidovic, N., & Golubchik, L. (2005). Leveraging architectural models to inject trust into software systems. In *Proceedings of the 2005 Workshop on Software Engineering for Secure Systems—Building Trustworthy Applications*, (vol. 30, pp. 1-7). IEEE.

Bansal, S., & Baker, M. (2003). *Observation-based cooperation enforcement in ad hoc networks*. Palo Alto, CA: Stanford University.

Barber, B. (1983). *The logic and limits of trust*. New Brunswick, NJ: Rutgers University Press.

Basso, A., Goldberg, D., Greenspan, S., & Weimer, D. (2001). Emotional and cognitive factors underlying judgments of trust e-commerce. In *Proceedings 3rd ACM Conference on Electronic Commerce*. ACM Press.

Becchetti, L., Castillo, C., Donatol, D., Leonardi, S., & Baeza-Yates, R. (2006). Using rank propagation and probabilistic counting for link-based spam detection. In Proceedings of WebKDD. WebKDD.

Berger, S. et al. (2009). Security for the cloud infrastructure: Trusted virtual data center implementation. *IBM Journal of Research and Development*, 53(4), 560–571. doi:10.1147/JRD.2009.5429060.

Bethencourt, J., Sahai, A., & Waters, B. (2007). Ciphertext-policy attribute based encryption. In *Proceedings of the 2007 IEEE Symposium on Security and Privacy*, (pp. 321–334). IEEE.

Bhattacherjee, A. (2002). Individual trust in online firms: Scale development and initial test. *Journal of Management Information Systems*, 19(1), 211–241.

Bhatti, R., Bertino, E., & Ghafoor, A. (2006). X-federate: A policy engineering framework for federated access management. *IEEE Transactions on Software Engineering*, 32(5), 330–346. doi:10.1109/TSE.2006.49.

Bickmore, T., & Cassell, J. (2001). Relational agents: A model and implementation of building user trust. In *Proceedings of the SIGCHI Conference on Human Factors in Computing Systems*, (pp. 396-403). ACM.

Bigley, G. A., & Pearce, J. L. (1998). Straining for shared meaning in organization science: Problems of trust and distrust. *The Academy of Management Executive*, 23, 405–421.

Bi, J., Wu, J., & Zhang, W. (2008). A trust and reputation based anti-SPIM method. In *Proceedings of IEEE INFOCOM* (pp. 2485–2493). IEEE. doi:10.1109/INFOCOM.2008.319.

Bilge, A., & Polat, H. (2010). Improving privacy-preserving NBC-based recommendations by preprocessing. [WI-IAT.]. *Proceedings of WI-IAT, 2010*, 143–147.

Blaze, M., Bleumer, G., & Strauss, M. (1998). Divertible protocols and atomic proxy cryptography. In *Proceedings of International Conference on the Theory and Application of Cryptographic Techniques* (EUROCRYPT), (pp. 127–144). EUROCRYPT.

Blaze, M., Feigenbaum, J., & Lacy, J. (1996). Decentralized trust management. In *Proceedings of IEEE Symposium on Security and Privacy*, (pp. 164-173). IEEE.

Blaze, M., Ioannidis, J., & Keromytis, A. D. (2002). Trust management for IPSEC. *ACM Transactions on Information and System Security*, 5(2), 95–118. doi:10.1145/505586.505587.

Boneh, D., Crescenzo, G. D., Ostrovsky, R., & Persiano, G. (2004). Public key encryption with keyword search. In *Proceedings of Int'l Conf. Advances in Cryptology* (EUROCRYPT '04). EUROCRYPT.

Boon, S., & Holmes, J. (1991). The dynamics of interpersonal trust: Resolving uncertainty in the face of risk. In R. Hinde, & J. Groebel (Eds.), *Cooperation and Prosocial Behavior*. Cambridge, UK: Cambridge University Press.

Bossardt, M., Dubendorfer, T., & Plattner, B. (2007). Enhanced Internet security by a distributed traffic control service based on traffic ownership. *Journal of Network and Computer Applications*, 30(3), 841–857. doi:10.1016/j.jnca.2005.07.006.

Brickell, E. F., Camenisch, J., & Chen, L. (2004). Direct anonymous attestation. In *Proceedings of the ACM Conference on Computer and Communications Security*, (pp. 132-145). ACM.

Briggs, P., Burford, B., De Angeli, A., & Lynch, P. (2002). Trust in online advice. *Social Science Computer Review*, 20(3), 321–332.

Buchegger, S., & Boudec, J. L. (2002). Performance analysis of the confidant protocol. In *Proceedings of the ACM International Symposium on Mobile Ad Hoc Networking and Computing (MobiHoc)*, (pp. 226-236). ACM.

Buchegger, S., & Le Boudec, J. Y. (2004). A robust reputation system for P2P and mobile ad-hoc networks. In *Proceedings of the 2nd Workshop Economics of Peer-to-Peer Systems*. IEEE.

Buchegger, S., & Boudec, J. Y. L. (2003). The effect of rumor spreading in reputation systems for mobile ad-hoc networks. In *Proceedings of WiOpt Modeling and Optimization in Mobile, Ad Hoc and Wireless Networks*. IEEE.

Cahill, V. et al. (2003). Using trust for secure collaboration in uncertain environments. *IEEE Pervasive Computing / IEEE Computer Society [and] IEEE Communications Society*, 2(3), 52–61. doi:10.1109/MPRV.2003.1228527.

Cai, H., Li, Z., & Tian, J. (2011). A new trust evaluation model based on cloud theory in e-commerce environment. In *Proceedings of the 2nd International Symposium on Intelligence Information Processing and Trusted Computing (IPTC)*, (pp. 139-142). IPTC.

Calero, J. M. A., Edwards, N., Kirschnick, J., Wilcock, L., & Wray, M. (2010). Toward a multi-tenancy authorization system for cloud services. *IEEE Security and Privacy*, 8(6), 48–55. doi:10.1109/MSP.2010.194.

Campadello, S., Coutand, O., Del Rosso, C., Holtmanns, S., Kanter, T., & Räck, C. … Steglich, S. (2005). Trust and privacy in context-aware support for communication in mobile groups. In Proceedings of Context Awareness for Proactive Systems (CAPS), (pp. 115-125). CAPS.

Cao, N., Wang, C., Ren, K., & Lou, W. (2012). Privacy-preserving multi-keyword ranked search over encrypted cloud data.[IEEE.]. *Proceedings of INFOCOM, 2011*, 829–837.

Castelfranchi, C., Falcone, R., & Pezzulo, G. (2003). Integrating trustfulness and decision using fuzzy cognitive maps. In *Proceedings of the First International Conference of Trust Management* (iTrust 2003) (LNCS), (vol. 2692, pp. 195-210). Berlin: Springer.

Chang, Y. C., & Mitzenmacher, M. (2005). Privacy preserving keyword searches on remote encrypted data. In *Proceedings of Int'l Conf. Applied Cryptography and Network Security (ACNS '05)*, (pp. 442-455). ACNS.

Chen, Y. (2010). *A privacy-enhanced reputation system for mobile ad hoc services*. (Master Thesis). Aalto University, Espoo, Finland.

Chen, Y., & Yan, Z. (2012). Gemini: A handbag for pervasive social communications. In *Proceedings of IEEE TrustID 2012*. IEEE.

Chen, Y., Yan, Z., & Niemi, V. (2011). Implementation of a reputation system for pervasive social networking. [IEEE.]. *Proceedings of IEEE TrustID, 2011*, 857–862.

Cheung, K. H., & Misic, J. (2002). On virtual private network security design issues. *Computer Networks, 38*(2), 165–179. doi:10.1016/S1389-1286(01)00256-0.

Chin, S. H. (2009). On application of game theory for understanding trust in networks. In *Proceedings of the International Symposium on Collaborative Technologies and Systems* (CTS '09), (pp. 106-110). CTS.

Chuong, C., Torabi, T., & Loke, S. W. (2009). Towards context-aware task recommendation.[JCPC.]. *Proceedings of JCPC, 09*, 289–292.

Corritore, C. L., Kracher, B., & Wiedenbeck, S. (2003). On-line trust: Concepts, evolving themes, a model. *International Journal of Human-Computer Studies. Trust and Technology, 58*(6), 737–758.

Cramer, H., Evers, V., Ramlal, S., Someren, M., Rutledge, L., & Stash, N. et al. (2008). The effects of transparency on trust in and acceptance of a content-based art recommender. *User Modeling and User-Adapted Interaction, 18*(5), 455–496. doi:10.1007/s11257-008-9051-3.

Creed, W. E. D., & Miles, R. E. (1996). Trust in organizations: A conceptual framework linking organizational forms, managerial philosophies, and the opportunity costs of controls. In *Trust in Organizations: Frontiers of Theory and Research*. London: Sage Publications. doi:10.4135/9781452243610.n2.

Crocker, L., & Algina, J. (1986). *Introduction to classical and modern test theory*. Mason, OH: Thomson Leaning.

Culnan, M. (1999). *Georgetown internet privacy policy study: Privacy online in 1999: A report to the federal trade commission*. Washington, DC: Georgetown University.

Curtmola, R., Garay, J. A., Kamara, S., & Ostrovsky, R. (2006). Searchable symmetric encryption: Improved definitions and efficient constructions. In *Proceedings of ACM Conf. Computer and Comm. Security* (CCS'06), (pp. 79-88). ACM.

CyberAtlas. (2002). *Privacy worries plague Ebiz*. Retrieved July 5, 2002 from http://cyberatlas.internet.com/markets/retailing/article/06061_1183061,00.html

Davis, F. D. (1989). Perceived usefulness, perceived ease of use, and user acceptance of information technology. *Management Information Systems Quarterly, 13*(3), 319–339. doi:10.2307/249008.

Davis, F. D., Bagozzi, R. P., & Warshaw, P. R. (1989). User acceptance of computer technology: A comparison of two theoretical models. *Management Science, 35*, 982–1002. doi:10.1287/mnsc.35.8.982.

Davis, F. D., Bagozzi, R. P., & Warshaw, P. R. (1992). Extrinsic and intrinsic motivation to use computers in the workplace. *Journal of Applied Social Psychology, 22*(14), 1111–1132. doi:10.1111/j.1559-1816.1992.tb00945.x.

Dempster, A. P. (1968). A generalization of Bayesian inference. *Journal of the Royal Statistical Society. Series A (General), 30*, 205–247.

Denning, D. E. (1993). A new paradigm for trusted systems. In *Proceedings of the IEEE New Paradigms Workshop*, (pp. 36-41). IEEE.

Deutsch, M. (1960). Trust, trustworthiness, and the f scale. *Journal of Abnormal and Social Psychology, 61*(1), 138–140. doi:10.1037/h0046501 PMID:13816271.

Deutsch, M. (1962). Cooperation and trust: Some theoretical notes. *Nebraska Symposium on Motivation. Nebraska Symposium on Motivation, 10*, 275–318.

Deutsch, M. (1973). *The resolution of conflict: Constructive and destructive processes*. New Haven, CT: Yale University Press. doi:10.1177/000276427301700206.

Dey, A. K. (2001). Understanding and using context. *Journal of Personal and Ubiquitous Computing, 5*, 4–7. doi:10.1007/s007790170019.

Dillon, T., Wu, C., & Chang, E. (2010). Cloud computing: Issues and challenges. In *Proceedings of 24th IEEE International Conference on Advanced Information Networking and Applications*, (pp. 27-33). IEEE.

Dimoka, A. (2010). What does the brain tell us about trust and distrust? Evidence from a functional neuroimaging study. *Management Information Systems Quarterly, 34*(2), 373–396.

Douceur, J. R. (2002). The sybil attack.[LNCS]. *Proceedings of IPTPS, 2429*, 251–260.

Dubois, D., & Prade, H. (1980). New results about properties and semantics of fuzzy set theoretic operators. In *Fuzzy Sets Theory and Applications to Policy Analysis and Information System*. New York: Plenum Press. doi:10.1007/978-1-4684-3848-2_6.

Dunn, J. R., & Schweitzer, M. E. (2005). Feeling and believing: the influence of emotion on trust. *Journal of Personality and Social Psychology*, 88(5), 736–748. doi:10.1037/0022-3514.88.5.736 PMID:15898872.

Ekberg, J.-E., Asokan, N., Kostiainen, K., & Rantala, A. (2008). Scheduling execution of credentials in constrained secure environments. In *Proceedings of the 3rd ACM Workshop on Scalable Trusted Computing*, (pp. 61-70). ACM.

England, P., Lampson, B., Manferdelli, J., Peinado, M., & Willman, B. (2003). A trusted open platform. *IEEE Computer*, 36(7), 55–62. doi:10.1109/MC.2003.1212691.

Felten, E. W. (2003). Understanding trusted computing – Will it benefits outweigh its drawbacks. *IEEE Security and Privacy*, 1(3), 60–62. doi:10.1109/MSECP.2003.1203224.

Fenkam, P., Dustdar, S., Kirda, E., Reif, G., & Gall, H. (2002). Towards an access control system for mobile peer-to-peer collaborative environments. In *Proceedings of Eleventh IEEE International Workshops on Enabling Technologies: Infrastructure for Collaborative Enterprises*, (pp. 95-100). IEEE.

Firdhous, M., Ghazali, O., & Hassan, S. (2011). Trust management in cloud computing: A critical review. *International Journal on Advances in ICT for Emerging Regions*, 4(2), 24–36.

Fishbein, M., & Ajzen, I. (1975). *Beliefs, attitude, intention and behavior: An introduction to theory and research*. Reading, MA: Addison-Wesley.

Fogg, B. J., & Tseng, H. (1999). The elements of computer credibility. In *Proceedings of the CHI '99*. ACM Press.

Fogg, B. J., Marshall, J., Kameda, T., Solomon, J., Rangnekar, A., Boyd, J., & Brown, B. (2001). Web credibility research: A method for online experiments and early study results. In *Proceedings of the Conference on Human Factors in Computing Systems CHI 2001*. ACM Press.

Fogg, B.J., Marshall, J., Laraki, O., Osipovich, A., Varma, C., Fang, N., et al. (2001). What makes web sites credible? A report on a large quantitative study. In *Proceedings of the Conference on Human Factors in Computing Systems CHI 2001*. ACM Press.

Fogg, B.J., Kameda, T., Boyd, J., Marchall, J., Sethi, R., Sockol, M., & Trowbridge, T. (2002). *Stanford-Makovsky web credibility study: Investigating what makes web sites credible today*. A Research Report by the Stanford Persuasive Technology Lab.

Fogg, B. J. (2002). *Persuasive technology: Using computers to change what we think and do*. San Francisco, CA: Morgan Kaufman. doi:10.1145/764008.763957.

Fox, A. (1974). *Beyond contract: Work, power, and trust relations*. London: Faber.

Gambetta, D. (2000). Can we trust trust? In *Trust: Making and Breaking Cooperative Relations*. Oxford, UK: University of Oxford.

Ganeriwal, S., & Srivastava, M. B. (2004). Reputation-based framework for high integrity sensor networks. In *Proceedings of the ACM Security for Ad-Hoc and Sensor Networks*, (pp. 66–67). ACM.

Gefen, D. (2000). E-commerce: The role of familiarity and trust. *Omega: Internet. J. Management Sci.*, 28(6), 725–737.

Gefen, D., Benbasat, I., & Pavlou, P. (2008). A research agenda for trust in online environments. *Journal of Management Information Systems*, 24(4), 275–286. doi:10.2753/MIS0742-1222240411.

Gefen, D., Karahanna, E., & Straub, D. (2003). Trust and TAM in online shopping: An integrated model. *Management Information Systems Quarterly*, 27(1), 51–90.

Gil, Y., & Ratnakar, V. (2002). Trusting information sources one citizen at a time. In *Proceedings of the 1st International Semantic Web Conference*. IEEE.

Goh, E. J. (2003). *Secure indexes*. Retrieved from http://eprint.iacr.org/

Goh, E., Shacham, H., Modadugu, N., & Boneh, D. (2003). Sirius: Securing remote untrusted storage. In *Proceedings of Network and Distributed Systems Security Symposium (NDSS)*, (pp. 131–145). NDSS.

Gollmann, D. (2007). *Why trust is bad for security*. Retrieved May 2007, from http://www.sics.se/policy2005/Policy_Pres1/dg-policy-trust.ppt

Google Apps. (n.d.a). Retrieved from http://www.google.com/enterprise/apps/business/

Google Apps. (n.d.b). *Engine*. Retrieved from http://code.google.com/appengine/

Google. (n.d.). *Computer engine*. Retrieved from https://cloud.google.com/products/compute-engine

Goyal, V., Pandey, O., Sahai, A., & Waters, B. (2006). Attribute-based encryption for fine-grained access control of encrypted data. In *Proceedings of the 13th ACM Conference on Computer and Communications Security*, (pp. 89–98). ACM.

Grabner-Kräuter, S., & Kaluscha, E. A. (2003). Empirical research in on-line trust: A review and critical assessment. *International Journal of Human-Computer Studies, 58*(6), 783–812. doi:10.1016/S1071-5819(03)00043-0.

Grandison, T., & Sloman, M. (2000). A survey of trust in internet applications. *IEEE Communications and Survey, 3*(4), 2–16. doi:10.1109/COMST.2000.5340804.

Granovetter, M. S. (1985). Economic action and social-structure. *American Journal of Sociology, 91*, 481–510. doi:10.1086/228311.

Green, M., & Ateniese, G. (2007). Identity-based proxy re-encryption. In *Proceedings of the International Conference on Applied Cryptography and Network Security* (ACNS), (pp. 288–306). ACNS.

Guha, R., & Kumar, R. (2004). Propagation of trust and distrust. In *Proceedings of the 13th International Conference on World Wide Web*, (pp. 403-412). IEEE.

Guha, R., Kumar, R., Raghavan, P., & Tomkins, A. (2004). Propagation of trust and distrust. In *Proceedings of the 13th Int. Conf. on WWW*, (pp. 403-412). IEEE.

Guo, Z., Yan, Z., & Wang, F. (2010). A methodology to predicate human-being's movement based on movement group. In *Proceedings of ACM/IEEE CPSCom*, (pp. 612-619). ACM/IEEE.

Gupta, M., Judge, P., & Ammar, M. (2003). A reputation system for peer-to-peer networks. In *Proceedings of the 13th international workshop on Network and Operating Systems Support for Digital Audio and Video (NOSSDAV '03)*. ACM.

Gyongyi, Z., Garcia-Molina, H., & Pedersen, J. (2004). Combating web spam with TrustRank. In *Proceedings of VLDB*, (pp. 576-587). VLDB.

Hall, R. S., Heimbigner, D., Van Der Hoek, A., & Wolf, A. L. (1997). An architecture for post-development configuration management in a wide-area network. In *Proceedings of the 17th Int'l Conf. Distributed Computing Systems*, (pp. 269-278). IEEE.

Hamed, H., Al-Shaer, E., & Marrero, W. (2005). Modeling and verification of IPSec and VPN security policies. In *Proceedings of 13th IEEE International Conference on Network Protocols*, (pp. 259 – 278). IEEE.

Hancock, J. T., Toma, C., & Ellison, N. (2007). The truth about lying in online dating profiles. In *Proceedings of the ACM CHI*, (pp. 449–452). ACM.

Haskins, R., & Nielsen, D. (2004). *Slamming spam: A guide for system administrators*. Reading, MA: Addison-Wesley Professional.

He, R., Niu, J., Yuan, M., & Hu, J. (2004). A novel cloud-based trust model for pervasive computing. In *Proceedings of The Fourth International Conference on Computer and Information Technology*, (pp. 693-700). IEEE.

Herlocker, J. L., Konstan, J. A., & Riedl, J. (2000). Explaining collaborative filtering recommendations. In *Proceedings of the 2000 ACM Conference on Computer Supported Cooperative Work CSCW '00*, (pp. 241-250). ACM.

Herrmann, P. (2001). Trust-based procurement support for software components. In *Proceedings of the 4th International Conference of Electronic Commerce Research* (ICECR04), (pp. 505-514). ICECR.

Herrmann, P. (2003). Trust-based protection of software component users and designers. In *Proceedings of the First Int'l Conf. Trust Management*, (pp. 75-90). IEEE.

Herscovitz, E. (1999). Secure virtual private networks: The future of data communications. *International Journal of Network Management, 9*(4), 213–220. doi:10.1002/(SICI)1099-1190(199907/08)9:4<213::AID-NEM328>3.0.CO;2-E.

Hu, J., & Burmester, M. (2006). LARS: A locally aware reputation system for mobile ad hoc networks. In *Proceedings of the 44th ACM Annual Southeast Regional Conference*, (pp. 119-123). ACM.

Huang, D., Zhang, X., Kang, M., & Luo, J. (2010). MobiCloud: Building secure cloud framework for mobile computing and communication. In *Proceedings of the Fifth IEEE International Symposium on Service Oriented System Engineering* (SOSE), (pp. 27-34). IEEE.

Huang, D., Zhou, Z., Xu, L., Xing, T., & Zhong, Y. (2011). Secure data processing framework for mobile cloud computing. In *Proceedings of 2011 IEEE Conference on Computer Communications Workshops* (INFOCOM WKSHPS), (pp. 614–618). IEEE.

Huang, A. B. (2002). The trusted OC: Skin-deep security. *Computer, 35*(10), 103–105. doi:10.1109/MC.2002.1039525.

Hwang, K., & Li, D. (2010). Trusted cloud computing with secure resources and data coloring. *IEEE Internet Computing, 14*(5), 14–22. doi:10.1109/MIC.2010.86.

Hyytia, E., Virtamo, J., Lassila, P., Kangasharju, J., & Ott, J. (2011). When does content float? Characterizing availability of anchored information in opportunistic content sharing.[IEEE.]. *Proceedings - IEEE INFOCOM, 2011*, 3137–3145. doi:10.1109/INFCOM.2011.5935160.

Jensen, C., Potts, C., & Jensen, C. (2005). Privacy practices of Internet users: Self-reports versus observed behavior. *International Journal of Human-Computer Studies, 63*(1-2), 203–227. doi:10.1016/j.ijhcs.2005.04.019.

Jia, W., Zhu, H., Cao, Z., Wei, L., & Lin, X. (2011). SDSM: A secure data service mechanism in mobile cloud computing. In *Proceedings of 2011 IEEE Conference on Computer Communications Workshops* (INFOCOM WKSHPS), (pp. 1060–1065). IEEE.

Joinson, A. N., Reips, U., Buchanan, T., & Schofield, C. B. P. (2010). Privacy, trust, and self-disclosure online. *Human-Computer Interaction, 25*(1), 1–24. doi:10.1080/07370020903586662.

Jøsang, A. (1999). An algebra for assessing trust in certification chains. In *Proceedings of the Networking Distributed System Security Symposium*. IEEE.

Jøsang, A., & Ismail, R. (2002). The beta reputation system. In *Proceedings of the 15th Bled Electronic Commerce Conference*. Bled.

Jøsang, A. (2001). A logic for uncertain probabilities. *International Journal of Uncertainty. Fuzziness and Knowledge-Based Systems, 9*(3), 279–311.

Jøsang, A., Ismail, R., & Boyd, C. (2005). A survey of trust and reputation systems for online service provision. *Decision Support Systems*, 618–644.

Jøsang, A., Ismail, R., & Boyd, C. (2007). A survey of trust and reputation systems for online service provision. *Decision Support Systems, 43*(2), 618–644. doi:10.1016/j.dss.2005.05.019.

Kallahalla, M., Riedel, E., Swaminathan, R., Wang, Q., & Fu, K. (2003). Plutus: Scalable secure file sharing on untrusted storage. In *Proceedings of the USENIX Conference on File and Storage Technologies* (FAST), (pp. 29–42). USENIX.

Kamvar, S., Scholsser, M., & Garcia-Molina, H. (2003). The EigenTrust algorithm for reputation management in P2P networks. In *Proceedings of 12th International Conf. of WWW*, (pp. 640-651). IEEE.

Karvonen, K. (2001). Designing trust for a universal audience: A multicultural study on the formation of trust in the internet in the Nordic countries. In C. Stephanidis (Ed.), *First International Conference on Universal Access in Human-Computer Interaction*, (vol. 3, pp. 1078-1082). Mahwah, NJ: Erlbaum.

Katzenbeisser, S., & Petkovic, M. (2008). Privacy-preserving recommendation systems for consumer healthcare services.[ARES.]. *Proceedings of ARES, 08*, 889–895.

Kaufman, L. M. (2009). Data security in the world of cloud computing. *IEEE Security and Privacy, 7*(4), 61–64. doi:10.1109/MSP.2009.87.

Khan, K. M., & Malluhi, Q. (2010). Establishing trust in cloud computing. *IT Professional, 12*(5), 20–27. doi:10.1109/MITP.2010.128.

Kikuchi, H., Kizawa, H., & Tada, M. (2009). Privacy-preserving collaborative filtering schemes.[ARES.]. *Proceedings of ARES, 09*, 911–916.

Kim, J., & Moon, J. Y. (1998). Designing towards emotional usability in customer interfaces-trustworthiness of cyber-banking system interfaces. *Interacting with Computers, 10*, 1–29. doi:10.1016/S0953-5438(97)00037-4.

Kini, A., & Choobineh, J. (1998). Trust in electronic commerce: Definition and theoretical considerations. In *Proceedings of the 31st Hawaii International Conference on System Science*, (vol. 4, pp. 51-61). IEEE.

Koehn, D. (1996). Should we trust in trust? *American Business Law Journal, 34*(2), 183–203. doi:10.1111/j.1744-1714.1996.tb00695.x.

Kolan, P., & Dantu, R. (2007). Socio-technical defense against voice spamming. *ACM Transactions on Autonomous and Adaptive Systems, 2*(1).

Kortuem, G., Schneider, J., Preuitt, D., Thompson, T. G. C., Fickas, S., & Segall, Z. (2001). When peer-to-peer comes face-to-face: Collaborative peer-to-peer computing in mobile ad hoc networks. In *Proceedings of the First International Conference on Peer-to-Peer Computing*, (pp. 75-91). IEEE.

Kosko, B. (1986). Fuzzy cognitive maps. *International Journal of Man-Machine Studies, 24*, 65–75. doi:10.1016/S0020-7373(86)80040-2.

Kujimura, K., & Nishihara, T. (2003). Reputation rating system based on past behavior of evaluators. In *Proceedings of the 4th ACM Conference on Electronic Commerce*, (pp. 246 – 247). ACM.

Lee, J., Kim, J., & Moon, J. Y. (2000). What makes Internet users visit cyber stores again? Key design factors for customer loyalty. In *Proceedings of the Conference on Human Factors in Computing Systems CHI 2000*. ACM.

Lee, S., Sherwood, R., & Bhattacharjee, B. (2003). Cooperative peer groups in NICE. In *Proceedings of IEEE Conference on Computer Communications* (INFOCOM 03). IEEE CS Press.

Lee, J., & Moray, N. (1992). Trust, control strategies and allocation of function in human-machine systems. *Ergonomics, 35*(10), 1243–1270. doi:10.1080/00140139208967392 PMID:1516577.

Lee, K. C., & Chung, N. (2009). Understanding factors affecting trust in and satisfaction with mobile banking in Korea: A modified DeLone and McLean's model perspective. *Interacting with Computers, 21*(5-6), 385–392. doi:10.1016/j.intcom.2009.06.004.

Lewicki, R. J., & Bunker, B. (1995). Trust in relationships: A model of trust development and decline. In *Conflict, Cooperation and Justice*. San Francisco, CA: Jossey-Bass.

Lewis, D., & Weigert, A. (1985). Trust as a social reality. *Social Forces, 63*(4), 967–985.

Li, Q., Hao, Q., Xiao, L., & Li, Z. (2009). Adaptive management of virtualized resources in cloud computing using feedback control. In *Proceedings of 1st International Conference on Information Science and Engineering* (ICISE), (pp. 99-102). ICISE.

Li, X., Valacich, J. S., & Hess, T. J. (2004). Predicting user trust in information systems: A comparison of competing trust models. In *Proceedings of the 37th Annual Hawaii International Conference on System Sciences*. IEEE.

Liang, Z., & Shi, W. (2005). PET: A personalized trust model with reputation and risk evaluation for P2P resource sharing. In *Proceedings of 38th Annual Hawaii Int. Conf. on System Sciences*. IEEE.

Li, D., Meng, H., & Shi, X. (1995). Membership clouds and membership cloud generators. *Journal of Computer Research and Development, 32*(6), 15–20.

Li, H., & Singhal, M. (2007). Trust management in distributed systems. *Computer, 40*(2), 45–53. doi:10.1109/MC.2007.76.

Liiv, I., Tammet, T., Ruotsalo, T., & Kuusik, A. (2009). Personalized context-aware recommendations in SMARTMUSEUM: Combining semantics with statistics. [SEMAPRO.]. *Proceedings of SEMAPRO, 09*, 50–55.

Li, J., Li, R., & Kato, J. (2008). Future trust management framework for mobile ad hoc networks. *IEEE Communications Magazine, 46*(4), 108–115. doi:10.1109/MCOM.2008.4481349.

Lin, C., Varadharajan, V., Wang, Y., & Pruthi, V. (2004). Enhancing grid security with trust management. In *Proceedings of IEEE International Conf. on Services Computing*, (pp. 303-310). IEEE.

Li, T., Gao, C., & Du, J. (2009). A NMF-based privacy-preserving recommendation algorithm.[ICISE.]. *Proceedings of ICISE, 09*, 754–757.

Liu, W., Aggarwal, S., & Duan, Z. (2009). Incorporating accountability into internet email. In *Proceedings of SAC '09*, (pp. 975-882). SAC.

Liu, Z., Joy, A. W., & Thompson, R. A. (2004). A dynamic trust model for mobile ad hoc networks. In *Proceedings of the 10th IEEE International Workshop on Future Trends of Distributed Computing Systems* (FTDCS 2004), (pp. 80-85). IEEE.

Liu, Z., Yau, S. S., Peng, D., & Yin, Y. (2008). A flexible trust model for distributed service infrastructures. In *Proceedings of 11th IEEE Symposium on Object Oriented Real-Time Distributed Computing*, (pp. 108-115). IEEE.

Liu, D., Meng, X., & Chen, J. (2008). A framework for context-aware service recommendation.[ICACT.]. *Proceedings of ICACT, 08*, 2131–2134.

Liu, Y. T., Gao, B., Liu, T. Y., Zhang, Y., Ma, Z. M., He, S. Y., & Li, H. (2008). BrowseRank: Letting web users vote for page importance. In *Proceedings of SIGIR*, (pp. 451-458). ACM. Janecek, A. G. K., Gansterer, W. N., & Kumar, K. A. (2008). Multi-level reputation-based greylisting.[ARES.]. *Proceedings of, ARES08*, 10–17.

Lodi, G., Panzieri, F., Rossi, D., & Turrini, E. (2007). SLA-driven clustering of QoS-aware application servers. *IEEE Transactions on Software Engineering, 33*(3), 186–197. doi:10.1109/TSE.2007.28.

Lohse, G. L., & Spiller, P. (1998). Electronic shopping. *Communications of the ACM, 41*(7), 81–87. doi:10.1145/278476.278491.

Luhmann, N. (1979). *Trust and power*. Chichester, UK: Wiley.

Lumsden, J., & MacKay, L. (2006). How does personality affect trust in B2C e-commerce? In *Proceedings of 8th International Conference on Electronic Commerce: The New e-Commerce: Innovations for Conquering Current Barriers, Obstacles and Limitations to Conducting Successful Business on the Internet*. ACM Press.

Luo, Y., Le, J., & Chen, H. (2009). A privacy-preserving book recommendation model based on multi-agent. [WCSE.]. *Proceedings of WCSE, 09*, 323–327.

Lynch, L. (2011). Inside the identity management game. *IEEE Internet Computing, 15*(5), 78–82. doi:10.1109/MIC.2011.119.

MacCallum, R. C., & Austin, J. T. (2000). Applications of structural equation modeling in psychological research. *Annual Review of Psychology, 51*, 201–226. doi:10.1146/annurev.psych.51.1.201 PMID:10751970.

Malek, S., Esfahani, N., Menasce, D., Sousa, J., & Gomaa, H. (2009). Self-architecting software systems (SASSY) from QoS-annotated activity models. In *Proceedings of the Int'l Conf. Software Eng. (ICSE) Workshop Principles of Eng. Service-Oriented Systems*, (pp. 62-69). ICSE.

Manchala, D. W. (2000). E-commerce trust metrics and models. *IEEE Internet Computing, 4*(2), 36–44. doi:10.1109/4236.832944.

Marsh, S. (1994). *Formalising trust as a computational concept*. (Doctoral Dissertation). University of Stirling, Stirling, UK.

Maurer, U. (1996). Modeling a public-key infrastructure. In *Proceedings of the European Symposium of Research on Computer Security* (LNCS), (vol. 1146, pp. 325–350). Berlin: Springer.

Mayer, R. C., Davis, J. H., & Schoorman, F. D. (1995). An integrative model of organizational trust. *Academy of Management Review*, 20(3), 709–734.

McCrickard, D. S., Czerwinski, M., & Bartram, L. (2003). Introduction: Design and evaluation of notification user interfaces. *International Journal of Human-Computer Studies*, 58(5), 509–514. doi:10.1016/S1071-5819(03)00025-9.

McGibney, J., & Botvich, D. (2007). A trust overlay architecture and protocol for enhanced protection against spam. In *Proceedings of the Second International Conference on Availability, Reliability and Security* (ARES 2007), (pp. 749-756). ARES.

McKnight, D. H., & Chervany, N. L. (2000). What is trust? A conceptual analysis and an interdisciplinary model. In *Proceedings of the 2000 Americas Conference on Information Systems* (AMCI2000). Long Beach, CA: AIS.

McKnight, D. H., & Chervany, N. L. (2003). The meanings of trust. *UMN University Report*. Retrieved December 2006, from http://misrc.umn.edu/wpaper/WorkingPapers/9604.pdf

McKnight, D. H., & Chervany, N. L. (2001). Trust and distrust definitions: One bite at a time. In *Trust in Cyber-Societies*. Berlin: Springer. doi:10.1007/3-540-45547-7_3.

McKnight, D. H., Choudhury, V., & Kacmar, C. (2002). Developing and validating trust measures for e-commerce: An integrative typology. *Information Systems Research*, 13(3), 334–359. doi:10.1287/isre.13.3.334.81.

McKnight, D. H., Cummings, L. L., & Chervany, N. L. (1998). Initial trust formation in new organizational relationships. *Academy of Management Review*, 23, 473–490.

Mejia, M., Peña, N., Muñoz, J. L., Esparza, O., & Alzate, M. A. (2011). A game theoretic trust model for on-line distributed evolution of cooperation in MANETs. *Journal of Network and Computer Applications*, 34(1). doi:10.1016/j.jnca.2010.09.007.

Meyer, T. A., & Whateley, B. (2004). Spambayes: Effective opensource, Bayesian based, email classification system. In *Proceedings of CEAS*. CEAS.

Michiardi, P., & Molva, R. (2002). Core: A collaborative reputation mechanism to enforce node cooperation in mobile ad hoc networks.[LNCS]. *Proceedings of Advanced Communications and Multimedia Security, 2828*, 107–121. doi:10.1007/978-0-387-35612-9_9.

Microsoft Azure. (n.d.). Retrieved from http://www.microsoft.com/azure/

Mikic-Rakic, M., Malek, S., & Medvidovic, N. (2008). Architecture-driven software mobility in support of QoS requirements. In *Proceedings of the First Int'l Workshop Software Architectures and Mobility*, (pp. 3-8). IEEE.

Milgram, S. (1972). The familiar stranger: An aspect of urban anonymity. In *The Individual in a Social World* (pp. 51–53). Reading, MA: Addison-Wesley.

Misztal, B. A. (1996). *Trust in modern societies: The search for the bases of social order*. New York: Polity Press.

Moore, G. C., & Benbasat, I. (1991). Development of an instrument to measure the perceptions of adopting an information technology innovation. *Information Systems Research*, 2(3), 192–222. doi:10.1287/isre.2.3.192.

Mui, L. (2003). *Computational models of trust and reputation: Agents, evolutionary games, and social networks*. (Doctoral dissertation). Massachusetts Institute of Technology, Cambridge, MA.

Muir, B. M. (1987). Trust between humans and machines, and the design of decision aids. *International Journal of Man-Machine Systems*, 27, 527–539. doi:10.1016/S0020-7373(87)80013-5.

Muir, B. M. (1994). Trust in automation part I: Theoretical issues in the study of trust and human intervention in automated systems. *Ergonomics*, 37(11), 1905–1922. doi:10.1080/00140139408964957.

Muir, B. M. (1996). Trust in automation part II: Experimental studies of trust and human intervention in a process control simulation. *Ergonomics*, 39(3), 429–469. doi:10.1080/00140139608964474 PMID:8849495.

Muller, S., Katzenbeisser, S., & Eckert, C. (2008). Distributed attribute-based encryption. In *Proceedings of the 11th Annual International Conference on Information Security and Cryptology*, (pp. 20–36). IEEE.

Myerson, R. B. (1991). *Game theory: Analysis of conflict.* Boston: Harvard University Press.

Nielsen, J. (1999). *Trust or bust: Communicating trustworthiness in web design.* Retrieved from http://www.useit.com/alertbox/990307.html

Nielsen, J., Molich, R., Snyder, S., & Farrell, C. (2000). *E-commerce user experience: Trust.* New York: Nielsen Norman Group.

Novák, V., Perfilieva, I., & Močkoř, J. (1999). *Mathematical principles of fuzzy logic.* Dordrecht, The Netherlands: Kluwer Academic. doi:10.1007/978-1-4615-5217-8.

Nurmi, D., et al. (2009). The eucalyptus open-source cloud-computing system. In *Proceedings of 9th IEEE/ACM Int'l Symp. Cluster Computing and the Grid (CC-GRID 09)*, (pp. 124–131). IEEE/ACM.

O'Donovan, J., & Smyth, B. (2005). Trust in recommender systems. In *Proceedings of IUI'05*, (pp. 167-174). IUI.

Olden, E. (2011). Architecting a cloud-scale identity fabric. *Computer, 44*(3), 52–59. doi:10.1109/MC.2011.60.

Olson, J. S., Zheng, J., Bos, N., Olson, G. M., & Veinott, E. (2002). Trust without touch: Jumpstarting long-distance trust with initial social activities.[ACM.]. *Proceedings of, CHI2002,* 141–146.

Oppliger, R., & Rytz, R. (2005). Does trusted computing remedy computer security problems? *IEEE Security and Privacy, 3*(2), 16–19. doi:10.1109/MSP.2005.40.

Osborne, M. (2004). *An introduction to game theory.* Oxford, UK: Oxford University Press.

Ott, J., Hyytiä, E., Lassila, P. E., Kangasharju, J., & Santra, S. (2011). Floating content for probabilistic information sharing. *Pervasive and Mobile Computing, 7*(6), 671–689. doi:10.1016/j.pmcj.2011.09.001.

Page, L., Brin, S., Motwani, R., & Winograd, T. (1998). *The pagerank citation ranking: Bringing order to the web.* Palo Alto, CA: Stanford University.

Pavlou, P., & Gefen, D. (2004). Building effective online marketplaces with institution-based trust. *Information Systems Research, 15*(1), 37–59. doi:10.1287/isre.1040.0015.

Pearl, J. (1988). *Probabilistic reasoning in intelligent systems: Networks of plausible inference.* San Francisco, CA: Morgan Kaufmann.

Pennington, R., Wilcox, H. D., & Grover, V. (2004). The role of system trust in business-to-consumer transactions. *Journal of Management Information Systems, 20*(3), 197–226.

Perez, S. (2009). *Why cloud computing is the future of mobile.* Retrieved from http://www.readwriteweb.com/archives/why_cloud_computing_is_the_future_of_mobile.php

Perlman, R. (1999). An overview of PKI trust models. *IEEE Network, 13*(6), 38–43. doi:10.1109/65.806987.

Pirretti, M., Traynor, P., McDaniel, P., & Waters, B. (2010). Secure attribute based systems. *Journal of Computer Security, 18*(5), 799–837.

Polat, H., & Du, W. L. (2005). Privacy-preserving top-n recommendation on horizontally partitioned data. In *Proceedings of the 2005 IEEE/WIC/ACM International Conference on Web Intelligence*, (pp. 725-731). IEEE.

Pu, P., & Chen, L. (2006). Trust building with explanation interfaces. In *Proceedings of the 11th International Conference on Intelligent User Interfaces IUI '06*, (pp. 93-100). IEEE.

Pu, P., & Chen, L. (2007). Trust-inspiring explanation interfaces for recommender systems. *Knowledge-Based Systems, 20*(6), 542–556. doi:10.1016/j.knosys.2007.04.004.

Putnam, R. D. (1995). Bowling alone: America's declining social capital. *Journal of Democracy, 6*(1), 3–10. doi:10.1353/jod.1995.0002.

Raya, M., Papadimitratos, P., Gligory, V. D., & Hubaux, J. P. (2008). On data-centric trust establishment in ephemeral ad hoc networks. In *Proceedings of IEEE INFOCOM* (pp. 1912–1920). IEEE. doi:10.1109/INFOCOM.2008.180.

Regan, K. (2003). Secure VPN design considerations. *Network Security,* 5–10.

Reiter, M. K., & Stubblebine, S. G. (1998). Resilient authentication using path independence. *IEEE Transactions on Computers, 47*(12), 1351–1362. doi:10.1109/12.737682.

Resnick, P., & Zeckhauser, R. (2001). *Trust among strangers in Internet transactions: Empirical analysis of eBay's reputation system*. Retrieved from http://www.si.umich.edu/Bpresnick

Resnick, M. L., & Montania, R. (2003). Perceptions of customer service, information privacy, and product quality from semiotic design features in an online web store. *International Journal of Human-Computer Interaction, 16*(2), 211–234. doi:10.1207/S15327590IJHC1602_05.

Resnick, P., Kuwabara, K., Zeckhauser, R., & Friedman, E. (2000). Reputation systems. *Communications of the ACM, 43*(12), 45–48. doi:10.1145/355112.355122.

Resnick, P., & Varian, H. R. (1997). Recommender systems. *Communications of the ACM, 40*(3), 56–58. doi:10.1145/245108.245121.

Resnick, P., & Zeckhauser, R. (2002). Trust among strangers in Internet transactions: Empirical analysis of eBay's reputation system. In M. Baye (Ed.), *Advances in Applied Microeconomics: The Economics of the Internet and E-Commerce* (Vol. 11, pp. 127–157). London: Elsevier. doi:10.1016/S0278-0984(02)11030-3.

Riedl, R., Hubert, M., & Kenning, P. (2010). Are there neural gender differences in online trust? An FMRi study on the perceived trustworthiness of eBay offer. *Management Information Systems Quarterly, 34*(2), 397–428.

Riegelsberger, J. (2003). Interpersonal cues and consumer trust in e-commerce. In *Proceedings of the Conference on Human Factors in Computing Systems* (CHI'03). New York: ACM.

Riegelsberger, J., & Sasse, M. A. (2001). Trust builders and trustbusters: The role of trust cues in interfaces to e-commerce applications. In *Towards the E-Society: Proceedings of the First IFIP Conference on E-Commerce, E-Society, and E-Government*. London: Kluwer.

Riegelsberger, J., Angela Sasse, M., & McCarthy, J. D. (2005). Do people trust their eyes more than ears? Media bias in detecting cues of expertise. In *Proceedings of the Conference on Human Factors in Computing Systems* (CHI'05). New York: ACM.

Riegelsberger, J., Sasse, A. M., & McCarthy, J. D. (2005). The mechanics of trust: A framework for research and design. *International Journal of Human-Computer Studies, 62*(3), 381–422. doi:10.1016/j.ijhcs.2005.01.001.

Rotter, J. B. (1967). A new scale for the measurement of interpersonal trust. *Journal of Personality, 35*, 651–665. doi:10.1111/j.1467-6494.1967.tb01454.x PMID:4865583.

Rotter, J. B. (1971). Generalized expectancies for interpersonal trust. *The American Psychologist, 26*, 443–452. doi:10.1037/h0031464.

Rousseau, D. M., Sitkin, S. B., Burt, R. S., & Camerer, C. (1998). Not so different after all: A cross-discipline view of trust. *Academy of Management Review, 23*(3), 393–404. doi:10.5465/AMR.1998.926617.

Rukzio, E., Hamard, J., Noda, C., & Luca, A. D. (2006). Visualization of uncertainty in context aware mobile applications. In *Proceedings of Mobile HCI*. ACM Press. doi:10.1145/1152215.1152267.

Sahai, A., & Waters, B. (2005). Fuzzy identity-based encryption. In *Proceedings of 24th International Conference on the Theory and Application of Cryptographic Techniques*, (pp. 457–473). IEEE.

Sanchez, R., Almenares, F., Arias, P., Diaz-Sanchez, D., & Marin, A. (2012). Enhancing privacy and dynamic federation in IdM for consumer cloud computing. *IEEE Transactions on Consumer Electronics, 58*(1), 95–103. doi:10.1109/TCE.2012.6170060.

Sarigöl, E., Riva, O., Stuedi, P., & Alonso, G. (2009). Enabling social networking in ad hoc networks of mobile phones. *Proceedings of VLDB Endow., 9*(2), 1634–1637.

Sarkio, K., & Holtmanns, S. (2007). Tailored trustworthiness estimations in peer to peer networks. *International Journal of Internet Technology and Secured Transactions, 1*(1/2), 95–107. doi:10.1504/IJITST.2007.014836.

Satyanarayanan, M., Bahl, P., Caceres, R., & Davies, N. (2009). The case for VM-based cloudlets in mobile computing. *IEEE Pervasive Computing / IEEE Computer Society [and] IEEE Communications Society, 8*(4), 14–23. doi:10.1109/MPRV.2009.82.

Schechter, S. E., Dhamija, R., Ozment, A., & Fischer, I. (2007). The emperor's new security indicators. In *Proceedings of 2007 IEEE Symposium on Security and Privacy*, (pp. 51-65). IEEE.

Schmidt, S., Steele, R., Dillon, T. S., & Chang, E. (2007). Fuzzy trust evaluation and credibility development in multi-agent systems. *Applied Soft Computing*, *7*(2), 492–505. doi:10.1016/j.asoc.2006.11.002.

Schwartz, A. (2004). *SpamAssassin*. Sebastopol, CA: O'Reilly Media, Inc..

Seetharam, A., & Ramakrishnan, R. (2008). A context sensitive, yet private experience towards a contextually apt recommendation of service.[IMSAA.]. *Proceedings of IMSAA*, *2008*, 1–6.

Shafer, G. (1976). *A mathematical theory of evidence*. Princeton, NJ: Princeton University Press.

Shafer, G. (1990). Perspectives on the theory and practice of belief functions. *International Journal of Approximate Reasoning*, *3*, 1–40.

G. Shafer, & J. Pearl (Eds.). (1990). *Readings in uncertain reasoning*. San Francisco, CA: Morgan Kaufmann.

Shan, R., Li, S., Wang, M., & Li, J. (2003). Network security policy for large-scale VPN. In *Proceedings of International Conference on Communication Technology*, (pp. 217-220). IEEE.

Shelat, B., & Egger, F. N. (2002). What makes people trust online gambling sites? In *Proceedings of Conference on Human Factors in Computing Systems* (CHI 2002). ACM Press.

Sheppard, B. H., Hartwick, J., & Warshaw, P. R. (1988). The theory of reasoned action: A meta analysis of past research with recommendations for modifications in future research. *Consumer Res.*, *15*(3), 325–343. doi:10.1086/209170.

Sheridan, T. (1980). Computer control and human alienation. *Technology Review*, 61–73.

Sillence, E., Briggs, P., Harris, P., & Fishwick, L. (2006). A framework for understanding trust factors in web-based health advice. *International Journal of Human-Computer Studies*, *64*(8), 697–713. doi:10.1016/j.ijhcs.2006.02.007.

Singh, A., & Liu, L. (2003). TrustMe: Anonymous management of trust relationships in decentralized P2P systems. In *Proceedings of IEEE International Conference on Peer-to-Peer Computing*, (pp. 142-149). IEEE.

Song, D., Wagner, D., & Perrig, A. (2000). Practical techniques for searches on encrypted data. In *Proceedings of the IEEE Symp. Security and Privacy*, (pp. 44-55). IEEE.

Song, S., Hwang, K., Zhou, R., & Kwok, Y. K. (2005). Trusted P2P transactions with fuzzy reputation aggregation. *IEEE Internet Computing*, *9*(6), 24–34. doi:10.1109/MIC.2005.136.

Spring, J. (2011). Monitoring cloud computing by layer, part 1. *IEEE Security and Privacy*, *9*(2), 66–68. doi:10.1109/MSP.2011.33.

Stanford, J., Tauber, E., Fogg, B. J., & Marable, L. (2002). *Experts vs. online consumers: A comparative credibility study of health and finance web sites*. Retrieved from http://www.consumerwebwatch.org/news/report3_credibilityresearch/slicedbread_abstract.htm

Stantchev, V., & Schrofer, C. (2009). Negotiating and enforcing QoS and SLAs in grid and cloud computing. In *Proceedings of the 4th International Conference on Advances in Grid and Pervasive Computing* (LNCS), (vol. 5529, pp. 25-35). Berlin: Springer.

Steinbrück, U., Schaumburg, H., Duda, S., & Kruger, T. (2002). A picture says more than a thousand words—Photographs as trust builders in e-commerce websites. In *Proceedings of Conference on Human Factors in Computing Systems CHI 2002*. ACM Press.

Stihler, M., Santin, A. O., Marcon, A. L., & da Silva Fraga, J. (2012). Integral federated identity management for cloud computing. In *Proceedings of the 5th International Conference on New Technologies, Mobility and Security* (NTMS), (pp. 1-5). NTMS.

Stuedi, P., Riva, O., & Alonso, G. (n.d.). *Demo abstract ad hoc social networking using MAND.* Retrieved from: http://www.iks.inf.ethz.ch/publications/files/mobicom08_demo.pdf

Stylios, C. D., Georgopoulos, V. C., & Groumpos, P. P. (1997). The use of fuzzy cognitive maps in modeling systems. In *Proceedings of the Fifth IEEE Mediterranean Conf. Control and Systems*[REMOVED HYPERLINK FIELD]. IEEE.

Subjective Logic. (n.d.). Retrieved from http://folk.uio.no/josang/sl/

Sundareswaran, S., Squicciarini, A., & Lin, D. (2012). Ensuring distributed accountability for data sharing in the cloud. *IEEE Transactions on Dependable and Secure Computing, 9*(4), 556–568. doi:10.1109/TDSC.2012.26.

Sun, Y., Han, Z., & Liu, K. J. R. (2008). Defense of trust management vulnerabilities in distributed networks. *IEEE Communications Magazine, 46*(2), 112–119. doi:10.1109/MCOM.2008.4473092.

Sun, Y., Han, Z., Yu, W., & Liu, K. J. R. (2006). A trust evaluation framework in distributed networks: Vulnerability analysis and defense against attacks. In *Proceedings of IEEE INFOCOM* (pp. 1–13). IEEE. doi:10.1109/INFOCOM.2006.154.

Suryanarayana, G., Diallo, M. H., Erenkrantz, J. R., & Taylor, R. N. (2006). Architectural support for trust models in decentralized applications. In *Proceedings of the 28th Int'l Conf. Software Eng.*, (pp. 52-61). IEEE.

Su, X., & Khoshgoftaar, T. M. (2009). A survey of collaborative filtering techniques. *Advances in Artificial Intelligence.* doi:10.1155/2009/421425.

Tada, M., Kikuchi, H., & Puntheeranurak, S. (2010). Privacy-preserving collaborative filtering protocol based on similarity between items.[AINA.]. *Proceedings of AINA, 10*, 573–578.

Tajeddine, A., Kayssi, A., Chehab, A., & Artail, H. (2011). Fuzzy reputation-based trust model. *Applied Soft Computing, 11*(1), 345–355. doi:10.1016/j.asoc.2009.11.025.

Tang, Y., Krasser, S., He, Y., Yang, W. I., & Alperovitch, D. (2008). Support vector machines and random forests modeling for spam senders behavior analysis. In *Proceedings of IEEE GLOBECOM*, (pp. 1-5). IEEE.

Tang, Y., Lee, P. P. C., Lui, J. C. S., & Perlman, R. (2012). Secure overlay cloud storage with access control and assured deletion. *IEEE Transactions on Dependable and Secure Computing, 9*(6), 903–916. doi:10.1109/TDSC.2012.49.

Tan, Y., & Thoen, W. (1998). Toward a generic model of trust for electronic commerce. *International Journal of Electronic Commerce, 5*(2), 61–74.

TCG. (2003). *TCG TPM specification v1.2.* Retrieved from https://www.trustedcomputinggroup.org/specs/TPM/

TCG. (2003). *TPM specification v1.2.* Retrieved from http://www.trustedcomputinggroup.org/resources/tpm_main_specification

Theodorakopoulos, G., & Baras, J. S. (2006). On trust models and trust evaluation metrics for ad hoc networks. *IEEE Journal on Selected Areas in Communications, 24*(2), 318–328. doi:10.1109/JSAC.2005.861390.

Trifunovic, S., Legendre, F., & Anastasiades, C. (2010). Social trust in opportunistic networks. In *Proceedings of IEEE INFOCOM Workshops*, (pp. 1-6). IEEE.

Turel, O., Yuan, Y., & Connelly, C. (2008). In justice we trust: Predicting user acceptance of e-customer services. *Journal of Management Information Systems, 24*(4), 123–151. doi:10.2753/MIS0742-1222240405.

Uddin, M., Zulkernine, M., & Ahamed, S. I. (2008). CAT: A context-aware trust model for open and dynamic systems. In *Proceedings of the ACM Symposium on Applied Computing* (SAC '08), (pp. 2024-2029). ACM.

Vaughan-Nichols, S. J. (2003). How trustworthy is trusted computing? *IEEE Computer, 36*(3), 18–20. doi:10.1109/MC.2003.1185209.

Venkatesh, V., & Bala, H. (2008). Technology acceptance model 3 and a research agenda on interventions. *Decision Sciences, 39*(2), 273–315. doi:10.1111/j.1540-5915.2008.00192.x.

Venkatesh, V., & Davis, F. D. (2000). A theoretical extension of the technology acceptance model: Four longitudinal field studies. *Management Science, 46*(2), 186–204. doi:10.1287/mnsc.46.2.186.11926.

Venkatesh, V., Morris, M. G., Davis, G. B., & Davis, F. D. (2003). User acceptance of information technology: Toward a unified view. *Management Information Systems Quarterly, 27*(3), 425–478.

Walsh, K., & Sirer, E. G. (2005). Fighting peer-to-peer SPAM and decoys with object reputation. In Proceedings of P2PECON, (pp. 138-143). P2PECON.

Wang, G., Liu, Q., & Wu, J. (2010). Hierachical attibute-based encryption for fine-grained access control in cloud storage services. In *Proceedings of the ACM Conf. Computer and Communications Security* (ACM CCS). Chicago, IL: ACM.

Wang, X., Du, Z., Liu, X., Xie, H., & Jia, X. (2010). An adaptive QoS management framework for VoD cloud service centers. In *Proceedings of 2010 International Conference on Computer Application and System Modeling* (ICCASM), (pp. 527-532). ICCASM.

Wang, Y., & Varadharajan, V. (2005). Trust2: Developing trust in peer-to-peer environments. In *Proceedings of the IEEE International Conference on Services Computing*, (vol. 1, pp. 24–31). IEEE.

Wang, C., Cao, N., Ren, K., & Lou, W. (2012). Enabling secure and efficient ranked keyword search over outsourced cloud data. *IEEE Transactions on Parallel and Distributed Systems, 23*(8), 1467–1479. doi:10.1109/TPDS.2011.282.

Wang, C., Wang, Q., Ren, K., & Lou, W. (2010). Privacy-preserving public auditing for data storage security in cloud computing.[IEEE.]. *Proceedings - IEEE INFOCOM, 2010*, 1–9. doi:10.1109/INFCOM.2010.5462173.

Wang, J., Kodama, E., Takada, T., & Li, J. (2010). Mining context-related sequential patterns for recommendation systems.[CAMP.]. *Proceedings of CAMP, 10*, 270–275.

Wang, J., Wang, F., Yan, Z., & Huang, B. (2011). Message receiver determination in multiple simultaneous IM conversations. *IEEE Intelligent Systems, 26*(3), 24–31. doi:10.1109/MIS.2010.33.

Wang, Y. D., & Emurian, H. H. (2005). An overview of online trust: Concepts, elements and implications. *Computers in Human Behavior, 21*, 105–125. doi:10.1016/j.chb.2003.11.008.

Wan, Z., Liu, J., & Deng, R. H. (2012). HASBE: A hierarchical attribute-based solution for flexible and scalable access control in cloud computing. *IEEE Transactions on Information Forensics and Security, 7*(2), 743–754. doi:10.1109/TIFS.2011.2172209.

Williamson, O. E. (1993). Calculativeness, trust and economic organization. *The Journal of Law & Economics, 30*, 131–145.

Windows Azure Virtual Machines. (n.d.). Retrieved from http://www.windowsazure.com/en-us/

Wong, M., & Schlitt, W. (2006). *Sender policy framework (SPF) for authorizing use of domains in e-mail, version 1.* RFC 4408 (Experimental). Retrieved from http://www.ietf.org/rfc/rfc4408.txt

Wood, D., Stoss, V., Chan-Lizardo, L., Papacostas, G. S., & Stinson, M. E. (1988). Virtual private networks. In *Proceedings of International Conference on Private Switching Systems and Networks*, (pp. 132-136). IEEE.

Wrightsman, L. S. (1991). *Assumptions about human nature: Implications for researchers and practitioners.* Newbury Park, CA: Sage.

Wu, B., Goel, V., & Davison, B. D. (2006). Topical TrustRank: Using topicality to combat web spam. In *Proceedings of the 15th international conference on World Wide Web*, (pp. 63-72). IEEE.

Wu, B., Goel, V., & Davison, B. D. (2006). Topical TrustRank: Using topicality to combat web spam.[IEEE.]. *Proceedings of WWW, 06*, 63–72.

Wu, I., & Chen, J. (2005). An extension of trust and TAM model with TPB in the initial adoption of on-line tax: An empirical study. *International Journal of Human-Computer Studies, 62*(6), 784–808. doi:10.1016/j.ijhcs.2005.03.003.

Xiao, Y., Lin, C., Jiang, Y., Chu, X., & Shen, X. (2010). Reputation-based QoS provisioning in cloud computing via dirichlet multinomial model. In *Proceedings of IEEE International Conference on Communications* (ICC), (pp. 1-5). IEEE.

Xiao, H., Zou, Y., Ng, J., & Nigul, L. (2010). An approach for context-aware service discovery and recommendation. [IEEE.]. *Proceedings of IEEE ICWS, 10*, 163–170.

Xiong, L., & Liu, L. (2004). PeerTrust: Supporting reputation-based trust for peer-to-peer electronic communities. *IEEE Transactions on Knowledge and Data Engineering, 16*(7), 843–857. doi:10.1109/TKDE.2004.1318566.

Yamagishi, T., & Yamagishi, M. (1994). Trust and commitment in the United States and Japan. *Motivation and Emotion, 18*, 129–166. doi:10.1007/BF02249397.

Yan, Z. (2007). *Trust management for mobile computing platforms.* (Doctoral dissertation). Helsinki Univ. of Technology, Helsinki, Finland.

Yan, Z., & Chen, Y. (2010). AdContRep: A privacy enhanced reputation system for MANET content services. In *Proceedings of UIC 2010* (LNCS), (vol. 6406, pp. 414-429). Berlin: Springer.

Yan, Z., & Chen, Y. (2011). AdChatRep: A reputation system for MANET chatting. In *Proceedings of SCI2011 in UbiComp2011*, (pp. 43-48). ACM.

Yan, Z., & Cofta, P. (2004). A mechanism for trust sustainability among trusted computing platforms. In *Proceedings of the First International Conference on Trust and Privacy in Digital Business* (TrustBus'04) (LNCS), (vol. 3184, pp. 11-19). Berlin: Springer.

Yan, Z., & MacLaverty, R. (2006). Autonomic trust management in a component based software system. In *Proceedings of ATC06* (LNCS), (vol. 4158, pp. 279-292). Berlin: Springer.

Yan, Z., & Niemi, V. (2009). A methodology towards usable trust management. In *Proceedings of ATC'09* (LNCS), (vol. 5586, pp. 179-193). Berlin: Springer.

Yan, Z., & Niemi, V. Dong, Y., & Yu, G. (2008). A user behavior based trust model for mobile applications. In Proceedings of Autonomic and Trusted Computing ATC08 (LNCS), (vol. 5060, pp. 455-469). Berlin: Springer.

Yan, Z., & Prehofer, C. (2007). An adaptive trust control model for a trustworthy component software platform. In *Proceedings of ATC'07* (LNCS), (vol. 4610, pp. 226-238). Berlin: Springer.

Yan, Z., & Yan, R. (2009). Formalizing trust based on usage behaviours for mobile applications. In *Proceedings of ATC09* (LNCS), (vol. 5586, pp. 194-208). Berlin: Springer.

Yan, Z., & Zhang, P. (2011). AdPriRec: A context-aware recommender system for user privacy in MANET services. In *Proceedings of UIC2011* (LNCS), (vol. 6905, pp. 295-309). Berlin: Springer.

Yan, Z., Kantoal, R., Shi, G., & Zhang, P. (2013). Unwanted content control via trust management in pervasive social networking. In *Proceedings of IEEE TrustCom2013*. Melbourne, Australia: IEEE.

Yan, Z., Kantola, R., & Shen, Y. (2012). Unwanted traffic control via hybrid trust management. In *Proceedings of IEEE TrustCom 2012*. Liverpool, UK: IEEE.

Yan, Z., Liu, C., Niemi, V., & Yu, G. (2009). *Trust information indication: Effects of displaying trust information on mobile application usage.* Retrieved from http://research.nokia.com/files/NRCTR2009004.pdf.

Yan, Z., Liu, C., Niemi, V., & Yu, G. (2010). Effects of displaying trust information on mobile application usage. In *Proceedings of ATC'10* (LNCS), (vol. 6407, pp. 107-121). Berlin: Springer.

Yan, Z., Liu, C., Niemi, V., & Yu, G. (2010). *Trust information indication: Effects of displaying trust information on mobile application usage* (Technical Report NRC-TR-2009-004). Nokia Research Center. Retrieved from http://research.nokia.com/files/NRCTR2009004.pdf

Yan, Z., Niemi, V., Dong, Y., & Yu, G. (2008). A user behavior based trust model for mobile applications. In *Proceedings of ATC'08* (LNCS), (vol. 5060, pp. 455-469). Berlin: Springer.

Yan, Z., Zhang, P., & Deng, H.R. (2011). TruBeRepec: A trust-behavior-based reputation and recommender system for mobile applications. *Journal of Personal and Ubiquitous Computing*. doi: 10.1007/s00779-011-0420-2

Yan, Z., Zhang, P., & Virtanen, T. (2003). Trust evaluation based security solution in ad hoc networks. In *Proceedings of the 7th Nordic Workshop on Secure IT Systems* (NordSec03). NordSec.

Yang, Y., & Sun, Y. Kay, S., & Yang, Q. (2009). Defending online reputation systems against collaborative unfair raters through signal modeling and trust. In *Proceedings of SAC'09*, (pp. 1308-1315). SAC.

Yan, Z. (2008). A comprehensive trust model for component software.[IEEE.]. *Proceedings of SecPerU*, *08*, 1–6. doi:10.1145/1387329.1387330.

Yan, Z. (2008). Autonomic trust management for a pervasive system.[IEEE.]. *Proceedings of Secypt*, *08*, 491–500.

Yan, Z. (2010). Security via trusted communications. In P. Stavroulakis, & M. Stamp (Eds.), *Handbook on Communications and Information Security* (pp. 719–746). Berlin: Springer. doi:10.1007/978-3-642-04117-4_33.

Yan, Z. (2010). *Trust modeling and management in digital environments: From social concept to system development*. Hershey, PA: IGI Global. doi:10.4018/978-1-61520-682-7.

Yan, Z. (2010). Security via trusted communications. In P. Stavroulakis, & M. Stamp (Eds.), *Handbook on Communications and Information Security*. Berlin: Springer. doi:10.1007/978-3-642-04117-4_33.

Z. Yan (Ed.). (2010). *Trust modeling and management in digital environments: From social concept to system development*. Hershey, PA: IGI Global. doi:10.4018/978-1-61520-682-7.

Yan, Z., Chen, Y., & Shen, Y. (2013). A practical reputation system for pervasive social chatting. *Journal of Computer and System Sciences*, *79*(5), 556–572. doi:10.1016/j.jcss.2012.11.003.

Yan, Z., Chen, Y., & Zhang, P. (2012). An approach of secure and fashionable recognition for pervasive face-to-face social communications.[IEEE.]. *Proceedings of IEEE WiMob*, *2012*, 853–860.

Yan, Z., Dong, Y., Niemi, V., & Yu, G. (2009). Exploring trust of mobile applications based on user behaviours. In *Proceedings of InTrust 2009 (LNCS)* (Vol. 6163, pp. 212–226). Berlin: Springer.

Yan, Z., Dong, Y., Niemi, V., & Yu, G. (2011). Exploring trust of mobile applications based on user behaviors: An empirical study. *Journal of Applied Social Psychology*.

Yan, Z., Dong, Y., Niemi, V., & Yu, G. (2013). Exploring trust of mobile applications based on user behaviors: An empirical study. *Journal of Applied Social Psychology*. doi:10.1111/j.1559-1816.2013.01044.x.

Yan, Z., & Holtmanns, S. (2008). Trust modeling and management: from social trust to digital trust. In R. Subramanian (Ed.), *Computer Security, Privacy and Politics: Current Issues, Challenges and Solutions*. Hershey, PA: Idea Group Inc. doi:10.4018/978-1-59904-804-8.ch013.

Yan, Z., Kantola, R., & Shen, Y. (2011). Unwanted traffic control via global trust management.[IEEE.]. *Proceedings of IEEE TrustCom*, *2011*, 647–654.

Yan, Z., Kantola, R., & Zhang, P. (2011). A research model for human-computer trust interaction.[IEEE.]. *Proceedings of IEEE TrustCom*, *2011*, 274–281.

Yan, Z., & Niemi, V. (2009). A methodology towards usable trust management. In *Proceedings of Autonomic and Trusted Computing ATC09 (LNCS)* (Vol. 5586, pp. 179–193). Berlin: Springer. doi:10.1007/978-3-642-02704-8_14.

Yan, Z., Niemi, V., Chen, Y., Zhang, P., & Kantola, R. (2013). Towards trustworthy mobile social networking. In *Mobile Social Networking: An Innovative Approach*. Berlin: Springer.

Yan, Z., & Prehofer, C. (2011). Autonomic trust management for a component based software system. *IEEE Transactions on Dependable and Secure Computing*, *8*(6), 810–823. doi:10.1109/TDSC.2010.47.

Yan, Z., & Yan, R. (2009). Formalizing trust based on usage behaviours for mobile applications. In *Proceedings of Autonomic and Trusted Computing ATC09 (LNCS)* (Vol. 5586, pp. 194–208). Berlin: Springer. doi:10.1007/978-3-642-02704-8_15.

Yan, Z., & Zhang, P. (2006). Trust collaboration in P2P systems based on trusted computing platforms. *WSEAS Transactions on Information Science and Applications*, *2*(3), 275–282.

Yan, Z., & Zhang, P. (2006). A trust management system in mobile enterprise networking. *WSEAS Transactions on Communications, 5*(5), 854–861.

Yan, Z., Zhang, P., & Deng, R. H. (2012). TruBeRepec: A trust-behavior-based reputation and recommender system for mobile applications. *Journal of Personal and Ubiquitous Computing, 16*(5), 485–506. doi:10.1007/s00779-011-0420-2.

Yao, L., & Li, Y. (2009). Research on trust in e-commerce of C2C based on game-theory. In *Proceedings of International Conference on Management and Service Science,* (MASS'09), (pp. 1-4). MASS.

Yap, G., Tan, A., & Pang, H. (2007). Discovering and exploiting causal dependencies for robust mobile context-aware recommenders. *IEEE Transactions on Knowledge and Data Engineering, 19*(7), 977–992. doi:10.1109/TKDE.2007.1065.

Ye, Y., Jain, N., Xia, L., Joshi, S., Yen, I.-L., Bastani, F., et al. (2010). A framework for QoS and power management in a service cloud environment with mobile devices. In *Proceedings of the Fifth IEEE International Symposium on Service Oriented System Engineering* (SOSE), (pp. 236-243). IEEE.

Yu, S., Wang, C., Ren, K., & Lou, W. (2010). Achieving secure, scalable, and fine-grained data access control in cloud computing.[IEEE.]. *Proceedings - IEEE INFOCOM, 2010,* 534–542.

Yu, Z., Zhou, X., Zhang, D., Chin, C., Wang, X., & Men, J. (2006). Supporting context-aware media recommendations for smart phones. *IEEE Pervasive Computing / IEEE Computer Society [and] IEEE Communications Society, 5*(3), 68–75. doi:10.1109/MPRV.2006.61.

Zahedi, F., & Song, J. (2008). Dynamics of trust revision: Using health infomediaries. *Journal of Management Information Systems, 24*(4), 225–248. doi:10.2753/MIS0742-1222240409.

Zhang, H., Duan, H., Liu, W., & Wu, J. (2009). IPGroupRep: A novel reputation based system for anti-spam. In *Proceedings of the Symposia and Workshops on Ubiquitous, Autonomic and Trusted Computing,* (pp. 513-518). ACM.

Zhang, J., Xu, W., Peng, Y., & Xu, J. (2010). MailTrust: A mail reputation mechanism based on improved TrustGuard. In *Proceedings of the International Conference on Communications and Mobile Computing* (CMC), (pp. 218-222). CMC.

Zhang, P., Sun, H., & Yan, Z. (2011). Building up trusted identity management in mobile heterogeneous environment. In *Proceedings of IEEE 10th International Conference on Trust, Security and Privacy in Computing and Communications (TrustCom),* (pp. 873-877). IEEE.

Zhang, X., Han, B., & Liang, W. (2009). Automatic seed set expansion for trust propagation based auti-spamming algorithms. In *Proceedings of the Eleventh International Workshop on Web Information and Data Management,* (pp. 31-38). IEEE.

Zhang, Z., Wang, X., & Wang, Y. (2005). A P2P global trust model based on recommendation. In *Proceedings of 2005 International Conf. on Machine Learning and Cybernetics,* (vol. 7, pp. 3975-3980). IEEE.

Zhang, D., & Yu, Z. (2007). Spontaneous and context-aware media recommendation in heterogeneous spaces. [IEEE.]. *Proceedings of the IEEE VTC, 07,* 267–271.

Zhang, J., Xu, W., Peng, Y., & Xu, J. (2010). MailTrust: A mail reputation mechanism based on improved TrustGuard.[CMC.]. *Proceedings of, CMC10,* 218–222.

Zhang, P., & Yan, Z. (2011). Adaptive QoS management for mobile cloud services. *China Communications, 10,* 36–43.

Zhang, X., Han, B., & Liang, W. (2009). Automatic seed set expansion for trust propagation based auti-spamming algorithms.[WIDM.]. *Proceedings of WIDM, 09,* 31–38. doi:10.1145/1651587.1651596.

Zheleva, E., Kolcz, A., & Getoor, L. (2008). Trusting spam reporters: a reporter-based reputation system for email filtering. *ACM Transactions on Information Systems, 27*(1). doi:10.1145/1416950.1416953.

Zhou, M., Jiao, W., & Mei, H. (2005). Customizable framework for managing trusted components deployed on middleware. In *Proceedings of 10th IEEE Int'l Conf. Eng. of Complex Computer Systems,* (pp. 283-291). IEEE.

Zhou, M., Mei, H., & Zhang, L. (2005). A multi-property trust model for reconfiguring component software. In *Proceedings of the Fifth International Conference on Quality Software* (QAIC2005), (pp. 142–149). QAIC.

Zhou, M., Mu, Y., Susilo, W., & Yan, J. (2011). Piracy-preserved access control for cloud computing. In *Proceedings of TrustCom11* (pp. 83–90). TrustCom.

Zhou, Z., Xu, H., & Wang, S. (2011). A novel weighted trust model based on cloud. *Advances in Information Sciences and Service Sciences*, *3*(3), 115–124. doi:10.4156/aiss.vol3.issue3.15.

Zimmerman, J., & Kurapati, K. (2002). Exposing profiles to build trust in a recommender. In *Proceedings of the Conference on Human Factors in Computing Systems CHI 2001*. ACM Press.

Zouridaki, C., Mark, B. L., Hejmo, M., & Thomas, K. R. (2006). Robust cooperative trust establishment for MANETs. In *Proceedings of the Fourth ACM Workshop on Security of Ad Hoc and Sensor Networks*, (pp. 23-34). ACM.

Zucker, L. G. (1986). Production of trust: institutional sources of economic structure, 1840–1920. *Research in Organizational Behavior*, *8*, 53–111.

About the Author

Zheng Yan received the B. Eng in electrical engineering and M. Eng in computer science and engineering from Xi'an Jiaotong University in 1994 and 1997. She received a second M. Eng in information security from National University of Singapore in 2000. She received the Licentiate of Science and the Doctor of Science in Technology in electrical engineering from Helsinki University of Technology in 2005 and 2007. She is currently a professor at the Xidian University, China, and a docent at the Aalto University, Finland. She joined the Nokia Research Center, Helsinki, in 2000, working as a senior researcher until 2011. Before Nokia, she worked as a research scholar at the Institute for Information Research from 1997 to 1999 and a software engineer at the IBM partner SingaLab from 1999 to 2000, Singapore. She has authored more than 80 publications and edited one book. She is the inventor of 25 patents and patent applications. She has given 6 keynotes and invited talks in international conferences and universities. Her research interests are in trust, security, and privacy; mobile applications and services; social networking; data mining; cloud computing; and pervasive computing. Prof. Yan serves as an organizational and technical committee member for more than 40 international conferences and workshops. She is an editorial board member of the *Journal of Convergence*, an editor of *KSII Transactions on Internet and Information Systems*, a special issue leading guest editor of *IET Information Security, Future Generation Computer Systems, Information Fusion, IEEE Systems Journal*, and *Computers & Security*, and acts as a reviewer for many reputable journals. She has organized IEEE TrustID2011/2012/2013 with IEEE TrustCom, IEEE DASC 2012, a special track about Pervasive Social Computing with UIC/ATC2010 and IEEE iThings 2012, etc. She is a member of the IEEE. Her recent awards are: Outstanding Leadership Award at IEEE iThings 2012; Outstanding Service Award at IEEE TrustCom 2012; Outstanding Service Award at IEEE TrustID 2012; "100 Expert Plan" award of Shaanxi Province, specially recruited expert of Shaanxi Province, China (2011); Sisu Award in Nokia Research Center, Helsinki (2010); Best Organizer Award in UIC/ATC2010 (2010); EU ITEA Bronze Achievement Award (2008).

Index

pervasive clouds 68-69, 88-89

Pervasive Social Networking 8, 130-133, 135-137, 139-143, 145, 151, 154, 159, 165-167, 170, 172, 249

Pervasive System 216, 223

Privacy 2, 5, 8-9, 11, 25, 29, 32-33, 35-36, 38, 40, 42, 44, 46-47, 49-51, 54-55, 58-59, 62-63, 67-68, 76, 78, 80-82, 84, 87-92, 100, 125, 130-138, 140, 143, 145, 148, 156, 158-160, 163, 165-167, 170, 176, 178, 184-189, 191-192, 194, 198, 221, 224, 237, 241, 246, 248, 251

R

Recommender Systems 137, 168, 183, 191-192

Reputation 4-5, 10, 14-15, 20, 22, 24, 26, 28-29, 31-32, 39-42, 44-45, 48-51, 59, 62, 64, 69, 73-83, 85-89, 94, 96-100, 125, 127-128, 130, 132-140, 142-148, 159-161, 163, 166-171, 176-178, 183, 186, 189-194, 197, 202, 222, 226-227, 230-232, 235-238, 240-243, 245-251

Reputation Systems 29, 31-32, 39, 41-42, 45, 48, 50-51, 130, 134-135, 167-168, 171, 178, 191, 222, 231, 236

Root Trust Module 31-33, 38, 42, 178, 199-200, 202, 204, 207, 216

S

Security 1-6, 8-11, 22, 24-27, 29, 31-33, 38, 40-44, 46-52, 54-59, 61-62, 64, 67-68, 71, 76, 78, 81-82, 87-88, 90-92, 95, 97, 120, 126-128, 130-134, 150, 159, 163, 165-171, 176-179, 184, 187, 190, 192, 194, 198, 200, 202-203, 205-206, 212, 220-224, 226, 236, 249, 251

Social Networking 1, 8, 45-46, 69-70, 74-76, 94, 99, 130-137, 139-143, 145, 151, 154, 159, 165-167, 169-170, 172, 178, 242, 249

Spam 46, 51, 94-99, 101, 106, 125-128, 137, 166, 169-171, 193, 250

Spam Filtering 94-95, 97-98

Subjective Logic 17, 20, 25, 28

system entity 77, 79, 81, 83, 95, 97, 100-103, 110, 126, 212, 214

T

traffic control 29, 94-103, 108-111, 117, 119-121, 123, 126-130, 133, 137, 145, 154, 163, 166, 170, 194

Trusted Computing 4, 9, 25, 31-33, 38-39, 42, 45, 49-50, 128, 171, 177, 184, 194, 196, 199-202, 205, 207, 216, 220-221, 223-224, 227, 240

Trust Evaluation 11, 13, 15, 17-25, 28, 30, 32-33, 43-45, 48, 50-51, 54-55, 69-70, 75-76, 83, 85, 94-95, 97-98, 100, 102, 108-109, 126, 130, 140, 166, 169, 178, 193, 196-197, 199, 202-203, 205-206, 223-224, 226-227, 229-230, 237, 239-240, 250

Trust Management 1, 7-11, 15, 21, 23, 25-26, 29, 31-33, 39, 41-48, 50-52, 54-55, 64, 67-68, 76, 89-90, 93-97, 100-102, 120, 126-129, 131-136, 138, 140-141, 148, 165-170, 172, 175, 177-178, 184-187, 190, 193-194, 196-199, 205-227, 229, 232-235, 240, 242, 247-249, 251-252

Trust Model 10, 13-17, 23-29, 32, 40, 43, 45, 50-51, 142, 168, 190, 194, 197, 223-224, 229, 232-235, 240, 247-248, 251

U

unwanted traffic 29, 94-103, 105-130, 132-133, 137, 145, 154, 163, 166, 170, 194

Unwanted Traffic Control 29, 94-103, 108-111, 117, 119-121, 123, 126, 128-130, 133, 137, 145, 154, 163, 166, 170, 194

Usability 7, 15, 32, 39, 42-46, 55, 63, 68, 70, 76, 88-89, 166, 184, 190, 198, 221, 226-227, 231-232, 236-237, 246-248

Usable Trust Management 8-9, 15, 44-45, 47, 51, 89, 136, 138, 170, 175, 194, 226-227, 232-233, 235, 247-248, 251-252

User Acceptance 15, 68, 132, 138, 161, 167, 186, 188, 193, 226, 228, 235, 250

user interface 15, 47, 135-136, 141, 159, 162-164, 175-176, 179, 185-186, 227-229, 231, 235, 242, 246-247

User Trust 7-8, 14, 16, 26, 48, 64, 132, 136, 174-177, 184, 186-187, 195, 237, 240, 249